INSIGHT GUIDE

JORDAN

DISCOVERY CHANNEL

APA PUBLICATIONS
Part of the Langenscheidt Publishing Group

ABOUT THIS BOOK

Editorial

Project Editor
Michael Ellis
Managing Editor
Dorothy Stannard
Editorial Director
Brian Bell

Distribution

UK & Ireland
GeoCenter International Ltd
The Viables Centre , Harrow Way
Basingstoke, Hants RG22 4BJ
Fax: (44) 1256-817988

United States
Langenscheidt Publishers, Inc.
46–35 54th Road, Maspeth, NY 11378
Fax: (718) 784-0640

Canada
Prologue Inc.
1650 Lionel Bertrand Blvd., Boisbriand
Québec, Canada J7H 1N7
Tel: (450) 434-0306. Fax: (450) 434-2627

Worldwide
Apa Publications GmbH & Co.
Verlag KG (Singapore branch)
38 Joo Koon Road, Singapore 628990
Tel: (65) 865-1600. Fax: (65) 861-6438

Printing

Insight Print Services (Pte) Ltd
38 Joo Koon Road, Singapore 628990
Tel: (65) 865-1600. Fax: (65) 861-6438

©2000 Apa Publications GmbH & Co.
Verlag KG (Singapore branch)
All Rights Reserved

First Edition 1994
Fifth Edition 1999
Reprinted 2000

CONTACTING THE EDITORS
Although every effort is made to
provide accurate information, we
live in a fast-changing world and
would appreciate it if readers
would call our attention to any
errors or outdated information
that may occur by writing to us:
**Insight Guides, P.O. Box 7910,
London SE1 1WE, England.
Fax: (44 20) 7403-0290.**
insight@apaguide.demon.co.uk

This guidebook combines the interests and enthusiasms of two of the world's best known information providers: Insight Guides, whose titles have set the standard for visual travel guides since 1970, and Discovery Channel, the world's premier source of nonfiction TV programming.

The editors of Insight Guides provide practical advice and general understanding about a destination's history, culture, institutions and people. Discovery Channel and its website, www.discovery.com, help millions of viewers explore their world from the comfort of their home and also encourage them to explore it firsthand.

How to use this book

The book is structured to convey an understanding of Jordan and its culture and to guide readers through its sights.

◆ The Features section, with a yellow colour bar, covers the country's history and culture in authoritative essays written by specialists.

◆ The Places section, with a blue bar, provides full details of all the sights and areas

worth seeing. The chief places of interest are coordinated by number with the maps. Additional chapters on the West Bank and Syria have been included for people who are visiting these countries as part of a wider tour of the region.

◆ The Travel Tips listings section, with an orange bar, at the back of the book, offers a convenient point of reference for information on travel, accommodation, restaurants and other practical aspects of the country. Information may be located quickly using the index printed on the back cover flap.

The contributors

This new edition was edited by **Michael Ellis** and builds on the original book produced by **Dorothy Stannard**. For this edition, Amman-based journalist **Amy Henderson** updated the existing text, contributed features on food and hiking and wrote the text to the picture stories Architectural Legacy, Café Societies and Scuba-diving.

New material was also provided by writer **Chris Bradley**, who leads adventure travel tours to Jordan. His contributions include the Camel, the River Jordan, the Dead Sea, the Badia and the text for the picture story on the Bedouin Inheritance.

Completing the team working on this edition is **Stephanie Genkin**. She extended the chapter on The West Bank and updated the chapter on Syria.

Contributors to the original edition include **Rowlinson Carter** (most of the history), **Paul Lalor** (Jordan's post-war history and the chapter on the Palestinians and Salt), **Rami Khouri** (Jarash and the North, the Jordan Valley and Petra), **Jane Taylor** (East to Azraq and Wadi Rum), **Alison McQuitty** (the King's Highway), **Pamela Watson** (Syria), **Mariam Shahin** (Aqaba), **Rebecca Salti** (Life of the Bedouin and the Craft Tradition), **Peter Vine** (Wildlife), **Roger Williams** (Artists' Impressions) and **Floresca Karanasou** (Travel Tips, plus Amman, which she wrote with Paul Lalor).

The book was proof-read by **Sylvia Suddes** and indexed by **Simon Hartley**.

Map Legend

— · · —	International Boundary
— — —	Province Boundary
— · —	National Park/Reserve
— — —	Ferry Route
✈ ✈	Airport: International/Regional
🚌	Bus Station
P	Parking
ℹ	Tourist Information
✉	Post Office
† ⴕ	Church/Ruins
†	Monastery
☾	Mosque
✡	Synagogue
🏰	Castle/Ruins
∴	Archaeological Site
∩	Cave
⌇	Statue/Monument
★	Place of Interest

The main places of interest in the Places section are coordinated by number with a full-colour map (e.g. ❶), and a symbol at the top of every right-hand page tells you where to find the map.

INSIGHT GUIDE
Jordan

CONTENTS

Introduction

History

Features

Magical
Wadi Rum

Travel Tips

Insight on ...

Information panels

Places

THE SANDS OF TIME

In the shifting sands of the desert, a nation has emerged from
the bubbling ferment of history

Jordan is a 20th-century creation in an ancient cockpit of history. Called Trans-jordan in 1919, it rose out of the detritus of the Ottoman Empire after World War I, between the Jordan River and an arbitrary line running through the sands of the Arabian desert. Although the throne was brand-new, its first occupant, Abdullah – the present King Hussein's grandfather – traced his lineage back over 1,400 years to the Prophet Mohammed.

A sharp contrast between the fertile Jordan Valley (known as the "sown") and the desert hinterland has been at the bottom of Jordan's history from the earliest times. The valley was busy, the desert remote. It is conceivable that the first stirrings of distinctly human activity in the East African Great Rift Valley two million years ago gradually worked north via the Red and Dead seas when these were dry extensions of the same geological rift. In any case, stone tools found at the ancient site of Pella, in the north of Jordan, suggest that a comparable level of human activity had been attained in the Jordan Valley some 800,000 years after the original rumblings in Africa.

The oldest surviving town

An astounding milestone in human development was achieved at Jericho in 7000 BC. Beneath the walls that famously came tumbling down in the Old Testament were other walls of immense archaeological significance: the first evidence of nomads abandoning their traditional way of life in order to practise systematic agriculture around a permanent home. Out of that particular acorn grows the whole idea of towns, city-states, statehood, cash economies and so forth – the checklist of urban civilisation. This pioneering effort proved to be way ahead of its time and, as far as Jericho was concerned, it was put on ice for a few thousand years.

PRECEDING PAGES: coffee pots, a national symbol; designer rugs; the Desert Patrol; aboard the Hejaz Railway. **LEFT:** a people of the desert.
RIGHT: the fabric of Bedouin life.

An ancient thoroughfare

In the meantime, civilisations flourished in Egypt and Mesopotamia on the strength of rivers which took care of agricultural necessities, thereby creating societies with a previously unknown commodity, surplus labour. The Jordan River was not as generous, but its valley

served as a landbridge between Egypt and Mesopotamia, Africa and Asia, and Arabia and Europe. Crowded in biblical times with a tongue-twisting cast of Canaanites, Hittites, Perizzites, Girgashites, Amorites, Jebusites, Edomites and so on, this busy thoroughfare was intermittently subjugated by the great empires of the time: Egyptian, Assyrian, Babylonian, Persian, Macedonian, Roman, Byzantine, Arabian, Mamluke and Turkish.

For a while, even Genghis Khan's grandson, the mighty Kublai Khan, considered adding it to the Mongol Empire during the 13th century. Similar thoughts occurred to more recent despots, Napoleon Bonaparte and Adolf Hitler.

For the record

Jordan enters recorded history shortly before its absorption into the Egyptian Empire. Tribal anarchy and famine drove the Hebrews under Abraham to Egypt. Four centuries later, by which time the Egyptians had imposed a measure of law and order in the Promised Land, Moses led them back. Focusing on these migrations, the Bible loses sight of ancient trade imperatives. Eastern silks, spices and other things unobtainable in the Mediterranean basin could be shipped up the Red Sea, but the more reliable route, avoiding reefs and pirates, was overland by camel caravan from Yemen.

TRADE ROUTES

Petra, Jordan's most outstanding historical site, grew rich on developing trade, as did Mecca, further south in Saudi Arabia and Palmyra to the north, in the heart of what is now Syria. Rabbath Ammon (now Amman) and Gerasa (present-day Jarash) also prospered as trading posts. Petra eventually folded under the advance of Rome, and when Rome itself collapsed, its inheritance passed to the Graeco-Roman Eastern Empire, Byzantium. Jordan was farmed out to the Ghassanids, Christian vassals of Byzantium, before being conquered by the Arabs in the 7th century, when it became part of an Islamic Empire later dominated by the Turks.

The desert hinterland was ignored or positively avoided by the trade routes and the transient empires that controlled them, as it was also by the indigenous population of the Jordan Valley. The desert tribes, on the other hand, were perpetually engaged in a warlike ritual over this "wild land of blood and terror".

In the words of T. E. Lawrence many years later: "Each hill and valley in it had a man who was its acknowledged owner and who would quickly assert the right of his family or clan to it, against aggression. Even the wells and trees had their masters..." Others were allowed to drink from the wells and make firewood of the trees, but no more than was absolutely necessary. To overstep the mark was an act of war. The ritual was, Lawrence wrote, a kind of "crazed communism".

Between the valley and the sands

The distinction between valley and desert people has by no means disappeared. The former, taller and more heavily built, are believed to be basically the Canaanites of old with an uneven sprinkling from passing empires. The desert tribes are an almost pure strain, and are ethnically indistinguishable from the desert populations of neighbouring countries such as Syria and Saudi Arabia. Consensus says that the valley Arabs have been receptive to cultural currents swirling around the Mediterranean basin, while their desert counterparts have stuck steadfastly to their own traditions.

The population of Transjordan, as created in 1919, was predominantly (about 75 percent) of desert tribal origin. The subsequent absorption of the West Bank and the influx of Palestinian refugees during the 1948 and 1967 wars put the desert tribes and the mixed population of "valley" and "coastal" peoples on a roughly equal numerical footing. However, it should be added that statistics are being revised in anticipation of the conclusion to final status negotiations on the future of the West Bank. The political debate bristles with contemporary rhetoric; in the shadows, though, the course of Jordan's history swings, as always, on a pendulum between the stark contrasts of desert and sown. ❏

LEFT: Neolithic statue in the Archaeological Museum in Amman.
RIGHT: the desert hinterland, once "a wild land of blood and terror".

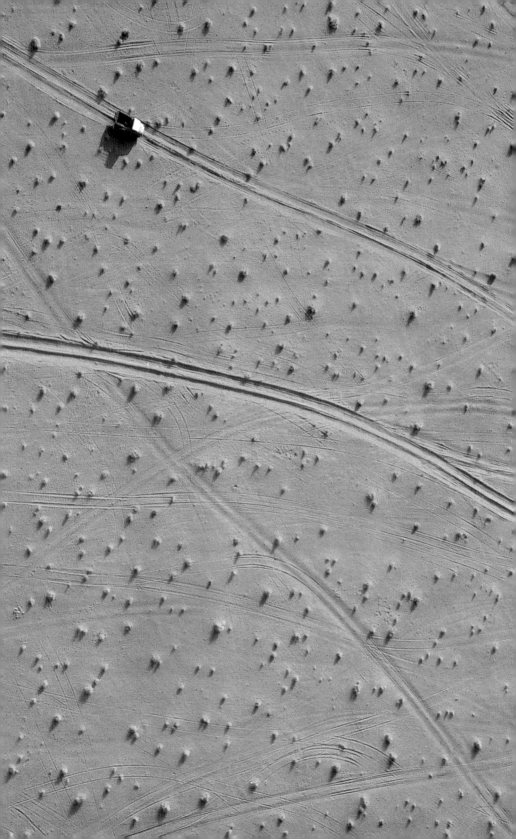

Decisive Dates

9000 BC: First inhabitants settle on the West Bank of the Jordan River near modern Jericho.

3000–1550 BC: Early Bronze Age; Amorites and Canaanites arrive in Jordan.

c. **1280 BC:** Moses leads Israelites out of Egypt; 40 years later they settle east of the Jordan River.

c. **1225 BC:** Joshua captures Jericho; Palestine is divided among the 12 tribes of Israel.

c. **1000 BC:** David is proclaimed King of the Israelites; he conquers Jerusalem and makes it his capital.

960–922 BC: Reign of Solomon. Expands kingdom

through treaties and marriages, and builds the first Temple in Jerusalem. The kingdom is divided on his death into Judah in the south and Israel to the north.

722 BC: The Assyrians, led by Sargon II, destroy the Kingdom of Israel, replacing the inhabitants with settlers from Syria and Babylonia.

612 BC: The Babylonian army under Medes captures Nineveh, the Assyrian capital.

597–587 BC: Jerusalem, Palestine and Jordan fall to the Babylonian King Nebuchadnezzar.

538 BC: Nabataeans establish a kingdom based at Petra in southern Jordan.

332–1 BC: Alexander the Great conquers Syria, Palestine and Egypt.

323 BC: Alexander dies and his Middle Eastern

domain is divided: Ptolemy I is given Egypt and parts of Syria, and Seleuces is granted Babylon.

198 BC: The Seleucid army under Antiochus III defeats the Ptolemies' army; both states are consolidated under the Seleucid flag.

188 BC: Antiochus III is defeated by the Roman army; Roman Empire absorbs his kingdom.

170 BC: Antiochus IV sacks Jerusalem.

167 BC: Jews revolt under Judas Maccabeus.

64 BC: Damascus falls to Pompey's Roman army. Palestine falls in 63 and is renamed Judaea.

63 BC – AD 106: The Decapolis, or the League of 10 Cities, is formed in the area.

40 BC: Parthian kings of Persia and Mesopotamia invade the Decapolis; Mark Antony leads the army which repels them.

37 BC: In Rome, Herod the Great is proclaimed King of Israel; the Temple is rebuilt in Jerusalem.

c. **4 BC – AD 39:** Life of Jesus Christ.

AD 66: Jews revolt against the Romans.

106: Nabataean Kingdom incorporated into the Roman Empire.

325: Constantine, the Byzantine Emperor, converts to Christianity.

525–565: The reign of Justinian. Churches are built at Christian holy sites.

629: Christians and Muslims battle for the first time near Karak; Mohammed takes Mecca.

638: Jerusalem falls to the Muslim Arabs led by Caliph Omar.

642: Arabs conquer Egypt.

658: Omayyad dynasty founded in Damascus. A brilliant period in arts and architecture ensues.

750: Omayyads are overthrown by Abbasids, who move the caliphate to Baghdad.

1095: Pope Urban II launches first Crusade to retake Jerusalem from the Muslims.

1099: Crusaders establish a kingdom in Jerusalem, and build fortresses in Jordan and Syria.

1250: Mamlukes take power in Cairo. They eventually rule over an area from Egypt to Syria.

1516: Syria and Palestine are absorbed into the Ottoman Empire.

1901: The Jewish National Fund is created to buy Arab lands for Zionist settlements.

1909: Revolt by the Young Turks in Istanbul encourages nationalistic feelings among populations under Ottoman rule.

1914–18: World War I; Ottoman Empire sides with Germany.

1916: The Arab Revolt. The Arab Pan-nationalist Movement, under Emir Feisal's leadership, joins forces with the British to drive out Ottoman Turks.

1917: British troops occupy Jerusalem and Aqaba.
1920: The Conference of San Remo reconfirms the secretly negotiated 1916 Sykes-Picot agreement, denying the Arabs an independent state and giving Britain a mandate to rule Palestine and France authority over Syria and Lebanon.
1923: Britain recognises Transjordan's independence under its protection, with Abdullah, Feisal's brother, as its king. The Arab Legion is formed under a British officer, J. B. Glubb (Glubb Pasha).
1930s: Large numbers of Jews fleeing from the Nazis arrive in Palestine, sparking riots.
1939–45: World War II; Jordan offers its Arab Legion to fight with the Allies.
1946: Britain gives up mandate. Transjordan becomes an independent monarchy.
1947: United Nations vote to partition Palestine; Hashemite Kingdom of Jordan is created.
1948: Britain's mandate over Palestine expires; State of Israel proclaimed; the first Arab-Israeli war begins as the last British troops depart.
1950: Abdullah formally annexes the Gaza Strip, West Bank and East Jerusalem into his kingdom.
1951: King Abdullah is assassinated at Al-Aqsa Mosque in Jerusalem.
1952: Hussein is declared king at 17 after his father, Talal, is declared mentally unstable.
1955: Jordan becomes a member of the United Nations; Egypt nationalises the Suez Canal.
1960: Iraqi government overthrown; Palestinians, with Egypt's backing, try to depose King Hussein, who offers citizenship to all Palestinian refugees.
1964: The PLO and its more militant cousin, Al-Fatah, are formed.
1967: The Six-Day War between Israel and the Arab armies leaves Jordan devastated: Jerusalem and the West Bank are lost.
1969: Yasser Arafat is elected chairman of the PLO. Terrorist acts against Israel increase.
1970: King Hussein clamps down on the PLO's growing power, culminating in Black September. The civil war between local Palestinians and the government leaves the PLO routed.
1974: King Hussein recognises the PLO as the sole representative of the Palestinian people.
1980: Jordan backs Iraq in its eight-year war against Iran; Syria goes with Iran.
1988: King Hussein gives up legal and administrative claims to Jerusalem and the West Bank.

1989: Price rises for basic staples, as dictated by the IMF as part of an economic recovery package for Jordan. Bread riots ensue. In Ma'an, southeast of Petra a tribal stronghold, 11 die.
1990: Iraq invades Kuwait in August. Large sections of Jordan's population back Iraq. Around 300,000 Palestinians arrive in Jordan, having been expelled from Kuwait and Saudi Arabia.
1992: Israeli-Palestinian peace talks begin in Madrid. Law passed legalising all political parties.
1993: Jordan's first multi-party democratic elections are held shortly after Palestinians announce peace deal with Israelis.
1994: Jordan and Israel sign a peace treaty.

1997: Parliamentary elections return a tribally-dominated parliament after 10 opposition parties boycott in protest against a crackdown on public freedoms. Members of Israel's Mossad attempt assassination of Hamas leader in Amman, bringing relations between Jordan and Israel to a standstill.
1998: The King travels to the United States for a second course of treatment against cancer, first diagnosed in 1992, drawing to the fore the question of his succession. A peace deal is struck between Yasser Arafat and Israeli prime minister Binyamin Netanyahu.
1999: King Hussein dies of cancer, shortly after nominating his eldest son, Abdullah, as his successor in place of his brother Hassan, Crown Prince for 33 years. Abdullah is sworn in as King. ❑

LEFT: detail at Iraq al-Amir, near Amman.
RIGHT: sarcophagus dating from the 13th–7th century BC displayed in Amman's Archaeological Museum.

A HOLY LAND

The early history of Jordan is one of migration and trade, cities bought and fought over, the creation of religious doctrines and the battles that ensued

Unresolved confusion over names and dates torments visitors hoping to locate historical and biblical references in Jordan, and that has ever been the case. Early travellers, many of them clergymen attached to various Palestine exploration societies, first had to overcome obstructions put in their way by the Turkish authorities who had ruled the Holy Land virtually since the time of the Crusades. First-hand experiences were pooled, so by the end of the 19th century visitors on their way to Jordan – as distinct from Palestine or the West Bank – understood that 96 places mentioned in the Bible awaited them.

Early settlement

Ironically, fixed settlement became a viable proposition in the Jordan Valley not long after Abraham's departure for Egypt to escape the tribal anarchy and famine that had plagued the region. Egypt was on the point of building an empire, and as the imperial frontier pushed towards Mesopotamia, the area it encompassed benefited from unprecedented, if less than perfect, law and order. Bedouin tribes remained a law unto themselves, but urban development took root at Madaba in the plain of Moab and at Jarash in the mountains of Gilead.

Under the umbrella of Egyptian security, it was a relatively short step from nomads exchanging their peripatetic existence for permanent homes to the emergence of a host of petty kingdoms with taxing Old Testament names. Edom is among the most memorable if only because its founder, Esau, has always brightened up religious study as a hairy man, contrasting with his brother Jacob, a smooth man (Genesis 27:11). If you lose your bearings in the welter of Old Testament names, it may help to remember that Karak is at the heart of ancient Moab, Petra at the heart of Edom.

The whereabouts of Sodom and Gomorrah is more problematic. By tradition these evil

twins were devoured in Abraham's lifetime by a storm of fire and brimstone which deposited the ashes at the bottom of the Dead Sea. Old maps invariably showed them under fathoms of water but still engulfed in flames. In recent times, divers carrying extra weights to counteract the excessive buoyancy of the water have

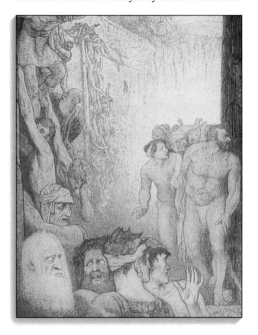

scoured the sea-bed without success. Various theories have put the site of the cities on the Plain of Jordan and the shores of the Dead Sea. Scholars favouring the Lisam peninsula, which juts into the sea below the Mountains of Moab in the east, have been encouraged by the fairly recent discovery of a necropolis containing some 20,000 tombs, many untouched since the bodies were laid to rest about 2500 BC.

The Exodus

By 1280 BC the Israelites had outstayed their welcome in Egypt and had to embark on the Exodus under Moses. The direct route lay through Edom, but in spite of Moses' promise

---

LEFT: Madaba's 6th-century mosaic map of Palestine.
RIGHT: the destruction of Sodom and Gomorrah.

not to veer left or right from the beaten track of the King's Highway, the Edomites refused to allow him and his party through their territory. The detour amounted to 40 years in the wilderness before the weary refugees were able to climb Mount Nebo in Moab and survey the Promised Land. Moses died in Moab without ever crossing to the West Bank of the Jordan. He was buried in a valley "over against Bethpeor: but no man knoweth of his sepulchre unto this day". While his grave remains a mystery, there is general

agreement among experts these days that Mount Nebo is one of three peaks about 10 km (6 miles) west of Madaba.

The Israelites had to fight their fellow Semites for a place in the Promised Land. Battles took place everywhere; the most interesting on Jordanian territory was probably fought at Rabbath Ammon (now Amman), the Ammonite capital. King David of Israel approached Rabbath Ammon on the pretext of consoling the Ammonite king on the recent death of his father. The king was not to be comforted by David's thoughtful message. Instead, the messengers were seized and had their beards hacked off, followed by a crude re-tailoring of their clothes which left their buttocks all but exposed. This insult in itself was cause enough for war, but David had another reason for ordering battle to commence. The lovely Bathsheba, on whom he had his eye, was inconveniently married to Uriah the Hittite. David made a point of ordering the luckless husband into the thickest part of the action with the happy thought that he could not possibly survive. Uriah duly perished, David was free to marry Bathsheba, and the son she subsequently bore him was the future King Solomon. David may have delighted in his coup, but was not inclined to show magnanimity towards the conquered population, who were roasted alive in a kiln.

For all its candour about the human foibles of the Israelite kings, the Old Testament gives a rather partisan account of the wars, with the Israelites enjoying a suspiciously high rate of success. A different flavour is imparted by the Mesha or Moabite stone, a block of basalt inscribed with 34 lines of writing in a script that falls somewhere between ancient Phoenician and Hebrew, which was discovered just north of Jordan's Wadi Mujib in 1868. This is the voice of King Mesha of Moab, crowing about his victories over the Israelites in the 9th century BC. He is particularly pleased about a battle in which he killed 7,000 Israelites, hastening to add, however, that he scrupulously spared the women. He could afford the gesture because, he says, "Israel is laid waste for ever."

Whether or not King Mesha actually checked the run of Israelite military success, there is no disputing the historical fact that the state eventually carved out by David and Solomon became the leading power in the region. Urusalim (Jerusalem) was captured around 1000 BC and replaced Hebron as the capital of the Israelite kingdom.

On the death of Solomon in 922 BC, the kingdom divided into Israel in the north and Judah in the south, the respective capitals being Samaria and Jerusalem. Both kingdoms were overwhelmed by the Assyrian invasion of 722 BC. The Israelites were carried away to captivity in Mesopotamia but, by agreeing to pay tribute, Judah was left intact, albeit as a vassal state. There was no second reprieve, however, when Nebuchadnezzar II of Babylon conquered the empire in 587 BC. Jerusalem was sacked, Solomon's Temple on Mount Moriah was completely destroyed, and the population was carried off to captivity in Babylon.

Cyrus I of Persia conquered Babylon half a century later, whereupon the men of Judah were allowed to return to Jerusalem. They rebuilt the Temple and fostered special treatment from Persia by remaining aloof from local rebellions against Persian rule. Deir Alla in the Jordan Valley – where Jacob recuperated after wrestling with an angel – was evidently a Persian settlement, but there are no significant monuments in Jordan of this Persian era.

Ammon, for instance, acquired a Greek name, Philadelphia. As always, the desert tribes were so remote that they were unaffected by the profound cultural transformation on all sides.

Although Alexander did not live long enough to consolidate his colossal empire, he revitalised trade between east and west and for Jordan, straddling a historic trade route, this was bound to be immensely profitable. The key stretch was the overland camel caravan route from Aden and Yemen up the east coast of the Red Sea to Damascus and points beyond.

The first major staging post was Mecca, and its future role at the centre of Islam was not

Alexander the Great, conqueror of Persia and its possessions in 332 BC, was responsible for drawing the Near East into the orbit of Graeco-Western civilisation. Having previously scorned Macedonians as barbaric foreigners, the Greek diaspora was quick to mount the bandwagon of Alexander's astonishing military success. Trading posts and settlement followed in the wake of the triumphant Macedonian army. The industrious Greeks were not inclined to stray very far from the coast, but their influence certainly reached into the Jordan Valley. Rabbath

unconnected with its traditional pre-eminence in trade and commerce. Another of the staging posts was Palmyra in Syria, and between the two, caravans were serviced and taxed at Petra.

Petra and the Nabataeans

Very little is known about Petra in the earlier days of ancient Edom. Biblical references to the Edomite capital of Sela probably refer to the western wall of the canyon. The Nabataeans, a tribe of nomads originating in western Arabia, seem to have settled around Petra in the 6th century BC.

They made the most of Petra's strategic position and prospered wonderfully. Inevitably, they

LEFT: Moses surveys the Promised Land.
ABOVE: the Dead Sea Scrolls.

attracted dangerous predators, none more so than Antigonus, one of Alexander the Great's Seleucid heirs. His energies were divided between several unsuccessful attacks on Petra and attempts to take a larger slice of Alexander's legacy from the other principal heirs, the Ptolemies of Egypt. The latter had a foothold in Jordan at Gadara, later Umm Qais, a less important staging post than Petra. The Seleucids eventually seized Gadara from the Ptolemies in 218 BC; but were in turn dispossessed by the Jews in 100 BC.

CAESAR'S GIFT

It is said that Cleopatra requested Petra as a gift from Caesar. He baulked at the idea, so she settled for Jericho instead.

West of the Jordan in the meantime, the Seleucid Antiochus Epiphanus made a searing impact when he took Jerusalem by storm in 170 BC, slaughtering most of the inhabitants and selling the rest into slavery. The Temple was re-dedicated to Jupiter, an outrage which Daniel called "the Abomination of Desolation". The Jewish backlash was led by the Maccabees, a strait-laced sect who caused consternation among the Edomites by insisting on their circumcision. The pious Maccabees later suffered a dramatic fall from grace.

Petra could afford to maintain forces capable of seeing off enemies like Antigonus. It could even afford to buy Roman recognition of its independence when the Roman legions in 63 BC seized Syria and Palestine. Having reached an accommodation with Rome, the Nabataeans then suffered a terminal lapse of judgment by taking the side of the Parthians in a dispute they were having with Rome.

The agreement was torn up and Rome moved in. As the new masters of Petra, the Romans began their customary re-modelling of the place to suit their own taste. If the remnants are impressive today, the impact at the time must have been overwhelming.

"A complete moral collapse," observes an eminent biblical scholar. The Maccabees took one of their private arguments for arbitration to the new Roman master of Damascus, Pompey. He lost his temper with the lot of them, battered down the walls of Jerusalem and marched into the Temple. He also overwhelmed the Nabataeans, hoping to replace their efficient trading tentacles with a kind of common market of 10 semi-independent cities, which he called the Decapolis (*see page 170*).

As there were never enough Roman-born citizens to administer the rapidly expanding empire, even top positions were delegated to local men. Some acquitted themselves with distinction; others, like Herod the Great, were notably poor choices. Herod joined the imperial service as governor of Galilee and in 31 BC was nominated as King of Judaea, in which capacity he effectively ruled the Jordan Valley. His mind was apparently unsettled by something of an identity crisis. He was, it was said, "by birth an Idumaean (i.e. Edomite), by profession a Jew, by necessity a Roman, by culture and by choice a Greek." Soaking in the hot springs at Zarqa Ma'in ("Callirhoe" in the Bible), he concocted architectural schemes which would either intimidate or placate his restless subjects. Machaerus, now known as

away to her father in Petra before the plan was executed, but John found the whole affair distasteful and said so. For this, John was himself thrown into Mukawir and later beheaded.

Herod's vindictiveness towards John presaged the acute paranoia which led him to massacre any segment of society whose loyalty he suspected. By the time he died at Jericho in 4 BC of internal ulcers and putrid sores, Herod had so much blood on his hands that the Jewish historian Josephus omits to mention the minor matter of Bethlehem's murdered babes.

Herod's successors could be equally uncongenial. Few subjects sympathised with his

Mukawir, was one of a string of fortresses serving the first purpose; the Western Wall at the Temple in Jerusalem was built to please the Jews. As Cleopatra had evidently lost interest in Jericho, he stepped in with an offer to lease it.

Herod's dispute with John the Baptist began and ended at the Machaerus or Mukawir fortress. The origin of their animosity was Herod's thought of incarcerating in Mukawir the wife (one of 10) who was obstructing his designs on her sister. The wife managed to slip

LEFT: Roman remains at Petra.
ABOVE: decorative fragments at Qasr al-Hallabat, a Roman fort-turned Omayyad palace.

grandson Herod Agrippa, Caligula's great friend, as he suffered an agonising death, his insides eaten away by worms. Emperor Claudius at once demoted the kingdom to the status of a province under a Roman governor. Pontius Pilate (AD 26–37) then horrified the Galileans by using their blood in sacrifices and the Jews by milking their Sacred Fund to pay for a new aqueduct. As far as Christians are concerned, Pontius Pilate's overwhelming ignominy was of course earned by his role in the Crucifixion. For the purposes of this book, however, the life and times of Jesus must necessarily be confined to the occasions on which he ventured east of the Jordan River.

Jesus Christ

Tracing Christ's movements in Jordan through biblical references is complicated by changes in place-names. The region east of the Jordan River was administered by the Romans as Peraea, one of four divisions of Palestine, but this name does not appear in the New Testament. On the two occasions when Jesus visited the quarter, it is referred to as "the country of the Gadarene", in other words the area around Gadara, or Umm Qais, the trading post which the Jews seized from the Seleucids in 100 BC. On the more notable of Jesus's visits to Gadarene country, he met two tomb-dwellers

possessed by evil spirits and cast their demons into a herd of pigs (Matthew 8: 28–34).

Gadara today is only a ruined shadow of the city it was at this period and continued to be until the 7th century. According to the Jewish historian Josephus, Gadara at the time of Christ was predominantly a heathen rather than Jewish city, which would of course account for the presence of a herd of domestic pigs.

While Christ's own preaching was mainly an appeal to Jews to rectify their own religion, St Paul of Tarsus introduced the idea of aiming the Christian message at heathens like the population of Gadara. This new objective was considerably helped by the Jews being preoccupied

by rebellion against Rome, which reached a gory climax in the destruction of Jerusalem by Titus in AD 70, a massacre in which Jewish converts to Christianty were equal victims.

Christianity readily fitted into the Greek intellectual traditions which had prevailed in the Near East since Alexander the Great's conquest. Compared with the struggle for survival in Rome itself, Eastern Christians could indulge in a debate over the extra iota which turned the Greek word Homoousios into Homoiousis. The former meant that Father and Son were "of the same essence"; the latter that they were merely "of like essence". The distinction dug a chasm between the so-called Monophysitic and Orthodox schools of thought. While Constantine's edict of toleration in 324 made life easier for Christians in the Roman Empire as a whole, the debate over the extra iota reached a pitch that saw Christians killing Christians in what had been their original sanctuary. The conflict continued unabated for centuries to come.

Fully occupied by the skirmishes endemic in desert life, the tribes were totally indifferent to both religious schism and the titanic wars between Byzantium and Persia which characterised the 6th and 7th centuries. Their religion remained rooted in the worship of sacred objects and heavenly bodies. The parallel streams of their ritual were bridged by a *sanctus sanctorum*, a large meteorite preserved in a cubicle temple in Mecca, the Ka'aba. The same black stone is the focal point of Muslim pilgrimage to Mecca, but it was no less revered by pagans long before the birth of the Prophet.

Christianity's equivalent to the Black Stone was the True Cross, kept in the Church of the Holy Sepulchre in Jerusalem. When the Persians captured Jerusalem in 614, they burned the church and carried off the cross. Heraclius, the dashing young emperor of Byzantium, avenged the outrage by defeating the Persians 13 years later and personally carrying the recaptured True Cross along Via Dolorosa to its rebuilt home. Heraclius hoped that in his hour of triumph he could effect a reconciliation between Orthodox and Monophysite leaders. Alas not, but his victory over Persia was tantamount to re-drawing the map of the Near East, an achievement celebrated by the contemporary mosaic map still to be seen in the Orthodox Church of St George at Madaba (*see page 224*).

Otherwise, the fruits of Heraclius's victory

were short-lived: inexplicable reports were received of armies advancing on three fronts, and the possibility of the Persians returning could not be ruled out.

The arrival of Islam

The intruders were Muslim Arabs, devotees of the Prophet Mohammed who had died three years before in Medina. To begin with, Mohammed's call to arms against unbelievers was aimed not at Jews or Christians, but at the population of Mecca, who had driven him out of their city and monopolised

THE PROPHET'S WORD

Those killed on God's behalf were promised an eternal paradise of cool streams, delicious fruit and an unlimited number of virgins.

miraculous show of unity given their backdrop of perpetual anarchy. It is not known whether Mohammed intended to carry his revolution beyond the Arabian peninsula and he left no instructions about a successor. Abu Bakr, one of his earliest adherents, was proclaimed Caliph, but there were already hints of rival claims, which were to spark Muslim civil wars and put a chasm between Sunni and Shi'ite sects.

Early in 633, Abu Bakr organised three columns to invade Byzantine territory. One

the proceeds of pilgrimages to the Black Stone. In his battle for Mecca, Mohammed promised an eternal paradise of sensory delights for those killed doing God's will. Nomads who knew only the hardship of life in the desert could hardly wait. Eight years after Mohammed's flight to Medina (the Hegira), Mecca was captured, and the Black Stone was at once absorbed into the religious ritual of the victorious Muslims.

Most of the tribes of Arabia had submitted to Islam before Mohammed's death in 632, a

LEFT: Byzantine mosaic at Madaba.
ABOVE: a trade caravan arrives in Aqaba.

followed the coastal route to reach the plains of Beersheba. The others skirted the edge of the desert as they advanced north. In early encounters with Byzantine troops, the desert Arabs demonstrated a degree of mobility that made them formidable opponents in open country, although they had little knowledge of siege warfare. Even so, they were able to capture a number of fortified positions. After decades locked in combat with Byzantine Greeks over the infamous extra iota, Monophysite Christian defenders were not averse to throwing open their gates to fellow Arabs whose commitment to one God, however recent, might well prove compatible with their own. ❏

THE CRUSADES

*In the 11th century, the Byzantine emperor Alexius Comnenus called for the first
Crusade; at stake was the survival of Christianity in the Holy Land*

All through the summer of 636 (the Prophet Mohammed had been dead for three years), Muslim Arab and Christian Byzantine armies glared at one another along the banks of the Yarmouk River, the boundary between Jordan and Syria. The afternoon of 20 August then produced a fierce sandstorm.

Dome of the Rock on the spot in Jerusalem where Mohammed, who actually died in Medina, is believed to have ascended into heaven.

Ruling from Damascus, the Omayyad dynasty indulged their nostalgia for life in the desert by building, east of Amman, a string of castles and hunting lodges where they stayed for a few

Keeping the driving sand behind them, the Arab horsemen scythed through the suddenly blinded Byzantines, and with this swift dispatch ended 1,000 years of Graeco-Roman-Byzantine domination in the region. Within a year, the Arabs controlled most of the Near East, including Jerusalem.

Desert retreats

The Arabs were magnanimous victors, assimilating the unfamiliar skills of their subject peoples and tolerating Judaism and Christianity as long as their adherents paid their taxes.

There appears to have been some reciprocity. Byzantines lent a hand in 691 to help build the

weeks each year. Those at Azraq and Hallabat were built on the remains of Roman forts.

When the Abbasids overthrew the Omayyads in 750 and moved their capital to Baghdad, Jordan was reduced to a backwater whose population reverted to Bedouin ways. As the Abbasids did not retain the Omayyads' fondness for desert life, the castles fell into disuse.

The Abbasids reached unprecedented levels of artistic and intellectual achievement under Harun ar-Rashid, immortalised in the tales of *Arabian Nights*. Not for the first time, the death of a dazzling leader led to the partition and rapid disintegration of his empire among spiteful sons.

Jordan was swept along in a shift of power from the moribund Abbasids in Baghdad to the militant Shi'ite Fatimists in Egypt. Under the Fatimid Caliph al-Hakim at the beginning of the 11th century, the long tradition of Arab religious toleration broke down. He made Christians wear black and hang wooden crosses from their necks. Jews, too, were ordered into distinctive dress; in the public baths, they had to wear bells.

It was understood at the time that al-Hakim was going mad, the more so when he banned

COOL CALIPH

When the Abbasid Caliph Mehedi made the pilgrimage to Mecca, he made sure the camels carried special containers for snow – specially for cooling his drinks.

The First Crusade

Christians again found the way barred, but this time by Seljuk Turks who captured Baghdad in the course of conquering most of Asia Minor. Hordes of undisciplined troops made the pilgrim trail impassable. In 1069 the Byzantine emperor Alexius Comnenus warned that Christianity in the east was imperilled; his call for a Crusade was later endorsed by Pope Urban II.

The First Crusade consisted of four separate feudal armies. They met up in Constantinople,

chess and the sale of female footwear, the latter being his brainwave for sweeping prostitution off the streets. In 1009, however, he went to the lengths of ordering the destruction of the Church of the Holy Sepulchre in Jerusalem.

Christians everywhere went up in arms, but the danger of war receded when Hakim went off on one of his constitutional donkey rides at night and to everyone's relief failed to return. Christians rebuilt the church and, for a while, pilgrims once again made their way to Jerusalem unmolested.

LEFT: embarking for the Crusades.
ABOVE: Knights of St John charge the Saracens.

captured Nicaea in June 1097 after a siege of six weeks and Antioch a year later. But nothing in Europe had prepared the troops for conditions in the desert, where suits of armour were infernos and disgustingly impractical for occupants brought low by chronic dysentery.

In the circumstances, the Crusaders did not reach Jerusalem until June 1099. The daunting defences seemed to shrink next to the exhilaration of at last being there. "When they heard the name of Jerusalem called," William of Tyre recorded, "they began to weep and fell on their knees, giving thanks to our Lord… Then they raised their hands in prayer to Heaven and, taking off their shoes, bowed down to the ground and kissed the earth." The thoughts of the engineers, though, were on an absence of timber for siege machines without which the city walls looked impregnable.

The solution to the engineers' dilemma was provided, bizarrely, by Tancred, a Norman knight whose dysentery and modesty forced him constantly "to dismount, go away from the group and find a hiding-place". Having withdrawn into a deep recess beneath a hollow rock on one such occasion, Tancred spotted a large quantity of sawn timber. This windfall went into siege machines which breached the walls of Jerusalem on 15 July 1099.

CREATION OF THE KNIGHTS TEMPLAR

On his return to Jerusalem from the Idumaean country, Baldwin I busied himself administering his kingdom. The most imporant item of business on his agenda was the foundation of Military Orders out of the community of monks, who since 1070 had looked after poor and sick pilgrims visiting the city. The monks, based in a wing of the royal palace, the former Al-Aqsa Mosque in the Temple area, adopted a distinctive red cross on a white tunic as the insignia of their new order, the Knights Templar. Although the Military Orders owed allegiance to the Pope, they provided the kingdom with a welcome regular army of trained soldiers.

Controlling Jerusalem

Godfrey de Bouillon, Duke of Lorraine, was put onto the throne of the proclaimed "Latin Kingdom of Jerusalem" but with famous modesty declined to wear a crown in a place where Jesus had worn thorns. He was succeeded by his brother Baldwin I, whose priority was to secure an adequate coastline and build a line of inland fortresses which would give him mastery over Arab caravan routes. But the activity of construction warned Toghetekin of Damascus, who also wanted to corner the revenue.

In 1108, Toghetekin attacked a recently completed fortress east of Lake Tiberias. Its custodian, Gervase of Basoches, was put to death and his scalp, a shock of wavy white hair, paraded on a pole. But Baldwin and Toghetekin had greater interests elsewhere, and it made sense to share the proceeds rather than cause them to dry up by turning the trade routes into a battleground. They agreed a truce in northern Transjordan, supposedly to last 10 years.

It was characteristic of the times that a truce in northern Transjordan in no way inhibited Baldwin and Toghetekin from battling elsewhere. The land between the Dead Sea and the Gulf of Aqaba was important to them both. For Toghetekin, it was a base from which to raid Judaea; for Baldwin, it protected the Kingdom of Jerusalem from Egypt's desire to join with the eastern Muslim world. While the sympathies of the Bedouin population lay with Damascus, the Christians had the support of Greek monasteries in the Idumaean wilderness. Crusaders and Damascenes clashed in Wadi Moussa, near Petra, but again they agreed on a tactical disengagement. The Damascenes withdrew, leaving Baldwin to smoke their Bedouin allies out of their caverns and steal their flocks.

Baldwin decided in 1115 that the Idumaean country would have to be permanently occupied, and the necessary first step was to build a great castle at one of the few fertile spots, Shawbak. He named the castle Montreal (Royal Mountain) before pushing further south to the Red Sea at Aqaba. While the Crusaders bathed their horses, the local inhabitants took to their boats and fled. Baldwin fortified the town with one citadel and built a second on the little island of Jesirat Far'un, which the Franks called Le Graye, just offshore. With garrisons in both strongholds, the Franks dominated the roads to Arabia and Egypt, enabling them to raid caravans at their ease and effectively separating Egypt from the heartland of Islam.

The creation of a regular army (*see* "The Creation of the Knights Templar", *page 32*) went some way towards relieving Baldwin's concern that the influx of Westerners was diluting the warrior and clerical ethos of the kingdom with bourgeois attitudes receptive to the indolent habits of the East. Matters such as the imperfect truce with Toghetekin in Transjordan required constant vigilance – the demarcation of their fron-

LAP OF LUXURY

The knights and their ladies lived in silken and fur-lined splendour, drinking the wine of Palestine and hunting with hawks as the Omayyads had done before them.

was thus with a view to tightening control along the Dead Sea that the great fortress of Karak was built. Even so, there was no serious Frank colonisation of the area and the Bedouin tribes continued their nomadic life.

Karak was built on the crest of a hill, a twilight world of stone-vaulted chambers, halls, stables and corridors behind deep moated walls. To Western pilgrims, a glimpse of Outremer life in castles such as Karak, to say nothing of Jerusalem, was shocking because of its luxury and licence. "We

tier necessitated cutting a castle in half at one point, rendering it useless, while a fort built by Toghetekin near Jarash was considered altogether out of order and razed.

Baldwin's death symbolised the supplanting of the pioneer Crusaders by a second generation from the West who wished to exercise more systematic control of the country east and south of the Dead Sea as Muslim caravans found ways of circumventing Montreal, Baldwin's castle, and an increasing number of desert raiders slipped by to attack the coastal plain. It

---

LEFT: the first sight of Jerusalem.
ABOVE: a treaty is made with Saladin.

who had been occidentals have become orientals," Fulcher of Chartres observed. An Arab traveller noted approvingly that on being invited to dinner at the home of an elderly Outremer knight, he was assured that all meals were prepared by Egyptian women and pork never crossed the threshold.

The Cruellest knight

From 1150 onwards, Jerusalem sent increasingly heated messages to the West reporting Muslim encroachment and predicting that another Crusade would soon be necessary, and it was at this point that a cruel young knight named Reynald de Chatillon entered the scene.

More than any other single person, Reynald proved fatal to Christian Jerusalem.

In 1160, Reynald went north to plunder the seasonal movement of grazing herds from the mountains to the plain. Slowed down by a huge number of captured cattle, camels and horses, he was himself captured and carried away, bound on a camel, to gaol in Aleppo.

During his unlamented absence of 16 years, the Franks were confronted by their most formidable Muslim adversary to date – Saladin, a Kurdish mercenary who had risen to become vizier of Egypt. He captured most of Syria in the course of tightening the noose around the

timber from the forests of Moab and tested on the Dead Sea) to raid sea-caravans on the Red Sea and to attack Mecca itself. He captured Aqaba, which had been in Muslim hands since 1170, but the fortress on Ile de Graye held out. While Reynald remained with two of his ships to blockade the island, the rest of his fleet sailed merrily down the Red Sea. They caused havoc by plundering richly laden merchantmen from Aden and India, sinking a pilgrim ship heading for Jedda, setting fire to shipping in almost every port on the Arabian coast, and even sending a landing party ashore to pillage an undefended caravan that had crossed the desert from

Crusader states. Aleppo remained independent, but only because a Frankish army came to its assistance and lifted Saladin's siege. Gumushtekin, the ruler of Aleppo, showed his gratitude by releasing all Christian prisoners, and among them was one Reynald de Chatillon.

Back in his domain, Reynald resumed his thievery, and in 1181 fell on a caravan on its way to Mecca and made off with its goods. Saladin retaliated by throwing into chains 1,500 Christian pilgrims forced to land in Egypt because of bad weather. Reynald still refused to return the goods and war became inevitable.

Undeterred by news that Saladin was marching north, Reynald launched a fleet (built with

the Nile. The Muslim world was horrified, and even the Frankish princes were ashamed.

Saladin rides in

Saladin left Damascus in September 1183 with Reynald in his sights. Reynald, never a man to show concern, did not allow Saladin's reported advance to interfere with his plans for a gala wedding between his 17-year-old stepson, Humphrey of Toron, and Princess Isabella, aged 11. Distinguished guests, jugglers, dancers and musicians from all over the Christian East arrived at Karak throughout November. And on 20 November, so too did Saladin.

The Muslim army went to work straight

away. They attacked the lower town and managed to force an entrance. Reynald was able to escape back into the castle only because one of his knights held the bridge over the moat until it could be destroyed behind him.

The walls of Karak held out against the pounding of Saladin's nine mangonels, and on 4 December reports of a Crusader force approaching past Mount Nebo persuaded him to lift the siege and return to Damascus. Saladin tried again the following year, but the result was the same. Under pressure of other business, it then suited both Franks and Saladin to declare a truce.

Peace meant that Muslim caravans could again travel through Frankish lands, and once again the sight of a large pot of gold passing by from Egypt was more than Reynald could resist. The merchants were diverted into the castle at Karak. Saladin exploded with rage, and war resumed.

Saladin assembled the largest army he had ever commanded. On 1 July 1187, he crossed the Jordan at Sennabra, took Tiberias in less than an hour, and led his army on to Hattin, a village with pastures and plenty of water, where the road descended towards the lake. The Frankish army, including Reynald, approached Saladin's position along a road with no water. On the afternoon of 3 July they gained the plateau above Hattin, but heat and thirst had taken a grievous toll.

Reynald's last stand

The Christians spent a miserable night, racked by thirst and the sound of prayers and songs from the Muslim camp below. Worse still, the Muslims set fire to the scrub covering the hillside, sending up gusts of choking smoke. The attack began at first light. Many of the knights and infantry were slaughtered at once, but the survivors fought with desperate courage.

Saladin greeted the handful of survivors graciously. He seated the Christian King Guy next to him and offered a goblet of rose-water, iced with the snows of Mount Hermon. When Guy handed the goblet to the knight sitting next to

> ### IN LOVE AND WAR
> While rocks were hurled at the walls, the bridegroom's mother personally prepared a selection of tasty dishes which were sent to Saladin with her compliments.

him, Saladin had a quick word with his interpreter. Under the laws of Arab hospitality, food or drink given to a captive meant that his life was safe. "Tell the King," Saladin said, "he gave that man drink, not I." The man in question was Reynald de Chatillon. Saladin ran through a list of Reynald's crimes but there was no sign of repentance. He ended the litany with a swipe of his sword, sending Reynald's head rolling. Jerusalem fell to Saladin on 2 October 1187. A series of misguided Crusades then ensued.

The Outremer Franks failed to regain Jerusalem or Transjordan, but they held on to coastal cities for most of the 13th century. They were sustained by the export of sugar, taxes on transit trade, and dissension among Saladin's descendants. In 1291, however, Al-Mansur Qalawun, a Mamluke, positioned a huge siege train against the walls of Acre, the main Christian stronghold on the coast, and took it after a fight which saw every last defender killed.

The usual cry for a Crusade was heard, but Europe was now preoccupied by the Hundred Years' War. Religious warfare was far from over, but the saga of Crusaders in the Holy Land died in the dust of Acre after 194 years. ❏

LEFT: Richard the Lionheart and the Master of the Knights of St John.
RIGHT: siege of Antioch, ancient capital of Syria.

MAMLUKES AND OTTOMANS

As the Crusades drew to a close, the Mamlukes ushered in a remarkable age of military might and cultural flowering. Then came the Ottomans

With the expulsion of the Crusaders at the end of the 13th century, Jordan was absorbed into an expanding Mamluke Empire. The foundations of this empire rested on the remarkable fact that Mamlukes were slaves (the word "Mamluke" means "belonging to") who not only approved of slavery but turned it into a kind of self-perpetuating, oligarchical meritocracy.

The term Mamluke was first applied in Saladin's day (12th century) to young boys who were bought or captured abroad in order to be trained for the professional corps of the army. Experience led to a preference for children of the tough Circassian and Caucasian nomadic tribes, hence the tradition that Mamlukes were generally white, even if they adopted Islam and grew up speaking Arabic. Far removed from family and tribal ties, Mamlukes could be relied upon to give their masters undivided loyalty.

Unlike domestic slaves, Mamlukes could not be sold on. Servitude was exclusive to the original purchaser, and when he died his Mamlukes were at liberty to market their mercenary services either as individuals or, in cooperation with other Mamlukes, as a private army. These private armies proliferated as Mamlukes grew rich on military plunder and bought their own Mamlukes; non-Mamlukes were thus turned into subjects of the former slaves.

The Mamluke Empire lasted for nearly three centuries before Mamlukes were reduced to a military caste in Egypt. As such they were still around to fight Napoleon on the banks of the Nile, although the last of their number were massacred soon afterwards, in 1811.

Their legacy in Jordan, though modest, does not always get the attention it deserves. The Qalaat ar-Rabad at Ajlun, for example, is a fine piece of Mamluke military architecture, and the Montreal Crusader castle at Shawbak is, as it stands, a Mamluke 14th-century restoration of the 12th-century Crusader original.

LEFT: Mamlukes, the Circassian military caste.
RIGHT: Mamluke warrior in battle dress.

Qalaat ar-Rabad, the aforementioned castle at Ajlun, was a link in the typically ingenious communications network by which the Mamlukes ran their empire from Cairo. Lofts in the castle contained pigeons ready to relay messages attached under their wings, and at times they even carried air freight.

THE FALL OF THE MAMLUKES

The Mamluke era has been called "a combination of extreme corruption and savage cruelty with exquisite refinement in material civilisation and an admirable devotion to art". Mamlukes could afford luxuries because, partly through their hold on Jordan, they controlled lucrative trade routes. It was the Portuguese explorer Vasco da Gama who eventually wrecked their prosperity by discovering the alternative sea route to India. Five years after his historic voyage in 1498, the Mamluke government in Egypt was bankrupt and unable to maintain an army capable of meeting the growing threat of the Ottoman Turks.

The Ottoman takeover

The end of Mamluke rule in Jordan drew nearer with the Ottoman victory over the Persians at Chaldiran in 1514. Ironically, Ottoman success owed much to the Janissaries who – with an infantry composed of boys, taken from their families to be trained – bore a similarity to the Mamlukes. Salim the Grim, whose grandfather Mehmed II captured Constantinople in 1453, occupied Jordan on behalf of the Ottomans in 1516.

Whereas the Mamlukes had ruled Jordan

> ### A BOWL OF CHERRIES
>
> A Mamluke in Cairo with a desire for Lebanese cherries sent an order by pigeon. Three days later 600 birds arrived, each carrying a single cherry in a silk purse.

from Cairo and Damascus, the Ottomans attempted to do so from Constantinople several weeks distant. They saw waging war on Christendom as a pious duty, and it was best discharged by going west into Europe. Although the likes of Suleiman the Magnificent built superb monuments in parts of the empire, the area east of the Jordan River was a neglected appendage, administered from the trading town of Salt.

In the desert, the real rulers were Bedouin who lived on the proceeds of inter-tribal plunder and tolls exacted from travellers. As Lawrence observed of a later period, "camel-raiding parties, self-contained like ships, might cruise confidently along the enemy's cultivation-frontier, sure of unhindered retreat into their desert-element which the Turks could not explore". In the 1880s, the Ottomans hoped to collect taxes from the tribes, but such thoughts came to nothing.

Internationally speaking, the Ottomans could be forgiven for not knowing where they stood in the 19th century. Britain, Turkey's ally against Napoleon, immediately afterwards supported a Mamluke revolt against Turkish suzerainty in Egypt. The British navy sank the Turkish fleet in the interest of Greek independence in 1826, but Britain and Turkey were allies again in the next year against Russia. And so it went.

While relations with Britain were obviously unpredictable, there was at least a constant factor in enmity with Russia. From Catherine the Great onwards, Russian designs on Turkey's Balkan possessions were decked out as a latter-day Crusade: Christians liberating Orthodox believers from the Muslim yoke. The brunt was borne by Circassian Muslims, and it was in these circumstances that Turkey settled Muslim Circassian refugees in Jordan. They revitalised Amman and, with a long tradition as Mamlukes and Janissaries, gravitated towards service in the Ottoman imperial army.

In 1900 the Sultan Abdul Hamid embarked on improving communications between Damascus and the Arabian provinces by building the Hejaz railway line to Medina. It followed the old pilgrim trail to Mecca and thus cut through the heart of Jordan. While it had previously suited Turkey to keep inter-tribal warfare bubbling, stability was now essential to protect the line.

A Turkish governor appointed to Karak in the interest of security was confronted by a tribal rebellion in 1910. This was partly an echo of convulsions in Istanbul following the Young Turk revolution two years earlier, and its successful suppression flattered to deceive. The empire's communications were long and brittle. Moreover, its subject peoples were restless – especially the Arabs. ❏

LEFT: 19th-century pilgrims dressed in readiness for the journey to Mecca.
RIGHT: the Mamluke architecture of Ajlun Castle.

THE ARAB REVOLT

*First muted by Hussein, Sherif of Mecca, the Arab Revolt was supposed to free the
Arab world from the yoke of the Ottoman Empire and create a unified Arabian state*

For Hussein, Sherif of Mecca, the apparently terminal condition of the Ottoman Empire, which had been dubbed the "Sick Man of Europe" at the beginning of the 20th century, inspired the dream of a vast Arab confederacy that would recreate the past glory of the Abbasid Empire. Hussein envisaged him-

ening posture of these powers, he evoked his authority as Caliph – the spiritual head of the Islamic faith – to declare a *jihad* (holy war) on the European powers. In theory, this made it incumbent upon Muslims everywhere to take up arms against Europeans. This threat was not taken lightly by Britain, France or Russia, as

self and his sons ruling this reawakened empire, establishing a powerful role for the Hashemite line of the Prophet Mohammed.

In February 1914 his second son, the Emir Abdullah, was sent to Cairo to speak to Lord Kitchener, the British Agent and Minister of War. The object of Abdullah's visit was to find out how Britain would react in the event of an Arab revolt against Turkey. Kitchener was interested in the potential of such a campaign, but, preoccupied with the possibility of war with Germany, remained non-commital.

Later that year, the Sultan of Turkey could feel British, Russian and French hands tightening around his throat. In response to the threat-

each of these powers had huge numbers of Muslim subjects – Britain alone, for example, ruled 70 million in India.

Abdullah's suggestion of a revolt was held up to the light for closer consideration, and its appeal was starkly apparent to Europe. If Turkey's Arab subjects were in a rebellious mood, their Islamic loyalty to the Turkish Caliph could be compromised by a countemand from the Sherif of Mecca, even though spiritually he occupied the rung below the Caliph.

The crimson banner

Hussein now procrastinated, holding out for guarantees of his Abbasid dream in return for military support. Before the matter was resolved, British forces suffered a humiliating evacuation from Gallipoli and increased their pressure on Hussein accordingly. On 5 June 1916, Ali and Feisal, the Sherif's first and third sons, raised the crimson banner outside Medina to signal the start of the Arab Revolt. Some 30,000 Arabs assembled in response to Hussein's call, volunteers aged between 12 and 60.

But a siege of Medina, the terminus of the Hejaz railway from Damascus, was deliberately not pressed, or not pressed with any great conviction. "We must not take Medina," a British adviser mused. "The Turk was harm-

army from Egypt to Damascus. According to his cover story, he was examining the "wilderness" in which Moses and the Israelites spent 40 years after being denied use of the King's Highway by the Edomites. In 1916, Lawrence was given the responsibility of estimating the leadership qualities of Hussein's sons. He concluded that Feisal was the most promising.

Large numbers of Turkish troops were successfully tied down in Medina, allowing the Arab irregulars the opportunity to dictate the pace of the battle, as they fought their way up the Red Sea to Aqaba, a port ideally placed to receive British arms shipments from Egypt.

less there... We wanted him to stay at Medina, and every other distant place, in the largest numbers. Our ideal was to keep his railway just working, but only just, with the maximum of loss and discomfort."

The adviser was young T. E. Lawrence, the future "Lawrence of Arabia", and his rank of second-lieutenant belied his true status in British Army Intelligence. Two years earlier, he had posed as an archaeologist in order to survey a possible invasion route for the British

The Howeitat

The positioning of Aqaba's defences was based upon the presumption that an attack would come from the sea. Instead, Lawrence plotted an attack via a looping course through the desert, and by doing so would enable a small number of Arabs to take the Turks by surprise.

Abu al-Lissal had to be taken en route, a test of the fighting qualities of the Howeitat tribesmen and in particular Auda, their warrior chief. In 30 years of incessant warfare, he was reputed to have killed 75 men with his own hand.

Surveying the Turkish positions in Abu al-Lissal, Lawrence remarked, rather mischievously, that from what he had seen c'

LEFT: Sherif Hussein ben Ali, Emir of Mecca, with Sir Ronald Storrs, who became Governor of Jerusalem.
ABOVE: Arab forces on the march.

Howeitat so far, they fired a lot of shots to hit very little. In *The Seven Pillars of Wisdom*, Lawrence described Auda's swift response to such an insulting accusation. "Almost pale with rage, and trembling, he tore his head-cloth off and threw it on the ground beside me. Then he ran back up the hill like a madman, shouting to the men in his dreadful strained and rustling voice." Lawrence chased after him but all Auda would say was "Get your camel if you want to see the old man's work."

SPIRITS OF THE PAST

Holed up with his men in the castle at Azraq, Lawrence sensed how "past and present flowed over us like an uneddying river. We dreamed ourselves into the spirit of the place."

Within no time at all, they were in the midst of a furious downhill camel charge, with Auda's men firing from the saddle. Lawrence, up front on his racing camel, shot out of the saddle when his mount tripped, and had to sit out the action. By the time he had recovered his senses, the battle was over. Some 300 Turks had been killed and 160 taken prisoner – all for the loss of just two Howeitat.

Donning uniforms from the dead Turks, the Arabs rode down the Negab Pass and across

INFIGHTING AMONG THE SHEIKHS

While the Arab forces under Feisal's command began to resemble a regular army – they were joined by experienced Arab deserters from the Turkish army – Lawrence's guerrilla strike force revelled in unorthodoxy. "The men were a mad lot," Lawrence wrote, "sharpened to distraction by hope or success." As every fourth or fifth man was a sheikh who would recognise no other sheikh, Lawrence had to act as referee. In the course of one operation lasting six days, he had to adjudicate on "twelve cases of assault with weapons, four camel-liftings, one marriage, two thefts, a divorce, 14 feuds, two evil eyes, and a bewitchment."

the Guweira plateau towards the port of Aqaba. The surprise assault from the landward side worked to perfection. Turkish outposts were thrown into panic and quick surrender, and the Arab force raced through a sand-storm to capture Aqaba and triumphantly splash in the sea.

Victory at Aqaba wrapped up the Hejaz phase of the war. General Allenby now led the British advance from Sinai to Syria and the Arab troops became his right wing.

The practicalities of war in Jordan had hardly changed since the days of the Crusades or even the Romans. Any spot of intrinsic strategic value invariably boasted some ancient fortification which was either occupied by Ottoman forces or used by Lawrence and his men between hit-and-run attacks on the railway line.

On the other hand, the fall of Jerusalem could hardly have deviated further from historical precedents. The mayor first offered the keys of the city to a couple of British army cooks who had gone out looking for water and got lost. But they didn't want the responsibility of holding the keys to Jerusalem, and so refused them, as did two sergeants who came ambling by. The mayor was pleased to find a private finally willing to accept them, and thus changed hands a prize washed in blood since biblical times.

In the meantime, the Arab army pushed up British army, took Dir'a, and were then poised for their triumphant entry into Damascus. By this time it was obvious that Hussein's Abbasid dream would not automatically be granted, so the proclamation in September 1918 of an Arab government under Feisal was an attempt to pre-empt the uncertainty. More powerful forces soon intervened, however, though, in compensation, Feisal was later offered Iraq.

Out of the wreckage of the defeated Ottoman Empire arose Transjordan. Abdullah, who had first explored with Lord Kitchener the idea of an Arab revolt five years earlier, would rule the new country, albeit under British tutelage. ❏

through the corn-belt east of the Dead Sea, taking Shawbak, Tafila, Karak and Madaba. Numbers swelled as more tribes joined the rebellion, the army's backbone being stiffened by artillery. Lawrence had a Rolls-Royce armoured car, though he usually kept his Arab dress.

A dream fulfilled?

After the capture of Amman, the Arab force began their advance along the gorge of the Yarmouk River. The Arabs linked up with the

LEFT: General Allenby enters Jerusalem.
ABOVE: Paris Peace Conference, 1919, with Feisal in the centre and T. E. Lawrence to his right.

DRESS SENSE

Lawrence usually adopted an Arab mode of dress when working with the tribes. "If you can wear Arab kit when with the tribes," he advised his British colleagues, you will acquire their trust and intimacy to a degree impossible in uniform." The use of native "kit" gained an extra dimension when Lawrence hired three gypsy women – and borrowed one of their dresses – for a reconnaissance of Amman. Their appearance proved too inviting for some Turkish soldiers, forcing the ladies to take to their heels. The experience brought Lawrence to the conclusion that behind enemy lines he would in future discard Arab dress, in favour of Army uniform.

LAWRENCE OF ARABIA

The legend of Lawrence is beguiling, inspiring and, at times, amusing. He did much
for the cause of the Arab Revolt, but ultimately his loyalty was to the British Empire

Lawrence of Arabia – "T. E." (Thomas Edward) to his friends – was a legend before he was 30. In Arab dress, a golden dagger in his belt, Lawrence could mount a moving camel with a kind of pole-vault action using its tail. He was an expert shot with either hand, as useful with a pistol as the lightweight Lewis machine gun packed in a basket on his camel. Seen against a backdrop of endless desert dunes, the figure of Lawrence was an irresistible antidote to terrible tales of trench warfare on the Western Front.

In due course, the legend attracted iconoclasts, notably a biography by Richard Aldington which implied that Lawrence was pre-eminently a posturing, melodramatic homosexual, but Lawrence's image – in part the consequence of Peter O'Toole's mesmeric performance in David Lean's 1962 film *Lawrence of Arabia* – remains largely heroic and romantic. However, with the gradual unpeeling of official British secrets after the statutory 50 years, it now seems that Lawrence was more closely attached and loyal to British Intelligence than had hitherto been suspected. His cause was less Arab independence than a vendetta against French imperial expansion.

A boy of destiny

Lawrence was born in 1888 in Wales, the son of an Anglo-Irish landowner called Chapman who had left his wife and four daughters to elope with the girls' governess, Sarah Maden. Both changed their names to Lawrence but never married. Thomas Edward was the second of their four sons, a boy with an unusually brisk step and an unwavering gaze. A dose of mumps in adolescence probably stunted his growth: his 5 ft 5 inches (1.7 metres) looked less because of his disproportionately large head.

Young Lawrence apparently had some kind of premonition about his future. He toughened

LEFT: Lawrence in a portrait by Augustus John.
RIGHT: a bedouin whose father had fought with Lawrence in the Arab Revolt.

himself by sleeping on bare floorboards, bicycling till he dropped and going days without food. An interest in medieval castles led to the study of famous battles. Reflecting on his brilliant military career in the desert, Lawrence liked to say breezily that "of course" he had no army training and had only read "the usual schoolboy stuff". In reality, there was probably not an army general in Britain, let alone a schoolboy, who had trawled through all 25 volumes of Napoleon's dispatches between the textbook strategy of everyone from the Roman Procopius to Clausewitz and Foch.

Archaeology and reconnaissance

Whilst at Oxford University, Lawrence caught the eye of D. G. Hogarth, an archaeologist and – on the quiet – a British Intelligence expert on the Middle East. Interest in the region then focused on the tottering Ottoman Empire, a tantalising fruit for European imperial powers, not least because of the oil reserves in the Ottoman provinces. Germany stole a march on rivals by arranging to build a rail-link between Berlin and Baghdad – with an oil concession extending 17 km (12 miles) on either side of the line.

London saw the scheme as a threat to British India, the Suez Canal and its own oil interests. It was therefore not pure coincidence that, at Oxford, Hogarth made preparations for an archaeological expedition to a Hittite site at Carchemish, which happened to overlook construction of the Berlin-Baghdad railway. Among Hogarth's recruits was Lawrence, who, at Hogarth's insistence, took crash courses in Arabic and photography.

When the Carchemish dig closed for the hot summer months, Lawrence roamed further afield with a young Arab who was known as Dahoum. It was on one of these excursions that Lawrence was first arrested, and held prisoner at Azraq as a suspected deserter from the Turkish army. A bribe to one of the guards eventually secured his release.

The stigma of betrayal

It seems that Lawrence was haunted by having misled the Arabs, Feisal in particular, into believing that they were fighting for a single independent Arab state. He knew all along, it is now clear, about the Anglo-French Sykes-Picot plan to partition the Arab world into British and French spheres of influence. Lawrence tried to console himself with the thought that a deception that helped to defeat Germany and Turkey was better than losing the war.

Nevertheless, the strain of operating under misleading colours took its toll on Lawrence after the Paris Peace Conference. In the face of Zionist pressure at the conference for the creation of a Jewish national home in Palestine, Lawrence came round to thinking that all parties would best be served by a semi-autonomous Arab state under British protection – financed and advised by Zionists! When this was rejected and a large part of the still-born Arab state was given to France, Lawrence escaped public view by enrolling in the ranks of first the Royal Air Force (as "John Hume Ross") and afterwards of the Royal Tank Corps (as "Private T. E. Shaw"). He did, however, remain on good terms with the likes of Winston Churchill, and made a genuine contribution to the design of a new speedboat and a device that anticipated the hovercraft.

On 13 May 1935, Lawrence set out from his cottage, Clouds Hill, on his beloved Brough Superior motor-cycle. In swerving to avoid a cyclist, Lawrence crashed and fractured his skull. He died six days later, although rumour did its utmost to keep him alive – as a secret agent in World War II, as a recluse living in the international zone of Tangier, and so on. For his army of admirers, a simple motor accident was no way to end the legend. ❑

FACT OR FICTION?

Lawrence's most notorious arrest interrupted a clandestine reconnaissance of Dir'a during the Arab Revolt. His account in *The Seven Pillars of Wisdom* of being led captive to Hajim Bey, the Turkish governor, in order to be beaten and raped – by the guards if not successfully by the Bey himself – is so effusive in its language and detail that some scholars are inclined to make a connection with his masochistic tendencies in later life. Real, exaggerated or perhaps even imaginary, the Dir'a ordeal is thought to have contributed to the subsequent mental and emotional problems Lawrence suffered, which occasionally made him suicidal.

LEFT: Lawrence in Jerusalem, with King Abdullah on the right of the picture.
RIGHT: Lawrence astride his beloved motorbike.

ENTER THE HASHEMITES

*Hashemite dreams of a Pan-Arab nation failed to take account of
complex post-war deals concocted by Western powers*

When Emir Abdullah arrived in Ma'an by rail from the Hejaz in 1920, Transjordan was teetering on the edge of chaos. The order that had been established by the Ottomans during the second half of the 19th century had broken down in World War I, and the efforts of the Emir's brother Feisal to extend his authority from Damascus had been unsuccessful. In July 1920, Feisal's fledgling kingdom soon fell apart when he was driven out of Syria by the French, who now controlled the country in line with secret wartime agreements struck with Britain.

The British, unsure of what to do with Transjordan, had recognised three separate governments, in Irbid, Salt and Karak, and sent British advisers to each one. The government based in Salt was moderately successful because the local Christians and Circassians continued to pay their taxes and officials appointed by Feisal's short-lived kingdom in Damascus were able to maintain order. But the authority of the administrations in Irbid and Karak was strictly limited, and the country was a patchwork of local sheikhdoms. The Bedouin had begun to raid again and the line between desert and sown fluctuated from day to day. As the Lebanese historian Kamal Salibi has put it, "a state of utter lawlessness" prevailed in the countryside.

Within a very short time, Emir Abdullah had managed to restore order and created a new state where one had never existed before. That state was Transjordan.

A grand plan

Transjordan was not Emir Abdullah's initial objective and it was never his final one. When he alighted from the train in Ma'an, he announced his intention of marching on Syria to regain it for the Hashemites. From his point of view, the Arab Revolt had been fought to establish a broad Arab kingdom in the area under his family, which was uniquely qualified to rule on

LEFT: King Abdullah.
RIGHT: Abdullah and his entourage.

account of its descent from the Prophet Mohammed. Britain had promised to lend its support to this scenario in return for Hashemite backing in World War I.

However, Britain had made conflicting promises during the war, and under the Sykes-Picot agreement – a secret pact between France

and Britain – Syria and Lebanon were to come under French dominion, Iraq and Palestine under British. This carve-up of the Middle East was further complicated by Britain's commitment to the idea of a Jewish National Home in Palestine, established in the Balfour Declaration. Though underhand, the deal between France and Britain was ratified by the League of Nations in 1920.

So while Emir Abdullah's announcement at the railway station in Ma'an accurately reflected his Arab Nationalist convictions, he must have known that the British would not support him against the French. The sad experience of his brother Feisal in Syria had made that clear.

The Emir's immediate and most pressing aim was to salvage something from the broken promises made by Britain in World War I.

Transjordan, poor, undeveloped and lawless, had not been allocated to anyone in the Great Power land-grab and increasingly it must have seemed like a good starting-point for the Emir's wider ambitions. However, he had very little money and his army was small. His initial objectives therefore were to secure material and moral support from Britain.

SPOILS OF WAR

In the Sykes-Picot agreement struck in 1916, following a successful outcome of the war, France was to gain control over Syria and Lebanon, Britain was to get Iraq and Palestine.

The Emir and his aims were also attractive to many of the inhabitants of Transjordan. His Hashemite heritage served him well and he quickly developed links with local Bedouin tribes. Settled communities like the Christians and the Circassians, whose lives were disrupted by persisting lawlessness, also welcomed him. Abdullah consolidated these links by staying with Christian families, such as the Abu Jabers and Sukkars of Salt and with the Circassian Muslim al-Mufti family in Amman.

Establishing the Emirate

Wary at first, the British quickly recognised that it was in their own interests to back Abdullah. The local administrations established by Feisal from Damascus were largely incompetent and discredited. Abdullah, with British help, would restore order in a territory for which they had no firm plans. Support for the Emir would also help to right the wrongs Britain had done the Hashemites after the Arab Revolt.

On 15 May 1923, therefore, the Emirate of Transjordan came into existence, albeit on the understanding that this new country would be closely supervised by Britain while it proceeded on the road to full independence.

He also lived and held court in Bedouin-style encampments on the outskirts of Amman and in Shuneh in the Jordan Valley. The Emir's most important card, however, was that he controlled the only military force in the country. He was determined to establish his authority and restore law and order.

The rumble of discontent

In spite of this determination, the Emir's task was not an easy one. As early as 1921, at Kura, near Irbid, a sheikh named Kulayb al-Shurayda led villagers against the Emir's tax collectors. A more serious threat was presented over the next two years by the Adwan Bedouin tribe, who were joined by educated locals from towns such as Irbid, Salt and Karak.

The Adwan protested against the favouritism shown to the Beni Sakhr tribe and the townsmen demanded a more democratic form of government. They also raised the slogans "Transjordan for the Transjordanians" and "foreigners out", reflecting their anger about the way in which power was being monopolised by Syrians, Hejazis and other Arabs employed by Emir Abdullah in line with his pan-Arab convictions.

> **BALFOUR DECLARATION**
>
> A letter of 2 November 1917 from the British foreign secretary to Lord Rothschild of the British Zionist Federation declared Britain's support for a Jewish homeland in Palestine.

In 1928, partly in response to widespread street demonstrations, a constitution was promulgated and a part-elected, part-appointed parliament was introduced. Its function was largely advisory, but it served the Emir's purpose of bringing Transjordanians into the system and he made sure that it carefully reflected the different constituencies in the country.

By the mid 1930s, the Emir Abdullah was able to claim: "We entered Transjordan to find four governments, each one sep-

arate from the other…Our first aim was to put the country together and secure its need to achieve unity. And here it is today…enjoying the complete unity to which sister countries in its neighbourhood still aspire."

If he was to survive and forge a state from Transjordan, the Emir had no alternative but to turn to the British. A new military force, which later became the Transjordanian army (the Arab Legion), was created under the command of a British army captain, Peake Pasha. Typically, Abdullah tried to solve both rebellions peacefully by personal intervention, and only when all else failed did he order his army into action. It is also a Hashemite hallmark that the leaders of the revolts were later pardoned.

LEFT: Abdullah witnesses the establishment of the British mandate in Palestine, July 1920.
ABOVE: inspection of the Arab Legion.

A state of independence

On 22 March 1946, Transjordan secured its independence. Two months later the title Emir was changed to King and the country was renamed Jordan. Four years later Jordan absorbed the West Bank. Both King and country had come a long way since 1920. But at what cost? To this day King Abdullah remains a controversial figure in the Arab world. The King's critics accuse him of serving British interests in the region to secure his own survival and aggrandisement. During World War II, Transjordan remained loyal to Britain and helped crush Arab nationalists in Iraq who saw Britain's difficulty as their opportunity.

Admirers of King Abdullah portray him as a pragmatic politician who was years ahead of his time. For them, he correctly evaluated the balance of power in the region from the start. Working within the constraints it imposed, he managed to carve out the state of Jordan as a first step towards a larger Arab Kingdom. As a Hashemite, it is argued, he had more claim to

The taint of colonialism

King Abdullah's critics were in the vast majority during the late 1940s and throughout the 1950s. Colonial rule was coming to an end all over the region and governments that were tainted by association with the colonial powers were attacked everywhere. Increasingly, the call was for independence and Arab strength through unity.

The failure of the Arab states to prevent the loss of Palestine, the creation of Israel and the exodus of 700,000 Palestinians from their homeland in 1948 finally blew the lid off the pot. After 1948, successive governments were

Arab leadership than any other individual or any other ideology.

Foiled in Syria, the King had turned his attentions towards Palestine, where he recommended a conciliatory course rather than the "all or nothing" approach advocated by the Palestinian leader of the time, Haj Amin al-Husseini, the Mufti of Jerusalem. King Abdullah's admirers point out that had it not been for the Jordanian army in the 1948 war, all of Palestine would have been lost to Israel. They also argue that the union of the East Bank and West Bank was carried out at the request of the Palestinians themselves, at a time when their leadership was in a state of complete disarray.

overthrown one after the other in Syria, and the Prime Minister of Lebanon was assassinated in 1951. The next year, King Farouk of Egypt was removed from power by a group of army officers, among them Gamal Abdel Nasser.

It was against this turbulent background that King Abdullah proceeded on his regular journey to Al-Aqsa mosque in Jerusalem for the Friday prayer on 20 July 1951. As he made his way into the mosque, the King was shot dead by a Palestinian gunman, an assassination witnessed by his shocked grandson and eventual successor, Hussein. ❑

ABOVE: the funeral of King Abdullah, 1951.

An Officer and a Gentleman

Within the Arab world, Glubb Pasha – the British officer who set up Jordan's Desert Patrol and turned them into a crack fighting force – is much better known than Lawrence of Arabia. And unlike Lawrence, Glubb was a genuinely modest and self-effacing man.

Born into a military family as John Bagot Glubb in 1897, he was raised in an atmosphere of loyalty to the British Empire and confidence in the future. In due course he came to serve on the Western Front in World War I, and in 1917 was badly wounded by shrapnel and part of his chin was blown off. The Bedouin would later nickname Glubb "Abu Hunaik" (father of the little jaw).

For 10 years after the war, Glubb served in Iraq, where his particular task was to pacify the desert and guard Iraq's borders against Bedouin raiding from the south. To this end, he developed the revolutionary idea of employing Bedouin to police themselves. Glubb developed his links and love for the Bedouin during this time, when even the most humble desert-dweller knew him as Abu Hunaik.

Glubb then served in the Emirate of Transjordan, where he set up the Desert Patrol of the Arab Legion, as the British-officered Transjordanian army was known. Composed only of Bedouin, soldiers of the Desert Patrol had their own distinctive uniforms, comprised of a long khaki coat modelled on traditional Arab garb, a red belt and a red and white Arab headdress (*shimag*).

Within two years, Glubb had brought raiding to an end, and the Desert Patrol had begun to evolve into the elite striking force of the Transjordanian army, completely loyal to its commander and the Emir Abdullah. As a result of increasing trouble in Palestine and World War II, the army was expanded and Bedouin were taken on in increasing numbers.

In recognition of his achievement, Glubb replaced Peake Pasha as commander of the Arab Legion in 1939, taking on the mantle of Pasha, an honorary title awarded to senior Jordanian officials. Under Glubb's command, the Arab Legion served with distinction in Iraq and Syria during World War II. During the 1948 war against Israel, the Jordanian army's achievements far outstripped those of any other Arab fighting force. However, in these troubled times, Glubb's dual loyalties, to Britain (blamed by Arabs for the creation of Israel) and to Jordan came under strain.

Winds of change were blowing through the region. The cause of Arab nationalism, led by Gamal Abdel Nasser in Egypt, swept through the area. Increasingly, Glubb was castigated as British imperialism's chief agent in the Arab world.

When King Hussein came to the throne in 1953, he was barely 18 years old, and found it difficult to cope with Glubb's old-fashioned ways. The King wanted to rule without British interference; he was also sympathetic to calls for the Arabisation of the army, which was still dominated by British officers.

Sadly, Glubb failed to recognise that his time had passed, and in 1956 was dismissed from the King's service. This was a rude awakening for a man who had served in Jordan for 26 years.

Glubb retired to the English countryside, making a living by writing and lecturing. Over the next 28 years he wrote more than 22 books, most of them on Arab history, and spoke at meetings throughout Britain and the United States.

King Hussein paid a final tribute to Glubb at his funeral at Westminster Abbey in 1986. The King described a man of "impeccable integrity, who performed quietly and unassumingly the duties entrusted to him by his second country, Jordan, at a crucial moment in its development." ❑

RIGHT: Glubb Pasha with a young Hussein.

THE REIGN OF KING HUSSEIN

Riding out the turmoil of more than 40 difficult years, King Hussein
was the longest-serving ruler in the modern Middle East

Following the assassination of Abdullah, his son, Talal, was the designated successor. But in a secret parliamentary session in 1952, Talal was deposed in favour of his eldest son, Hussein, on grounds of mental illness. As Crown Prince Hussein was not yet 18, a regency council was appointed until he reached the legal age of accession in May 1953.

While King Abdullah had created Jordan, it was his grandson's task to consolidate this achievement. Like his grandfather before him, King Hussein quickly came under attack from the Arab nationalist forces which were rampant during the 1940s and 1950s. Many Trans-jordanians were also caught up in the radical politics of the day.

Learning to cope with crises

The first few years of the young King's reign were characterised by riots, demonstrations and general unrest throughout the country. The crowds were protesting in particular against the special relationship with Britain. Matters came to a head in December 1955 as the King leaned towards joining the Baghdad Pact, a British-inspired bloc of countries designed to check the spread of communism into the Middle East.

For most Arabs, Israel and the imperialist powers were their real enemies, not communism. A policy of "non-alignment" seemed to hold out the promise of real independence for the Arab states. In September 1955 the President of Egypt, Gamal Abdel Nasser, signed an arms deal with Czechoslovakia, signalling that his country would no longer be dependent on military supplies from the West.

Local and regional pressure forced King Hussein to recognise that Jordan was swimming against the historical tide. The young King also seems to have had some sympathy with trends in the region. Following the anti-Baghdad Pact riots of December 1955, the King promised the country free elections within a

few months, and in March 1956 he dismissed Glubb Pasha, the British commander of the Jordanian army. Glubb Pasha was replaced by a promising young Jordanian officer, Ali Abu Nuwar. Despite these moves, the King was to face the greatest threat to his throne so far in April of the following year.

"A plucky little King"

A familiar combination of local and regional developments were the background to the crisis of April 1957. The Jordanian elections of 1956 resulted in a radical parliament and government under the leadership of Suleiman Nabulsi. At the end of the same year, Britain, France and Israel launched the Suez war against Egypt. The tripartite aggression, as it is known in the Arab world, ended with the withdrawal of the three powers under American pressure. Arabs saw the war as a victory for Nasser, Egypt's leader. Increasing support for him was coupled with a peak of anger against the old colonial powers, Britain and France, and the new enemy, Israel.

LEFT: King Hussein in full regalia.
RIGHT: a youthful King Hussein.

In Jordan, differences between the King and the Nabulsi government on the distribution of power and regional and international alignments reached new heights. Nabulsi and his supporters called for a stronger parliament and for closer links with radical Arab states like Egypt and Syria and also with the Soviet Union and China. The King was determined to maintain his authority and leaned towards more conservative Arab states such as Saudi Arabia. He had also shown interest in the Eisenhower Doctrine

DOMINO EFFECT

With Arab nationalism triumphant in Egypt, Syria and Iraq, observers predicted that it was "only a matter of time" before Jordan went the same way.

that time) and called for a general strike and street demonstrations against the regime. The King took immediate and dramatic action. He formed a new government under Ibrahim Hashem, and using Bedouin and other loyal troops imposed martial law and a countrywide curfew. All political parties were immediately dissolved and leading opposition figures were arrested.

These moves were welcomed by the United States as a necessary step against encroaching communism. The American press carried arti-

recently announced by the United States, which promised to give aid to countries struggling against communism.

Unrest mounts

Differences between the Nabulsi cabinet and the King led to the resignation of the government on 10 April 1957, and the King attempted to form a new cabinet. In this general air of crisis, the new army Chief of Staff, Ali Abu Nuwar, attempted a military *coup d'état*, but the attempt was nipped in the bud by Bedouin units loyal to the King.

On 24 April, Nabulsi supporters met in Nablus in the West Bank (still part of Jordan at

cles about "the plucky little King". However, Egypt and Syria viciously attacked Jordan, and regionally trends seemed to be in their favour.

In 1958, Syria and Egypt announced the formation of the United Arab Republic. Feeling surrounded and threatened, King Hussein responded by uniting with his Hashemite cousins in Iraq. But in July 1958, there was a bloody coup in Baghdad and Iraq's royal family was massacred.

The next few months and years were difficult. In October 1958, the Syrian air force tried to bring down a plane piloted by the King. In February 1959, General Sadeq al-Shara'a led another coup attempt, and then in August of the following year, one of the most promising of a new generation of politicians, Prime Minister Haza al-Majali, was assassinated.

However, the King stood fast and through a combination of tough security measures and enlightened policy, both he and the country survived. Democracy was laid to one side for the sake of stability. Jordan was ruled by a government appointed by and responsible to the King. The army was placed under the command of Habes al-Majali, an ultra-loyal supporter of the King, and the intelligence and internal security services were built up. At the same time, a booming economy and relatively free elections

become more pressing. Israel's national water plan threatened to deprive Jordan of the precious resource and intelligence reports revealed that Israel had developed an atomic bomb.

When Gamal Abdel Nasser called for an Arab summit to discuss these and other issues, King Hussein responded with alacrity. However, the meeting in Cairo in 1964 proved to be the peak of a slippery slope that led to the disastrous 1967 war with Israel.

The road to war

At the 1964 summit meeting it was felt that the Palestinian question was being forgotten by the

in 1961 encouraged many Jordanians to develop a stake in the country and the regime.

By 1964, the Arab regional situation had also improved from the King's perspective. The union between Egypt and Syria had broken up in 1961, and attempts at unity between Iraq, Egypt and Syria in 1963 had also failed. Trends seemed to be in the direction of the more inclusive form of Arab unity favoured by the King. Meanwhile the need for united action had

LEFT: violence rocks Amman in September 1970.
ABOVE: Baqa'a, a Palestinian refugee camp.
RIGHT: pro-Iraq demonstrations during the 1990–91 Gulf War.

world and that the Palestinians needed a focus for preserving their identity. The PLO was therefore created, but it was agreed that it should co-operate with Jordan. The summit also made a decision to avoid offensive action against Israel until the Arab states were ready for war. But there were other Palestinian organisations operating in the area, among them Yasser Arafat's Fatah. Their strategy was to take the war to Israel and provoke a conflict which they believed the Arab states would inevitably win. Increasingly, the PLO was pushed to take a similar stand as the Fatah.

Jordan clamped down on the operations of the PLO and Fatah within their borders, but towards the end of 1966 a number of raids against Israel managed to get through. As the King had anticipated, Israel's response was ferocious. Eighteen people were killed in a punitive attack against the West Bank town of Samu'a on 13 November 1966. Arab summit resolutions were forgotten in the ensuing wave of anger. Jordan was widely blamed for not arming villagers along the ceasefire line, and so they were unable to defend themselves against the Israeli attack. Riots flared up in Jordan's major

PALESTINIAN RESISTANCE

In the aftermath of the 1967 war, Palestinian guerrilla groups increased their presence in Jordan, and parties banned since 1957 soon re-emerged.

Despite warnings of certain defeat from people like ex-Prime Minister Wasfi at-Tell, the Jordanian King felt compelled to join the Arab side. Within six days, the war was over; the Arabs were utterly defeated. Jordan was the biggest loser, with Israeli forces in occupation of the West Bank. At a stroke, Jordan had lost a large part of its population and the source of 40 percent of its gross national product. The defeat also created the conditions for what was perhaps the greatest threat yet to the Kingdom of Jordan.

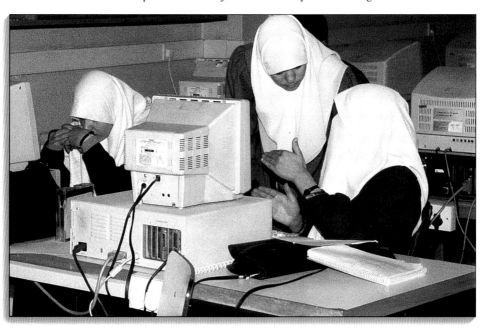

towns in frustration and indignation. The Arab states now descended into a destructive spiral of outbidding each other in actions against Israel. In April 1967, six Syrian warplanes were shot down by Israel. In May, partly in response to Jordanian accusations of cowardice, President Nasser of Egypt requested a withdrawal of UN forces that had been based on the Sinai Peninsula since the 1956 war. He also closed the straits of Tiran to Israeli shipping, effectively shutting off access between the Israeli port of Eilat and the Red Sea. The actions of Egypt were provocation enough for a country already fired up for war; Israeli forces attacked the Arab states in June 1967.

Black September

The Jordanian army was badly mauled in the 1967 war and the King's authority was openly questioned in its wake. Economically, the country was in a mess and also had to provide for about 350,000 Palestinian refugees from the West Bank. Palestinian guerrilla organisations (referred to collectively as the Palestinian Resistance) began to operate above ground, but their undisciplined behaviour in Jordan's towns and villages alienated many of their supporters. The radical leftist politics of the Popular Front for the Liberation of Palestine (PFLP) and the Democratic Front (PDFLP) frightened the Palestinian and Jordanian middle class. Jordanians were particularly upset by the chauvinistic behaviour of most of the Palestinian organisations, and increasingly took refuge in a new Jordanian nationalism.

By 1970, the Palestinian guerrillas had developed into "a state within a state" and posed an unacceptable challenge to the King's authority. In September 1970 (which Palestinians call "Black September"), Jordan's army moved against the Resistance. After 10 days of fighting more than 3,000 people were killed according to Palestinian estimates. By then, the army had the upper hand and by July 1971, the Resistance had been forced out of Jordan.

However, the relationship between the PLO (which now represented all Palestinian organisations) and the Jordanian government continued to complicate matters. The two sides got together again towards the end of the 1970s, but efforts to reach a joint position on common problems broke up in 1986. While the King claimed the West Bank and the PLO argued that it represented all Palestinians, even in the East Bank, there was no room for progress.

Meanwhile the King was coming under pressure to democratise the system in Jordan. He was accused of using the West Bank situation as an excuse for not holding elections. The

Boom time ahead

As the country entered a more stable phase after 1970, political and economic factors accelerated this process. The 1970s and early 1980s were a boom time. The country benefited from the collapse of Lebanon and the oil boom in the Gulf. By the mid-1970s, more than 28 percent of the population was working abroad. By 1980, Jordan had a 9 percent growth rate and no unemployment. Palestinians invested in real estate in Jordan, signalling their commitment.

LEFT: tradition and modernity comfortably coexist.
ABOVE: discussions between King Hussein and Yasser Arafat.

intifada, which began in 1987, made it clear that the Palestinians of the West Bank looked to the PLO for leadership. More seriously, riots broke out in south Jordan, the heartland of Hashemite support, in April 1989.

King Hussein responded to these pressures. In 1984 the constitution had been changed to permit elections without the participation of West Bankers, but the real breakthrough came in July 1988 when the King renounced claims to the West Bank. In return the PLO promised to keep out of Jordanian politics. This paved the way for a greater degree of democracy.

On 8 November 1989, Jordanians went to the polls in the first free elections since the 1950s.

It was also a first for Jordanian women, who had been given the right to vote in 1974. A National Charter was later drawn up by a special commission, which stressed national unity and equality of citizenship. A new law was passed which legalised political parties.

Islamic fundamentalism

It was not all plain sailing in the years ahead, however. The 1990–91 Gulf War presented several difficulties (*see panel below*). The rising influence of Islamicists was another thorny problem, and when, shortly before the 1993 elections, the King changed the electoral law,

most observers agreed that this step was aimed at reducing the power of Islamic activists. The changes were initially criticised for reinforcing tribal and conservative voting patterns. Later, the King was accused of manipulating the outcome of the elections to ensure the smooth passage of Jordan's controversial peace deal with Israel, and to push through other legislation disagreeable to the public.

The changes also inspired fear that the elections would be cancelled because of the unexpected Palestinian–Israeli peace accord of September 1993, but in the event 800.000 people went to the polls in November to vote for

THE GULF WAR

The 1990–91 Gulf War placed King Hussein in a particularly difficult position. Jordanian public opinion backed Saddam Hussein and large demonstrations backing Iraq marched through the streets of Amman. In the end, King Hussein's neutrality (he favoured a peaceful resolution of the problem from within the region) cost Jordan vital aid and earnings from the Gulf States (many Jordanians and Palestinians working in the Gulf were expelled) and dented relations with the United States. On the plus side, however, the King's popularity within Jordan soared as a result of what was seen as a principled stand.

candidates from some 20 parties. It was widely agreed that the composition of the new parliament reflected the country's respect for the King, and was an endorsement of his call for moderation. But the change to the election law remains a point of contention to this day; it was a factor leading to a boycott by nine opposition parties, led by the Islamicists, during the election of 1997.

In 1994, following Israeli withdrawal form parts of the Occupied Territories, Jordan signed an historic peace treaty with Israel. Theagreement was greeted with optimistic hopes of increased prosperity for the whole region. Soon Israelis were visiting Petra as tourists.

The end of an era

But dark clouds were gathering on another front. In the early 1990s, the King developed cancer of the lymphatic system, and his ailing health began to raise uncomfortable questions about life after his death, such as who would succeed him, and even whether the country has the stability to survive without his unifying presence.

But the King mounted a valiant fight against cancer, and when he returned from treatment in the United States in 1992 with a clean bill of health, most of the country came out on the streets to welcome him home, a testament to

in place of Hassan. The sudden switch was significant, and shortly afterwards the King was forced to return to the US for emergency treatment. Boarding his plane to the States, he looked ill and frail. A week later he was on the way home again, but this time on a life-support machine. Within days the King was dead.

King Hussein's funeral drew a dazzling array of world leaders, including four American presidents past and present, President Yeltsin, himself very ill, and a brace of sworn enemies such as President Assad of Syria and Benjamin Netanyahu of Israel.

Stepping into his father's shoes will not be

the people's genuine love and respect for their king. And following a relapse in 1998, when the King addressed his subjects via satellite from the Mayo Clinic in the US, not a car could be seen driving in Amman. When he returned home, apparently well, he was again greeted by an ecstatic welcome.

During Hussein's absence the country was governed by his brother, Prince Hassan, his designated successor since 1965. However, in January 1999 the King announced that he was making his eldest son, Abdullah, Crown Prince

easy for King Abdullah. Though Jordan is more united than it has been at any time in its history, regional and domestic developments are testing the strength of its social fabric. Regular bread riots and 27 percent unemployment are dangerous symptoms. The poor economy is further aggravated by slow progress in the Middle East peace process, lingering economic sanctions on Iraq, and damaged relations with the Gulf states since the Gulf War. Sharp public criticisms of government policy have led the regime to clamp down on public freedoms. Jordan is a poor country, and its future, and that of the democratic process, rests on the support of its friends during the years to come. ❏

LEFT: female candidate during the 1997 election.
ABOVE: the funeral of King Hussein in February 1999.

THE JORDANIANS

Jordan is a conservative country where ancient pride runs deep, old allegiances matter and fortunes are forged by fate

Take the Bedouins of the biblical desert *wadis*, combine with the peasants and villagers of the hill towns and the Jordan Valley, add a dash of shrewd urban merchants and a sprinkling of Armenian artisans, Druze mountainmen, Circassian warriors and Bahai gentlemen and you begin to have some idea of Jordan's rich ethnic mix.

Lying east of the biblical river that gave the country its name, Jordan is as new as it is old, as rich as it is poor and as powerful as it is weak. It is new in its contemporary framework and composition and rich in its educated citizens, with the highest number of university graduates per capita in the Arab world. For years Jordan received most of its financial capital through remittances from expatriates working in the wealthy Gulf states or in developing Arab countries such as Yemen, Oman and Sudan.

Its cultural and ethnic multiplicity as well as its relatively flexible political and legal infrastructure has made it unique in the region. In few other countries have Muslim revisionists and Westernised Arabs lived side by side so peacefully. It is home to the full spectrum of Muslim and Christian sects, though the vast majority of people (over 90 percent) belong to the Sunni branch of Islam.

Conservative society

With no outlet to the sea except for the slim port of Aqaba, Jordan's people are conservative in nature and tradition – Jordanians are known even within the Arab world for their more introverted character. That said, they are among the most hospitable people on earth and *marhaba* and *ahlan wa-sahlan*, variations on "welcome", are constant refrains. Formalities and politeness are important social norms, especially with strangers (*franji* or *aganeb*), and in-

tricately bound up with pride and self-esteem. When faced with camera-touting, shorts-clad foreigners, Jordanians are torn between their urge to welcome and the assault on their inherent conservatism.

Amman, the largest and most populated city in Jordan, containing more than 1½ million peo-

ple, is one of the cleanest and most efficient cities in the Arab world. But scratch the surface of this modern city and you will find ancient pride and old allegiances. People born in Amman are still likely to identify with the town from which their families originally came, and will claim they are from, say, Salt, Jerusalem or Nablus rather than from Amman. People also identify with the relationship that their forefathers had to the land and will refer to themselves as *fellahin*, meaning farmers or villagers; *Bedu*, meaning Bedouin, or *madanieen*, meaning city folk.

A similar regard for heritage is found in the reverence paid to the Bedouin, often considered Jordan's indigenous inhabitants (although they are not the only ones). Clan word carries weight not only locally but also in Amman and six of the 80 seats in parliament are reserved for Bedouin leaders (which makes them over-represented).

Regional differences

Although Jordan is small, it has strong regional differences. Amman's neighbour, Salt, is traditionally hostile to outsiders, and its conservative character is mirrored by its picturesque Ottoman architecture and enclosing mountains, which protect the Saltis and bar the

tongues as well as the beauty of the women. Their cultural affiliation with Syria has influenced their social and political outlook since the 19th century. Natives of Irbid, Anjara and Ajlun were among the first Jordanians to join pan-Arab political parties in the 1930s. Irbid and Jarash have also witnessed a large influx of Palestinians, who play a major role in the political and cultural life of the north.

The most significant town in southern Jordan is Karak, whose people are descendants of migrants from the West Bank town of Hebron up to 400 years ago. Like the Hebronites, the Karakis are often light-skinned and fair-haired,

stranger. Known for their haughty pride and stubborn ways, Saltis are the butt of jokes throughout Jordan, a role they share with the people of Tafila (a mixed community of indigenous pastoral Arabs and Kurdish settlers, living in a region between Karak and Petra).

Northerners – the residents of Jarash, the industrial town of Zerqa and the University city of Irbid – have a different history from Jordanians living in the south. Influenced by Damascene culture and outlook, the northerners are considered shrewder and more business-oriented than southerners. They are frequently fairer and taller, betraying Syrian origins, and are known for their cool heads and sharp

as many of them are descendants of Crusaders. For the most part they are Muslims, but the town also has one of the most prominent Christian populations in Jordan. Almost exclusively of Arab origin, the Karaki Christians are believed to be one of the oldest Christian communities in the world.

Ma'an, another southern town and a major centre on the north–south trade route for several centuries, retains its links with transport to this day. Over 90 percent of its male population work in the transport sector. When the

ABOVE: home cooking.
RIGHT: a picnic in Seven Hills Park, near Amman.

economy belly-flopped in 1989, Ma'an was the scene of anti-government riots (believed to have triggered democratic changes).

Work and wages

With unemployment running at about 15 percent of the population, and, following the return of some 300,000 expatriates expelled from Kuwait in the wake the 1990–91 Gulf War, a surfeit of professional labour available, work is a question of getting what you can. Though self-employment is the dream of many Jordanians, around 50 percent of the workforce comprises government employees. Their salaries are low – a newly qualified university graduated teacher and a less educated civil servant with 10–15 years experience would both earn about £140 (US$210) a month, while an assistant professor at the University of Jordan may receive a salary in the region of £450 ($670) – although this would come with a raft of benefits, such as cheap health care, subsidised shopping facilities, a social security system and pension plan.

Private sector salaries are also fairly low, but again there are attractive fringe benefits. Bank clerks, for example, who earn a figure in the region of £150 ($225) a month, get 14-month

THE ROLE OF HOME AND FAMILY

Most Jordanian families invest heavily in land and property, taking a large mortgage (and then taking up to 30 years to pay it off) or else living in inconspicuous homes for years while saving for a villa or a grove of oranges or olives in the Jordan Valley. Homes are usually built so that further floors can be added when the sons marry, and three- or four-storey homes often contain extended families, who lunch and dine together.

As well as making economic sense, this family cohabitation takes care of possible social problems. Grandparents act as babysitters and daughters-in-law nurse ageing parents. Daughters-in-law are also expected to do most of the cooking, although all female members of the family usually participate in kitchen-related duties. Men hardly ever share in domestic tasks.

The average Jordanian family still has seven children, and the country has one of the highest birth rates in the world. Though Western-sponsored seminars on contraception are welcomed by the upper classes and condoms and the Pill are available without prescription, greater birth control is not an active part of government policy. To date, the most that the government has done to encourage birth control is to run a television campaign promoting breastfeeding – and thus birth spacing.

yearly salaries, as well as health and social security benefits. In addition, large companies often give employees a yearly bonus or gift reflecting profits.

Nonetheless, any visitor going to even the smallest shopping centre in Jordan will immediately realise that no Jordanian family can possibly survive on such salaries, especially when rent on even a small flat in a cheap area is about £60 ($90) a month. As a consequence, many people, especially civil servants, have two jobs, with occupations such as writing, supermarket work, acting as an estate agent or driving taxis providing popular ways of moonlighting.

Superstitions and the coffee cup

Superstitions and belief in fate ("what is written") and the supernatural are rife. When someone falls sick or has an accident, it is believed to be a result of *rire* (jealousy) and *hassad* (envy). To dispel malevolence and the "evil eye" incense is burned, a lamb is offered to the poor and a blue medallion is worn or hung in the home or car. If a person is believed to be afflicted by the evil eye, he or she will be bombarded with incense and readings from the Holy Koran or Bible. Silver plaques with verses from holy books promising fertility, luck, health and a long life guard the bedside of many a Jor-

Family values are paramount and have dictated a particularly strict moral code, to which consecutive waves of political refugees used to a more liberal climate in Palestine, Lebanon and more recently Iraq have had to adapt. Prostitution rings have been closed down, public drunkenness is not tolerated, and gambling is against the law – a jurisdiction that has won widespread support. Even belly-dancing is confined to the large hotels.

As a consequence of this strict moral climate, Jordan has a low crime rate. Murder is invariably a so-called "crime of honour", especially in the countryside, and is almost always to do with a woman allegedly flouting sexual taboos.

danian child. Women consult "coffee ladies", who read their fortune in the dregs of a cup.

Many of the superstitions are religion-related. When, a few years ago, a young Jordanian Christian lost the ability to walk, she swore that she would dress like the Virgin Mary for a year if God restored the use of her limbs. A few months later she was cured and sure enough she walked around in a long robe and wooden cross for a year.

Reported visions of the Virgin Mary are numerous. Muslims and Christians are known to flock to homes of *seiers* or "anointed ones", hoping to catch a glimpse of the most revered woman in Christendom and Islam.

A woman's place

Being a patriarchal society, the ruling and running of Jordan is still to a very great extent male-dominated. Two women briefly held ministerial posts in the early 1980s, but it was over a decade before another woman gained a government position – Rima Khalaf in 1995. As Planning Minister, she served in three consecutive governments, making her the longest serving woman in a key ministerial post.

Despite these facts of the adult world, the education of children of both sexes is given a high priority in Jordan. Girls receive a mandatory primary education, most are encouraged to finish secondary school, and more than half the 20,000 students at Amman's University of Jordan are female.

Women have the same political rights as men and according to the Jordanian constitution they have "equal rights". However, a number of civil status laws and the penal code claiming the Koran as a reference undermine this constitution. Liberal thinkers who have lobbied for years to change this anomaly are finally beginning to realise some success. In 1998, for example, women gained the right to carry their own passports without the permission of husbands or male "guardians" – a small but significant step forward. Ironically, women are often the most conservative when it comes to changing the sexual imbalance.

But evidence of female submission is not found in veiled faces and modest dress (as recently as 1978 one had to look hard to find a veiled woman walking down the streets of Amman). The revival of the veil has more to do with personal quest and a rejection of Western imperialism. In the aftermath of the war in neighbouring Lebanon and the eight-year Iran-Iraq War people looked to religion in search of peace and tranquillity and many women turned away from the traditionally flashy Arab style of dress to a more modest garb. In addition, this change accompanied an economic depression, which often made simple dress an economic necessity.

> ### VOTES FOR WOMEN
> Though it failed to elect any women, the 1989 election showed that men were more likely to vote for a female candidate than women.

Marriage, births and deaths

Of all the events that take place in a lifetime, weddings are the most important; in terms of

LEFT: the costly business of a wedding.
ABOVE: Italian fashions for Jordan's privileged few.

cost, they are second only to buying a home. Indeed men from the middle- and lower-income groups often don't marry until they reach their thirties because they cannot afford to marry sooner. For similar reasons, polygamy has almost died out and is rarely found at all in cities.

Most marriages are still the product of family introductions, if not outright matches made by female members of the bride's and/or groom's family, though upper-middle-class Jordanians usually court one another in a Western fashion and marriage is

rarely forced upon an unwilling couple. An eligible groom should have a respected family lineage, wealth, education, be of the same religion as the bride and should be marrying for the first time. The same goes for the bride, but she must also be virtuous. The dowry for meeting such conditions can be vast.

About one in five marriages ends in divorce, though in half of these cases it occurs during the period between the signing of the legal contract and consummation, the time when the couple are "preparing to live together". Though legally married and permitted to sleep together during this period, couples don't usually consummate their marriage until the night of the "wedding party", often as much as a year later.

Divorce for women still carries a stigma and few divorcees remarry. Most return to their parental homes or to the home of their nearest living male relative, on whom they then depend for their economic survival. Women rarely live alone.

Once married, a woman's primary role is to produce children. The birth of a child is the happiest of all occasions and money and time are invested in preparing for the new arrival – the mother's family is responsible for providing the child's first wardrobe and furniture. A male is almost always preferred as a first child and a woman with many sons is considered more powerful than a woman with daughters. Jordanian mothers thus spoil sons more than daughters and as a result girls tend to be independent at an earlier age. But children of both sexes are treasured, and their education is highly valued. Although child vendors are not as common as in many developing countries, Jordanians have noticed their numbers increase as the country's economic pinch sharpens.

Ritual occasions

Male circumcision is an important ritual among Muslim families. At one time it took place at the age of 13, usually at the hand of the local barber, and was followed by a big celebration. Today almost all baby boys are circumcised in a hospital soon after birth.

When a death occurs, the *aza* (condolence period), when respects are paid to the immediate family of the deceased, is another important ritual. It is considered essential to attend the *aza* of a neighbour or colleague and even of relations of neighbours, colleagues, business contacts and in-laws. It takes place in the home of the deceased or that of a relative. Men and women sit in separate rooms – sexual segregation is practised at both Muslim and Christian *azas* – and black, unsweetened Arabic coffee is served. For 40 days after a death, an *aza* is reopened every Monday and Thursday.

The colour of mourning in Jordan is black. This is contradictory to Islamic custom which dictates that mourning women wear white or beige. Black has been the colour of mourning in Jordan since Byzantine times. ❏

HEAVY BURDEN

The dowry for the bride's family can consist of presents equivalent to the bride's weight in gold.

LEFT: food for a sweet-toothed nation.

The Royals

When the young King Hussein assumed his constitutional duties on 2 May 1953, his love of flying, motor-cycling, water sports, racing-car driving, and amateur ham radio generated a rather adventurous and daring image in the Western press. He was frequently portrayed as a dashing young Arab monarch, who bridged the ways of the Orient and the Occident, and was as comfortable talking to presidents of NATO member states as to Bedouin tribal leaders at home.

The King recognised early on that despite the emotional appeal of mid-century pan-Arab ideological currents, the key to the survival of Jordan and its royal family was the improvement of people's daily living conditions, a sense of national and political identity, and hope and security for the future. To this end, the Royal family has tried to remain accessible to people and to receive their complaints, suggestions and personal requests, whether through formal gatherings or more informal encounters. Jordanians who feel they have been done an injustice often boast they will take their claim to the King personally – and in many cases, a request for a meeting with him will get a positive response.

Personal charisma was an important element of King Hussein' success, and King Abdullah is credited with having the same easy charm as his father. The royals take a paternal but genuine interest in their subjects, going up in a helicopter after a bad snowstorm or rainfall to check on hard-hit areas, paying personal condolences at the homes of Jordanians who have died in the line of duty. In 1992, during the worst snowfall of the century, Prince Hassan, and some hardy guards and companions trekked out to check on the condition of isolated villages that had been cut off.

Along with King Abdullah, some two dozen active adult princes and princesses carry out public activities. Several are pursuing careers in private business or the armed forces, and most provide patronage for, or actively participate in, the activities of charitable societies. Queen Noor, King Hussein's American widow, who over the years steadily won the hearts of the Jordanian people, personally instigated the Noor Al Hussein Foundation, focusing on children's and women's needs, the arts, rural development and the environment.

RIGHT: King Abdullah at his father's funeral.

Increasingly, royal family members can be seen leading charity walks or participating in sports and cultural activities, mixing easily and casually with what they always refer to as "the Jordanian family". Like his father, King Abdullah is very much at home behind the wheel of a rally car,and also enjoys flying, parachuting and diving.

Born in Amman in 1964 to Princess Muna (aka Toni Gardiner), Hussein's English-born second wife, King Abdullah trained as a career soldier at Sandhurst in England. He is married to a Palestinian, from a prominent family with roots in the West Bank town of Turkalm, a link likely to please the estimated 50 percent or so of Jordan's population

that is Palestinian. This fact is believed to have contributed to King Hussein's decision to change the succession.

Before his death, King Hussein spoke of fulfilling the goals of the Great Arab Revolt by transforming Jordan into a credible example of an Arab/Islamic state based on democratic pluralism and respect for human rights. It is an historical anomaly that a monarch that reigned for over four decades was the driving force of democratisation. It reflects the Royal Family's awareness that the long-term stability and progress of Jordan must rely on the participation of the people rather than on military means, foreign aid, or the personal and political contacts of the monarch. ❑

THE BEDOUIN WAY OF LIFE

*The heyday of tribal life in Jordan may be over, but the Bedouin still thrive,
mixing new technology with old traditions*

As amber streaks of dawn illuminate the lilac hills, Fatma, a willowy young shepherdess, herds her flock of sheep and goats out of their corral and down the hill to graze in the nearby valley. While the goats stop to nibble on sprigs of wild thyme, she rests on a boulder, pulls out a twisted roll of black goats' hair from the sack hanging on her wrist and begins to spin.

As she rolls the wooden spindle (*maghzal*) against her thigh to twist the fibres into yarn, Aisha, a 15-year-old girl from the neighbouring tent who accompanies Fatma each day, breaks into song as she rounds up the strays who have wandered from the herd. Beco, their sheep dog, bounds after her, adding his voice to Aisha's.

As they follow the flock, the girls are joined by Aisha's mother, Eida, leading her donkey. Water containers are tied to the sides of the animal and one of Aisha's little sisters is perched on top. As Eida stops to fill her jerry cans from an artesian well, two water trucks drive up. Fatma quickly draws her long black *mandeel* across the lower half of her face and tucks it in at the side.

Back at their hillside encampment on the edge of a pine forest Kifaya, Fatma's mother, feeds and waters kid goats. Her long black dress, called a *thaub,* is embroidered with grapevines intertwined with pink and yellow flowers in a pattern from Ramallah. Fatma and Aisha wear the *madraga*, the full-length black gown of another cut worn by the Bedouin women of the East Bank of Jordan. The bright silky blouses of pink and fuchsia worn under their open-necked gowns show off the young women's olive skin and large black eyes.

In 10 days Kifaya will help her daughter set up a loom in order to weave the 24 skeins of goat hair she has spun since shearing time last spring. Fatma will then weave a long narrow strip to replace one of the seven needed to con-

struct the goat-hair tent that her family will pitch in readiness for the approaching winter at Rama, near the Dead Sea.

Each June, when the heat of the Dead Sea area becomes too intense for the animals, Fatma's family pack up their belongings, load them and their livestock on to two trucks, and

move up to the central highlands for better pastures, water and a cooler climate. This summer the family has expanded to three tents – one for each of Fatma's two married brothers and one for her parents, herself and her siblings. In summer they use tents of burlap, which are cooler and lighter to transport than the black tent called "house of hair" that they leave in Rama.

On the home front

Once the herd has bedded down for a midday nap in the shade of some pines, the herdswomen return home to find Kifaya baking *shrak*, a Bedouin bread. She plucks a ball of dough off a tray and tosses it from one palm to

---

PRECEDING PAGES: leaning on the "house of hair".
LEFT: face of the Bedu.
RIGHT: the ancient craft of weaving.

the other until it becomes a large, paper-thin circle which she deftly throws over the hot *saj*, a wide metal bowl turned upside down on three stones over a fire of brush and goat dung. After just a few seconds the bread is golden-brown and she passes it to Fatma who tears off a piece and scoops up a bite of *rajouf*, a Bedouin dish made of lentils. A meal in itself, the bread is made from the wheat grown by the family wherever they camp. It is eaten at breakfast and supper with tea or buttermilk.

BEDOUIN SOAP

In the evening, Fatma's family and neighbours follow the latest developments in a soap opera about a Jordanian Bedouin family on a TV hooked up to a car battery.

with water. Chickens scurry about among feed sacks, troughs and jerry cans. A clay water pot, butane gas cylinder, large round pan for washing clothes and a kettle black from many fires all have their appointed place in the scene.

Inside, the tent is separated by a curtain. One side is for the men and their guests and the other is where the women carry out the housekeeping. On the women's side, storage areas are piled high with provisions, pans, a hot plate and a barrel of flour, while brightly coloured clothes

After the meal, Fatma's brother loads sacks of manure on to a tractor and her mother fills a water trough for the kid goats. Meanwhile her father, known as Abu Musallam, meaning the father of Musallam (the name of his eldest son), opens a silver tobacco case, and rolls himself a cigarette using *hisheh*, the local tobacco. Seated on a stuffed woollen mattress, he is dressed in an ankle-length gown and the jacket of a grey wool suit. A white *hatta*, folded into a triangle, is draped over his head and held down by a double ring of thick black cord called *aqal*. He sips *miramiya*, a sweet tea flavoured with sage.

At the edge of the courtyard between the tents are two goat pens and an oil drum filled

hang drying from a guy-rope.

"In spring we milk the sheep and goats twice a day. Every year we slaughter a large female goat and make the goatskin into a *si'n* (churn)," Fatma explains. Swung back and forth from a tripod of poles, this invaluable tool is used by the women to make *saman* (clarified butter) and cheese, some of which the family sells to buy fruit and vegetables. Also made in springtime are *jameed*, yoghurt cakes, which are spread on top of the tents to dry in the sun and used to make the sauce for *mansaf*.

Kifaya wears a tiny ring in her nose and has two teeth capped with gold. Inside the sash tied around her waist she carries her coin purse and her *kohl*, the eyeliner worn by women and their babies to protect them from the elements. Earrings of gold coins dangling from tiny chains add to Fatma's beauty. Aisha, who has learnt poetry from her grandparents, wears a gold ring inscribed with a verse from the Koran.

Nomads no more?

There has been massive settlement of the Bedouin over the past decades, a development that reflects both a benevolent government and a desire for a more comfortable lifestyle. Though there are 10 major tribes in Jordan, the number of families who still move about in

a Jordanian sociologist. "The semi-nomadic people raise crops as well as livestock, and their settlement in villages is seasonal. After spending the winter in villages, they return in spring and summer to their nomadic lifestyle. As more of their numbers have settled to take advantage of the schools and clinics provided by the government in villages, towns and cities, the lines are no longer clear between urbanism, Bedouin and village life. Today it is individual families who move from place to place, not the tribe. Now the kids are in school and families want electricity. For them, the Bedouin life is no longer considered comfortable."

tents is a tiny fraction of the whole population. Yet wherever one goes the Bedouins' long narrow tents can be spotted from afar, pitched on remote mountainsides or on the outskirts of cities, whether they belong to the Sirhan tribe in the northeast, the Beni Sakhr in central Jordan, the Howeitat in the south, or to a Palestinian tribe from the Bir Sheba area in Wadi Araba.

"The nomad by definition keeps moving from one place to the other, following grazing and sources of water," explains Dr Sabri Rbitat,

LEFT AND ABOVE: portraits of the Bedouin – a man in a red and white *keffiyeh*, tattooed woman near Petra and Adwan siblings.

WHAT'S IN A NAME?

Girls in Bedouin society are often given names whose meanings reflect the nature of the community's outdoor life. These may be poetic names, evocative of the conditions in which the Bedouin exist or of nearby natural phenomena: "Ishbeh", for example (meaning a blade of grass), "Shatwa" (a spring shower) or "Sharqiya" (the east wind that was blowing on the day the girl was born). Some girls' names are rather more prosaic: for example "Kifaya" (meaning that's enough [girls]!); others, such as Aisha, Fatma and Miriam, have religious significance (in this case they are the names of the daughters of the Prophet Mohammed).

The affluent Bedu

But greater comfort and affluence is not merely a case of a Japanese pick-up truck replacing a camel, or the acquisition of a new refrigerator or TV set. There are examples of considerable wealth among the Bedu. Over in Abdoun, the most exclusive part of Amman, Sultan Abdul-Majeed al-Adwan, one of the leaders of his tribe, lives in a sumptuous villa. Hardly a day passes, however, when he isn't visited by members of the Adwan tribe who live in South Shuneh, close to the King Hussein bridge. Members of his tribe come to ask him a variety of favours; they may wish Sultan to lead their

family delegation in the *jaha* (the formal process of asking for a bride's hand in marriage) or may ask him to represent them in an *atweh*, a tribal method of settling disputes between the members of two families.

Sultan's country residence is a 660-year-old castle, which he inherited from his forefathers, who built it on their lands overlooking the Sail Hisban canyon near Na'ur, and which he renovated in 1993. Lovingly furnished, it gathers together the relics of his family's past – the furniture his grandfather brought from Damascus for his grandmother and photographs of his father, grandfather, and great-grandfather, who lived during the heyday of tribal life in Jordan.

On the wall of the courtyard hangs the *mansaf* tray last used by his father to serve 25 sheep on a bed of 200 kg (485 lb) of rice when he was visited by the young King Hussein in 1962.

Walking on eggshells

Sultan explains some aspects of Bedouin etiquette: "If you are a guest, you should approach a tent from behind, and stop before entering, to be polite. The guest is welcome for three and a third days. Then he is no longer welcome. There is a saying that the serpent is more acceptable than the guest who overstays his visit. He is received as a prince, but when he is in the house he is more like a prisoner, he has to be so careful not to look at the wife or the daughter and to be on his best behaviour. When he leaves, they see him off like a minister. It would be impolite to see him off too well, as it would look like the host is glad to see him go!

"When one has many guests, the coffee (poured traditionally from an elegant pot called a *dalleh*) is first offered to the main guest, while tea is offered from the right. If a guest wants more coffee, he holds out his tiny porcelain cup to be served again. Once he has had enough, he shakes it to indicate he wants no more.

"When eating the *mansaf* of bread, meat and rice, one must eat it with the right hand only, never using the left hand which is held behind the back. Everyone gathers around the tray and, without any utensils, uses their fingers to form a ball of rice and sauce into a mouth-sized bite. One should eat only from the food directly before one – not that in front of a neighbour. They should never touch the head of the sheep (placed in the centre of the *mansaf*) because it is the symbol of welcoming the guest. If the guest eats all the meat, rice or sauce, it shows he is greedy, but if he finishes all the bread, it means the host wasn't as generous as he should have been, as bread is inexpensive."

Bedouin marriage

Sultan goes on to explain the subtle web of etiquette surrounding betrothals and weddings: "The *jaha*, the asking of a bride's hand, is governed by strict protocol. Before going to the bride's family the family of the groom enlists the support of the most respected members of the community. The father of the bride or the head of her tribe welcomes the visitors and one cup of coffee only is poured for the main guest.

Determining the identity of this important person is complicated by elaborate politesse. The cup is passed around until someone accepts it. As it is passed among the group, each demurs in turn, saying 'no, it should be so-and-so, not me' and 'no, it's for someone else.' The one who finally accepts the 'cup of the *jaha*' doesn't drink it but begins a speech: 'In the name of God the all-merciful and compassionate, we are the *jaha*. We would like to be your in-laws. We want your daughter for our son...' He must never mention the name of the girl. Then he praises the girl's tribe and declares what good friends they are of her tribe or clan.

married. The women are separate and the men sit under a black goat-hair tent. Guests bring a gift (*nuqout*). This used to be a sheep, rice or money. Now, in the modern mix of tradition and technology, it could be a TV, silver or a piece of crystal. They sing and praise the bride, say the groom is a brave man and very generous and that his father is a leader who comes from a good strong tribe. Some still celebrate for three nights before the wedding with singing and gunfire, building up to a crescendo the night they bring the bride. A week later she pays a visit to her parents and takes them a sheep, rice, sugar and clarified butter." ❏

"In the villages, a group of women go on Thursday afternoon to fetch the bride from her tribe. They used to go on 100 to 200 horses. When the bride saw them coming, she was supposed to run away so they wouldn't make snide comments that she was eager to be married. They first bathed her and then put red henna on her palms and also on the soles of her feet. They then took her with them.

"Then the official ceremonial lunch is held on Friday, the day after the marriage have been

LEFT: Adwan father and son in front of the massive ancestral *mansaf* pan, used for a royal visit in 1962.
ABOVE: baking *Shrak*, the tasty Bedouin bread.

FAMILY FIRST

It used to be that if a man wanted to get engaged to a young woman from outside his tribe, the girl's male cousins had priority over him, even if her parents had agreed to the match. This rule applied right up to the wedding day itself. There was a saying that the cousin "brings down the bride from the top of the horse on the bride's way to her wedding". This used to cause a lot of trouble among the tribes, often leading to bloody feuds, and the practice was eventually outlawed. However, marriage between cousins is still common among the Bedouin, and not unusual in Jordanian society as a whole. Family always comes first.

THE PALESTINIANS

Refugees for over half a century, Jordan's Palestinians have proved remarkably resilient, putting down roots and dominating banking and trade

At Umm Qais in the north of Jordan, the site of a Graeco-Roman town, there is a great view over the Sea of Galilee on the other side of the ceasefire line between Israel and Jordan. Cars from many different Arab states – Saudi Arabia, Syria, Iraq and the Gulf – are parked here nearly every day; they belong to diaspora Palestinians returning to see what was once their homeland. It is a sombre place and tourists often miss the sadness in their haste to view the ruins and eat at Um Qays's excellent restaurant.

In 1947 there were about 1.3 million Palestinian Arabs living under the British Mandate in Palestine. Two years later, more than 700,000 of them were dispersed through the Middle East, driven from their homes by Israeli forces. When in 1967 Israel occupied the West Bank – the last part of historical Palestine – 150,000 existing refugees moved on again and another 300,000 became refugees for the first time.

Most of these Palestinians settled in Jordan, where they were granted Jordanian citizenship. Some are allowed to visit their homeland – if the Israeli authorities permit it (Israel still controls the Palestine Authority's borders) – but only a small fraction have been given leave by Israel to return to live.

The imprint of Palestine is everywhere in Jordan, especially in the towns. It is in the names of shops – the Jerusalem restaurant, the Ramle butcher's – in the refugee camps of Wahdat and Jabal al-Hussein, and in the posh Abdoun area of the capital, amidst mansions funded by money made in the Gulf. Eager to improve their condition and retrieve what they have lost, Palestinians have the highest university graduate rate in the Arab world; their alumni can be found at the highest levels in every Arab state, and, as a people, Palestinians have contributed enormously to all facets of life in the region.

LEFT: a Palestinian wearing the characteristic black and white *keffiyeh.*
RIGHT: a Palestinian bakery in Amman.

In Jordan, Palestinians dominate the private sector in banking, retail and international trade; only in government and the army is their influence marginal. Such a strong Palestinian presence in Jordan has created political problems, reflected in controversy about their number. Some analysts put the proportion of Palestini-

ans (those who arrived in 1948 and after) at 65 percent of the population; others claim the number just 35 percent. In truth, it is impossible to draw sharp lines between Jordanians and Palestinians, and, until relatively recently, the issue would never have been raised.

Under the Ottomans who ruled from the 15th century onwards, there was unrestricted movement throughout an empire that stretched from North Africa to modern Iraq and from Turkey to the Yemen. Links between the east and west banks of the Jordan River were particularly close: Salt with Nablus, Nazareth and Jerusalem; Karak with Hebron, and, in the north, Irbid with Beisan, Tiberias and Galilee.

Famous names

Some of the most famous names in today's Jordan reflect the strength and continuity of these links over hundreds of years. In 1993, and again in 1997, the Prime Minister was a Majali, most of whom migrated from Hebron to Karak centuries ago. The Nabulsi family have also played an important role in Jordan's modern history. They moved from Nablus to Salt in the late 19th century and still have relatives in the West Bank.

This close association survived the British Mandate. The Palestinians had had better access to education than those east of the Jordan

River and many of them found jobs in Emir Abdullah's administration. Peasants on both side of the river continued to cross back and forth in pursuit of seasonal labour.

However, the division of the Middle East into spheres of influence dictated by Britain and France, the creation of the Emirate of Transjordan and Britain's commitment to establishing a Jewish national home in Palestine, introduced new realities that contained the seeds of conflict.

Differences appeared and grew wider. Emir Abdullah's primary purpose was to sustain and develop his Emirate. The main objective of the Palestinian leader, Haj Amin al-Husseini, the Mufti of Jerusalem, was to foil British plans to turn Palestine into a Jewish national home. The Mufti adopted a firm anti-Zionist, anti-British stand, while Emir Abdullah recommended a conciliatory line.

The decimation of the Palestinian national movement in the 1936–39 rebellion against the British, followed by the 1948 war with Israel, permitted the Emir to gather his Palestinian allies in Jericho in 1948. At this meeting they agreed to the absorption of areas still held by the Jordanian army (namely the West Bank) into Jordan. Familiar problems persisted, however, over objectives and priorities. Emir Abdullah and King Hussein concentrated on the consolidation of the Hashemite Kingdom, while most Palestinians wanted to liberate Palestine and return home.

In the 1950s and early 1960s a new Palestinian leadership emerged that eventually coalesced in the form of the PLO, which came into being in 1964. Palestinians everywhere saw this as a welcome sign that they were once more taking charge of their own destiny. The Jordanian government, however, feared the effects of "a dual authority" on its efforts to forge a state out of the Palestinians and Jordanians who made up society.

The disastrous defeat in the 1967 war against Israel brought these differences to a head. In the post-war vacuum, Palestinian guerrillas developed their strength in Jordan and soon constituted "a state within a state", effectively challenging the sovereignty of the King. In September 1970 all-out conflict broke out between them and the revitalised Jordanian army. By July 1971, King Hussein's forces had driven the guerrillas out of the country.

JORDAN AND THE PLO

The PLO's sole right to represent all Palestinians was upheld by the 1974 Rabat Arab Summit, threatening King Hussein's efforts to secure national unity in Jordan and his claim to the West Bank. The PLO and the Jordanian government failed to find a compromise at the end of the 1970s, and successive talks broke up acrimoniously in 1986. Breakthrough came in July 1988, eight months after the outbreak of the *Intifada* in the West Bank and Gaza against Israeli occupation. Persuaded by popular support for the PLO, the King renounced his claims to the West Bank. In return, the PLO promised to stay out of Jordanian politics on the East Bank.

On the ground today

Many Palestinians claim that they face discrimination in the army and other sectors of public life. In turn, many Jordanians complain about Palestinian control of the private sector and about how the conflict between the Palestinians and Israelis dominates so much of their lives.

In general, however, most citizens of Jordan recognise that life under the Hashemites is better than the most likely alternatives, and all want to put paid to the threat posed by the slogan "Jordan is Palestine",

A QUESTION OF IDENTITY

The question of who is a Palestinian and who is a Jordanian remains one of the country's most sensitive issues.

have a stake in Jordan, as the million-dinar mansions in Abdoun testify. The middle classes have also benefited from the economic booms, and even less wealthy Palestinians and refugees would think twice about sacrificing the relative security of what they have in Jordan for what is on offer elsewhere in the Middle East.

Some Jordanian nationalists have called on Palestinians to make a choice between their Palestinian and Jordanian identities. They complain that the Palestinians want to have it both

raised by Israelis opposed to the creation of a Palestinian state. The fighting between Palestinian and Jordanian forces in September 1970 showed what efforts to implement such a cynical slogan could lead to.

Among most Palestinians, the commitment to Palestine remains very strong. However, many who arrived in Jordan in 1948 have put down roots. The same is true, if to a lesser extent, of those who came in 1967. Palestinian businessmen and others who have prospered

LEFT: the streets of Baqa'a refugee camp.
ABOVE: sweet seller in Baqa'a.
RIGHT: a Palestinian aubergine seller.

ways – to retain their rights and privileges in Jordan without jeopardising their national rights in Palestine. However, King Hussein always made it clear that there was no question of asking Palestinians to make such choices.

If a full Palestinian state eventually evolves out of the Palestinian Authority, Palestinians may be free to choose between a home in Palestine or Jordan. Perhaps some kind of confederation can be worked out between the two states that reflects the historical links between the two banks of the river. If, however, the final status of the West Bank and Gaza remains ambiguous, there may be problems ahead for Jordan and the region as a whole. ❑

THE CRAFT TRADITION

Read a woman's life story in her embroidery or weaving, delight in Hebron glass

and jewellery, and carry it all back home in functional, well-made basketry

To gain an appreciation of Jordan's crafts, especially the arts of embroidery and weaving, there is no better source than Widad Kawar, whose stunning collection of traditional costumes and Bedouin weavings is a source of inspiration and research for craftspeople, international scholars and modern Arabs seeking to rediscover their heritage.

Originally from Bethlehem, Widad Kawar began collecting the traditional dresses of her homeland in the late 1950s. The protection of this fragile legacy became even more urgent in 1967, when war accelerated the diaspora of the Palestinian people. Supported by her husband, a Jordanian businessman, she began by collecting heirlooms of women in the refugee camps and moved on to collecting those of women on the East Bank. At the same time she gathered the home-made implements and carpets they used. Her collection has been exhibited in museums in Europe and in the far east.

Embroidery

While Jordanian men traditionally socialised over coffee, tea and the water pipe, the women were never idle. They plied their crafts, especially embroidery, while visiting one another at home, in courtyards and along footpaths, passing on to the younger generation their proverbs, folklore, and family history as well as their skills.

As a young girl learned the stitches, she was initiated into her culture. Patterns, colours and fabrics revealed her village, tribe, social status, material wealth, and the period in which she lived. Individuality was expressed in the way each woman assembled the pieces of her dress.

A young girl's skill in embroidery was noted by the older women and was equated with her capabilities as a homemaker. The finer her stitches, they said, the better her groom. Until recently nearly every Jordanian or Palestinian

girl, whatever her social class, embroidered her own trousseau. The six to 12 loosely cut robes she made were worn over a lifetime, and her bridal dress served for many a special occasion – and in some cases was her shroud.

Trousseaus on both sides of the Jordan River included embroidered cushions as beautiful and

varied as the dresses. Today it is the cushions that have carried this art into modern everyday life in Jordan, where in many a home – from simple abodes to the King's palace – the decor is not complete without one or more matching sets. Their colours can range from a riot of red, maroon, purple and pink, spiked with orange, green, and gold, to a more sober combination that emphasises the artistry of the needlework, such as indigo embroidery on an off-white background. The simple cross-stitch is the basis for the myriad designs, and the motifs that recur in infinite variety tend to be drawn from nature: trees, flowers, feathers, waves, and geometric triangles or zigzag patterns.

PRECEDING PAGES: Palestinian embroidery.
LEFT: examples from Bani Hamida House.
RIGHT: Widad Kawar's traditional costumes.

Since the mid-1980s embroidery has embellished articles besides cushions. Elegantly embroidered quilts based on the popular "horse hoof" design hold their own in a Paris home furnishings show; the "tree of life" motif is now embroidered on to large wall hangings; and Oriental village scenes in delicate pastels, complete with a mosque or a church, are recreated in embroidery and appliqué on watered silk.

International recognition

The revival and international reputation of Jordanian crafts is largely thanks to the patronage of the Noor al-Hussein Foundation, an organi-

Traditional crafts have also been incorporated into high fashion. In the 1970s a handful of enterprising women, such as Mariam Abu Laban and Leila Jurius, began to match traditional Jordanian and Palestinian needlework with rich Middle Eastern fabrics, such as striped silk and watered silk. By so doing they created elegant gowns and jackets with a modern flair. Other designers followed suit, resulting in collections modelled seasonally on runways at Jordan's luxury hotels. Queen Noor supports this fledgling fashion industry, often wearing such gowns and suits for public appearances at home and abroad.

sation dedicated to encouraging and promoting Jordanian artisans, and also to the efforts of non-profit-making organisations. Save the Children's Bani Hamida Women's Weaving Project and Jordan River Designs, which together employ nearly 2,000 Bedouin and refugee women, have put Jordanian crafts on the world map, as too has the Jarash Women's Society's embroidery and weaving project, an initiative that was instigated by Catholic Relief Services.

Upmarket designers, boutiques and home furnishing shops from around the world, and certainly in the international cities such as New York, Paris and London, now carry an array of hand-made products of Jordan.

Weaving

Like embroidery, Bedouin weavings are expressions of a way of life. They serve many purposes in the nomadic environment: the outer walls and room dividers of the tents, the cushions and bedding-bags that comprise the furniture, rugs, saddle-bags, coffee-bags, food containers, and other practical items. All these items are woven by hand out of sheep's wool and goat and camel hair.

It takes at least two months to wash, card, spin, ply, dye the wool, set the loom, weave and sew the pieces together (which more than justifies the high cost of traditionally woven rugs in the shops). Traditionally this process is shared between husband and wife: he shears the wool and washes it; both card and spin the fleece into yarn; and in the past women dyed the wool using bark, earth, indigo, plants and insects as colourants (now the husband delivers the wool to the dye-master in the nearby town). When the wool is ready, they both set up the ground loom, on which the woman weaves the rug. Sometimes two women sit side by side, passing the shuttle and beating the weft threads into place with the horn of a gazelle. For each

THE ART OF WEAVING

To maintain the right tension in the fabric, the weaver wraps the yarn around her toe in such a way that the rug, the loom and the woman become as one.

members of the Ma'ay'a family still continue this long tradition, along with Mr Hayek, whose name means weaver in Arabic.

Traditional weaving is encouraged by national development projects. Save the Children's Bani Hamida Women's Weaving Project, involving 900 women in 12 villages, the Queen Alia Fund in Sadaqa in the Karak area, Mleih and Dana in the south strive to revive craft traditions and create jobs and income for rural women at the same time. Under their guidance, the Bedouins'

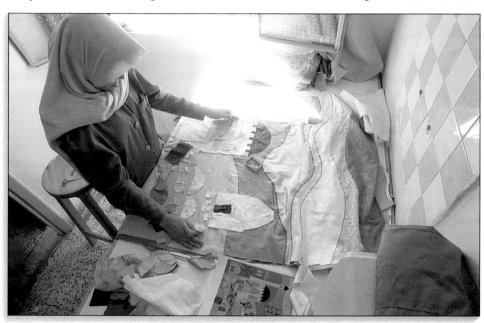

rug, a groundloom is constructed anew, with whatever material is available. The stones, sticks and stakes normally used in the loom may be replaced by a shovel and a couple of orange crates or ammunition boxes. It is some-times hard to believe that such rudimentary tools and a simple weaving technique can pro-duce pieces that are so exquisite.

In towns, male weavers tend to make use of the less strenuous and more expensive upright looms (the groundloom costs no more than the price of a few tent stakes). In Madaba a few

LEFT: intricately embroidered quilts are in demand.
ABOVE: appliqué in watered silk.

traditional colour combinations – deep-reds, in-digo and black, green, orange and mustard and natural sheep colours – have been joined by attractive pieces in a softer palette of modern pastels.

Pottery and ceramics

Jordan's natural clay deposits have been utilised for centuries. Archaeological digs are littered with shards dating from prehistoric times, and the early Islamic period witnessed a magnifi-cent blossoming of ceramic arts, as pieces in Jordan's main museums testify. Until recently simple sun-cured pottery, baked in a dung and straw-fired pit, was used for food storage as well as for serving-vessels and oil-lamps. The most common pots were the large coil-and-slab *jarra*, often 75 cm (2½ ft) tall. Once used to store water and olive oil and to pickle and preserve olives, these can now be seen gracing the gardens of elegant villas in Amman.

Today, talented young artisans are bringing new life and a new look to this age-old art form. One of the best modern ceramicists is Mahmoud Taha, well-known for his tile murals. Hazim Zu'bi and sisters Rula and Reem Atalla have introduced designs using contemporary Islamic calligraphy and petraglyph images. Another potter, Maha Faraj, heads the ceramics

project of the Queen Alia Fund near the Royal Medical City. In the new tourist village of Taybet-Zaman near Petra, replicas of the delicate rust-coloured pottery of the ancient Nabataeans are now being produced.

Jewellery

Like ceramics, jewellery has a long history in Jordan. Caches of gold jewellery from the 9th to the 5th centuries BC have been found near Petra, and goldwork, cameos and jewellery of copper, bronze, silver, iron, and glass from the later Bronze Age to Roman times have been unearthed near Amman. Today gold jewellery – formerly exclusive to royalty and the upper

classes – is collected by rich and poor alike. Most women and some men in all social strata possess at least a few gold pieces (although the Koran discourages men from wearing the precious metal). In Amman's gold *suq* you can see citizens of all walks of life buying and selling the 21-carat jewellery. A nice souvenir is a tiny gold coffee pot (*dalleh*) – a symbol of Jordan – worn on a chain.

Traditionally the silversmith met the demands of the common people. Until recently, a Bedouin bride wore her personal wealth in her silver jewellery, and had the right to dispose of it as she liked. As with gold today, the pieces were bought or sold according to the woman's own plans, or the rise or fall in the family's fortunes.

The silver jewellery of the Bedouin comes in dazzling variety: bracelets, chokers, rings, hair ornaments, long chains and rows of coins attached to head-dresses or necklaces. It is embellished by the use of incising, embossing, hammering, repoussé (raised in relief), twisting, and granulation (soldered patterns of tiny silver balls). The latter technique was common from the Byzantine period and was reintroduced to Transjordan in the 1920s by silversmiths from the Hejaz. Filigree work probably originated with Yemeni silversmiths working in the area in the late 1800s. Arabic calligraphy is sometimes engraved on flat surfaces, or enhanced with black Circassian enamelled niello decoration. Small pendant ornaments in the shape of fish or crescent moons are made by sand-casting molten silver.

Silver beads are often combined with glass beads or precious stones used as amulets – blue glass from Syria against the evil eye, green malachite from Aqaba or green agate for good health, brown agate for warding off evil spirits, and white agate in order to keep a husband's love alive. Beads of brown and golden amber, rose coral from the Red Sea, mother-of-pearl, white cowry shells (female symbols) and ancient Venetian glass are often incorporated into Bedouin pieces.

Blown glass

"Hebron glass", named after the West Bank city renowned for this kind of glass, comes in shades of cobalt blue, bottle green, turquoise, amber and rose, and glows like jewels when displayed on a sunny windowsill. Workshops where the skills are practised are found at Na'ur, on the old road to the Dead Sea, in Madaba on the way to Mount Nebo and in the King Abdullah Gardens in Amman where larger items are produced. Originally made from sand, the glass is now made by recycling old bottles.

Basketry

One of the most ubiquitous part-time crafts is basket-making. Baskets and trays are woven for every imaginable use and come in every size. With handles, they are used to store grain or carry fruits and vegetables from market, while a deep laundry basket with lid is large

Wood

Wood has always been scarce in Jordan, and the antique wooden parlour chairs, tables, elegant large mirrors, and lovely old bridal chests inlaid with mother-of-pearl that you see in the more upmarket shops usually come from Syria. But traditional implements used to prepare Arab coffee in Jordan were often carved of local cured oak or pistachio. The mortar and pestle (*mihbash* and *yad*), the shallow tray in which the roasted coffee beans were placed to cool (*mabradah*), the wooden mould to stamp bread and cakes, mixing bowls and cooking spoons were all made by local carvers. ❑

enough for a small child to hide in. Even bee-hives were once plaited of cane.

Today, a basketry project begun by the Bisharat family in the northern village of Mukheibeh, perched high above the Yarmouk River, produces baskets of split bamboo and palm leaves that are sold in flower shops all over Jordan. Large round mats are also woven from bamboo fronds by Druze women in Azraq. Patterned or plain, a hand-woven Jordanian basket makes a lightweight and practical gift or souvenir.

LEFT: reviving an ancient craft.
ABOVE: a glass-blower in Kan Zaman, near Amman.

CRAFT SHOPS AND MUSEUMS

Many crafts and antiques are available in specialist shops around the country and especially in the markets of Amman, such as Al-Shami bazaar. Also look out for old games such as the *mangala*, which uses a wooden board carved in the shape of a cupcake pan; it is inherited from Roman times, and is still played in some Jordanian villages. For a general overview of crafts in Jordan, visit the Jordanian Museum of Popular Traditions and the Jordanian Folklore Museum, which are on either side of the Amphitheatre in Amman (*see page 147*). For further details of where to buy crafts and see workshops, see the *Travel Tips* section.

BUILDING ON THE PAST

The buildings of Jordan mix and match architectural styles spanning 2,000 years of history – from the Romans to the Ottomans

As a succession of empires and civilisations swept through the Middle East, following trade routes, spiritual paths or a desire to extend their sphere of control, each new power was influenced by the architectural styles and devices of its predecessors. Throughout Jordan, sites were rebuilt or reworked, and, in some cases, their stone and other raw materials were carted off for a new use elsewhere.

The Desert Castles have been home to many different civilisations, from the Romans to the Omayyads to the Crusaders. Qasr Hallabat, for example, was once part of a Roman fortress along the road linking Damascus to Aqaba, and the incomplete Qasr Al Mushatta exhibits a fusion of classical art and the repetetive geometric patterns particular to Islam. The Omayyads adapted elements of their predecessors' architecture: mosaics from the Byzantines; chunky Persian bricks; and smooth, gypsum-covered walls from the Sassanians.

The castles of Karak and Shawbak suffer the misnomer of Crusader fortresses, but the Mamlukes were responsible for most of the remains visible today. Their workmanship is more refined than that of the Crusaders, who had to build their forts in haste.

▽ **BUILDING IN THE MAKING**
By law, new buildings in Amman must be faced with local stone. The aim is to preserve the traditional integration of stone and wood structures and the land.

△ **MODERN MOSQUE**
The King Abdullah Mosque, built in the 1980s, is one of Amman's more recent landmarks. Here traditional motifs are given a modern twist.

▷ **REFINED URBAN LIVING**
The architecture of Salt reflects the sophistication of the city in the 19th and early 20th centuries. Classical and Ottoman flourishes abound.

▽ CARVED FACADES

Petra's Khazneh (Treasury), carved into the soft sandstone in the 1st century BC, is one of Jordan's most famous images. Most of Petra's buildings were carved rather than built.

◁ ECLECTIC TASTES

The Nabataeans mined every architectural style known to them. Petra, for example is mainly a bizarre mix of Greek, Roman and Egyptian influences. The designs on the Street of Facades (left) were an Assyrian invention.

△ DESERT STRONGHOLDS

The Omayyads built Jordan's so-called "desert castles" east of Amman, but the origins of many of these fortresses stretch back to Roman times.

▷ ROMAN RELICS

The Romans' use of various kinds of columns, capitals and floral motifs was later adopted in Nabataean and then Islamic architecture.

THE IMAGE MAKERS

The frescoes on the interior walls of the bathhouse in Qusayr Amra, east of Amman, reveal the naturalism of Islamic art before the ban on such images under an edict by Caliph Yazid II (720–24). The frescoes, which somehow escaped the widespread destruction that followed the edict, show a delightful and uninhibited sensuousness, with gazelles, monkeys, camels, birds, a guitar-strumming bear and even bathers in different states of undress. Depictions of animate subjects are also found in mosaics. Although a trademark of early Christianity, these were crafted by the Romans before them, and were later adopted by the Omayyads. The mosaics in Madaba, date from Byzantine times. Most feature classical themes – hunting and fishing, mythological scenes and exotic birds and animals.

JORDANIAN FOOD

*"The guest is the hostage of the host", says an old Arabic proverb,
so when you're heading to Jordan be sure to pack a healthy appetite*

Food, and lots of it, is likely to be an important part of any Jordanian tour. In the Arab World, a bountiful homemade spread is a way of honouring guests, and in the finest tradition of hospitality Jordanian hosts spare no effort in preparing a meal. Four or five people are usually plied with enough food for 10 at least. In return, hosts expect their guests to eat amply, and even when their appetites are truly sated, pleas for mercy will only earn them another serving.

Although a meal can feel relatively heavy, the local diet is fortunately very healthy – based mainly on fresh vegetables, garlic, a mixture of spices and herbs, and olive oil. These are joined by a few other staples, such as yoghurt, *lebaneh* (a semi-dried yoghurt, roughly the consistency of a cream cheese and with a flavour similar to sour cream) and *tahini* (a paste made from sesame seeds). Although the basics of the diet are few, they are used with skill to create a huge and imaginative array of culinary delights.

A plethora of palates

Jordanians are quick to acknowledge that Jordanian cuisine is not exclusively their own, but an amalgamation of different Mediterranean dishes, in particular from Lebanon, Syria, Palestine and Egypt. Common among them are *hummus* (a paste of mashed chick peas and *tahini* topped with olive oil, crushed garlic, chilli peppers and parsley), *ful* (beans), *mutabal* (mashed aubergine mixed with *tahini* and garlic) *felafel*, *shawarmah* or *tabouleh* (a salad of finely chopped parsley, onions, tomatoes and cracked wheat mixed with lemon and olive oil). Arabs quip that these are Arab versions of fast food, and hundreds of roadside restaurants are dedicated to selling them. These dishes, accompanied by a pitta-like bread that serves as a scoop, can also be served as appetisers or as part of a *meze*, a buffet of small, light dishes.

LEFT: indulging in the national dish, *mansaf*, a feast of lamb and rice.
RIGHT: Arabic pastries in a shop in Amman.

Jordanians trouble themselves with very few high-hat dining rules dictating how and when food should be served: *hummus*, for example, is equally appropriate at breakfast, or with an evening meal, while *meze* may be served alongside a main lunch or dinner dish but can equally well be a meal in itself. The most important

aspect of dining is congregational, especially in the case of lunch, the largest meal of the day, when life grinds to a halt for at least two hours for an extended family get-together.

A daily feast

Lunch usually includes a stewed dish, such as lamb or chicken, served over rice. Favourites are *maloukhieh*, a leafy-green vegetable cooked with chicken pieces; *bamieh*, okra stewed in tomato sauce with garlic and lamb or beef; *masakhen*, a dish of chicken on a bed of *shraq* (a very thin bread) smothered in onions all baked in oil and sprinkled with a citrus-flavoured spice called *samac*. Another recommendation is *maqloubeh*, which can include lightly fried chicken with any fried vegetable – Jordanians have a preference for aubergine or cauliflower – stewed in a crock with uncooked rice piled between layers of chicken and vegetable. Once the rice is cooked through, the crock is upended onto a platter before it is served (hence the name *maqloubeh*, which literally means "upside-down").

Jordanians of Palestinian origin have a penchant for a baked dish known as *fatteh*. The base for *fatteh* is Arabic bread, broken into bits, over which is layered a mixture of vegetables and meat – *fatteh hummus*; *fatteh maqdous*

ans make a clear distinction between being invited to a mere lunch or dinner and being invited to a *mansaf*. It is a true feast: usually a whole stewed lamb, served on a steaming heap of rice and *shraq*, doused in hot *jameed* (dried yoghurt), sprinkled with *snobar* (fried pine nuts) and served on an enormous platter.

This gastronomic event is reserved for special occasions, such as when hosting an honoured figure in society, or celebrating births, weddings or graduations, or welcoming home family members that have been abroad for a long time. Everyone loves *mansaf*, and it is prepared, eaten and discussed with a reverence

(with aubergine and minced meat), *fatteh djaj* (chicken) – followed by a cold topping of yoghurt or *tahini*.

Stuffed vegetables are a mark of culinary skill. Their preparation is labour intensive, and if you are offered either *wara dawali* (minced lamb, ghee, nutmeg, cinnamon and rice stuffed in vine leaves) or *cusa mashi* (courgettes stuffed with the same), you'll know you are being highly honoured.

The national dish

Jordanians proudly claim only one dish as their own: *mansaf*, a Bedouin invention that has become the Jordanian national dish. Jordani-

usually reserved for religious ritual.

Rules govern both a *mansaf*'s preparation and consumption. In Bedouin tradition, for example, the size of a *mansaf* is relative to the esteem in which the guest is held – the bigger the *mansaf*, the more honoured the guest (see the picture of the dish used by the Adwan family on the occasion of a visit by King Hussein in 1962, *on page 82*). Generally, however, Bedouins refer to chunks of meat "the size of a cat's head" as the standard measure by which to carve the meat (a task which should only be carried out by the host).

The dish is eaten standing and, messy and challenging though it may seem, using only the right hand, which expertly rolls the meat, rice and bread into neat bite-sized balls. (The left hand, according to the instructions of Islam, is the hand used for bodily hygiene, and should never touch food: therefore, when one is tackling a *mansaf*, it should remain behind the back.) As a further test of dexterity, only the thumb, fore- and middle fingers should be used to pop the ball into the mouth, without lips and fingers touching.

It reflects poorly on a host's generosity if a guest ever reaches the bottom of the dish, but it is equally poor behaviour for guests to eat anything except what is immediately in front of

containing a layer of soft cheese, served hot and drenched in syrup – *qatayif*.

Tea and coffee are served immediately following a meal, and many Jordanians are committed believers in herbal drinks – a few of which you may need after a *mansaf*. Aniseed is drunk to calm the nerves, fennel seeds to alleviate wind, camomile to clear the sinuses, thyme to ease a cough, and sage and mint may be taken to calm an upset stomach and aid digestion.

"Sahtain!", Jordanians will wish you after a meal – "two healths". It's unlikely to be much consolation for an overtaxed stomach. ❏

them. And should you have a liking for exotic delicacies such as the tongue, remember this treat goes to the host's guest of honour.

A sweet tooth

Like most people of the Middle East, Jordanians crave sweetness, and various guises of pastry dripping in honey – *baklava* – are consumed in delicate portions throughout the land. Other desserts include a sweet milk pudding with pistachios – *mahalbiyya wa festaqis* – and cake

LEFT: chefs at the restaurant of the Hotel Intercontinental, in Amman.
ABOVE: a meal shared.

THE RAMADAN FAST

In the Muslim calendar, the ninth month is known as Ramadan. During this month, most Muslims observe a fast throughout the hours of daylight, and only eat a meal – *ittar* – after sunset. At the end of the month, Eid al-Fitr is the feast held to mark the end of the fast, when special food is eaten, new clothes are purchased and alms are given to the poor.

For non-Muslim visitors, hours of business for restaurants and shops tend to be erratic during Ramadan, and it is difficult to get a meal before sunset. Also, as a matter of courtesy, it is best not to eat or drink in public during daylight in Ramadan.

WILDLIFE

*The deserts of Jordan once teemed with living creatures. The plant and animal life
that has survived the modern age is beginning, with help, to flourish again*

For such a small country Jordan encompasses dramatic contrasts. Snow frequently caps hills in winter whilst summer temperatures in the desert may exceed 36°C (97°F). Different areas also experience very different climates simultaneously. While the mountains of Ajlun in the north and Shawbak in the south are subject to a Mediterranean climate (hence the snow), the main part of the country basks in a desert climate. Between these extremes are at least four other climatic regions, creating a spectrum of wildlife habitats.

Contrary to popular belief, the desert itself is endowed with abundant plants and animals, thanks to a fertile distant past. A drive across Jordan's deserts by four-wheel-drive vehicle, or perhaps over its well-surfaced roads in an ordinary car, is packed with clues to the dramatic changes to natural conditions that have taken place over the years. One only has to stand at the great Omayyad castles at Amra or Kharaneh, both in the midst of arid desert, to realise that the landscape must have been somewhat different when the Omayyad caliphs built here. Great hunters, the caliphs built these castles in the heart of "big-game country", where natural forests provided shade, refuge and food for gazelles and other mammals.

Destruction of tree cover, primarily for wood-burning, was one of the biggest causes of change. Protection of surviving woodlands is therefore a priority of the **Royal Society for Conservation of Nature**, an organisation that has been active in protecting Jordan's wildlife habitats and setting up wildlife reserves.

The Arabian oryx

Jordan has played a key role in rescuing the Arabian oryx from the jaws of extinction through a captive breeding and reintroduction campaign known as Operation Oryx, in which

PRECEDING PAGES: Arabian oryx, rescued from the jaws of extinction.
LEFT: an ostrich at Azraq.
RIGHT: ibex in Wadi Mujib Wildlife Reserve.

oryx held at the **Shaumari Reserve** are bred and swapped with animals from other captive populations to maintain a strong blood-line.

Whilst there are currently 143 Arabian oryx at Shaumari, and animals from this centre are also released into the wild in Oman, the Society has extended the programme to include other

threatened animals including the Nubian ibex, the Syrian wild ass (onager), the ostrich, and the common gazelle. The centre at Shaumari, established in 1975, has a total area of 22 sq. km (8½ sq. miles). Apart from the captive breeding programme it is a natural reserve where 11 mammals, 134 birds and 130 plant species have been recorded.

Within only a few miles of Shaumari is the wetland area of Azraq (*see page 198*), a magnet for millions of birds passing between Eurasia, Arabia and Africa. The variety and abundance of birds is remarkable; at least 120 different species can be regularly seen, and the total list of species spotted numbers over 300.

More surprising, however, is the number of waterfowl that congregate in this desert oasis, including teal, gadwall, wigeon, pintail, garganey, shoveler, pochard, and tufted duck. In 1977 the Ramsar Convention declared Azraq to be a wetland of international importance for migratory waterfowl.

Azraq is also an excellent location for close observation of birds of prey such as osprey, honey buzzard, black kite, Levant sparrowhawk, buzzard, short-toed eagle, steppe eagle, spotted eagle, lesser spotted eagle, hen harrier, pallid harrier, marsh harrier, peregrine falcon, red-footed falcon, kestrel and lesser

kestrel. Visitors from Europe who are aware of the decline of many of these species will be surprised by their numbers at Azraq. For instance, the corncrake, one of the recent casualties of European agricultural development, turns up at Azraq each year, probably arriving from the steppe-lands of Asia. The Azraq Reserve spreads over a modest area of some 12-sq. km. (4½-sq. mile), but includes pools, marshes, water meadows and salt dunes.

The **Wadi Mujib Wildlife Reserve** is a wild and beautiful area occupying a 212-sq. km. (82-sq. mile) area of steep mountainside and valley, extending from the Dead Sea at 400 metres (1,300 ft) below sea-level to the eastern highlands, which rise 800 metres (2,600 ft) above sea level. Explorations on foot are sometimes rewarded by sightings of the Nubian ibex, along with a wealth of other fauna, and a long list of plants that includes several rare orchids. Jordan is home to at least 22 species of wild orchids: many of them are threatened by habitat depletion so care should be taken to leave them undisturbed.

Protected places

The southernmost wildlife habitat (excluding the marine life in the Gulf of Aqaba) is Wadi Rum, where huge rocky outcrops of sandstone rise out of a pink desert speckled with Bedouin encampments. The designated **Wadi Rum Wildlife Reserve** covers an area of 510 sq. km (200 sq. miles). Beyond the immediate valley lie range after range of rocky hills inhabited by ibex, gazelle, hedgehog and porcupine.

Further plans are afoot to extend wildlife management. A proposed reserve at Burqu' will cover 950 sq. km (370 sq. km) in the northeast of Jordan, close to the borders with Syria and will include the Burqu' Palace within its boundaries. Such a vast area of totally protected habitat is necessary if Jordan's efforts to reintroduce Arabian gazelle, Dorcas gazelle, onager and ostrich to their natural habitats are to succeed. Another desert area earmarked for protection, the **Rajil Wildlife Reserve**, about 50 km (30 miles) from Azraq in the eastern desert, is an area rich in gazelle, red fox, hare, hyena and wolves as well as desert plants.

At Karak, the surrounding plateau has a wealth of interesting wildlife and a reserve covering 410 sq. km (158 sq. miles) has been surveyed. Tentatively named the **Abu Rukbah**

THE LAST LEOPARD

The Dana Wildlife Reserve (*see also page 111*) lies in south Jordan, where the Shara range reaches 1,300 metres (4,260 ft) and where an exceptionally rugged landscape includes precipitous canyons and deep winding gorges that defeat even the best four-wheel-drive vehicles. Here, some of Arabia's most exhilarating mountain scenery is home to the country's last few leopard and two of their prey, the mountain gazelle and Nubian ibex. The RSCN constantly monitor the various species with the aim of protecting and promoting their development. The high ground of the reserve has a natural woodland, formed by pine, oak and juniper.

Wildlife Reserve after the main road that passes through the plateau, its elevated, rugged terrain is the perfect habitat for mountain and desert gazelle.

The desert landscape of Wadi Bayir is destined to become the **Bayir Wildlife Reserve**, with an area of 440 sq. km (170 sq. miles). It is earmarked for the release of Arabian oryx, gazelle, onager and ostrich.

Two other reserves currently on the drawing board include the **Jarba Wildlife Reserve**, focusing on Wadi Jarba, where mountain

THE NATIONAL FLOWER

Jordan's national flower is the black wild iris. It is as likely to be seen growing along the roadside in the plateau lands as in any of Jordan's wilder locations.

bers during spring. Look out also for the emerald green grasshopper and its dramatic relative, the preying mantis.

Lizards are frequently seen throughout the country. While walking through the sandstone pathways of Petra, you may well encounter the Petra wall lizard, *Lacerta danfordi,* which suns itself on the rocks in the morning light. A sharp eye is needed to distinguish the Mediterranean chameleon which stands motionless among the branches of bushes, following its prey with its

gazelle will be reintroduced, and the **Jabal Mas'ada Wildlife Reserve** which will extend over 460 sq. km (286 sq miles) of the Wadi Araba, including the Masada mountain in the southern sector of Jordan. This area already includes mountain gazelle, ibex, striped hyena, fox, hare, wolf and badger.

Insects and reptiles

Insect-life is also widely distributed, and colourful butterflies, such as the small copper and small tortoiseshell, migrate in large num-

revolving eyes and capturing it on a tongue that is as long as its body. Although there are several poisonous snakes in Jordan, including the horned viper and the Palestine viper, visitors are unlikely to encounter them and there are very few instances of snake bite.

Having climbed Jordan's mountains, trekked across its plateau lands, scrambled up its *wadis* and wandered through its deserts, there is still more wildlife to encounter. There is no better way to cool off after an exhausting day exploring Petra or Wadi Rum than to swim in the clear waters of the Gulf of Aqaba and admire the corals and fishes of the Red Sea-Indian Ocean (*see the picture story on pages 274–75*). ❏

LEFT: a grey heron sits and waits.
ABOVE: a blue lizard.

HIKING AND CLIMBING

This chapter offers an overview for hiking and climbing in Jordan, but for serious treks and climbs specific geographical information should be obtained

Jordan suffers the unfortunate nickname of "the desert Kingdom" – implying that the land is dry, dull and void of life. In fact, the Middle East's four recognised bio-geographical regions are all unified within Jordan's borders: **Mediterranean** (the highlands of Um Qays and Irbid), **Irano-Turanian** (the area surrounding the highlands including Salt and Jarash), **Saharo-Arabian** (the area known as the Badia, or eastern desert, the Central Desert, Wadi Sarhan, Al Jafr Basin and Al Mudawwara Desert) and **Sudanian** (the Rift Valley to Rum and Aqaba). These are home to unique flora and fauna, some of which is discussed in the chapter on wildlife, *see pages 105–107*. Some 420 bird species have been identified in Azraq alone, earning Jordan's reputation as a centre for bird watching.

In spite of such promise, most terrain – with the exceptions of Wadi Rum and Petra – remains unexplored by nature enthusiasts. This is partly because official tourism planning has targeted cultural tourists and partly because of security considerations. However, the sudden expansion of the tourism industry since the mid-1990s has spawned concern about its impact on the country's many fragile ecosystems, and through the efforts of the RSCN (Royal Society for the Conservation of Nature), the government has brought many areas under protection. Along with a handful of eco-tourism offices, it is striving to facilitate this new genre of tourism.

North Jordan

The rich and rolling hills of north Jordan are relatively undisturbed areas, and offer great opportunities for short hikes – ruins such as **Ajlun Castle**, **Pella** or **Umm Qays** make perfect start or end points. A particularly rewarding climb is down the side of Umm Qays to the hot springs of **Himma**, where you can have a relaxing soak and enjoy a light

meal at the resthouse. In the north, popular hikes, descend from the hills towards the Jordan Valley through any one of dozens of wadis leading to some of the country's most fertile agricultural land. The area is not as deserted as some of the southern hiking territory, and you are bound to be invited for a chat over coffee with local residents. You should take a good map with you to be certain of where the militarised zones in the valley begin and end.

Eastern Desert

The eastern region lends itself to camel trekking rather than hiking. It is replete with archaeological treasures such as the **Desert Castles** (*see pages 199–209*). For the best appreciation of what you will see, it is better to take along a specialist. Discovery Tours (*see the Travel Tips, page 330*) is knowledgeable in the Eastern Desert area, and can help plan, and give advice on, trips here.

LEFT: striding out in Wadi Rum.
RIGHT: essential accessories.

The RSCN is busy rehabilitating the oasis in the **Azraq Wetlands Reserve**, and has had success reintroducing the elegant Arabian oryx in the **Shaumari Wildlife Reserve** (*see page 204 for both*). These two reserves provide opportunities to observe some of Jordan's rarest animal species, while the Azraq Oasis is also a stop-over for birds on migratory routes.

Wadi Mujib and the Dead Sea

Almost any point along the King's Highway, running along the crest of the mountains that separate the Jordan Valley from the rest of the Kingdom, can be a starting point for treks down through the mountains and wadis to the Dead Sea or even for a journey all the way to Aqaba, depending on time available. From **Madaba**, for example, you can hike down the mountainsides to **Ma'in** and the hot spring baths once patronised by Herod.

Accessible from the King's Highway or from the parallel Dead Sea road is the **Wadi Mujib**. Dubbed the Grand Canyon of Jordan, Mujib is again a protected area and it is recommended only for serious, experienced climbers who have a few days to spend. It does require a special permit from the RSCN, and no climbing gear is allowed.

WADI RUM

The possibilities for hiking and climbing in Wadi Rum are plentiful. Veteran Rum trekker Tony Howard has identified more than 400 routes, and his book *Treks and Climbs in Rum and Petra* is recommended reading for serious hikers and climbers. There are camping facilities at Rum, but alternatively – if you are feeling sufficiently resourceful – you can pitch a tent anywhere in the desert. If you are fortunate enough to receive an invitation, you might also spend a night in a Beit Sha'ar (Bedouin tent). The Bedouins' invitations are very genuine, but in order not to abuse hospitality it is appropriate to offer something – which may well be refused – in advance of your stay.

It is especially important in Rum to be mindful of both the elements and the culture; dress becomes particularly important here. Men and women should keep shoulders and legs covered when in the company of the Bedouin. This measure is also practical considering the intensity of the sun. Although hikers and climbers are relatively free to roam through Wadi Rum, its recent designation as a national park, again under the protection of the RSCN, may mean that some areas will soon be restricted or may only be visited with a guide. Therefore, before planning your itinerary, it is advisable to contact the RSCN for up-to-the-minute information.

Dana

The **Dana Nature Reserve** is the jewel of RSCN activity in Jordan and is a superb place for hiking and camping. In addition to wonderful views of Wadi Dana and Wadi Araba, it offers a variety of flora, fauna and ecosystems. There are also two fine camping facilities on the reserve, as well as a guest house and a hotel for backpacking budget travellers in the Dana Village. Although hiking is strictly confined to routes dictated by the RSCN, any one of six trails is rewarding.

The **Rummana Trail** (2.5 km/1½ miles, 2½ hours) is a medium-difficulty round trip hike leading from the Wadi Dana campsite, just below the tower entrance to the reserve, to the summit of Jabal Rummana, one of the highest points in the reserve. At the top of Jabal Rummana are the ruins of a military site used during the early Islamic period (300 BC–AD 900).

The medium-grade **Cave Trail** (4km/2½ miles, 2 hrs) leads hikers up the steep incline of Shagg Al Kelb (the Valley of the Dog) past 27 caves believed to have been occupied from the Nabataean through the early Islamic period. Niches carved into the cave walls and a cross carved into the entrance of another cave suggest that these abodes were also used as monasteries during the Crusades.

Dana's most interesting and fun trail is probably the **Feinan Trail** (14 km 8½ miles), which leads through Wadi Dana down to the Feinan Campsite. It is a relatively easy one-way climb that follows a dirt path, but is graded medium because of its length. The biogeography shifts from wooded highlands to shrubby steppe vegetation within the space of a few kilometres, and at the bottom of the wadi, the pools of Tur'ah are shrouded in aquatic vegetation. Towards the end of the hike is Kirbet Feinan, an archaeological site with evidence of occupation from Neolithic to Islamic periods. The remains of two Byzantine churches and a monastery can still be seen.

Petra

Like Wadi Rum, Petra is pretty much limitless in possibilities for exploration. Some of the

most popular short, less demanding hikes in and around Petra are to **ad-Dayr** (the monastery), the ascent to which is approached from behind the museum and restaurant at the end of the colonnaded street near Qasr Al Bint, or to the **High Place of Sacrifice**, which leads climbers up steep, narrow ancient processional way to the plateau atop Jabal Madhbah. More challenging routes include one to **Jabal Harun**, the highest peak in Petra, where the Prophet Aaron is presumed buried – enthusiasts site Jabal Harun as one of the most exhilarating climbs and one of the most spectacular sites to pitch camp for a night. By day, the peak is a

point for surveying the entire Petra area.

These hikes and many other climbs are well documented in *Petra – A Guide to the Capital of the Nabataeans* by Rami Khouri.

There is nothing to stop hikers from creating their own adventures in Petra, but beware during the rainy season. Additionally, if you intend to stray far, experts suggest you keep an eye on the goat dung littering the ground. Dung is an indication that the area you are in is accessible to people and known to the Bedouin who herd their flocks through the area. If you don't see dung, it indicates that neither the Bedouin or their unruly goats pass that way, and probably for very good reason ❑

ARABIAN HORSES

This most aristocratic of breeds is proud, intelligent and strong.

The Arabian horse not only wins races but also inspires romantic legends and poetry

Hidden among pine trees off the road to Fuhays in the suburbs of Amman is the Royal Jordanian State Stud. It is here, in a low-lying complex engirdled by clematis and roses that the King's 135 pure-bred Arabian horses are stabled, attended by 40 full-time grooms.

The stud has come a long way since the early 1920s, when the Emir Abdullah brought a small team of Arabs with him from the Hejaz. These horses, augmented by some given to him by local tribes, formed the foundations of today's stock. At the time, Emir Abdullah's interest was recreational rather than ideological, but in the 1960s, when interbreeding with thoroughbreds in the interests of horse-racing threatened the purity of the Arab breed in the region, his grandson King Hussein set up an official state stud. First under the management of a European couple, Mr and Mrs Lopez, and now under the hand of Princess Alia, Abdullah's great-granddaughter who traces her interest in Arabians to a childhood love of "a pony and a rocking-horse", the stud has blossomed into a thriving enterprise committed to preserving the local lines and supplying stock for Arab studs all over the world. The streamlined and efficient stables have a full-time vet and a team of three farriers. The copious amounts of manure nourish Amman's finest rose beds.

A breed apart

The Arabian (*equus Arabicus*) is more compact and delicate-looking than the thoroughbred, yet it is famed for its power as well as its beauty, but its most valuable asset historically was its endurance, a quality prized by the Bedouin, its human counterpart in weathering the hardships of the desert. As one early 20th-century traveller noted, "The Bedouin seem to belong to the Arabian horse as naturally as the date palm belongs to the sand-dune."

PRECEDING PAGES: the Mounted Police.
LEFT: Arabian horses form close bonds with humans.
RIGHT: competitor at the Royal Horse Show.

A tribe's horses were its chief pride, its partners in raiding, hunting and war. They were also associated with an important rite of passage. Once a young male Bedu had single-handedly captured a mare from within the midst of an enemy's camp he was admitted to the *mejlis*, the distinguished council of men who

gathered around the chief's camp-fire.

As a rule, mares were valued above stallions. Not only did they reproduce, but they were seen as more manageable in warfare and likely to be quieter when stealth was required and the whinny of a randy stallion could blow a Bedu's cover. It is thought to be for this reason that the blood-line of Arabs is traced through the mares.

Years of working and living together – horses often bedded down in the family tent – forged a bond of affection between the Bedouin and their horses which transcended usual human/animal relationships and inspired romantic legends and poetry.

Myth clouds the Arabian's origins. The breed

is believed to have originated either in central Arabia or near the Euphrates river in Mesopotamia some 4,000 years ago, but tradition, based on the fact that the main strains are known as *Al-Khamsa* (The Five), traces their descent to five horses said to have been owned by the Prophet Mohammed.

The Koran attributes their source to the south wind: "Then God took a handful of wind and fashioned from it a chestnut horse. He said, 'I have created you, Arabian horse; I have moulded you from the

> ### EQUINE INSPIRATION
>
> The Bedu would eulogise about their horses, referring to them as "drinkers of the wind", "the envy of all", and even comparing them with magic carpets.

back (they have 23 vertebrae, instead of the 24 of the non-Arab), long hindquarters which should be level with the back, a high tail, and fine legs (deceptively frail-looking, for they are in fact dense and strong). They can be grey (white), chestnut or black, and their colour at birth is no indication of their adult hue.

The Arab's superior intelligence makes it unsuitable for polo (they chase the ball) and its independence – perhaps more than its small build – makes it an unreliable show-jumper (though they can

wind; I have tied Good Fortune to your mane; you will fly without wings; you will be the noblest among animals... God then blessed the horse with sign of glory and happiness and marked his forehead with a star, and the horse leaped into space."

Flying horses

Modern-day breeders talk lyrically of symmetry, harmony, balance and the famous "float", the Arab's unique way of moving that brings to mind the magic carpet. The distinguishing physical characteristics of the breed are pointed ears, a concave face with a broad forehead, a large jaw and small muzzle, a small

jump quite well, they will often refuse). But some strains make good race horses, and all these qualities are prized by part-breeders, who improve the qualities of other breeds by mating them with Arabian stallions. Arabs are known for their prepotency – thus most other warm-blooded breeds contain an element of Arab in their blood, including the English thoroughbred and the pedigree hackney – even if a particular horse lacks some of the classic Arab traits, she may still pass them on to her foals.

As a rule, the animals are not used for breeding until they are four years old, after which mares then produce a foal every 11 months until their late teens or early twenties, with occasional time-off for a rest. The Royal Stables' longest-living stallion was 33 years old when he died, the sire of a foal just the year before.

There are various strains of breed, and the Royal Jordanian Stud has several rare lines, such as Umm Argub and Kehilah Krush. Maintaining these lines has been a delicate and difficult business. The Hamdani line, for instance, was almost lost in Jordan when female foals of the stud's only Hamdani mare were sent to Britain and Morocco

A DAY AT THE RACES

Amman holds an international horse show in the grounds of the stud each year. In addition Jordan's Royal Racing club plans to host Arab race meetings three or four times a year in Marqa, to the east of Amman.

Royal Mounted Guards and the army, one stallion, Ghazalleh, was found ploughing a field in the Jordan Valley.

Some of the horses hired out at Petra are thought to be pure Arabs, but the traditional means of tracking ancestry in such horses – verbally from father to son – has broken down. To help improve the general stock at Petra, the Royal Stables lend Petra two stallions a year for mating. The ratio of mares to stallions at the Royal Stables is 5–1. ❏

and the mare went on to produce only males. In the end stud was forced to buy back a mare.

The stud is also committed to preserving specifically local lines, even if they are not especially beautiful or prized. The greatest threat to such lines came immediately after King Abdullah's death, when, the horses' value and heritage not being fully appreciated, the late King's stable was disbanded. When King Hussein began reassembling the stock, he found the horses dispersed to all corners of Jordan. Though most were found serving with the

LEFT: awarding marks at the Royal Horse Show.
ABOVE: an Arab stallion poses for the camera.

A TOUGH LIFE

The horses are kept outside as often as possible as too much cosseting makes them susceptible to illness. When, during a particularly cold winter, infra-red lamps were rigged up to keep the horses warm, they quickly caught colds. Though foals are born throughout the year, the ideal time for a birth is as close to the beginning of the year as possible because a foal born at the end of December will be classed as a one-year-old by 2 January, even if it is only a few days old – a disadvantage for race horses, where age is a crucial factor. As a rule, the horses are not ridden until they reach the age of three.

THE CAMEL

The camel is intrinsic to life in the desert – as a vehicle, a carrier and as an inspiration for survival in one of the world's harshest environments

Of the two types of camel, the double-humped Bactrian and the single humped Dromedary, it is the latter that is found in the deserts of the Middle East. Originating in North America about 40 million years ago and related to the llama and alpaca of South America, the Arabian camel of today (*Camelus dromedarius*) was probably first domesticated in Arabia 2,500–1,500 BC, initially for milk production and later to carry heavy loads along the emerging overland trade routes. The journey from Qana or Hadramaut in South Arabia along the Incense Route to Gaza or Petra would take around 70 days covering 40 km (25 miles) per day, with thousands of camels, each carrying up to 500 kg (1,100 lbs).

As a pack animal in the desert, the camel is ideally suited to the harsh and difficult conditions, and is able to maintain a steady speed of 5 km (3 miles) per hour for up to 15 hours. Although it is capable of lasting about 20 days without water, it begins to suffer without far more frequent nourishment. During a prolonged absence of food or water, it uses up fat stored in its hump, and may lose as much as a quarter of its body weight.

A camel's body temperature is much the same as that of a human, but it has a much wider range and does not start to lose water by sweating until it has risen to around 41°C (106°F). It also urinates only about half a litre (about a pint) per day, roughly the same as a human, despite being four or five times larger. A healthy camel drinks about 20 litres (4½ gallons) of water each day, but after long periods without water can drink almost five times this amount in just 10 minutes.

As well as a good sense of smell, a camel is equipped with several unique features to help it combat sandstorms. It has a double row of heavy eyelashes to protect its eyes, hairy ear openings which filter out the sand and muscular nostrils which can close fully or partially.

During the mating season, males can be dangerous when they bite, kick and spit, and are prone to sudden fits of rage. After a nine month gestation period, the female gives birth to one calf, capable of walking within hours. Camels take 10 years to reach maturity. The natural coat

of the camel falls off during the moulting season, when the warm weather makes a thick covering unnecessary. The hair is used by the Bedouin for rugs, tents and clothing, and other useful products are camel milk and dried dung for burning.

In the Badia region – a basalt boulder-strewn landscape, impassable for even the toughest 4-wheel-drive vehicle – the Hajaneh still use camels to patrol the borders with Syria and Iraq. On foot and on camel, this Bedouin corp of the Jordanian army track smugglers and aliens entering the country. At their base near Safawi they have their own camel breeding programme and a force of some 500 camels. ❑

LEFT: beasts of burden and a source of meat, milk, hair for weaving and dung for burning.
RIGHT: good companions.

ARTISTS' IMPRESSIONS

Many artists have come to Jordan, and in particular to the site of Petra,
but few have been satisfied by their attempts to represent its glory

The European rush to rediscover antiquities in the 18th and 19th centuries gradually extended to the Orient. Though initially confined to professional explorers, this interest soon spread to dilettantes wealthy enough to undertake the lengthy and costly journeys such exploration involved. The development of the steamship in the early 19th century made such travel much easier (the Red Sea, for example, became navigable in all seasons), and by mid-century touring the Middle East had become a fashionable pastime for adventurous members of the wealthy middle classes. These early tourists were drawn by the sights described in travel literature (a new and booming industry) and by the evocative images of the Orient painted by the artists of the day, who flocked to the region hot on the heels of the explorers.

In the absence of press photographers, it was up to the artists of the day to capture the image of these newly "discovered" places and, via the laborious methods of paintings and lithographs, transmit to the world the wonders they had witnessed. In the early days this was no easy task. In many cases the journeys involved were long and arduous; there was plague and disease, a high possibility of losing one's baggage and a real possibility of losing one's life.

All these drawbacks were especially true of the rock-carved city of Petra, which had been rediscovered by the Swiss explorer Burckhardt in 1812 (*see page 255*). The inhabitants of Petra, the Howeitat and Omrah Bedouins descended from the original Nabataeans, were given to such hostility that pictures often had to be made in a great hurry. Some tribesmen believed that the artists possessed magic powers which enabled them to steal the ancient treasure away, and it was nearly a century before the journey to the city was considered safe.

PRECEDING PAGES: David Roberts' *El Deir, Petra.*
LEFT: local figures ("staffage") were often used to enliven 19th-century compositions, such as in this picture of Petra's theatre by Roberts.
RIGHT: self-portrait by Roberts.

Any archaeologist worth his salt would have possessed the ability to give a rough impression of a place, but it needed an exceptional draughtsman to convey the full majesty of a site as glorious as Petra. As the most accomplished draughtsman of his age, David Roberts was the man for such a task.

Painter Davie

"Painter Davie", of humble Scottish roots, was an amiable figure, and a good friend of Turner. In 1838 he set out on a tour of the Levant, starting in Egypt and going up to Jerusalem. His first stop was Cairo where an English traveller, John Pell, took him to meet the French artist, Louis-Maurice-Adolphe Linant. Linant was the first serious artist to have been to Petra, which he had visited 10 years earlier, but his work, which was rather heavy and laboured, had not been widely seen. When Roberts saw Linant's paintings, the scenes bowled him over.

The Scottish academician had been in two minds about taking on the additional hazard and expense of visiting Jeremiah's doomed city, but one look at Linant's drawings convinced him that the rewards would be well worth the effort. Such a journey, he was instantly convinced, would enable him to return to Britain with "one of the richest folios that ever left the East".

For this great adventure, Roberts was accompanied by John Pell and John Kinnear, an Edinburgh businessman and a keen admirer of Roberts's work. Roberts himself travelled in eastern clothes, which he had bought in order to

DAVIE'S DESPAIR

"I often throw away my pencil in despair of being able to convey any idea of it," Davie once wrote of his attempts to portray the magnificence of el-Deir.

instantly felt it to be still overshadowed by Jeremiah's curse. However, he wasted no time in making numerous sketches. It took all of his powers to capture the rose-red city's likeness and spirit, although like others who visited it before and after him, there were moments when he felt completely overawed.

He spent five and a half days at the site. It was hardly enough. He did not reach the tomb of Aaron, nor did he get a view of the Royal Tombs from the High Place of Sacrifice. His output was

look less conspicuous while sketching in Cairo.

One month after the party left Cairo it arrived in Aqaba where the men were obliged to employ as their escort Sheikh Hussein of the Alowein, who held sway in the lands leading to Petra and had been Linant's guide a decade earlier. But even he seemed unsure that he could give the "Franks" full protection against the local Bedouin, and at one point he refused to continue on the journey, declaring his charges to be "all mad" for even trying to enter the Wadi Musa.

Roberts's courage and determination won in the end but the continuing tension of the Arab tribes coloured his first sight of the city and he

nevertheless prodigious. Petra was ideal for his wonderfully dramatic and romantic style, and he held nothing back. Most of his drawings were surprisingly accurate.

He had good reason to be satisfied with his results and in good spirits he and his party left Petra and headed for Hebron. There he painted two watercolours of the town he found "almost English" in its cleanliness, and its children, "the most beautiful I have ever seen." But an outbreak of the plague forced them on to Jaffa and Jerusalem, where they joined the Easter faithful, visiting the monastery of Saint Saba, Bethlehem, Nablus, Ba'albek and all the other sites on the pilgrims' route.

There was no doubt that his journey did produce one of the richest folios of the region, and Roberts wrote on his return: "My sketches of the East have taken the world of art by storm." They were expertly worked up into watercolours and then lithographs and published in *The Holy Land* in 1842, accompanied by a rather turgid text by an unworldly Scots cleric, the Rev. George Croly.

Roberts's own reputation has gone up and down according to fashion, but *The Holy Land* has seldom been out of print and the original lithographs, plates torn from the early editions of the book, are highly priced.

equipment was strapped to a camel that had somehow taken a different route.

But Petra surpassed anything else he saw. And, like Roberts, he felt frustrated when faced with such magnificence. "My art is helpless to recall it to others," he complained. Writing to his sister, he conveys a strange description of Petra, food clearly not far from the front of his mind: "All the cliffs are a wonderful colour – like ham in stripes and parts are salmon colour."

Lear was there barely more than half a day when he was seized by local Bedouin tribesmen who sent him packing, robbed of everything from money to his hard-boiled eggs. ❏

Edward Lear

William Henry Bartlett, a topographic artist, was the next major artist to visit Petra, in 1845, where he was inspired to paint the unusually detailed watercolour *Principal Range of Tombs*. After Bartlett came Edward Lear, who made his misadventure to the Holy Land 16 years after Roberts. His first bit of bad luck was when, after leaving Hebron, he emerged from the Sufa Pass to find a scene of "astonishing beauty" only to remember that his painting

LEFT: view of Petra from the theatre from *Through Arabia* by M. Léon de Laborde.
ABOVE: *The Dome of the Rock* by David Roberts.

THE FINAL INDIGNITY

The final indignity came to Lear after his return to Britain. His major work of the trip, a painting of the eastern cliff entitled *Petra*, was hung in the Royal Academy in London in 1872, where it was placed above Whistler's portrait of his mother.

"As if in mockery," wrote the critic of the London *Times*, "Petra is placed immediately above Mr Whistler's 'arrangement in gray and black' which, thanks to its broad simplicity, would have lost nothing had the two pictures changed places, while, as they hang, Mr Lear's work is entirely sacrificed."

The curse of Jeremiah had struck again.

PLACES

A detailed guide to the entire country, with the principal sites carefully cross-referenced by number to the maps

Asmall country carved out of the heart of the Middle East, Jordan offers concentrated pleasures. The Nabataean city of Petra is the outstanding attraction, made all the more compelling by its seclusion. Its slender approach along a mile-long cleft has drawn adventurers (Burckhardt and Lawrence), artists (David Roberts) and poets ("rose-red city half as old as time" J. W. Burgon), not to mention Harrison Ford, Sean Connery and Denholm Elliot when Petra served as a suitably fabulous backdrop for the closing sequence of *Indiana Jones and the Last Crusade*.

But other sights and sensations beckon: the Graeco-Roman ruins of the Decapolis in the north, including Jarash and Pella; the 7th-century Omayyad palaces east of Amman; the ancient King's Highway, which snakes through some of the loveliest country in the Middle East; the pink canyons of Wadi Rum; and the multi-coloured coral reefs off Aqaba. Even Amman, a modern city built on hills, has an appealing energy and friendliness.

Distances in Jordan are short, so a little of everything can be sampled in a week. However, there is plenty to fill a longer stay (Petra alone is worth four days) and there are many incidental delights to be savoured – such as basking in hot springs at Himma, tingling in a full-body mudpack at the Dead Sea, or retracing some of the great biblical sites (even non-believers may find they are uplifted by more than soft breezes on Mount Nebu, where Moses surveyed the Promised Land).

The Places section which follows begins with Amman, a comfortable springboard and base, and crosses to its neighbour and rival Salt, an older town with a more oriental flavour, and then heads north and east. From there it journeys down the length of the Jordan Valley, pausing at the eerie Dead Sea, and then, regaining Amman, meanders along the King's Highway to Petra, via Crusader castles, Byzantine churches and flower-filled *wadis*. From Petra it strikes east to the Desert Highway to explore the desertscapes of Wadi Rum, and ends by dipping into the port-resort of Aqaba on the Red Sea.

Following the chapters on Jordan are short sections on the West Bank and Syria, designed for travellers taking a broader look at the Levant and roaming over its modern borders. ❏

PRECEDING PAGES: aerial view of Wadi Rum; the Royal Tombs at Petra; the lush land of the Jordan Valley in spring.
LEFT: a water-seller, Amman.

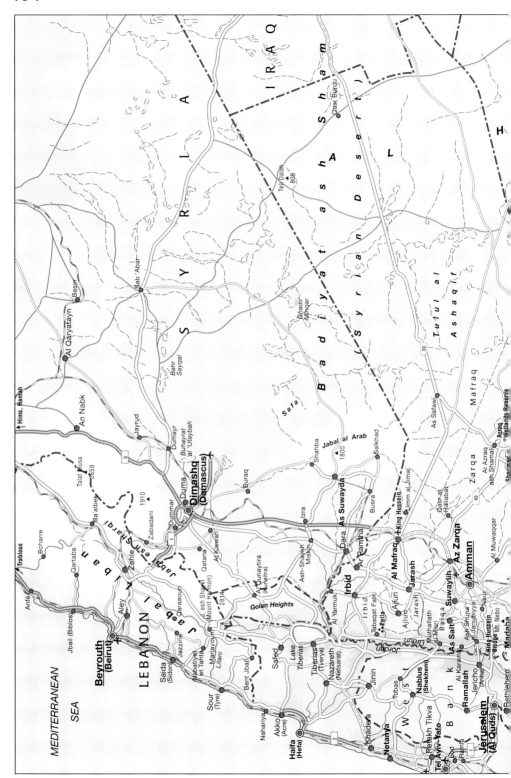

I R A Q

S Y R I A

S h a m

B a d i y a t   a s h   S h a m   (Syrian Desert)

H

Qasr Burqu

Tel Dalah ▲ 806

Tulul al Ashaqif

Hims, Hamah →

Al Qaryatayn

Basir

Sab 'Abar

Bahr Sayqal

Safa

Ghadir Mhqar

An Nabk

Hayrud

Dumayr

Buhayrat al 'Utaybah

Jabal al Arab

Shahba

Shahba ▲ 1800

Salkhad

As Safaw

Mafraq

Talat Musa 2659

Ba'albek

1910 ▲

Dummar

Zabadani

Duma

Dimashq (Damascus)

Buraq

Izra

As Suwayda

Busra

Umm al Jimal

Z a r q a

Al Azraq ash Shamali

Azraq Wetlands Reserve

Qasr al Hallabat

Al Muwaqqar

Sheikh

38

40

Bcharre

Qartaba

Anté

Zahle

J e b e l   e s h   S h a r q i

Qatana

Al Kiswah

Ash-Shaykh Miskin

Dara

Ar Ramtha

King Hussein

Al Mafraq

Trablous

Jbail (Biblios)

Aley

Qaraaoun

J. esh Shaykh (Mount Hermon)

A'Qunaytira (Qunetra)

2814 ▲

Golan Heights

Al Yarmuk

I r b i d

Irbid

Ajlun

Jarash

Jarash

Suwaylih

Amman

Naur

Saida (Sidon)

Jezzine

Nabatiyet et Tahta

Mrayayoun

Litani

Safed

Lake Tiberias (Tiverya)

Tiberias (Tiverya)

Tabaqat Fahl

Pella

Muthallath al Misri

Qasr al Hallabat

Beyrouth (Beirut)

L E B A N O N

Bent Jbail

Nazareth (Natsarat)

Jordan

J o r d a n

As Salt

Ash-Shuna al Janubiyah

Wadi Hussein

Bridge Mt. Nebo

Madaba

Sour (Tyre)

Jinin

W e s t   B a n k

Tubas

Nablus (Shekhem)

Jericho (Ariha)

Naharriya

Akko (Acre)

Khadera

Jinin

Ramallah

Haifa (Hefa)

Netanya

Petakh Tikva

Ramla

Jerusalem (Al Quds)

Bethlehem

Tel Aviv-Yafo

Lod

2

1

MEDITERRANEAN SEA

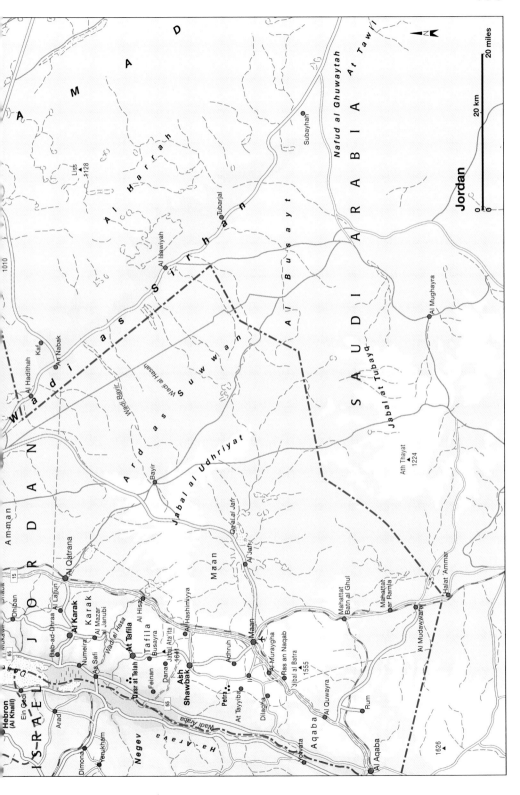

Jordan

20 miles

20 km

ISRAEL

Hebron
(Al Khalil)

Ein Gedi

Dimona

Yerukham

Arad

Dhiban

Shaia

Al Mukawir

Numeira

Bab-ad-Dhraa

Al Lajjun

Al Qatrana

Al Karak

Karak

Al Mazar

Al Janubi

Wadi al Hasa

As Safi

Feinan

Dana

Jibal Ata'ita

At Tafila

Tafila

Busayra

Al Hisa

Al Hashimiyya

Qasr at Telah

Ash Shawbak

Petra

At Tayyiba

Adhruh

Maan

Maan

Al Muraygha

Dilagha

Jibal al Batra 1555

Ras an Naqab

Al Quwayra

Rum

Yotvata

Aqaba

Al Aqaba

Al Jafr

Jbal al Jafr

Bayir

Jabal al Udhriyat

Ard as Suwwan

Wadi Bayir

Wadi al Hasah

Kaf

At Nabak

Al Haditha

W a d i   a s   S i r h a n

Al Isawiyah

Tubarjal

Al Harrah

Lists +128

1010

Subayhah

Nafud al Ghuwaytah

At Tawil

S A U D I   A R A B I A

Al Bu s a y t

Jabal at Tubayq

Ath Thayat 1224

Al Mughayra

Halat Ammar

Al Mudawwara

Mahattat Qar Ramla

Mahattat Batn al Ghul

Ha-Arava

Wadi Araba

Negev

J O R D A N

Amman

Maan

1626

A L M A D

1641

AMMAN

Though many visitors to Jordan treat its capital as a base camp for visits to archaeological sites such as Petra and Jarash, Amman is a vibrant place with its own monuments, history and pleasures

Scattered ancient monuments are juxtaposed with high-rise apartments and shining business establishments in this city of startling contradictions. Extreme poverty confronts extraordinary wealth, and it is readily apparent that the western-leaning governing minority and the more traditionally-minded majority inhabit different worlds which rarely mix.

Amman, sprawling over several mountains, is not a creaking, graceful monument to history like other Arab capitals. Unlike Damascus or Cairo, whose ancient alleyways have teemed with life for hundreds of years, Amman is mostly new, built in the latter half of the 20th century. Its early history is found only in scattered pockets: remnants of the ancient cities of Ammoun and Philadelphia remain in the Citadel, and a handful of houses from the days of the Ottoman empire are found downtown, all but drowning in more modern surroundings.

It is difficult to come to terms with Amman's seemingly haphazard geography. Roads lacking a rational order are bordered by simple buildings of similar design, constructed in a uniform white stone that gradually turns to a mellow gold with age or a setting sun. Road names, spelt out in black and yellow at nearly every intersection, are of little consequence to the city's inhabitants, who prefer to use landmarks for orientation.

LEFT: a view of the amphitheatre and downtown Amman.
BELOW: a street-side coffee shop.

A rich mix

Amman is a crossroads of civilisations, a status held during every period of occupation, and reflected now in the range of art, music, dance, cuisine and dress. It is the best place to explore Jordan's historic, cultural and ethnic diversity, and to see signs of social transition. Mule-drawn carts can be seen competing against sleek Mercedes, beat-up Toyotas and public transport for space on Amman's wide, smooth thoroughfares, and shepherds shuffle their flocks past the sprawling residential palaces of **Abdoun** and through congested **Shmaysani**. European and American fashions are often complemented by the *hejab* (head scarf); and while many books display the blacked-out marks of government censorship, the unpoliced Internet is now widely available in Jordan, and will soon be in every school in the kingdom.

Scores of unfinished buildings and towering cranes are reminders that this city of 1½ million is only just beginning to grow. Big city pressures and constant change have, however, failed to transform Ammanites into the hardened and indifferent city dwellers found in many capitals. Jordanians themselves are the city's charm, and their warmth and friendliness may even take Westerners aback. They are never reluctant to lend a hand, or too shy to answer questions about their own complex corner of the Arab World.

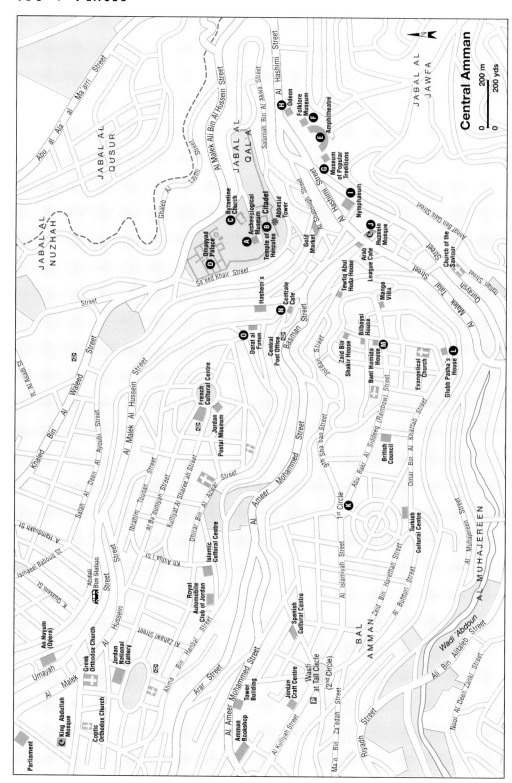

Central Amman

Early history

There is archaeological evidence of settlement in the Amman area for almost 9,000 years. Ain Ghazzal, off the Zerqa road on the outskirts of the city, is one of the largest Neolithic settlements (*c.* 6500 BC) ever discovered in the Middle East. The Citadel hill contains early Bronze-Age tombs (3300–1200 BC), and the site of a late Bronze-Age temple (1300–1200 BC) near the old airport at Marka suggests that these early inhabitants were quite well off.

By the beginning of the Iron Age (1200–539 BC) Amman had developed into the capital of the Ammonites referred to in the Bible. It was here, during a siege in the 10th century, that King David of Israel arranged the death of Uriah the Hittite, whose wife he coveted. Fortress towers ringed the outskirts of Amman (today one of the best preserved stands next to the Department of Antiquities' Registration Centre, near the 3rd Circle), but they were little protection against King David's determined attack. His forces toppled the Ammonites and, apart from a brief revival in the 9th and 8th centuries BC, the area was ruled successively by the Assyrians, Babylonians and Persians for several hundred years.

Amman's history during much of this time is unclear. However, it re-emerged into the limelight during the Hellenistic period, from the 4th century BC. The city was rebuilt and renamed Philadelphia by Ptolemy II (285–247 BC).

The area was conquered by the Seleucids in 218 BC and for two centuries it continued to prosper. In 63 BC, it was absorbed by the Roman Empire and Philadelphia became the southernmost city of the Decapolis, the 10 Graeco-Roman towns in the area. As the Roman Empire extended southward to Petra and beyond, Philadelphia found itself at the centre of the new Roman province of Arabia and of lucrative trade routes running between the Mediterranean and an interior which stretched to India and China as well as routes north and south. The city flourished and impressive monuments were constructed, including the temple of Hercules, the massive walls of the Citadel and the Amphitheatre and Odeon in downtown Amman. Mausolea like Qasr al-Quwaysmeh, in the village of the same name, and Qasr an-Nuwayjis, about 5 km (3 miles) from Sports City on the Zerqa road, also date from this period.

There were Christian martyrs in Amman during the Roman persecution. Tradition has it that a site near the village of Abu Alanda to the southeast of the city is the "Cave of the Seven Sleepers" mentioned in the Koran. The story goes that seven Christian boys fleeing persecution took refuge in the cave and fell asleep, only to wake three centuries later when Christianity had become the official religion of the Roman Empire based in Byzantium. There are other rock-carved Byzantine tombs in the vicinity.

Amman was a bishopric and the remains of two Byzantine churches can be found on the Citadel and in the garden of Darat al-Funun on Jabal al-Luwaybda. At Swayfieh, near 6th Circle, archaeologists have discovered the mosaic floor of another Byzantine church dating from the 6th century.

Philadelphia reverted to its Semitic name, Ammon, under the Islamic caliphate in Damascus and continued to flourish as a trade centre. It was the headquarters of

Map on page 138

BELOW: plying a trade in carrots.

the local Omayyad governor and capital of the surrounding Belqa'a district. The continuity of Amman's history is shown by the Omayyad Palace and other remains on the Citadel, all built on top of earlier structures.

With the shift in political power from Damascus to Baghdad under the Abbasid Caliphate (750–969) and to Cairo under the Fatimids (969–1171), Amman's fortunes declined. Nevertheless, writing in 985, the Arab geographer Muqaddasi referred to Amman as "the sword of the desert". He went on: "Amman, lying on the border of the desert has round it many villages and wheat fields. The Belqa'a district of which it is the capital, is rich in grains and flocks, it also has many streams, the waters of which work the mills. The castle of Goliath is on the hill overlooking the city."

During the Crusades and under the Mamlukes in Egypt, Amman was relegated to the shade by the rise of Karak in the south. By 1321, the Arab traveller Abu al-Fida reported that Amman was "a very ancient town and was ruined before the days of Islam… there are great ruins here and the river al-Zarqa flows through them." It was not until the end of the 19th century that Amman began to regain its former status.

In Ottoman times

Under the Ottoman Empire Amman remained a small backwater, with Salt the main town in the vicinity. In 1806 Amman was reported to be uninhabited, although the ancient buildings were used as temporary dwellings and store rooms by local farmers. There was plenty of water from the stream running through the valley and Bedouin often camped nearby.

Under pressure in Europe in the 19th century, the Ottomans sought to restore their authority to other parts of their empire. This process coincided with the exodus of large numbers of Circassian and other Muslims from the Caucasus in the wake of wars with the Christian tsar based in Moscow. They found refuge in the Ottoman Empire and, with the encouragement of Istanbul, some of them made their way to the area around Amman. The first to arrive were members of the Shabsugh tribe, and they are commemorated in the names of streets and buildings in downtown Amman today.

The Circassians were mostly farmers, but there were also goldsmiths, silversmiths, leather and dagger craftsmen and carriage-makers among them. Within a few years of their arrival they had built three mills along the river. They also constructed rough roads and used wheeled transport in Amman for the first time in hundreds of years. Local legend has it that they were the first to bring tea to Jordan. With all these talents, the Circassians disregarded and rather looked down upon commerce, and from the beginning of this century merchants from Salt, Syria and Palestine moved in to fill the gap in the market.

However, it was the construction of the Hejaz railway which brought Amman to the centre of the historical stage once more. Linking Damascus with Medina, the railway passed through Amman in 1902 and was completed in 1908. The railway changed the exclusively Circassian, agricultural character of the

BELOW: the King Abdullah Mosque.

town. Once more Amman became a centre on the route from Damascus to the Holy City. The population began to swell, and by 1905 there were some 3,000 people in what was becoming a market town with a mixed population.

Map on page 138

During the Emirate

When Emir Abdullah arrived in Transjordan from the Hejaz in 1920, it seemed for a while that Salt, the administrative centre of the area under the Ottomans, would become his capital. However, he eventually decided on Amman, marking a crucial stage in the modern history of the city. There were good reasons for choosing Amman. It was at the political and geographical centre of the country and the Hejaz railway linked the Emir with the Hashemite heartland to the south and with Damascus to the north.

Amman in the early 1920s was described by a British officer as "quite big for this part of the country and built along the bottom of a narrow valley with houses up the side of the hill. The houses are mostly one storey and extraordinary in shape, many of them suggesting a Swiss chalet, and others very much like Irish peasant cottages... with whitewashed outer walls." But there were no paved roads and few services.

A Syrian in a downtown café.

A modest start was made at creating an administration. On 11 April 1921, the first Council of Ministers was formed. The Chief Minister set up shop in a small building by the stream. In 1923, the Emir began to build the Hussein Mosque on a much older Omayyad one, a move which enraged St-John Philby (the father of British spy master Kim Philby), one of Abdullah's advisers at the time. Two years later Abdullah completed the construction of the Raghadan Palace on a hill across from the Citadel.

BELOW: the Darwish Mosque, built by a Circassian on Jabal Ashrafiya in 1961.

Begin your tour of Amman by taking a taxi to the Citadel.

Amman's main streets were realigned and widened in 1925 and new shops and houses spread along them. Between 1925 and 1927, offices for the Emir Abdullah and the British Residency were built. The telegraph system was reorganised and a bi-weekly motor service was created to connect Amman with Baghdad. Amman's first telephone directory appeared in 1926 and by the following year two newspapers were being published in the city.

The 1927 earthquake encouraged the construction of solid, stone buildings rather than the mud and wood homes preferred by the Circassians. As the *wadi* became more crowded, development began to spread up the nearby hills. Most of the influential people settled on Jabal Amman, near 1st Circle.

The modern kingdom

Despite a process of steady change, until 1948 Amman remained a sleepy capital on the edge of the desert with no more than 25,000 inhabitants. In residential areas, many streets were known by the name of their most important inhabitant. But after the 1948 war with Israel the population of Jordan jumped from about 400,000 to 1.3 million in one year. There was a similar surge in the population of Amman. Better-off refugees in Amman settled in the centre and west of the city, but the vast majority went to camps located in the east

BELOW AND RIGHT: street life in downtown Amman.

Following Jordan's annexation of the West Bank in 1951, merchants in Amman prospered by serving as middlemen for West Bank importers and between Palestinian producers and Arab markets. Attracted by the opportunities, rural-urban migration enlarged the population still further. By 1967, Amman had about 433,000 inhabitants and this was boosted by the influx of more than 150,000 Palestinian refugees in the wake of the war in that year.

When the job market opened up in the oil-rich Arab states of the Gulf in the early 1970s, the economic boom had enormous consequences on urban expansion in Amman. Between 1972 and 1982, the city grew from 21 sq. km (8 sq. miles) to 54 sq. km (21 sq. miles). Building expanded yet again with the return of the 300,000 or more Palestinians and Jordanians expelled from the Gulf and Kuwait after the 1991 Gulf War.

In the process, the city has spilled over and merged with nearby towns like Swaylah, Wadi as-Seer and Rusayfeh. Today the population of the Amman conurbation is estimated at 1.5 million. Unpaved roads have given way to paved streets and highways, and villas and high-rise apartments have replaced earlier simple dwellings. The demand for space has led to former residential buildings becoming centres of commerce. Cake and coffee shops, smart restaurants, hotels and banks have sprung up, especially in the **Shmaysani** area.

Meanwhile **Abdoun**, off 5th Circle, now has some impressive domestic architecture. The street leading from the Orthodox Club to the road for 5th Circle is like a gallery of modern building. Nearer the town centre, at Al-Abdali, is the **King Abdullah Mosque** with its distinctive blue dome. This was built during the early 1980s.

However, like all large cities, Amman has its problems. By the mid-1970s it was divided between an upper-income west with open spaces and good infrastructure and an east with middle- and lower-income neighbourhoods, overcrowding and few facilities. As the city expanded, a lot of much-needed agricultural land was covered by concrete, and seemingly incessant urban growth has seriously strained water resources.

Map on page 138

A portion of the Dead Sea Scrolls in the Archaeological Museum.

BELOW: daily bread.

Citadel walk

It is appropriate to start a tour of Amman by taking a taxi (it is a tough climb) to the **Citadel**, which not only clarifies the city's history but also gives a sense of its geography, which is confusing at street level. At the top, the Citadel hill looks like a building site. Archaeological digs continue to uncover new evidence of settlement from earliest times down to the recent past. However, the best excavated sites are Roman, Byzantine and Islamic.

Begin with the small but fascinating **Jordanian Archaeological Museum Ⓐ** (open 8am–5pm Wed–Mon; fee; tel 4638795) which has material from the Palaeolithic period onwards. It has a substantial collection of pottery and statuettes, fragments of statuary and coins, but four exhibits claim special attention: Neolithic wax-like figures, the Dead Sea Scrolls, ancient sarcophagi and the "Amman Daedalus".

The two wax-like figures were discovered at Ain Ghazzal in 1983, and date to the early Neolithic period (8000–6000 BC). They are reminiscent of the Greek Cycladic statues of the 3rd millennium BC which so influenced modern sculptors such as Henry Moore. But the figures discovered at Ain Ghazzal seem to be older and more expressive than the Cycladic statues.

The Dead Sea Scrolls are contained in a small alcove on the right at the end of the museum. They

Jordan and Syria were at the heart of the Omayyad empire, and it was during this dynasty's short-lived period of rule that the Dome of the Rock was built in Jerusalem and the Great Mosque in Damascus.

were found on the western shore of the Dead Sea in 1952, and one inscribed on metal tells of treasure hidden on the west bank of the Jordan River. Some scholars believe that this may refer to material removed from the Jewish Temple prior to its destruction by the Romans in the 2nd century (so far, all attempts to find this treasure have proved unsuccessful).

Another alcove on the other side of the room contains two of the most striking exhibits. The first of these comprises four sarcophagi. Discovered in the grounds of the Raghadan Palace in 1966, they are rare examples of burials practised between the 13th and 7th centuries BC. Just across from the sarcophagi is the "Amman Daedalus", a Roman copy of a Hellenistic original. The mythical Daedalus built the Minoan Labyrinth in Crete, but he is more famous for the wings he made to enable him and his son Icarus to escape the island. (Icarus's wings subsequently melted when he flew too close to the sun.) The incomplete statue imparts the liveliness and sense of movement characteristic of the finest Greek work.

Work at the Citadel since the mid-1990s has provided a fascinating insight into the progression and integration of successive cultures and dynasties. After visiting the museum, start a tour of the Citadel at the **Temple of Hercules B**, directly in front of the museum as you cross the street. The temple lies on a raised platform, dedicated to the Emperor Marcus Aurelius (AD 161–180). Three gigantic columns have been reconstructed here.

Just beyond the Temple of Hercules is a platform with a grand view over downtown Amman. From the walls of the Citadel, the eye passes over the small and larger amphitheatres below. Further to the right along the main streets, and hard to make out amongst the modern development, is the Nymphaeum.

BELOW: the Temple of Hercules.

Between it and the two minarets of the Hussein Mosque is the black and white Darwish Mosque on the hilltop behind Jabal Ashrafiya. This mosque was built on the highest point in Amman by a Circassian in 1961. The area around it offers more stunning views over the city.

From the Temple of Hercules, return to the road in front of the museum. To the right of the museum and slightly off the road is the site of a small **Byzantine church** ❻ marked by a number of Corinthian columns and the remains of a wall. A Byzantine city is thought to have flourished here for hundreds of years until its destruction at the hands of the Sassanids (Persians).

A path leads beyond the church to an area behind the museum. Archaeologists expect excavations of this "path" to uncover the remains of a road, which would have led the Romans to their high temples and the Byzantines to market. Today, the road directs visitors to one of the most exciting archaeological discoveries in recent times: the remains of an entire Omayyad city. Most Omayyad remains in the Middle East are isolated structures, so members of the Spanish archaeological team now excavating and restoring the area hope that this city will help shed light on Islamic urban planning, architecture and art; the site makes an interesting comparison with Andalusia's ancient emirate of Córdoba.

The road leads into the city's **main square**, or souk, where you can see the remains of several commercial stalls on either side. To the left are the steps that would have led to an impressive mosque, constructed by the Omayyads on the highest point of the Citadel. Archaeologists are now working to restore the water system that would have fed the fountain and a round pool used for ablutions inside the mosque.

Across the square is the **Great Audience Hall**, covered by a dome. The hall

Map on page 138

BELOW: striking a stance at the Citadel.

is thought to have been the main link between the palace and the rest of the city, which probably came under Omayyad control during the early 7th century. Archaeologists describe the building as a cocktail adaptation of Byzantine and Sassanid work. The intricate geometric carvings inside represent Sassanid tradition, while the cross-shaped building plan is typically Byzantine. The hall was probably used during the Omayyad period as a "hall of justice", whose second, northern doorway still opens towards the palace entrance.

Other details, in the hall and elsewhere, demonstrate the way the Omayyads absorbed other cultures' artistry into their own. Scant remains of mosaic floors inside the palace are also indicative of the Byzantine influence, while the smooth surfaces of some walls show that the Omayyads adopted the Sassanid technique of using gypsum in their buildings.

On exiting the northern door, look for the **"F" building** to your left, signed with a computer-generated depiction of what the structure probably looked like. Inside, several living quarters are situated around a central courtyard – a typical Omayyad residential arrangement, with extended families usually occupying the area around each courtyard. Eight other similar dwellings have been unearthed.

Proceed to the **Omayyad Palace Ⓓ**. Visitors will first pass through a patio, and a small entrance before reaching the **Throne Room**, from where the prince or governor, or possibly even the Damascus caliph, would have addressed visitors from behind a curtain, a Sassanian practice. The Omayyads enclosed the palace quarters in the original Roman temenos, or sacred precinct.

BELOW: the walkway to the Amphitheatre.

Returning to the Audience Hall, you will find the remains of the **bath house** immediately to your left. Its style is similar to that of Roman and Byzantine baths with minor differences; for example, the Omayyads provided more

generous seating in their baths, as holding congress and entertaining while bathing were favourite pastimes. You can also see the remains of the ceramic water system and, beyond that, an enormous restored water cistern. Continue straight towards the main road, and take a left for the main road to downtown Amman.

Map on page 138

Downtown

The Roman city centre is mostly under concrete and tarmac nowadays, but the restored **Amphitheatre** ❺ (169–77) conveys a sense of its size and importance. Built into the hillside, it seats about 6,000 people and is still used for performances today. There are three bands of seats: the tiers closest to the arena were for the nobles; the second for the military and the third for the ordinary citizens. Look out for a large stone inscribed with an eye, snake, dagger and bow (just discernible), lying on one side of the arena. This stone once topped the entrance to the amphitheatre and symbolised the emperor's protection.

Two small museums at either end of the Roman stage bring the history of Jordan and its capital up to date. The small **Jordanian Folklore Museum** ❻ (open 9am–5pm Wed–Mon; fee; tel 651742) tries to present a cross-section of Jordanian life. The statue of a Circassian in traditional dress guards the entrance. Inside, one exhibit shows how rugs are woven, and a display case has samples of different types of embroidery. There are also some old guns and a small display of traditional musical instruments. The latter include the *mihbash* (coffee-grinder), comprising a large wooden pestle and narrow-necked wooden mortar: a good grinder can beat out extraordinary rhythms.

At the entrance to the Jordanian Folklore Museum.

BELOW: a Circassian guard at the Royal Palace.

Town life is represented by a replica of the living-room of a fine house; the desert and the sown are represented by a Bedouin tent and the plastic camels of a bride and groom, and a small collection of agricultural implements, rakes and threshing boards.

At the other end of the stage is the **Jordanian Museum of Popular Traditions** ❼ (open 9am–5pm Wed–Mon; fee; tel 4651760), opened in 1971 by Sa'adiya at-Tell, the wife of Jordan's then Prime Minister, Wasfi at-Tell. It is an exceptional small museum, this time guarded by the statue of a Bedouin of the Desert Patrol, characteristically dressed in long khaki uniform, ornamental knife and red belt. The collection contains beautifully coloured and embroidered dresses from Jordan and Palestine and antique jewellery in silver, amber and coral. Look out for the display of heavy silver bracelets and exquisite headdresses. A side room contains a collection of mosaics from 4th–6th–century churches in Jordan.

The Roman **Odeon** ❽ begun in the early part of the 2nd century AD is to the right of the exit from the large amphitheatre. After more than 20 years of restoration work by the Jordanian Department of Antiquities, the Odeon reopened in 1997. The intimate little theatre hosted the National Music Conservatory for a commemorative concert.

Turn left along the main street past the Amman Municipality Public Library and keep left at the junction. This is called **Saqf as-Sayl Street** ("the roof of

TIP

A series of junctions
known as Circles (one
to eight) define the
geography of West
Amman. The modern
Abdoun area, for
example, is found
between the 5th and
6th Circles, and the
Emirate walk begins at
the 1st Circle.

BELOW:
detail, the King
Hussein Mosque.

the stream"), so-called because it is built over the stream which was so crucial in Amman's history. The Roman **Nymphaeum** ❶ (completed in AD 191), dedicated to the water nymphs, is about 100 metres (110 yards) further up on the right. The stone wall on the street is all that remains of the original building.

Turn right after the nymphaeum, past a shop selling spices and coffee and the fruit and vegetable market, and left at the next intersection for the **Hussein Mosque** ❷. It is decorated in pink and white stone, and a plaque on the wall reveals that the original mosque was built by Omar Ibn al-Khattab, the Second Caliph of Islam (634–644). Emir Abdullah built a new mosque on the site, and restoration work was carried out by King Hussein in 1987.

Directly opposite is the **Arab League coffee shop**, reached via a steep set of stairs round the corner to the right. Customers emerge in a large room filled with men playing cards and backgammon or just talking. The old wooden chairs, marble and brass-topped tables add to its atmosphere. Get a seat near the window across from the mosque, have a cool drink, coffee, tea or *narghileh* (hubble-bubble) and watch the world go by. Women who would prefer a less masculine domain may prefer **Jabri's**, at the bottom of King Hussein (or Salt) Street, about 200 metres (220 yards) away. Go past the entrance to the Arab League coffee shop, take a left along the main street and Jabri's is on the right.

The Emirate walk

For a walk through the early modern history of Amman and the Emirate down to modern times, take a taxi to Jabal Amman, to where Rainbow Street (Abu Bakr as Siddeq) off **1st Circle** ❸ comes to an end in a "T" junction. It was to this area that the influential people in the Emirate (including the current King's

grandfather and family) moved following the earthquake of 1927. They replaced the old Circassian houses of dried mud and wood with more secure stone houses. The beautiful houses and mansions in characteristic white and sometimes pink stone that are dotted along the route tell the history of Jordan before 1948.

It is appropriate that the first house on the left (as you walk back up Rainbow Street) once belonged to a leading Palestinian historian, Aref al-Aref, who came from Jerusalem in the early 1920s to work with Emir Abdullah and later returned to Palestine to become mayor of Jerusalem. The weathered stone and arched windows are framed by jasmine and a huge date palm.

Further up Rainbow Street, the **Mango villa** with its curving balconies is next on the left. The present structure dates from the 1950s, but an earlier part of the building is around the corner in Omar Ibn al-Khattab Street. Two brothers, Hamdi and Ibrahim Mango, were cloth merchants, who came to the Emirate from Nablus in Palestine. They made their fortune during World War II by selling a ship-load of cloth which they had imported just before the war. They were the first Jordanians to do business with the Japanese.

A little alleyway opposite the Mango villa leads to a small stone house which was home to the daughter of Mirza Pasha, an ex-Ottoman officer who came to Jordan in the early part of this century and became head of the Circassian community. Back on Rainbow Street, the compound on the right belonged to Said al-Mufti, another prominent Circassian who became Prime Minister during the Emirate. Emir Abdullah used to stay at the older Mufti house in the Wadi when he first arrived from the Hejaz. It has been destroyed long since and the current structure dates from the post-1927 period. One of the houses in the compound still has traces of the old Circassian buildings, with a low roof and long porch.

Map on page 138

BELOW:
Arab League coffee shop.

Glubb Pasha, "father of the little jaw" (see page 53), whose former residence can be seen along the route of the Emirate walk.

BELOW: the birthplace of the late King Hussein and his brother Hassan.

Turn left along Omar Bin al-Khattab Street (formerly Glubb Pasha Street). It curves for about 100 metres (109 yards) before coming to No. 40, where high walls on the right surround **Glubb Pasha's house** . Go back along the street for 10 metres, walk up the stairs on the same side as Glubb's house, and pass the Evangelical church, built in 1949, and the Ahliyah school, founded in 1926 by the Christian Mission Society of England. A large mansion on the right belongs to the Muasher family, Christians from Salt who came to Amman in the early years of the Emirate. They had a small grocery business but made their fortune during World War II.

Just across from the road, near the junction with Rainbow Street, is the house where the late King Hussein and Prince Hassan were born and lived with their father the late King Talal. Compared to some of the mansions hereabouts, it is a modest building. The family was relatively poor in those days and Emir Abdullah could accommodate only his immediate family at the Raghadan Palace. Older residents of the neighbourhood still recall how King Hussein and his family lived there for 17 years, interacting with their neighbours like any other family. Others claim that during the dead of night members of the royal family sometimes come to peek at their former home.

Straight on across Rainbow Street and just past a stone house on the corner, which once belonged to the Mara'i family of Syrian merchants, is what has become known as the **Bani Hamida house** ⓜ. This is the salesroom and administrative centre of a successful crafts project involving local Bedouin women. Beautiful flat woven rugs and other items are on sale. The house actually belongs to the Qussus family, Christians of the Halassa tribe from southern Jordan (a member of the Odat family was Minister of Justice under Emir-Abdullah), but it used to be home to Alec Kirkbride, who was the British Resident in Jordan for many years. His brother and parents lived in other Qussus houses nearby.

The **Bilbaysi house** of white stone, and the **Bilbaysi palace**, of alternating pink and white, are straight ahead. Older residents tell a rags-to-riches tale. They say that old Ismail Bilbaysi, whose family may have come originally from the town of Bilbays in Egypt, was himself from Nablus. He came to the East Bank in the early 1900s to work on the Hejaz railway as an unskilled labourer. He went on to become a delivery man for Shell – at the time, motor fuel was sold in containers holding 20 litres (4 gallons), which required a strong man such as Bilbaysi to shift – and then moved on to selling. In time he became Shell's sole agent in Jordan, and made his fortune from World War II.

The story goes that Bilbaysi accomplished all this without seeing any country other than Palestine and Jordan. When his son later became Jordan's ambassador to Switzerland he invited his father – who had developed eye problems – to Switzerland for the best available care. Ismail was reluctant, but allowed himself to be persuaded. On arrival, he was taken to hospital, where he underwent a successful operation. When it was over, his son tried to persuade him to stay in Switzerland so that he might see some of the country when the bandages were removed. But old Bilbaysi refused and he returned to Jordan where his eyes recovered.

Bilbaysi built the palace in 1954 and allowed King Abdullah to house his guests here (there was still no room at Raghadan). Locals claim that Rita Hayworth stayed here when shooting *Salomé*. King Abdullah rewarded Bilbaysi by making him a Pasha.

Map on page 138

Take the steps down past the high walls to the left, which enclose the **house of Prince Zaid Bin Shakir**, a relative of the King and ex-Prime Minister and Commander of the Armed Forces. Prince Zaid's father was one of Emir Abdullah's closest allies during the Arab Revolt. Turn left for about 30 metres/ yards and take the stairs down to the next street. The Rashdans' house is situated on the right. The Rashdans were from Irbid in the north and worked in government, reflecting once more Emir Abdullah's efforts to unite all parts of the country.

Go straight down the road for 100 metres/109 yards, keeping right at the fork, to the **house of Tewfiq Abul Huda**. Tewfiq Abul Huda was one of Emir Abdullah's earliest allies and prime minister of Jordan on several occasions. His home was built in 1927, and designed in the style of a Lebanese mountain house. The mason who planned and constructed the upper storey was a Lebanese Druze, Shekeeb Abu Hamdan. His grandson is an architect, and the offices of his practice are now housed here, surrounded by his grandfather's handiwork.

Go back towards the fork in the road. A small stone structure in a car park in front is all that remains of the **house of Ibrahim Hashem**. He was also with Emir Abdullah from very early on and locals joke about how he and Tewfiq Abul Huda used to take turns as Prime Minister. Certainly, a lot of important decisions

BELOW: Arabian fast food at Hashem's.

were made in this 50-metre/yard stretch of Amman and it is a shame that cars now park in what was Ibrahim Hashem's living-room. The remaining building is now used as a store room. Unfortunately, there is no law protecting Amman's historical buildings.

Fifty metres/yards down the road to the right, a set of stairs lead down to Emir Mohammed Street. Cross the road and turn right past Omar al-Khayyam Street. A small alley to the left leads to **Hashem's restaurant**, one of the oldest in the downtown area. It sells Arab fast foods, like *hummus* and *ful* (beans). In the old days, all classes of Jordanians used to meet and eat here; now it caters mainly for Egyptian and local workers.

Emir Mohammed and King Hussein (or Salt) streets intersect a few metres further along the main street. Above, is the **Centrale Café **, one of the oldest coffee shops in Amman and a nice place in which to relax and watch the hustle and bustle on the street below. The entrance is via a steep flight of stairs a little way up King Hussein Street, just after two small stalls selling excellent *shawarma*. Try to sit yourself next to the window so that you can look down the street to the Cairo Hotel on the right; the bullet holes you can see in its walls are a relic of the 1970 conflict between the Jordanian army and the Palestinian Resistance Movement.

Go back to Omar al-Khayyam Street and climb the street past the white - "service" taxis. Keep right uphill, then turn to the left. It is a steep climb, but worth it in the end. In front is the restored **Hamud house**, now known as the **Darat al-Funun** (Little House of the Arts), which was once home to Peake Pasha. In the 1920s and '30s Peake was woken up every morning by a military band whose tunes echoed through the hills and valleys of what was then a small town.

The house has been beautifully renovated by the architect and artist Amar Khammesh and is now an art gallery containing some of the best work contemporary Arab artists have to offer. All the exhibits are for sale and the artists provide a continuous supply of new material. The small sculpture displayed near the entrance of the gallery is by Mona Saudi, a leading Jordanian sculptor (*see page 68*), whose monumental *Architecture of the Soul* sits outside the Institut du Monde Arabe in Paris.

Budding artists and other interested folk can use the centre's library and video-room upstairs. This is one of the most interesting galleries in the Middle East, and is likely to breathe new life into local and regional contemporary art. The garden, where concerts are occasionally held, contains the remains of a Byzantine church.

Around Amman

Wadi as-Sir is one of the most attractive valleys in Jordan and it also contains one of the most interesting and underrated ancient monuments in the Middle East. The *wadi* lies about 12 km (8 miles) west of Amman, beyond 8th Circle and past the village of Wadi as-Sir itself. The scenery is spectacular at any time of the year, but the best time to visit the valley is in spring, when the landscape is verdant and lush and

BELOW: the coffee ceremony at Kan Zaman.

the slopes are dotted with poppies and wild irises. On such days, the hubbub of the capital's street life seems a world away, rather than the few kilometres that it is in reality.

Map on page 138

The road winds down the valley to the river and passes through several small villages before reaching **Iraq al-Amir**, Caves of the Prince; two of the caves bear ancient Hebrew inscriptions. The road continues only a little further, ending at **Qasr al-Abd**, the Palace of the Slave, perhaps the most important Hellenistic palace to have survived in the Middle East.

Just south of Amman, on a hilltop 12 km (7 miles) from 7th Circle, off the airport road, is **Kan Zaman**, a renovated 19th-century complex of stables, storehouses and residential quarters and now a major tourist attraction. The complex belongs to a prominent Jordanian family called the Abu Jabers. The family's forefathers moved from Nazareth to Salt at the beginning of the 19th century. By the middle of the century, they were growing cereals and raising livestock from their hilltop base.

Kan Zaman (which translates as "once upon a time") opened in 1989. It combines a turn-of-the-century atmosphere with some of the best food and crafts that Jordan has to offer. The stone-paved courtyard is lined with atractive shops selling handicrafts, jewellery and spices. Visitors can smoke a hubble-bubble at the coffee shop, or eat excellent Arabic food at the restaurant in the renovated stables. Be prepared too for the skirl of bagpipes, a popular Jordanian sound, and to see the waiters dance an Arab *dabkeh* here. There is also a piano restaurant at the other end of the courtyard called Al-Baydar, which translates as "the Threshing Floor". The restaurant serves local food that is cooked in the traditional *tanoor* clay oven. ❑

Bagpipes can often be heard at Kan Zaman.

BELOW: one of the few remaining trains on the Hejaz railway.

THE HEJAZ RAILWAY

Stretching from Damascus to Medina, the Hejaz Railway was begun in 1900 under the direction of the Ottoman Sultan. It was designed to transport Muslim pilgrims to Medina in the Hejaz, reducing the month-long journey by camel, donkey or foot to four days, and offering respite from the beating sun and toll-charging Bedouin. But, in addition to its ostensible function, the railway also served to unite Turkey's crumbling empire.

The line was built soley with Muslim funds, and soldiers were drafted in to undertake much of the construction work – it became a source of pride for the empire and a labour of devotion for the Muslim workers. Rising to a height of about 1,200 metres (4,000 ft) in some points, and plummeting to 90 metres (3,000 ft) below sea level near the Dead Sea, the track crosses 1,600 km (1,000 miles) of some of the most testing terrain on the globe.

During World War I, the railway became a vital line of communication for the Turks. By persistently blowing up trains, whilst never actually severing the line, Lawrence and his Arab irregulars drew Turkish attention away from the main battle fronts. In the latter part of the 20th century, the railway declined in use; today it teeters between extinction and a tourism-inspired revival.

CAFE SOCIETIES IN AMMAN

From smoke-filled dens to smart internet forums, the café industry in Amman has developed into a varied and competitive business

In Jordan, coffee is the life-blood of society. It is the foremost sign of hospitality and trust in every home and at every social occasion, from engagements to funerals. In business, a deal sealed over coffee becomes a binding commitment.

But, as Jordanian society undergoes rapid social change, so has its coffee-drinking habits. One of the Arab world's most enduring institutions – the coffee house tucked into the far corners of the *suq* – has evolved into a substantial commercial enterprise as varied as Jordanian society itself.

A THIRST FOR MORE THAN COFFEE

When Books@Café, the first internet café, opened in 1997, the country's alternative youth – a hitherto untapped sector – were attracted in droves, drawn by high-tech communication, occasional live music and an escape from the strict social rules governing public interaction between the sexes. The colourful café's lower floor is an open exhibition of amateur art, running alongside a display of quality handicrafts and a diverse, often daring, selection of foreign publications.

FOR THE WEALTHY

Jordan's jet-set can be spotted sipping coffee in the exclusive Café de Paris and Café Mokka, couched in the posh district of Abdoun. Fashionable, luxurious and discreet, much like their clients, they are well beyond the reach of ordinary Jordanians.

▷ FOR A CHANGE

The sweet, milky drink *sahlab*, served with a dusting of cinnamon, is only available in autumn and winter.

△ **SURF'S UP**
The latest trend in coffee-drinking venues is the internet café, where time loses its importance and conversation is global.

▽ **HOME FROM HOME**
For the retired and the unemployed, the Arab League coffee shop is a second home – a place to while away the hours.

A COFFEE WITH A SMOKE

The average man in Amman is still likely to patronise the traditional cafés in the downtown area. Places such as the Arab League coffee shop (*see page 148*) or the Central Café (*see page 152*) are windows onto everyday Jordanian life. Such cafés are particularly busy during the early evening, but in the day they offer a retreat for the growing numbers of unemployed. With a *finjan* (demitasse) of Turkish coffee or a cup of tea (like coffee, served sweet and strong) costing roughly 250 fils they rank as the cheapest source of entertainment in town. The traditional coffee houses are also the places to come for a smoke, and their rooms are usually cloaked in the heavy, sweet-smelling haze produced by the *argeelah* (water pipe). Under this cover, heads capped in red and white *kiffiyehs* bow over games of *taowleh* (backgammon) and *tarneeb* (trumps). Fuelled by coffee and the *argeelah*, such games can roll on for hours.

▽ **CAFFEINE RUSH**
Early evening is the peak time for business in the traditional coffee bars of Amman, such as the Arab League and the Central.

BOOKS@CAFÉ
fering 20 exotic flavours coffee and access to the rgeoning world of the ternet, this café draws the uth of Amman.

▷ **A TIME TO RELAX**
The new-age coffee shops offer young Jordanian women a little respite from the watchful eyes of a patriarchal society.

SALT

Though practically a satellite of Amman today, for long periods in the region's history Salt was the most important settlement between the Jordan River and the desert

Map on page 168

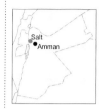

The townof **Salt** has attracted settlers since the Iron Age at least. The area enjoys a moderate climate, a plentiful supply of water and fertile soil (it gave its name to the sultana, the tasty dried grapes produced here for centuries). Located on the "frontier of settlement", the line between desert and sown, the town provided security from marauding Bedouin. It was also well placed on the north–south trade routes and those running from east to west, linking the interior with Jerusalem, Nablus, Nazareth and the Mediterranean coast. Its mixed Muslim-Christian population and its trading tradition helped create an atmosphere of tolerance and coexistence. Salt's golden age was at the end of the 19th century and the beginning of the 20th, and it is the legacy of this period that makes Salt unique in Jordan and beyond.

There are Roman tombs on the outskirts of the town, and during the Byzantine period it was known as Saltos Hieraticon. In the 13th century a fortress was built on the site of the citadel by the Mamluke Sultan al-Malik al-Mu'azzam, who was based in Cairo. Destroyed by the Mongols in 1260, the fortress was rebuilt a year later by a second Mamluke ruler from Egypt. Six centuries later, in 1840, it was demolished again by the forces of yet another Egyptian potentate, Ibrahim Pasha. The Citadel is now the site of a large mosque which towers over the modern town.

Throughout this time and with the decline of Amman, Salt played an important role in the region. When the Arab traveller Abu al-Fida visited the town in the 13th century, he described it as a prosperous small town with a castle and numerous orchards. In 1596, officials of the Ottoman Empire based in Istanbul noted that Salt was "the only town in the Belqa'a district". More than 200 years later, the Swiss traveller and Arabist, Burckhardt, described it as "the only inhabited place in the province of Belqa'a". He also recorded that there were 400 Muslim and 80 Christian families in the town at the time.

By the early 19th century, Salt was a well-off frontier town on the edge of the Ottoman Empire and the desert. Useful to all, it was ruled by none. In 1806, the people of Salt were said to be "free from every kind of taxation and to acknowledge no master." Down to the present day, Saltis have a reputation for being stubborn and independent.

The town was also the centre of lucrative trading between the region and urban industries in Palestine. Saltis were the middlemen for the supply of raw materials (3,500 camel-loads annually by mid-century) collected by local Bedouin for use in the tanneries of Jerusalem and the soap factories of Nablus. Raisins and grapes were also exported to Palestine. Travellers of the time wrote of a flourishing town with shops

PRECEDING PAGES: classical flourishes enliven the Ottoman architecture. **LEFT:** the steeply raked slopes of Salt. **BELOW:** a doorway to Jordan's past.

stocking cotton from Manchester, England and other goods produced locally. From 1867 onwards, the town's fortunes improved dramatically, and it is this golden age that makes Salt special.

Salt's Golden Age

In the mid-19th century, the Ottomans sought to reassert control over their empire in the Middle East. As part of this process, the Belqa'a region was incorporated into the area governed from Nablus and an administrative officer, with military forces at his disposal, was sent to Salt. The Ottomans also encouraged migration and settlement from other parts of the empire, and as the area became more secure people flocked in from Nablus, Nazareth, Jerusalem and further afield in search of opportunities in agriculture, trade, construction and government. Soon, officials based in Salt were collecting taxes from the surrounding countryside, as the Bedouin were steadily absorbed into the system.

Salt began to expand and new construction reflected its status. An Ottoman administrative office was built on what was to become the town square. In 1866, the first modern Christian church was built and the Church Missionary Society set up the first hospital. As trade increased, shops spread along Hamam Street and houses sprang up on the lower slopes of the hills meeting at the town centre. Merchants moved in from Palestine. Families such as the Touqans, Nabulsis and Mehyars migrated from Nablus, leading observers to speak of Salt as a mini recreation of Nablus. The Abu Jabers also arrived during the early 19th century, a family originally from Nazareth. But Salt had plenty of home-grown merchants as well, such as the Sukkars, Muashers and Sakets, and all of these family names are well known in Jordanian public life to this day.

BELOW:
selling produce from the nearby Jordan Valley.

Map on page 168

These families celebrated their good fortune by constructing fine houses, most of which have survived. Made from local yellow stone, they incorporate a variety of indigenous and European styles. Typically, they have one to three storeys with domed roofs and inner courtyards. The Abu Jaber mansion, built between 1892 and 1906, has frescoed ceilings painted by Italian artists and is reputed to be the region's finest example of a 19th-century merchant house.

Salt's fortunes declined after World War I. The first blow came when Emir Abdullah chose Amman as the capital of the new Emirate of Transjordan. The irreversible shift in political and economic power concluded with the Arab-Israeli wars of 1948 and 1967, when Salt was cut off from the Mediterranean and its natural markets in Nablus and the rest of Palestine.

For these reasons, Salt's population increased slowly from 15,000 in 1900 to 50,000 in 1993. Construction matched this pace with the happy result that while reinforced concrete has replaced local stone in many places, the town centre and other buildings remain almost as they were nearly 100 years ago. They provide a rare example of a turn-of-the-century Arab town in the Ottoman Empire.

A spice shop in Salt. The town's wealth was solidly founded on trade.

A walk around Salt

Buildings in Salt climb a tight cluster of hills. Arriving from Amman, one is suddenly confronted by layers of construction rising above. On a hill to the left, just before entering the town, is Salt secondary school, the first of its kind in the country. Built in 1924, it attracted teachers from all over the Arab world and a list of alumni reads like a *Who's Who* of Jordan. Straight ahead, a modern mosque dominates the town centre from the Citadel, the site of the 13th-century Mamluke fortress. Below, older yellow stone houses shine out amidst more modern concrete ones.

Start at **Salt Cultural Centre** (open Sat–Thur 8am–5pm), which includes a one-room folklore museum. Turn left at the main entrance and left again along what some know as Sharia al-Dayr (Monastery Street, after the monastery up the road) or Sharia Yarmouk (Yarmouk Street, after the nearby school) or Sharia al-Baladiya (Municipality Street, because it leads to the old Municipality building). On the right-hand side is what locals call the **Muasher house**, which marks the true beginning of the walk. A Christian merchant family, the Muashers are long-time residents of Salt from the Dababneh tribe believed to have originated in the Hawran region in the south of modern-day Syria and Lebanon.

In fact, this house also belonged to the Abu Jaber family originally. They built the house at the turn of the century and it was later sold to the Muashers. The house is unmistakable with its intertwined, liquorice-like columns on the second floor.

Walk back along the same street and up towards the town square. Older buildings on the left-hand side belonged to the Hammoud and Nabir families. Note the narrow stairs off the main street leading to other houses up the hill.

The **Latin Monastery** is on the right-hand side as you approach the square, behind high walls. The complex contains the oldest public building (1871) in

BELOW: making repairs.

One of the many worn but elegantly carved capitals that adorn the sandstone facades of Salt.

Jordan's modern age, a church (1890) and a fine courtyard, which was the site of important meetings between local notables and British officials from Palestine in 1921 prior to the establishment of the Emirate. There are two steel doors on the street; ring the bell to see inside.

A royal guest

The large house to be seen on the left when entering the square is the **Abu Jaber mansion** mentioned earlier. Its balconies and sheer size make it the most impressive building of its kind in the town. There is talk of turning the mansion into a museum as part of a broader plan to restore Salt's historic buildings and turn the town into a tourist centre.

Emir Abdullah stayed at the Abu Jaber house when he first arrived from the Hejaz in March 1921. Locals delight in telling how Abdullah was going to make Salt his capital, but they ran him out of town. According to Saltis, Bedouin from Abdullah's entourage had started pestering local women collecting water. One thing led to another, and the enraged townsmen drove Abdullah's men away by pelting them with stones. The Emir is said to have been so dismayed by this treatment, which he felt contradicted traditional rules of Arab hospitality, that he went off to Amman and declared it the capital of the Emirate of Transjordan. Relations between Abdullah and his Salti subjects never recovered from the blow, they say.

Keep left up the town square. A small entrance to the left beyond the Abu Jaber building and a row of shops leads up to a number of old houses behind the new government buildings on the square. Climb up the steps to where they fork. The house in front belonged to the Muasher family; the mansion at the top of the stairs to the right was built by the Sukkars, a Christian family from the Dababneh tribe. According to locals, Emir Abdullah stayed at this house. Note the European-style roof perched on the top storey.

To the right of the Sukkar house, along a small pathway behind the new government buildings, is a one-storey house which belonged to the Khateeb family from Jerusalem. Next door is a good example of the "peasant style" houses that characterised Salt prior to 1860. With an old olive tree in the garden, the lines and structure of the ruined building are clearly visible. It has one storey and, inside, two stone arches supporting the remains of a wood and clay roof.

Continue down the stairs past the house of the Saket family, old residents of Salt, to the town square. Cross the road and go back towards the Abu Jaber house and the modern **fountain** near the bottom of the square. This may be the site of Salt's first fountain, which is the source of another local legend. The story goes that in the 19th century a mason from the Far family of Nazareth was commissioned to build a fountain, which was to be paid for communally. But when Far finished the job, many Saltis refused to pay their share of the bill. So Far put a plug in the spring and, deprived of water, the defaulting Saltis paid up.

Near the fountain, directly across the square from the steps to the Muasher and Sukkar houses, a small yellow-walled lane leads up to the English church

BELOW: a wedding party crowds a narrow street.

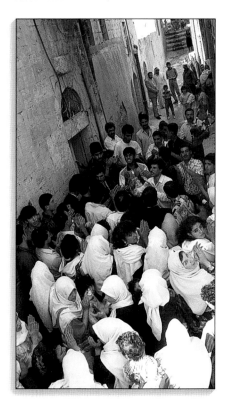

cum hospital cum school. The first door on the right is to the church, built in 1926. The second one higher up with E.H. (English Hospital?) engraved on it leads to the hospital (1882–1923) and the school, the very yellow building on the left, which is now disused. Sit a while in the old schoolyard and enjoy the view over the town. There are plans to turn the place into a small restaurant.

Go back down the steps and take the second left into Hamam Street. This narrow street is a working **market**. The yellow stone buildings are more than 90 years old, and the ambience goes back hundreds of years. Fruit and spices and other goods are on sale here, and 30 metres/yards along, just after a small entrance on the left, is the curving facade of the Touqan building. It is said that the Touqans fled from Nablus in the mid-19th century when that town was taken over by the army of Ibrahim Pasha from Egypt, who favoured the Abd - al-Hadi family. Fifty metres/yards further on, steps on the left lead to the Nabulsi house, another Nablus family. Note the wooden *mashrabiya* balcony, which allowed women to see out without being seen by passers-by.

Return to Hamam Street and, walking along it, pass a right-hand turn leading to the main street. Next on either side of the road are properties belonging to the Mehyar family, who may have arrived in Salt from Nablus in the 1860s or earlier. A little way along is the carved minaret of the "small mosque", built in 1906. This building, too, reflects the confidence and wealth of the time.

On reaching the main road, turn right towards the Cultural Centre and the end of the walk. Just before it on the left is a renovated **Touqan House**, which is now the Municipality building. The entrance hall provides a good example of the domed roofs which characterise these old houses – cool in summer, warm in winter – and upstairs there is a typical interior courtyard. ❑

Map on page 168

BELOW: talking shop in Salt.

JARASH AND THE NORTH

Centred on Jarash, the "Pompeii of the East", North Jordan has retained much of the mystery and beauty of its archaeological past, with fresh finds unearthing an ever more complex history

Map on page 168

N orth Jordan is a combination of archaeological treasure chest and pastoral idyll. Jordanians love the area for its greenery. For Ammanites especially, the tree-lined roads are a promising escape from the capital's hard, white angles and sometimes overwhelming development. Archaeologists' ears perk at the mention of the region, known internationally for one of the largest and best preserved Roman cities in the world, Jarash. The drive north from Amman is an invigorating one – the landscape changes from rugged browns to vibrant greens.

Region of the Decapolis

The area of north Jordan and south Syria – roughly from Aman to Damascus – was often referred to during the Roman era as the region of the Decapolis, meaning the "10 cities" in Greek. This was a region of great wealth, due to its rich agricultural lands, plentiful water from rainfall and perennial springs and rivers, valuable mineral resources, and its strategic location along some of the most important trade routes of antiquity. The spice, incense and silk routes all passed through or near the Decapolis.

It is not surprising, therefore, that this region should be dotted with some major archaeological sites, several of which can be visited on a pleasant day-trip from Amman that also takes in the three main topographic and climatic zones of the country – the semi-arid eastern desert, the central highlands, and the Jordan Valley to the west. The four most important sites in the northern highlands and desert plateau are Jerash, Umm Qays, Abila and Umm al-Jimal.

In their historical sweep, the antiquities of north Jordan cover a timespan of well over 5,000 years – from the establishment of cities in the Early Bronze Age to the Ayyubid/Mamluke settlements of the medieval Islamic era – and almost all the major sites continued to be inhabited right through to the 20th century.

The area contains many smaller antiquities sites and areas of natural beauty. The north is the most fertile part of the Jordanian plateau because of its higher altitude and greater rainfall. The best time of year to visit is the spring, when the plains are covered in wheat and barley and the rolling hills leading down to the Jordan Valley are blanketed in grass. The area is predominantly agricultural, with only a few medium-scale industries and service firms making up the balance of the economy. Many parts of the semi-arid eastern desert fringe turn green in spring, thanks to the seasonal farmers who tap run-off water or underground aquifers.

PRECEDING PAGES: the Cardo at Jarash. **LEFT:** Temple of Artemis, Jarash. **BELOW:** Temple of Zeus, Jarash.

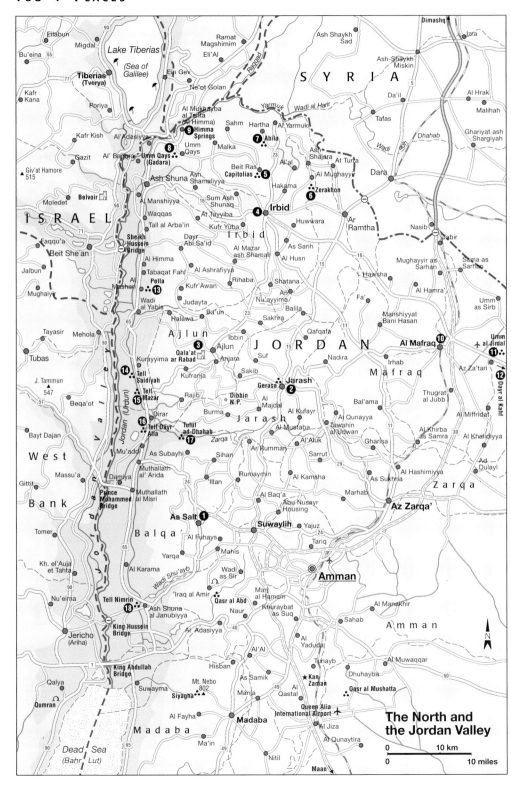

The North and the Jordan Valley

0   10 km

0   10 miles

Gaining an overview

To help flesh out the history of the region, it's worth stopping for an hour at the small but impressive Jordanian Heritage Museum at Yarmouk University in Irbid, with its excellent overview of the story of human development and civilisation in Jordan during the last half a million years.

Hotels at Irbid, Ajlun, Himma in the valley, and Azraq *(see* East to Azraq, *pages 199–209)* can be used for overnight bases. Travellers between Jordan and Syria have to pass through one of two border posts: Ar Ramtha or Jabir. It usually takes about an hour to cross the border, but can require longer if there is a long line of cars (such as during holidays). Traffic is lightest in the early morning.

Magic on the Roman frontier

Jarash ❷ (ancient Gerasa) is just off the main thoroughfare through modern Jarash – only a 45-minute drive north from Amman.

In spite of encroaching modernity, this is still one of the best preserved Roman cities in the world, and the spectacular ruins are rivalled in Jordan only by those of Petra. But, Petra relies partly on the amazing beauty of its setting, while Jarash is a man-made treasure, built over fertile rolling highlands.

As part of the Roman Decapolis, Jarash enjoyed a high degree of prosperity, wealth and civic development. Its diversity of economic activity – iron-ore mining, agriculture and trade – supported a rich culture well-versed in the art of luxurious living. Greek inscriptions at the South Theatre denote the names of wealthy donors and indicate a civic-minded society that numbered at least 20,000 during the city's golden era.

The monuments of Jarash also tell the tale of the empire's decline. The fragmented remains of splendid baths indicate the destruction wrought by successive earthquakes, while a concentration of churches – many built out of stones taken from pagan temples – indicate the rise of short-lived Byzantium, by which time Jarash was relatively insignificant.

Historical lineage

Graeco-Roman Jarash as we know it today was first built by the legions of Alexander the Great in the 2nd century BC. It flourished as a provincial trading city after the Roman General Pompey conquered the region in 63 BC. Along with its compatriot Decapolis cities of Philadelphia, Gadara and Pella, the city reached its peak in the 2nd century AD, when the Pax Romana allowed regional and international trade to flourish and encouraged local investment by wealthy merchants and landowners.

Jarash is a fine example of the grand provincial urbanism found in all Roman cities in the Middle East, comprising paved and colonnaded streets, soaring hilltop temples, handsome theatres, spacious public squares and plazas, baths, fountains and city walls pierced by towers and gates.

For the past decade, the Jordanian Department of Antiquities' Jarash International Project has brought together archaeologists and architects from eight

Maps
Area: 168
Site: 172

Jarash is often called the "Pompeii of the East" because of its fine state of preservation. Not only is virtually the entire city-centre still in place, but the carved architectural details are as fresh today as when they were first chiselled into the soft orange limestone 2,000 years ago.

BELOW: two visitors shelter in the shade of a broken column.

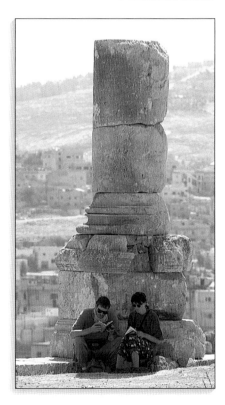

countries (the US, France, Poland, Spain, Italy, Australia, the UK and Jordan) to excavate new areas while conserving and restoring monuments. Their work has clarified nagging ambiguities about the earliest (Hellenistic) and latest (early Islamic) phases of the city's life. It confirms that Jarash existed virtually without interruption for over 1,000 years – spanning the Hellenistic, Roman, Byzantine and early Islamic (Omayyad and Abbasid) periods, from the 2nd century BC to the 9th century AD.

TIP

There are no hotels actually in Jarash, but the Dibeen Resthouse (*see Travel Tips*) is only a few kilometres away. Alternatively, Jarash can be incorporated into a day-trip from Amman.

Beneath its external Graeco-Roman veneer, Jarash also preserves a subtle blend of the orient and the occident. Its architecture, religion, languages and even the names of its citizens in antiquity reflected a process by which two powerful cultures initially clashed but ultimately meshed and coexisted – the Graeco-Roman world of the Mediterranean basin, and the ancient traditions of the Arab orient. The very name of the city reflects this interaction. The earliest settlement of indigenous Arab/Semitic people, in the pre-classical period of the 1st millennium BC, was called Garshu (as we know from a funerary inscription, found in Petra, in memory of a Jarash trader who died and was buried in the Nabataean capital).

The Hellenistic settlement founded in the 2nd century BC was called Antioch on the Chrysorhoas (or Antioch on the "Golden River", the Hellenistic name of the perennial stream which still runs through the city). Little of the Hellenistic city has been excavated, as most of it was removed when the Romans rebuilt it in the 1st and 2nd centuries AD.

BELOW: the Cardo in Jarash.

The Romans who came in 63 BC quickly Hellenised the former Arabic name Garshu into Gerasa. At the end of the 19th century, the Arab and Circassian inhabitants of the then small rural settlement in turn transformed Roman Gerasa

THE DECAPOLIS RIDDLE

The Decapolis is something of a riddle, for scholars still debate whether the term refers to a formal league or confederation of 10 cities bound by commercial, political and security bonds, or to something less systematic. It is mentioned in the New Testament as a "region", and Roman-era references suggest it may have been an administrative district, created when the General Pompey conquered the region in 63 BC.

Modern scholarship now agrees that at its height in the Roman period the Decapolis was probably a loose association of geographically contiguous Graeco-Roman provincial cities that shared cultural, commercial and political interests. Different lists of Decapolis cities from several historical periods provide the names of more than 10 cities, indicating that the definition of the region changed over time. The most recent scholarship identifies the cities as: Philadelphia (Amman), Gerasa (Jarash), Pella (Tabaqat Fahl), Gadara (Umm Qays), Scythopolis (Beisan or Bethshean), Damascus, Hippos, Canatha, Dium, and Raphana. The term Decapolis has never been found on coins or in inscriptions and literary sources originating in the area; all ancient references come from literary sources in places further afield.

into Arabic Jarash. In ancient times, the roads linking Jarash with Philadelphia to the south, Bosra and Damascus to the north, and Pella to the west would have been well travelled by local traders, international caravans and Roman legionary troops. When the Emperor Trajan occupied the Nabataean kingdom in south Jordan, north Arabia and Sinai in AD 106, the area underwent another major reorganisation. Half the Decapolis cities found themselves within the Roman province of Syria, while others, including Jarash, fell under the jurisdiction of the new province of Arabia.

But this reorganisation had little impact on the fortunes of these towns, which continued to develop. On the heels of peace came local investments in agriculture, industry and services, which in turn boosted both regional and international trade.

As Jarash flourished for more than 200 years thanks to income from exports and taxes from trade, it expanded out towards its meandering city walls, and filled in many of its urban spaces with public structures that still stand. In fact, you sense Gerasa's prosperity even before you arrive at the South Gate, because the first monument you reach on the road from Amman is the triple-gated **Hadrian's Arch** Ⓐ, standing alone some 450 metres (500 yards) south of the city walls. It was built to commemorate the Emperor Hadrian's visit to Gerasa in AD 129, when the city fathers planned to extend the city walls to link up with the arch, which would then form the town's main entrance from the south. However, the project was never completed, and the arch stands virtually on its own now; next to it is the massive **Hippodrome** Ⓑ, which is being excavated, and a cemetery in which you can still see the remains of a small Byzantine funerary church.

Maps
Area: 168
Site: 172

TIP

A visitor's centre and tourist office can be found in Jarash near the South Gate. Both are open daily from around 7.30am until sunset (7.30–8.30pm).

BELOW:
walking in the footsteps of history.

A walk through the ruins

Visitors enter the city today just as the Roman period inhabitants did – through the monumental, delicately carved **South Gate C**, now adjacent to the modern visitors' centre and restaurant. The gate has been recently reconstructed by a French-Jordanian team. Immediately inside it is a marketplace with a 3rd-century AD olive press visible in a room now below ground level.

From the South Gate, walk up into the spacious **Oval Plaza D**, a skewed oval-shaped space measuring 90 by 80 metres (295 by 262 ft) in size, with a fine arcade of Ionic columns. These columns retain the 1st-century architectural flavour of the site, which was largely remodelled in the 2nd century with Corinthian capitals and columns replacing the Ionic ones.

The Oval Plaza's non-symmetrical shape is unusual for classical cities, but is explained by its distinct role: it served to reconcile the two different axes of the Cardo and the Zeus Temple, which were aligned neither on a straight line nor at 90-degree angles. The plaza allowed the east-west axis of the Zeus Temple to fit into the north-south axis of the Cardo and the rest of the city. Visitors who walk into the plaza from the south find themselves naturally turning towards the north, to the start of the Cardo.

High to the west, overlooking the plaza, is the 1st-century AD **Temple of Zeus E**; it combines the classical temple look with the oriental tradition of sitting cultic installations on hilltops (like the biblical era "high places") and surrounding them with a *temenos* (an enclosed holy precinct). Recent excavations on the terrace in front of the temple have uncovered some pre-Roman, Hellenistic cultic structures, including an open-air altar.

Immediately west of the temple is the **South Theatre F**, ancient Gerasa's

You can test the theatre's enduring acoustics yourself by standing at the marked centre of the orchestra and speaking to anyone in the theatre from that point.

BELOW:
Hadrian's Arch.

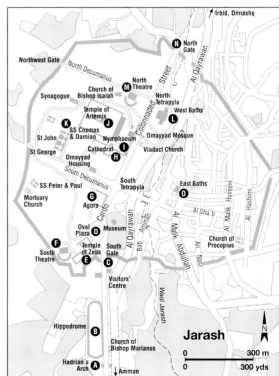

main gathering place for stage entertainment; it was completed in the early 2nd century AD and could accommodate 3,000 spectators. Inscriptions in Greek give the names of some of the wealthy Gerasenes who donated money to help pay for its construction. Today, with much of its stage area restored, its acoustics as sharp as ever, and some of its seats still "numbered" with engraved Greek letters, the South Theatre hosts the main events at the annual Jarash Festival of Culture and Arts (*see below*). There is a fine view from the rim of the theatre overlooking the Oval Plaza and much of the city.

The Oval Plaza leads visitors into the 12-metre (40-ft) wide and 800-metre (2,600-ft) long **Cardo**, the architectural spine and focal point of ancient Gerasa. In the 2nd century, the original Cardo was widened into its present Corinthian configuration (except at its northern end). The city's most important structures were arranged around the Cardo, including markets, temples, fountains and other public buildings.

As you walk up the street, you pass a series of important monuments, most of which are announced by large, thicker columns that stand out against the street colonnade. The large public building with an internal colonnade was perhaps the **Agora G**, or Forum. A richly carved entrance midway along the Cardo heralds a Roman temple that was transformed into a church in the Byzantine period; it is now known as the **Cathedral H**. Next to it is the **Nymphaeum I** (public fountain), on which you can see the original coloured paint from the Roman/Byzantine period still clinging to its upper-level niches. A little further north is the stately **propylaeum** (entrance) and processional way leading up to the **Temple of Artemis J** (daughter of Zeus, sister of Apollo, and patron goddess of the city). Her hilltop temple with soaring

Maps
Area: 168
Site: 172

Jerash on a T-shirt.

BELOW:
the Oval Plaza.

columns is nestled in a spacious, colonnaded *temenos* measuring 162 by 121 metres (531 by 396 ft); it was approached via a processional way that started across the river in the area of the modern city.

When the Byzantine Empire and Christianity dominated the region in the 4th century, some of Gerasa's pagan Roman temples were transformed into Christian churches. Many new churches were built from cut stones and columns taken from Roman era buildings that had collapsed from the frequent earthquakes which plagued the region in antiquity. With the discovery of three more churches in recent years, we know of at least 15 churches in Byzantine Gerasa; some of them still sport their mosaic floors. The **complex of three churches** dedicated to **St George**, **St John**, and **saints Cosmas** and **Damian**, west of the Temple of Artemis, has the best preserved mosaics from the 6th century; their subject matter includes representations of various animals as well as the churches' benefactors and bishops. Some of the church mosaics are also on display in the museum.

The massive **West Baths** were never excavated and remain in their state of collapse following a spate of successive earthquakes more than 1,000 years ago. Just to the west of the **North Tetrapyla** intersection with the North Decumanus is the **North Theatre** , which served as a performance stage as well as the city council chamber; you can still see the names of the local tribes that were represented in the city council engraved on the seats in Greek.

Beyond the North Tetrapyla is the **North Colonnaded Street**, a stretch of the original Cardo which was never widened or resculpted in the Corinthian order; it retains the more human-scale dimensions of Jarash during the 1st century AD, and leads to the large but ungainly **north gate** (whose strange shape

Artemis, patron goddess of Jarash, was renowned for her hunting prowess and eternal youth. She had a vindictive streak, however, and delighted in inflicting pain on women in childbirth.

BELOW: Chinese gymnasts at the Jarash Festival.

JARASH FESTIVAL

For two or three weeks every July, the renovated ruins of Jarash come alive with the festival. Performances span many nations and cultures and cover a wide range of the arts from, say, *Rigoletto* performed by an Italian operatic company to modern ballet on the steps of the Artemis Temple. Songs of Lebanese singers may ring out one night, while Shakespeare's *Taming of the Shrew* may take centre stage on the next. Chinese acrobats may spin on bicycles in the South Theatre, while elsewhere Spanish gipsies may sing and dance the flamenco in this ancient setting.

The festival was inaugurated in 1981 by Queen Noor, who has been its patron and guiding light ever since. The event is very popular, and is eagerly awaited each year. Funding is a great challenge in Jordan, but even during the 1990–91 Gulf War the festival still took place. As the events' organiser put it: "The festival offers an opportunity for Westerners to see Arabic folklore, hear oriental music and experience Middle Eastern cultrue. It also provides Jordanians with the chance to see art and cultural events of the West." During the festival, handicrafts are also displayed and sold, that great ancient corridor the Cardo providing the perfect showcase for Bedouin rugs, wrought ironwork, blown glass and embroidered gowns.

was, like the Oval Plaza, a means of reconciling the different axes of the Cardo and the external road entering Jarash from Pella).

From the Cardo, the Roman town expanded towards the city walls, forming different quarters for housing, commerce and cultic activities. At the height of its prosperity in the 2nd and 3rd centuries, Jarash and its immediate suburbs may have accommodated some 20,000 people. They were served by a splendid array of public facilities, including temples, theatres, markets, baths, plazas, fountains and a hippodrome. The massive **east baths ⦿**, in the centre of the modern town, indicate the extent of the city's spread, as well as the monumental size of some of its public facilities.

Many of the Roman structures were rebuilt or modified in the Byzantine era, when Gerasa ceased to be important for international trade and instead related more to other cities in the region. The city fortunes gradually dwindled, and successive attacks by Persian and Muslim forces in the early 7th century AD saw Jarash's historical course change once again.

After 636, the city fell to the control of Islamic forces emerging from Arabia. It continued to accommodate a small settlement of farmers, traders and potters for another 150 years, as recent excavations have clarified with the discovery of an Omayyad housing quarter off the South Decumanus, a small mosque across from the Artemis Temple propylaeum, and some pottery kilns; but when the Islamic world's capital shifted from Omayyad Damascus to Abbasid Baghdad in AD 750, Gerasa lost its strategic location on the road between Damascus and Islam's heartland in Arabia. As a result, its fortunes faded slowly thereafter, and the town could support little more than small squatter occupations after the 9th century.

Maps
Area: 168
Site: 172

BELOW LEFT:
South Theatre
BELOW RIGHT:
the entrance to the
Temple of Artemis.

Saladin's castle

One of the best preserved examples of medieval Arab/Islamic military architecture in the entire Middle East is **Ajlun Castle**, formally named **Qalaat ar-Rabad ❸**. It was built in 1184–85 by Izz ed-Din Ousama, one of the most capable governors of the Islamic leader Salaheddeen (Saladin), who defeated the Crusaders and evicted them from Jordan in 1189; the castle was the base from which Islamic forces defended this region against Crusader expansion (*see* The Crusades, *pages 30–35*).

The castle is very well preserved, and is a popular attraction for Jordanians and foreign visitors alike (beware, it is always crowded on Fridays). Its galleries, towers, staircases, and many chambers are like a medieval maze where visitors can spend an hour or two appreciating the structure itself as well as the magnificent views across the green hills all around. The view from the keep is especially thrilling.

Two small hotels nearby are good places to eat or spend the night. Alternatively, on the way down the hill after exiting the driveway to the castle, you'll find Bonita Ajloun restaurant. Lunch on the terrace allows a restful view of the castle and its surrounds.

Sites in the north

There are many other interesting sites in north Jordan that are not usually included in tourist circuits. **Irbid city ❹** itself is worth a visit because it retains the bustle and charm of provincial Middle Eastern towns that have not been totally disfigured by the consumerism and modernism that have made such a big impact on the larger cities. A trading centre to its farming hinterland for thou-

BELOW: vestiges of splendour.

sands of years, Irbid now has nearly 320,000 people and is Jordan's third larg-est city. Historically, it relied on a combination of agriculture and trading, which are still its main economic activities. There are some fine turn-of-the-century houses and public buildings in the city centre, where a small but rich **museum** can be visited at the office of the antiquities department.

The Decapolis city of **Capitolias** was located on the site of the modern vil-lage of **Beit Ras** ❺, astride the road north from Irbid. There are scattered archi-tectural pieces that can be seen here, along with some tombs, vaults, cisterns, and traces of foundation walls, but no major standing architecture.

About 20 minutes by car northeast of Irbid is **Zerakhon** ❻, a huge ancient walled city dating from the Early Bronze Age (3300–2200 BC), recently dis-covered and being excavated. It has well preserved remains of buildings (including a temple) and an urban water system that was a key reason for the town's existence for 1,000 years.

Recondite charm

The scattered remains of **Abila** ❼ are not frequently visited by foreign tourists today, but the site is well worth a visit by those who have the time. The large site is located amidst verdant agricultural fields at the modern Ain Quweilbeh spring, a 20-minute drive north of Irbid. While several of its ancient structures have been excavated, including churches, aqueducts, tombs, gates and public build-ings, Abila is especially fascinating because so much of it remains unexcavated, yet visible on the surface of the ground.

The large semi-circular depression in a hillside is where the theatre once stood, the path to the bridge over the stream hints at the route of the Roman road,

Map on page 168

A monument at Irbid.

BELOW: Levantine landscape around Ajlun Castle.

and the massive column drums and Corinthian capitals scattered incongruously in agricultural fields prod the visitor to imagine the temples, baths or marketplaces that remain buried.

The two hills that make up the site were occupied almost continuously from the Neolithic to the early-Islamic period, roughly from 7000 BC–AD 800. The site also includes an extensive cemetery with some of Jordan's finest Roman era painted tombs, but unfortunately these are not accessible to visitors due to water seepage and the danger of roof collapse. The site flourished for such a long period of time because of its rich water and agricultural resources, and its strategic location alongside ancient trade routes.

Exhilarating Umm Qays

The most dramatically situated Roman era town in Jordan is **Umm Qays ❽** (Roman Gadara). It sits on a long, high promontory overlooking the north Jordan Valley, the Syrian Golan Heights, and Lake Tiberias (Sea of Galilee) to the northwest, about two hours by car from Amman. The view from the site is exhilarating, and is made all the more attractive today by the new resthouse there, situated in an old Ottoman schoolhouse, with full meal and refreshment service. Owners of the resthouse are slowly restoring some of the former period homes as guest living quarters, though the task will not be complete for a couple of years. Summer dinners on the open terrace are an increasingly popular pastime among Amman residents. Take a powerful pair of binoculars with you to enjoy picking out sites in the distance.

BELOW:
restaurant at Ajlun.

The city was established in the Hellenistic period, and flourished as a strategic trading town for nearly 1,000 years, well into the early and medieval

Islamic eras. Its name in Arabic is thought to be related to the word *maqass*, which means junction in Arabic; this was an important junction on land trade routes linking the important north–south roads with the east–west passage to the Mediterranean Sea.

Map on page 168

Umm Qays today includes two distinct components – the ancient structures and town plan, and the late 19th-/early 20th-century Ottoman town clustered on the summit and largely built from stones reused from the classical town.

Among the most impressive ancient remains are a stunning black basalt theatre, the basilica and adjacent courtyard, which is strewn with beautifully carved black sarcophagi, the colonnaded main street and a side street clearly lined with shops, an underground mausoleum, two baths, a nymphaeum (public water fountain), a city gate, and the faint outlines of what was once a massive hippodrome. Gadara was renowned during the classical era as an inspired city of the arts, famous for producing notable playwrights, poets, satirists, orators, and philosophers.

Basilicas and tombs

A German archaeological team unearthed fascinating evidence of a 4th-century **Byzantine church**, possibly built over a Roman tomb where Jesus is supposed to have performed the miracle of the Gadarene swine in which two madmen were cured when their demonic spirits were transferred into a herd of swine that drowned after stampeding down a mountainside into nearby Lake Tiberias (Matthew 8:28). You can find the remains of the church and tomb by walking down the Decumanus Maximus (colonnaded) street for about 300–400 metres/yards, keeping an eye out for the city gate, in the shape of a circular

BELOW: a proud inheritor of Umm Qays's treasures.

TIP

A few kilometres-
northeast of Umm
Qays is **Himma** ⊙
with its hot springs.
These are well worth
visiting if you enjoy
the special pleasure of
soaking or swimming
in piping hot mineral
water. The pools are
open to men and
women on a shift
basis, and a modest
motel provides
accommodation.

BELOW: view of
barracks at
Umm al Jimal.

tower, to your left. Just beyond the gate is the eerie black basalt **mausoleum,** which can be seen more easily from the foot of the nearby flight of stairs. The area in front of the tomb is actually a Byzantine crypt, presumably built at the same time as the church. Strangely, the remains of the church lie squarely on top of the mausoleum with a hole in the centre of the floor that allowed people to peer into the tomb (*see below*).

The mystery deepens with the **basilica**, which, unusually, has five aisles instead of three. Only a dozen or so five-aisled churches have been found in the Middle East, all of them dating from the same period, all commemorating events in the life of Christ and all serving as important pilgrimage sites during the early Christian era.

Archaeological excavations of the crypt in 1988 discovered a skeleton bound in chains about the legs. A second account of the Gadarene swine appears in Luke 8:26–39 and refers to a possessed man who lived among the tombs and who had been chained and kept under guard. There is a similar reference to a demented and chained man in the Gospel according to St Mark. Archaeologists now postulate that the church, with its "peep hole" into the tomb, may have been built to honour the spot which Christian lore identified as the place where Jesus performed the miracle, and that the opening onto the crypt from the church floor is testament to the church's significance as an early pilgrimage site.

Visitors to Umm Qays can also get a feel for more recent history and life in 19th-century Jordan by strolling among the ruins of the late Ottoman village, with its large houses arranged around central courtyards. Two houses have been restored and are being used again: the **museum** in Beit Rousan, and the **German archaeological dighouse** in Beit Malkawi.

The road to Umm al Jimal

Map on page 168

Fedein is the ancient name of the walled town that existed at the site of modern **Al Mafraq** ❿, between Irbid and Umm al Jimal. Two distinct periods of ancient urbanism have been identified and excavated: an Iron-Age town with massive fortification walls that still stand several metres high, and a Byzantine/early Islamic walled town with the remains of a church, a beautifully decorated mosque, and other public buildings. Roman milestones from the area attest to its strategic location amidst the roads that criss-crossed northern Jordan in the classical and early Islamic periods. The site is still being excavated. Between Jarash and Mafraq, the quiet village of **Rihab** contains the remains of a dozen Byzantine churches, some of which are still being excavated.

The easternmost of the major northern cities, **Umm al Jimal** ⓫ can be reached by car in about two hours from Amman. It is situated at the edge of the eastern basalt desert plain, along a secondary road that was close to the junction of several ancient trade routes linking central Jordan with Syria and Iraq. Remains of the Roman road can still be seen today by taking a 10-minute drive to the west.

The city was inhabited for some 700 years, from the 1st to the 8th centuries, in three different stages: a rural village in the 2nd and 3rd centuries, a fortified Roman town in the 4th and 5th centuries, and a prosperous farming and trading city from the 5th to the 8th centuries. The key to Umm al Jimal's success was its inhabitants' ability to store winter rainwater in a series of covered and open reservoirs, which supplied water for human and animal consumption as well to irrigate summer crops. As a settlement with a reliable source of water and food, Umm al Jimal developed into a major caravan station.

A Byzantine-era cross, Umm al Jimal.

BELOW LEFT: the old stables at Umm al Jimal.
BELOW RIGHT: rebuilding the past.

Map on page 168

The name Umm al Jimal can mean either "mother of camels" or "mother of beauty" in Arabic. Its identification with ancient sites is still not determined (Thantia and Surattha have both been proposed as possible candidates). It is a dramatic and even chilling sight for visitors, for Umm al Jimal rises against the distant horizon like the skyline of a thriving metropolis; but as one draws near enough for the buildings and details to be discerned it becomes obvious that this is no more than a ghost town. Visiting in the early morning haze of winter is particularly thrilling, as the black basalt buildings take on a very eerie character indeed.

A walk through the ruins reveals a wide range of structures typical of a modest provincial town that lacked a formal urban plan – unlike the monumental splendour, architectural extravaganza, and imperial scale of more important towns such as Jarash, Gadara and Philadelphia. Among the most interesting structures are the tall barracks with their little chapel, several large churches, numerous open and roofed water cisterns served by conveyor channels, dozens of houses arranged in clusters (often around a common courtyard), the outlines of a Roman fort along the east side of the town, and the remains of several town gates.

Many of the structures at Umm al Jimal still stand two storeys high, thanks to the excellent engineering used in antiquity. Look out for examples of the very common "corbelling" technique (see picture of the Old Stables on page 181), in which long flat slabs of basalt stone laid over intersecting stones to form the roof of a typically long and narrow room or building. Arches were used to make the buildings larger, and nicely designed windows and doors (many still in place) helped to relieve structural pressure from the weight of the building material.

BELOW: local dress in Ramtha. **RIGHT:** view near Abila.

Other sites

North Jordan is also home to a number of other small archaeological sites that were trading towns or security posts in ancient times. Some of these, such as Burqu, with its Roman fort, and the walled town of Jawa, are well off paved roads and require a guide and four-wheel drive (see the chapter on the Badia, pages 213–4). Among the more accessible sites is **Umm as-Sirb**, northwest of Umm al Jimal, which reached the peak of its importance in the Byzantine period, when several large churches were built as part of a monastic complex. One church was converted into a mosque in the early Islamic period.

Umm al-Quttayn, about 40 km (25 miles) by car east of Umm al Jimal, has remains of four Byzantine churches and a large monastery (ad-Dayr), and it once also hosted a Roman cavalry unit. Umm al-Quttein was important historically because of its location at the edge of the settled zone of north Jordan/south Syria, to the east of which lay the more demanding basalt desert environment.

The impressive standing remains of the Roman fortress at **Dayr al-Kahf ⑫**, half-an-hour's drive east of Umm al Jimal and near the Syrian border, once formed part of the defensive system along the southeastern frontier of the Roman Empire. ❏

THE JORDAN VALLEY

The fertile land of the Jordan Valley has attracted settlers since biblical times; evidence of its past civilisations is a source of fascination for today's travellers

Map on page 168

T he Jordan Valley is the kingdom's garden of Eden. It elicits a mood of quiet fascination mixed with deep spirituality, all enveloped in a dramatic landscape that is enticing for both its physical beauty and its many historical and biblical associations. Archaeological evidence of early civilisation abounds in the valley, and although it is obvious that man settled here out of necessity – the land is some of the most fertile in the region – it is equally obvious, especially at dusk or after a soak in one of many steamy, hot springs, that it must have been immensely pleasurable too.

The valley today still thrives. It constitutes an integral part of Jordan's economy as attested by the swathes of banana plantations, citrus orchards and vegetable farms. At the southern limits of the sea, travellers along the highway might notice salt "mushrooms" cropping up from the water. These funny protrusions appearing like misplaced snow sculptures mark the potash extraction fields, the source of a multi-million dinar industry.

The lowest point on earth is also a playground for Jordan's upper class, many of whom own extravagant weekend getaways; while the Dead Sea's invigorating minerals attract large crowds of weekenders, especially in the spring and autumn.

Most importantly, the valley, river and sea form a natural border with Israel and the West Bank. The valley plains bear witness to Jordan's dramatic recent history, and remnants of the Arab-Israeli conflict, although slowly disappearing, can still be found. The King Hussein Bridge, for example, which once linked the kingdom to its West Bank territory, today seems astonishingly small and rickety. Houses that were casualties of the successive wars can be seen not far from the river, whose ever-dwindling waters are a reminder that this vital resource must be shared equitably and responsibly between three countries.

PRECEDING PAGES: valley fruit – a pomegranate. **LEFT:** a banana farm. **BELOW:** enjoying the valley's mineral springs.

A great valley is born

The Jordan Rift Valley-Dead Sea region is part of the Great Rift Valley that runs from Turkey to east Africa, which was formed by geological upheavals millions of years ago. The valley in its present form started to take shape between 100,000 and 20,000 years ago, as a result of the contraction of a salt-water sea that originally covered the entire 360-km (223-mile) stretch from the Red Sea port-resort of Aqaba in the south to Lake Tiberias (also known as the Sea of Galilee) in the north. It initially formed an inland lake (Lake Lisan, some 200 km/125 miles long and with a surface water level about 200 metres (656 ft) higher than the present Dead Sea) before shrinking again to leave behind Lake Tiberias and the Dead Sea; these two inland

The Jordan River

It is strange to think that Jordan, named after a river, is now one of the driest countries on earth. The River Jordan, for millennia the carrier of water to civilisations, begins its short journey at the foot of Mount Herman, straddling the border between Syria and Lebanon. The Jordan Valley is not so much the valley of the river itself, but a 20-km (12-mile) wide depression in which the river flows, part of the rift system linking the Bekaa Valley in the north to the Dead Sea, Wadi Araba and the Red Sea to the south.

Not far from its source, the river used to enter Lake Huleh, a low-lying swamp area, notorious as a breeding ground for malaria, but which has now been drained. The river slowly drops below sea level and flows for some 100km (62 miles) through northern Israel, overlooked by the Golan Heights, before entering Lake Tiberias (also known as the Sea of Galilee). This lake, some 200 metres (660 ft) below sea level, lies wholly

within Israel, with the outflowing waters of the Jordan used to produce hydro-electricity and irrigate extensive areas of cultivation. A little south of the lake, the main tributary of the Jordan, the 40-km (25-mile) long Yarmuk, flows in from the east, forming part of the Jordan/Syrian border. In this northern corner of Jordan, the old Hejaz railway link between Haifa and Dir'a crossed the Jordan River, some 260 metres (850 ft) below sea level, the lowest point ever reached by railway.

The three strategic bridges linking the West Bank then cross the Jordan, as it flows through its lower valley, known as the Ghor, a word derived from antiquity and denoting "a palm covered area which has been affected by gravitational subsidence, where snow never falls". This is the lowest lying land in the world, with the valley suffering high humidity and even higher temperatures, in a barren landscape. But given the fertile soil and an intricate system of canals, including the King Abdullah canal, running parallel to the river, a huge range of fruit and vegetables can ripen weeks before those in surrounding areas. It is the draining of the river for irrigation, particularly on the West Bank, that has reduced its flow to a mere trickle.

Access to the brown waters of the river itself is extremely limited due to the sensitivity of the border, and it is usually only glimpsed by travellers crossing one of the bridges. The river, hemmed in by sub-tropical vegetation, is only a few metres wide, and hardly as impressive as its name and history would suggest.

Jordanian archaeologists have uncovered a number of sites dating from the early Roman period in the Bethany area, to the south of the King Hussein Bridge. These include plastered pools, cisterns, habitable caves and churches along the banks of the perennial river flowing down Wadi Kharrar. Of course, the River Jordan appears in many biblical and Koranic stories involving Joshua, Moses and Elijah, and the most famous is the baptising of Christ by John the Baptist.

In August 1998, the first baptism to be carried out here since 1967 took place, and most of the sites are expected to be open to the public in the near future. ❑

LEFT: a narrow stretch of the Jordan River.

water bodies are surrounded on all sides by dry plains interspersed with side valleys (*wadis*) flowing from the eastern and western highlands.

Due to its low altitude, the valley is a natural hothouse characterised by mild winters, hot summers, rich agricultural lands and important mineral resources. Since the mid-1970s, it has benefited from a new programme of integrated rural development, based on exploiting the area's agricultural and mineral resources while providing a full range of social services for its growing population. This is a far cry from the early decades of the 20th century, when the valley was an inhospitable and dangerous place, known more for its malaria and occasional banditry than for its economic potential. The valley's permanent farming population of some 40,000 people in the early 1960s was almost totally uprooted during the politically turbulent and violent period of 1967–72. The integrated development effort was launched by the Jordan Valley Authority in 1973 with the aim of encouraging small, family-based farming units to cultivate 50,000 hectares (123,550 acres) of land using drip and sprinkler irrigation.

Map on page 168

SEA LEVEL

A buoyant experience

The **Dead Sea** itself is a draw for visitors from around the world, due to its unique water qualities, climate and historical and spiritual legacy. It sits amidst the dramatic mountains of the biblical kingdoms of Moab, Ammon and Edom to the east, and the rolling hills of Jerusalem to the west. Its buoyant waters are warm and the shoreline is coated in a soothing mud, rich in minerals.

A four-star hotel and resthouse offer facilities for dining, sleeping, swimming, and therapeutic treatments for people suffering from skin and other diseases, but women may feel uncomfortable at the resthouse, and it is advisable to swim and

A reminder that below you is the lowest piece of land in the world.

BELOW: limes being loaded for market.

Local women watch the world go by.

BELOW:
the women's
shift begins at
a hot spring.

relax at the hotel instead. Jordan anticipates a growing tourism market, however, and the construction of several more high quality hotel spas is planned in the Dead Sea area. Further north in the Valley are Himma thermal springs (accessible from Umm Qays: *see margin note, North Jordan, page 180*), with a modest motel, where you can sample the pleasures of water therapy in a more informal atmosphere.

A very ancient valley

The valley's water, land and warm climate have encouraged people to live, hunt and farm here since the earliest days of the human saga. There are over 200 known archaeological sites in the Jordan Rift Valley, and hundreds of others await discovery. The oldest evidence for human activity, stone tools discovered in the Wadi Himma region in the northern valley, date back almost one million years – to a time when the region probably looked very similar to today's savannah grasslands in East Africa.

Evidence of some of the world's earliest camp sites and semi-permanent villages comes from excavations near Pella, dating from the Natufian and Kebaran periods (10,000–18,000 years ago). The advent of year-round farming and livestocking settlements in the Neolithic period (8000–4500 BC) is also attested at several sites, though the most famous Neolithic village in the valley is across the river in Jericho.

Large sites such as Pella and Tell Nimrin show an almost uninterrupted sequence of human occupation going back at least 4,000 years, from the Bronze Age to the present. What follows is an overview of the most important sites that can be easily visited today, from north to south.

Panoramic Pella

Nestled in the foothills of the northern valley, exactly at sea level altitude just above the modern town of Al Mashari, **Pella ⑬** may be Jordan's richest site in terms of its historical sweep and architectural remains. It is also a delightful natural setting of rolling green plains, lush plantations and forested hills, watered by the perennial Wadi Jirm stream and overlooking the Jordan Valley plain below. On a clear day, you can look across the valley, through the hills of northern Palestine/Israel, and just discern the hills of Haifa on the Mediterranean coast.

The name Pella dates from the Hellenistic period, when soldiers of Alexander the Great named their new imperial settlements after the Macedonian birthplace of their leader. The site is known in Arabic as Tabaqat Fahl, the name of the nearby village ("Fahl" retains a linguistic link with the ancient names of Pella and Pihilum). Archaeological excavations have revealed a series of modest settlements and major walled towns at Pella for most of the past 6,000 years.

The site's impressive continuity is due to its rich natural resources and strategic location at the intersection of major north–south and east–west trade routes. A resthouse overlooking Pella from the east provides a splendid opportunity for rest and refreshments, along with one of the most satisfying panoramas in all Jordan. A 90-minute drive from Amman, Pella can be easily combined in a day-trip with the Dead Sea, Ajlun, Jarash, or Umm Qays.

On the central main mound of the site, where the archaeological dig-house is located, the earliest visible mudbrick house and fortification walls (in the deep trenches on the south side) date from Bronze and Iron Age walled towns, spanning the period 2000–600 BC. The Roman and Byzantine periods are represented by the small theatre by the stream, the colonnaded civic complex and church above it (reached over a monumental staircase), and the east and west churches.

BELOW: still standing – the columns of Pella.

The remains of domestic houses of the early Islamic (Omayyad) period are well preserved on the central mound; later Islamic structures can be seen at the 9th/10th-century Abbasid domestic area recently excavated in **Wadi Khandak** (in the valley north of the main mound) and in the restored 13th to 14th-century Mamluke period mosque on the main mound.

The entire rift valley is dotted with ancient tells (artificial mounds or small hills formed by the cumulative collapse of successive ancient settlements built of stone and mudbrick). Three of the most striking and substantial can be visited in the centre of the valley (west of the main road), and some of their excavated walls can be seen (though the sites have not been properly conserved for display). The long double mound of **Tell Saidiyah ⑭** was an important regional walled town for most of the Bronze and Iron Ages (3300–600 BC) and also had a large caravanserai in the early Islamic period. It has been inconclusively associated with the biblical sites of Zaphon and Zarthan.

The smaller **Tell Mazar ⑮** to its south (and visible from the summit of Saadiyyeh) was a substantial settlement in the Iron and Persian periods, from the 11th to the 4th centuries BC. Its name comes from the nearby *mazar* (pilgrimage site), of Abu Obeidah, an early Islamic general and companion of the Prophet

Map on page 168

Ploughing the rich, fertile earth of the Jordan Valley.

Mohammad who died and was buried there in AD 639. This is one of several such sites in the northern valley where companions of the Prophet died and were buried; these are not touristic sites, but pilgrimage sites that reflect the reverence accorded to some parts of the valley by Muslims.

The most dramatic of the three archaeological mounds is **Tell Dayr Alla **, towering over the main road at Dayr Alla village. Excavations have revealed almost continuous human habitation and use of the site from 1600–400 BC, for purposes such as a township, cultic centre, metalworking, a cemetery, grain storage, farming and a seasonal migration site. The tell rises 30 metres (98 ft) high, with its summit at an altitude of 200 metres (656 ft) below sea level. Some archaeologists believe it is the biblical site of Succoth.

About 7 km (4 miles) east of Tell Dayr Alla, and enclosed by a meandering, S-shaped bend in the Zarqa River, are the twin hills called **Tulul ad-Dhahab ** ("the little hills of gold"). They are not always easy to reach due to the waters of the Zarqa River (the biblical Jabbok). Excavated architectural remains and pottery shards indicate that both hills were fortified settlements in the Early Iron Age and Late Hellenistic/Early Roman periods. Remains of slag and furnaces confirm that iron smelting took place here, with the ore coming from the nearby Mugharat Wardah mines, 4 km (2 miles) to the north. Scholars in the 19th century identified these twin hills with the biblical sites of Penuel (where, according to the Genesis story, Jacob wrestled all night with an angel) and Mahanaim (where David was told of the death of his son Absalom). Neither of these site identifications has been verified by archaeological evidence.

BELOW: work mates take a breather.

The area south of Deir Alla (in the hills east of the main road) also has some **dolmens** still in their original position, especially at Damiya, Quttein and Matabi. These structures of four or five stone slabs (often associated with druids in Europe) were Bronze and Iron-Age burials, probably introduced into the area by immigrant populations from other parts of the Middle East. (Those who would like to see a dolmen without leaving Amman can view the dolmen that was excavated in the valley and precisely reconstructed on the campus of the University of Jordan.)

The southern valley

In the southern valley, at the edge of Ash Shuna al Janubiyya, is the large site of **Tell Nimrin **, situated next to the road leading north from the town. Recent excavations have verified that this area has been used as an agricultural settlement almost without interruption for around 4,000 years. From the main road, it is possible to see over 12 metres (40 ft) of stratified ancient remains in the exposed archaeological trenches. This is an unusually deep and rich sequence of historical material that allows scholars to note the various changes in environmental conditions, land use patterns and cultural traditions.

The view from the summit of Tell Nimrin has probably changed little over the millennia, and the site still houses a small village, predominantly centred on a life of farming. Like their ancestors before them, the residents of the village still use the water from the Wadi Nimrin to irrigate their lands.

Not far from Tell Nimrin is **Bethany** (Al Maghtas), an excavation area between the head of Wadi Kharrar and the Jordan River, where archaeological work is now on-going. Recently, this stretch of the Jordan River has been identified as the site of Jesus's baptism, and as the region where John the Baptist – revered in both Christianity and Islam – lived and worked. This area, mostly associated with early Christianity, corresponds to Bethabara on the mosaic map in the Church of St George in Madaba (*see page 224*).

Works in the thick greenery of the area so far have uncovered a 1st-century settlement with plastered pools and water systems believed to be used for baptism, and a 5th–6th-century (late Byzantine) settlement with churches, a monastery and other structures presumed to have catered to religious pilgrims.

The Jordanian Department of Antiquities is surveying some 20 sites in the Bethany area, most of which are assumed to have been stations along a pilgrimage route from Jerusalem to Jericho, the Jordan River, Bethany, the town of Livias (modern Tell al Rama) and Mount Nebo.

Archaeologists believe that the pilgrimage route commemorated places associated not only with John the Baptist and Jesus, but also with other great biblical prophets, including Joshua, Elijah and Elisha. Elijah's Hill (Jabal Mar Elias) at the head of Wadi Kharrar was revered in antiquity as the spot from which Elijah ascended to heaven in a chariot of fire after he parted the waters of the Jordan and crossed it with his successor, Elisha. A church situated immediately on the east bank of the river and dating to the Byzantine period may have been built to mark the precise spot of Jesus's baptism, but is also associated with the life of St Mary the Egyptian, a prostitute who repented at the Church of the Holy Sepulchre in Jerusalem and crossed the Jordan River to find rest. ❑

Map on page 168

BELOW: rich in minerals, the Dead Sea mud is liberally applied.

The Dead Sea

Situated less than an hour's drive from Amman, the Dead Sea is the lowest place on the earth's surface, fluctuating around 400 metres (1,310ft) below sea level, depending on the season. Though many large wadi systems empty their silty floodwaters from the surrounding mountains here, there is no outlet for the water. Combined with fiercely hot air temperatures, this produces a high rate of evaporation – almost 10 million tons of water per day. The evaporation leaves a mixture of salts and minerals – magnesium chloride, sodium chloride, bromide salts and potash – close to saturation point, giving the sea its glutinous surface.

Historically, the Dead Sea has been central to biblical and Koranic stories, and several sites on both sides of the lake are potential candidates for the "five cities of the plain" – Sodom, Gomorrah, Admah, Zeboiim and Zoar – which, according to Genesis, were destroyed by God (possibly around 2,300 BC).

One of these sites, Bab ad-Dhraa, has been excavated, revealing a strong town wall and a huge cemetery; this could be the site of Sodom. It can be seen shortly after the road to Karak turns away from the Dead Sea (*see page 231*). Many of the items found here are on display at the museum in Karak Castle.

About 15km (9 miles) to the south are similarly positioned ruins of Numeira (*see page 232*), a candidate for Gomorrah. The stories of "brimstone and fire raining down" would be consistent with actual accounts of earthquakes and eruptions caused by the movement of the Rift Valley continental plates.

Excavations near Safi (long associated with Zoar) at Dayr Ain Abata, the "Cave or Sanctuary of Lot" (*see page 232*), have unearthed a basilica church and small cave, possibly used by Lot and his daughters.

However, most visitors come to swim in the buoyant, milky-blue waters or to partake of the mineral and mud treatments. It is possible to stop and swim at any place along the coast, but it is important to wash in freshwater afterwards to remove the gluey mixture left on the skin. Most visitors pay to use the facilities at one of the resorts, or park near one of the in-flowing streams.

From the north the first resort is the Dead Sea Resthouse, closely followed by the new Movenpick and the Dead Sea Spa Hotel. All offer changing facilities, showers, clean sandy beaches, shaded areas and restaurants. The best times to visit are early morning and late afternoon. Try to avoid Fridays, unless you enjoy crowds

About 15km (9 miles) south of the Dead Sea Spa Hotel are columns, pools and the harbour of ancient Callirhoe, the bathing complex built by Herod the Great for his palace at Machaerus. Salt deposits are visible all along the coast until the large bridge over the river flowing from Wadi Mujib. Notice the marks on the canyon walls showing the depth the river reaches during torrential downpours.

Before Ghor Mazra'a and the road to Karak, you can see the Lisan Peninsula (*lisan* means tongue in Arabic), jutting out from the shore. Further south, Dead Sea products are collected for sale and distribution. ❏

LEFT: a couple plunge into the mud.

EAST TO AZRAQ

The area between Amman and Azraq is defined by a looping road linking the remarkable "desert castles". At the easternmost limit of this route is the Shaumari Wildlife Reserve

Map on pages 200–201

East of Amman and Az Zarqa, the steep, green hills that engirdle the capital area abruptly fall away to a flat and stark desert stretching to the country's easternmost border with Iraq. A vast territory that appears to be one desert is, in fact, three. A landscape littered with limestone pellets gives way to one cluttered with black basalt stones, which in turn gives way to the encroaching sands of Wadi Sirhan, which reaches off into Saudi Arabia. At the confluence of the three types of desert stands the much reduced Azraq oasis, its pools filled by a complex network of aquifers fed mainly from the Jabal Druze area of southern Syria (the passage of water taking up to 50 years). Surrounding the oasis is the Qa' al-Azraq, about 60 sq. km (23 sq. miles) of silt, beneath which lies such a concentration of salt that hundreds of tons each year are collected for both industrial and domestic use.

The ring of intriguing desert castles that appears to have risen, without rhyme or reason, from the flat and barren earth is the area's main attraction for visitors. Settlement is limited, though Bedouin still thrive here, their survival a testament to their timeless resourcefulness and endurance.

Lush past

Several hundred million years ago the area, like most of present-day Jordan, lay beneath the sea, which withdrew and re-inundated the land several times. The last inundation probably receded in the Eocene period, which began about 50 million years ago. A mere 1 million years ago, in the Pleistocene era, the broad shallow basin in which Azraq stands today was a huge inland lake of about 4,000 sq. km (1,500 sq. miles); then, as the waters slowly receded, the basin became a fertile plain with large swamps and pools and luxuriant vegetation at its centre.

Until only a few decades ago the desert teemed with wildlife. Gazelle, wild ass, ostrich and the magnificent white Arabian oryx roamed freely, preyed upon by wolf, hyena and the Bedouin. Azraq was a paradise of birds and animals, great and small, living in or around its waters or coming from the desert to drink. Some 12,000 to 40,000 years ago rhinoceros and hartebeest also inhabited its marshes; and stones found in a ruined Roman wall, carved with ostrich, snake, fish, hoopoe and wild ass, are eloquent testimonies to the abundance of 2,000 years ago. "Each stone or blade of it," wrote T.E. Lawrence in *The Seven Pillars of Wisdom*, "was radiant with half-memory of the luminous silky Eden, which had passed so long ago." Today there is little wildlife, and most is protected in reserves. The villain is not climatic change but 20th-century humans, who have cut down

PRECEDING PAGES: curvaceous Amra. **LEFT:** Qasr al-Harana. **BELOW:** the desert blooms eternal.

A lone rider in the desert hinterland.

trees, overgrazed pasture, pumped water for cities, and hunted with automatic weapons and four-wheel-drive vehicles.

The climate has changed little since the Romans, undaunted by the desert, built a string of forts here – the *limes arabicus* – along the boundaries of their Arabian province. The main fort-builders were Septimius Severus (AD 193–211) and, 100 years later, Diocletian. These frontier posts survived into the Byzantine era, some falling into disrepair, others restored for continued service until the Islamic Arab conquest in 636.

From the mid-7th to the mid-8th centuries, when the Omayyad caliphs established their court and the centre of Islam in Damascus, a scattering of settlements were built in the Jordanian desert. Each had a different function – fort, hunting lodge, trading-post, farm, caravanserai or meeting hall – but common to all were the organisation of water and an agricultural base. All were probably intended, whether by the caliph or his local ruler, to maintain regular contact with the Bedouin tribes on whose loyalty the Omayyads depended.

No desert asceticism applied here. The buildings included bath houses, spacious courtyards and great halls for audiences or for entertainment, adorned with columns and carvings, mosaics and frescoes. They were served by sophisticated hydraulic and heating systems, so that the stresses of a hard day's hunting or diplomacy could be soothed by fountains, pools and hot baths.

Sometime around the year 750, when the Omayyads were ousted by the Abbasids and the Islamic capital moved to Baghdad, many settlements in the Jordanian desert fell into disuse and ruin. The abandoned buildings became temporary encampments for Bedouin who lit fires in the decorated halls for heat or to cook food before moving on to deserts new.

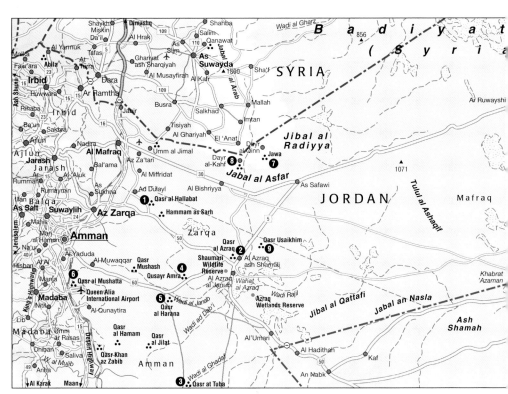

In 1896 Alois Musil, an Arabist from Prague, was told by some Bedouin of richly decorated buildings deep in the desert. Two years later he returned, and within a few days found two of these palaces, Qasr at-Tuba and Qusayr Amra. In the following months and years several more were discovered. None is exactly a palace (the meaning of the Arabic word *qasr*), nor a castle (as they are known in English); but all are charming examples of domestic architecture in Islam's earliest days, taking much inspiration from Byzantine and Persian art, but also showing the beginnings of an individual personality and style.

Map on pages 200–201

Visiting the "Desert Castles"

Today, with fast paved roads in place of the ancient desert tracks, a selection of the better preserved Omayyad palaces as well as the castle at Azraq can be seen in an easy day-trip from Amman. The roads form a neat circuit, with Azraq at the eastern end. Additionally, there are two unusually handsome complexes, Qasr al-Mushatta and Qasr at-Tuba, which lie outside this circuit, but it is worth making the effort to see them if you can. The former can be found near Queen Alia Airport, while the latter lies off the Desert Highway east of Qatrana. Qasr al-Tuba is the most difficult to reach, and a trip there necessitates a four-wheel drive vehicle.

The suggested route runs clockwise from Amman, but it can equally well be negotiated anti-clockwise. The trip can also be combined with a bird-watching visit to the Azraq Wetlands Reserve (*see page 204*), and to the Shaumari Wildlife Reserve (*see page 204*), home of the famous Arabian oryx. If more than one day is needed, simple accommodation can be found at Azraq, either in the Government Resthouse (whose large swimming pool is open mid-May to mid-October),

BELOW: Qasr al-Hallabat.

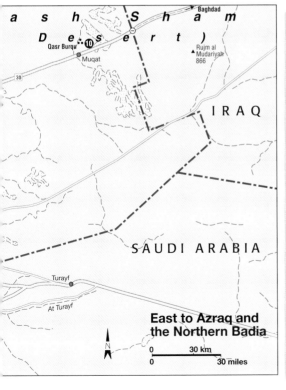

East to Azraq and the Northern Badia

0   30 km
0   30 miles

Inscriptions in Greek and Latin at Qasr al-Hallabat refer to building extensions and renovation work carried out at the castle complex.

BELOW:
the golden stone of
Hammam as-Sarh.

at the Sayad (Hunter) Hotel (also with a pool), or at the lodge of the Royal Society for the Conservation of Nature.

Taking the road north out of Amman towards Zarqa, after about 22 km (13½ miles) turn right at the sign to the Syrian and Iraqi borders. After another 12 km (7½ miles) take the right turn to Azraq and the Iraqi border; 7 km (4½ miles) further on, at a junction with a right turn to Azraq, continue straight ahead towards Mafraq. After 6 km (4 miles), a small blue sign points right towards **Qasr al-Hallabat ❶**. About 8 km (5 miles) further on, another blue sign points right to the castle itself.

This large desert complex started life as a Roman fort and ended as a luxurious country estate under the Omayyads. The original small fort was built around AD 111–114 to guard Trajan's new road to the south, the Via Nova Traiana; a Latin inscription mentions an extension in the early 3rd century; and another in Greek records a Byzantine restoration in 529.

The Omayyads, not content with mere restoration, virtually demolished the earlier structures to build their estate between the years 709 and 743. It was an extensive complex that they created, of which the castle, the mosque and the bath house are the most rewarding today. There was also a large reservoir, many cisterns and a walled agricultural enclosure.

The castle was lavishly decorated with frescoes and carved stucco, and with lively mosaics of animals and birds, fruits and geometric designs – now removed for safe keeping. Although this is a limestone area, many of the stones are basalt, and several carry sections of a long Greek inscription – an edict of the Emperor Anastasius I (AD 491–518) reorganising the province of Arabia. As they were all plastered over, they were clearly re-used purely for

Map
on pages
200–201

their architectural value. It is believed they might have been imported to Hallabat by the Omayyads from the ancient basalt city of Umm al Jimal, some 30 km (18 miles) to the north.

The mosque stands immediately to the east of the castle, some of its walls still at their full height. The doorway in the north wall, facing the remains of the *mihrab* (niche indicating the direction of prayer) has an attractive cusped arch.

The bath house, known as **Hammam as Sarh**, 2 km (1¼ miles) to the east of the castle beside the paved road, is a finely built limestone complex, originally finished with marble, mosaics and frescoes. The rectangular audience hall, now identifiable only by an outline of walls, had three parallel tunnel-vaults, and an alcove with a small room on either side, complete with latrines. A doorway in the north corner leads into the changing room (*apodyterium*) of the bath house, which doubled as a cool room (*frigidarium*). This opens into the room of medium heat (*tepidarium*) with a tunnel-vaulted recess, and then into the domed hot room (*calidarium*) which has two semi-circular recesses covered with semi-domes. Beyond this was the furnace which sent hot air under the raised floor of the calidarium. This complex is very similar in design to that of Qasr Amra.

Beside the baths stands a water storage tank into which water was poured having been raised from the well (18 metres/59 ft deep) by a pulley system operated by donkeys or horses endlessly walking around a confined circular space. There is also a *mihrab* nearby, indicating the remains of a late Ottoman open-air mosque.

To Azraq

The road running southeast from Hammam as Sarh turns right and, after 3 km (2 miles), joins the main Az Zarqa-Azraq road. After 55 km (34 miles) it reaches a junction at Al Azraq al Janubi (south), one of the two villages of the Azraq complex. Turning left, the tree-lined road to the rest-house can be seen on the left after 2 km (1¼ miles). Al Azraq ash Shamali (north) is another 2½ km (1½ miles) further on, with the Sayad Hotel on the left, and, 500 metres/550 yards ahead, is the great black basalt **Qasr al-Azraq** ❷.

Azraq's abundant waters made it as valuable to people as to wildlife. Palaeolithic camp sites have been found in the marshes, with flint tools fashioned by early Stone-Age inhabitants 100,000 years ago. The importance of the oasis continued – for the Bedouin who roamed the desert, and for traders – since Azraq stands at the head of Wadi Sirhan, the main caravan route between the Arabian Peninsula and Mesopotamia and Syria.

The first fort here may have been built by Septimius Severus (AD 193–211) as one of the eastern defences of the *limes arabicus*. But the earliest inscription relating to the castle is a dedication to Diocletian and Maximian, joint Emperors from AD 286 to 305. At the same time Diocletian built a new road to Azraq, the Strata Diocletiana, to improve lines of communications between the regions of Syria and southern Arabia.

The fort remained in use under the Byzantines, and

BELOW: a doorway at Azraq Castle.

Nature Reserves

Shaumari Wildlife Reserve lies south of Azraq, near the main road to Saudi Arabia. Its visitors' centre has a display of archaeological finds, a photographic exhibition of flora and fauna, and an audiovisual presentation on conservation.

But seeing real wildlife is the purpose of a visit here, and there is a tower for viewing animals, including the Arabian oryx, though sightings cannot be guaranteed. The most likely time to see them is late afternoon in late summer or autumn, before the rains begin. Then there is little natural water and the oryx come to the reserve's troughs.

Jordan's **Royal Society for the Conservation of Nature** (RSCN) was founded in 1966 but it was not until 1975 that the first nature reserve was established here on 22 sq km (8½ sq. miles) of desert, It was designated as a breeding centre for species that had become extinct or endangered in Jordan, prior to releasing them into the wild.

Specially targeted was the Arabian oryx (*Oryx leucoryx*), extinct in Jordan since the 1920s. The once teeming herds had dwindled throughout Arabia. Already in 1962, the Fauna Preservation Society and the World Wildlife Fund had launched "Operation Oryx" in Arizona, with a World Survival Herd of nine animals donated by Aden, Kuwait, Britain and Saudi Arabia. When numbers grew, subgroups were established. The RSCN proposed that Jordan should be the first country to reintroduce the oryx into the Arabian desert, and in 1978 four pairs were sent to Shaumari. The ruler of Qatar donated a male and two females, and from these 11 animals the Jordanian herd multiplied.

In 1983, when the herd numbered over 30, they were released into the whole area of the reserve. Though zoo-bred, their behaviour showed that they had not lost the instincts of the wild. They quickly split into smaller herds and established a hierarchy. Herd growth has continued, and today Shaumari has over 100 oryx. Other rehabilitation projects have also been undertaken, notably with the ostrich and the wild ass.

The **Azraq Wetlands Reserve**, 12 sq. km (4½ sq. miles) of marsh, mudflats and pools was proclaimed soon after Shaumari. It lies near Azraq Janubi, and visitors should check in first at the RSCN Resthouse, 600 metres towards Amman from the junction in Azraq Janubi, up a drive on the left.

About 300 bird species were recorded here in the 1970s – migrants, residents and seasonal visitors – but since then marshes and birds alike have diminished dramatically as water is pumped to meet the increasing demands of Amman.

A visit here can be rewarding, especially during the spring and autumn migration periods when a large variety of birds can be seen, including bee-eaters, swallows, flycatchers, warblers, wagtails, shrikes, snipe, pipits, hoopoes, larks, sandpipers, plovers, harriers, eagles, chats, ducks, crakes, storks and many more. A faint echo of Lawrence's "luminous, silky Eden" can be heard in the susurrus of wind in reeds, punctuated by the piping and fluting of birds, and the hoarse trumpetings of the marsh frogs. ❑

LEFT: an oryx at Shaumari Wildlife Reserve.

it was an occasional base for the Omayyads, perfect both for hunting and for meeting the desert tribes. After the fall of the Omayyads, it fell into disrepair and had to be rebuilt in 1237 by the Ayyubid governor, Azz al-Din Aybak, as recorded in an Arabic inscription above the main entrance. It was probably then that the little mosque in the middle of the courtyard was built. How far the castle was remodelled is unclear; plenty of Roman-cut stones were available, and several Roman doors (one weighing an incredible 3 tons) were reused exactly in the Roman fashion. They are still there, and still turning on their stone hinges. The Mamlukes and Ottomans also occupied Azraq Castle.

More recently "the blue fort on its rock" was T. E. Lawrence's base in the winter of 1917–18; his office was above the entrance gatehouse. Holed up here, Lawrence learned "the full disadvantages of imprisonment within such gloomy ancient unmortared places." As the rain came in and the men shivered, "past and present flowed over us like an uneddying river. We dreamed ourselves into the spirit of the place; sieges and feasting, raids, murders, love-singing in the night."

It was from Azraq that Lawrence and his men set out in September 1918 for the final assault on Damascus which marked the collapse of Turkish power and the end of World War I in the Middle East. "In front was our too-tangible goal," he wrote, "but behind lay the effort of two years, its misery forgotten or glorified. Names rang through my head…Rum the magnificent, brilliant Petra, Azrak the remote…"

Today the castle is less intact than when Lawrence was here, thanks to a severe earthquake in 1927. There is still the shell of an upper storey in some parts, and handsome arched stables with stone mangers and tethering blocks can be explored on the north side. The ancient well is on the east.

Map on pages 200–201

An ostrich at the Shaumari reserve.

BELOW: palms in a sadly depleted oasis.

Off the beaten track

The splendid **Qasr at-Tuba ❸**, in Wadi Ghadaf, is one of the hardest of the Omayyad palaces to reach. There is a choice of three routes there, but they all demand a 4 x 4 high-clearance vehicle, a compass and a guide. The route with the least rough driving runs 55 km (34 miles) south of Azraq, along the road that passes the turning to Shaumari. A track to the right leads to the palace. More difficult is a track from Qasr al-Kharaneh leading almost due south to Tuba (47 km/29 miles); criss-crossed by other tracks, the route is hard to make out. The third route runs 70 km (43 miles) east from Qatrana on the Desert Highway, half on paved road, half on rough tracks.

Qasr at-Tuba was the first palace found by Alois Musil in 1898, a great architectural skeleton, half lost in the desert sand. It was probably designed as a caravanserai on the trade route between Amman and the west, and Wadi Sirhan and southern Arabia. Wandering in its silent courts, surrounded by the limitless and haunting desert, it is not hard to imagine the men, horses and camels that once filled these ruins. It is thought Qasr at-Tuba was begun in 743–44, at the end of the decadent Caliph Walid II's reign, and remained unfinished at his death.

The complex consists of two symmetrical enclosures, together forming almost a double square – Siamese twins of palaces, each with suites of interconnecting rooms around a central courtyard. A round tower was set at each corner, and semi-circular towers at intervals along the sides. In the north corner the buildings are still nearly intact, including a magnificent barrel-vaulted hall; so too is most of the lower part of the west wall. The rest is an outline of foundations and tumbled walls, the latter originally built of three courses of stone, above which were sun-dried mud bricks. Stone also framed the door arches, and Musil originally found some finely carved stone door jambs and lintels – all these have long since disappeared.

For water, the inhabitants relied on some nearby pools, three huge wells, and the remains of round buildings where donkeys or horses operated a pulley system to raise the water.

Sensuous frescoes

The main road to Amman divides nearly 9 km (5½ miles) from Azraq, the left-hand fork passing the harmonious stone-built **Qusayr Amra ❹** on the right, after another 17½ km (11 miles). It stands in Wadi Butm, a shallow watercourse (dry most of the year), named after the *butm* (wild pistachio trees: *Pistachia atlantica*) once numerous here. Qusayr is the diminutive of *qasr*, and this "little palace" is the remains of a larger complex, probably including a fort, agricultural enclosures and living quarters, which was built in 711, under Caliph Walid I.

Today we see an audience hall with three barrel vaults and an alcove flanked by two small rooms, as well as a three-roomed bath house, including a domed *calidarium* with under-floor heating. All the walls and ceilings are covered with vivid frescoes – Amra's main attraction. Restored in 1971–3 by experts from the Madrid National Archaeological Museum, they are now in passably good condition despite centuries of neglect, smoke from Bedouin fires and grafitti.

BELOW:
extracting salt.

Map
on pages
200–201

The interest is not just for a particular style (for this aspect of the work is rather mixed), or for the joyous naturalism, but for what they reveal of the brilliant eclecticism of early Arab/Islamic art, drawing from Byzantine and Persian sources; and for the very fact that they still exist at all. The first edict ordering the destruction of images was under Caliph Yazid II (720–24), when these frescoes were sparklingly new. Mercifully they were overlooked – in fact, destruction was not rigorously imposed in secular buildings.

Here the painters were uninhibited in their depictions of human and mythological life: hunting scenes; athletes in training; the goddesses of poetry, philosophy and history; musicians and dancers; women and children bathers (in varying states of undress); and six figures, believed to be rulers conquered by Walid I – the Byzantine emperor, the Visigothic king of Spain, the Sassanian king and the Negus of Abyssinia (with inscriptions), and two without inscriptions who may have been the emperor of China and the Turkish khan. In addition, there are delicate gazelles, monkeys and birds, and a guitar-strumming bear; and set-pieces of the working life of various craftsmen.

Most interesting of all is the fresco in the dome of the *calidarium*, for it is the earliest known representation of the night sky portrayed in the round instead of on a flat surface. The Great and Little Bears, Andromeda, Cassiopeia, Sagittarius, Scorpio, Orion and others are all depicted – but the artist who worked on the ceiling appears to have copied them from a drawing that he transposed from right to left, thus altering the relationships of the constellations.

About 16 km (10 miles) west of Amra, immediately left of the main road, stands **Qasr al-Harana** ❺, the most complete of the Omayyad castles and the only one that appears military in purpose (though this may be more apparent

BELOW: Amra's frescoes survived the censors in a later, more puritanical age.

Structures old and new: the columns of Qasr al-Harana compete for prominence with the electric pilons of modern Jordan.

than real). This great four-square, two-storey structure has round towers on each corner and semi-circular ones in each wall, except on the south where the entrance is. It is built of large undressed stones, with layers of smaller stones between them, and with a decorative line of bricks in an open herringbone pattern running all round the building near the top. Originally it was plastered, but most of this has dropped off.

Small holes at intervals in the walls look like arrow-slits, but inside it is clear that they would have given the archers insufficient field of fire, and some would have needed 3-metre (9-ft) giants to reach them. In fact, they were probably for ventilation and light rather than for battle.

The entrance leads past large stables or store rooms on either side, and into a central courtyard, beneath which was a cistern. Suites of rooms are arranged in the traditional Arab pattern of a large rectangular room, with two smaller square rooms on each long side. Two handsome stone stairways lead to the upper floor, where several rooms still have some of their original decoration of arches and vaults, semi-domes and squinches, and plasterwork medallions, all reminiscent of Sassanian buildings. Above a door in one of the large rooms on the upper floor, a small painted Kufic inscription records the date in AD 710 when the castle was built.

The function of Qasr al-Harana remains uncertain. Its large stable area might, at first glance, suggest a caravanserai. But though the site is near a trade route, it is not actually on one; and with no evident springs, or other means of storing water, the one cistern would not have been able to supply a regular traffic of traders. Therefore, it may have been simply an occasional meeting place for the Omayyad authorities and the Bedouin tribes.

BELOW: Qasr al-Mushatta.

Around 37 km (23 miles) west of Harana is the village of **Al Muwaqqar**, once the site of a considerable Omayyad settlement, which has now completely disappeared. There is, however, a large ancient reservoir which is still used. Between Harana and Muwaqqar, but some distance north of the main road along an unmarked track, lies **Qasr Mushash**, a very large but ruined Omayyad agricultural estate, which is strictly for addicts of tumbled stones.

Map on pages 200–201

Near the airport

The largest and most richly decorated of Jordan's Omayyad palaces was **Qasr al-Mushatta** ❻, close to Queen Alia International Airport. It is reached by turning off the highway towards the airport, and then right just past the Alia Gateway Hotel. It is on the right of the perimeter road, after 11 km (7 miles).

The palace is a great square, walled enclosure with round towers at the corners and five semi-circular towers on each side, except on the south face, where a monumental gateway stood in the centre. Around this gateway were the finest of Mushatta's carvings, but in 1903 the Ottoman Sultan Abdul Hamid II gave them to Kaiser Wilhelm II. They now reside in the Pergamum Museum in Berlin. A few delicate carvings still bear witness to the palace's original glory.

The interior was never completed and most of it consists of outlines of walls and foundations around a large courtyard. North of this are the remains of the royal audience hall and residence – probably of Walid II, the extravagant and hated caliph who built Qasr at-Tuba around 743–44. The audience hall is basilical in form and has a trefoil apse that was once covered by a dome. On either side are barrel-vaulted halls. While stone was used for the out walls, the whole of this inner palace was built of bricks made of burnt mud. ❑

Capital detail, Qasr al-Mushatta.

BELOW: siphoning scarce resources.

THE BADIA

Map
on pages
200–201

*The sparse and inhospitable terrain of the Badia is an intense
landscape, pulsating with life based upon daily survival. The dry
sands also offer up some unlikely settlements of the past*

Covering 80 per cent of the total landmass of the country, the Badia is the
arid and semi-arid region of Jordan. It can be split roughly into three sections: the Northern Badia is the land to the east of the Amman-Mafraq
road, including the "Pan handle" bordering Syria and Iraq, and is an area characterised by low rolling hills, covered in black basalt boulders and silty mudflats
known as *qa'a*; Central Badia is east of the Desert Highway, roughly between
Amman and Karak, and is closest to the urban sprawl of the capital; the vast
Southern Badia is all of southern Jordan east of the Desert Highway, below
Karak and south of the Ras an-Naqab escarpment, where the desert plains give
way to the spectacular mountain landscape and sand dunes of Wadi Rum.

These regions are not kind to man or beast, with extremes of temperature,
unreliable water supply and difficult terrain. Only five per cent of Jordan's population lives here, mostly settled or semi-nomadic people of Bedouin descent.
The traditional wanderings of these Bedouin were dramatically affected by the
artificial national boundaries drawn up after World War I, when huge areas of
the Syrian and Northern Arabian deserts were split between Syria, Jordan, Iraq
and Saudi Arabia, with no regard to existing tribal boundaries. The main effect
on the desert people within these divisions was for them to follow a more sedentary lifestyle, well away from the strategic "straight
lines on maps" borders.

One of the main developments for the Northern
Badia came from the construction of the IPC (Iraq
Petroleum Company) pipeline between Kirkuk and
Haifa in the 1930s. The pumping stations known as
H4 and H5 became the centre of the settlements of
Ar Ruwayshid and As Safawi respectively.

Historic landscapes

The Northern Badia is the area covered in this chapter. It has not always been such a harsh and arid place,
as testified by the many ancient carvings depicting
lions, cattle and hunting scenes. Unique to the area
are the ancient "desert kites", kilometres of basalt
walls that were used to direct herds of wild animals –
gazelle, antelope and ostrich – to a restricted killing
ground. Hundreds of these weathered structures lie
all over the Badia.

Seldom visited, the impressive fort at **Jawa ❼**,
overlooking Wadi Rajil, is the best-preserved 4th-mil-
lennium BC town yet discovered anywhere in the
world. Very little is known about this "lost city of the
Black Desert" or the people who built, occupied and
abandoned it – all within a few decades.

There are the remains of houses and several preserved gates in the huge surrounding basalt wall, split
between upper and lower towns, but it is the water

PRECEDING PAGES:
a landscape of
sheep and sand.
LEFT: a shepherd
pours feed for
his desert flock.
BELOW: camel
territory.

supply system which is the most impressive aspect. A series of canals directed rainwater into large circular reservoirs, visible to the west of the upper town and still used today by the local people. Why Jawa is located in such a bleak, basalt-strewn, waterless place is a mystery, but it certainly has commanding views to the east and south, including to the entrance of the strategically important Wadi Sirhan, the great natural route into the heart of Central Arabia.

Some time later (possibly around the 2nd millennium BC) the abandoned ruins received a reprise when a "citadel" was built in the middle of the upper town. Some experts believe it to have been an overnight stop on a trade route that linked the Arabian Gulf to Palmyra in the north, and the Nabataean trade to the south. Sheer logistics dictate that it will remain unspoilt and little visited for some time, requiring a 4-wheel-drive and local guide for the 7 km (4 miles) from **Dayr al-Qinn village**. A new dig at Jawa by Jordanian archaeologists in the 1998–99 winter season should provide more clues to the exact purpose and positioning of the fort some 6,000 years ago.

Many of the older villages in this area have ruins of Roman forts nearby, often built as part of the "Strata Diocletiana" in the 3rd century, as a series of defences (including Azraq) to protect Roman interests from the problematic Arab raiders from the east. One of the more important was at **Dayr al-Kahf ❽** (the Monastery of the Caves) a village 13 km (8 miles) north of Al Bishriyya on the Mafraq-Safawi road. The large basalt fort has remains of three-storey towers, stables, a pool and church, with some fine examples of roofing techniques. Inscriptions indicate it was built in AD 306, with later extensions.

Another dramatic hilltop Roman fort is at **Qasr Usaikhim ❾**, some 16 km (10 miles) northeast of Azraq. Again 4-wheel drive is needed to reach the white

Sixty per cent of Jordan's water resources are estimated to be held in the Badia region; it also has tremendous potential for the exploitation of solar and wind energy.

BELOW: a lone herder picks his way through the boulders.

limestone hill, with the black basalt fort perched on top. This commanding position could easily monitor all trade in and out of Wadi Sirhan, and like many of these outposts possibly dates from Nabataean times.

The impressive but isolated fort at **Qasr Burqu** is about 20 km (13 miles) to the north of Muqat on the busy main road into Iraq. Once again 4-wheel- drive and local guide are needed to find the fort (mainly dating from the 3rd century) on the southeastern shores of a small lake. The construction of the dam secured a water supply for passing traders and possibly a later monastic community. Remains include a solid basalt tower, several rooms with inscriptions and a cistern, but the majority of visitors are primarily interested in the lake's migrating birds.

The Badia Project

Jordan has recognised the need to manage this region carefully to secure its future. Development of the Badia lands is of national importance, with the need to establish water, food and energy supplies to the fore, but changes must preserve and enhance the traditional way of life. In 1992 Crown Prince Hassan, working with British institutions, set up the Jordan Badia Research Development Project (JBRDP). Its remit is to study over 70 major factors such as natural and human resources, bio-diversity, technology transfer, desertification, reverse migration and tourism potential.

The JBDRP research area is a relatively untouched portion of the Badia, comprising around 15 per cent of the total region and based at Safawi. The target area of 11,000 sq. km (4,250 sq miles) contains a population of 16,000 spread over 35 villages, with half a million head of livestock. The test area was chosen to be specifically tough so that any results obtained could be applied to any other Badia land – including Jordan's neighbours.

The work, which is being undertaken with the help of the Royal Geographical Society of London and the University of Durham, is already yielding results. The use of vaccines on livestock has greatly improved productivity. Agricultural plans for the rich, silty volcanic ash soil are concentrating on less water-demanding and drought-tolerant plants.

Water harvesting programmes as practised by the Nabataeans are being formulated to make best use of what little rainfall there is, through reduced evaporation, as well as tapping into the massive subterranean supplies held in aquifers.

There's a touch of irony in the fact that the rigidly imposed "no-go" areas along the borders are now providing safe havens for the gazelle and oryx population, as well as for the fox, hare and wolf, all vital to the development of eco-tourism with animal/bird watching and nature treks. With many of Jordan's 6,000 or so archaeological sites straining under the pressure of too many visitors, diverting some to the Badia could be beneficial to both.

Tourism already exists in the Badia with most tours focusing on Wadi Rum (*see page 259*) and Azraq (*see page 203*), but few nights are spent here. The JBRDP plans to alter this. ❏

Map on page 200–201

TIP

The best times to see the lake's migrating birds are spring and autumn. Species include bea-eaters, warblers, wagtails, shirkes, hoopoes, larks, harriers, eagles and many more.

BELOW: the Bedouin has learnt to thrive in the Badia.

THE BEDOUIN INHERITANCE

The romantic notion of camel-riding nomads may be a far cry from the Bedouin of today, but their deeply valued traditions endure

Whether kings or coffee-sellers, Jordanians feel an affinity with the Bedouin and many of their customs stem from Bedouin traditions. It is easy to see why, considering that less than a century ago Jordan's towns were little more than villages with regular interaction with the Bedouin (townspeople would buy animals and animal produce and the Bedouin provisions). Bedouin society is perceived as honourable and its way of life as an ideal. Even in fashionable parts of Amman, its influences are seen in everything from jewellery and clothing to weddings and food.

HIERARCHY AND TERRITORY

The social organisation of Bedouin society centres on the tribe, to which every member owes allegiance and from which he receives protection. The head of the tribe, the "sheikh" is drawn from the leading family and is the arbiter of disputes, the greeter of guests and the representative to outsiders.

The major tribes include the Beni Khaled in the north, Beni Sakhr in the centre and the al-Howeitat in the south. All grazing land in the Badia belongs to the government and is theoretically available to all, but undrawn tribal boundaries established over hundreds of years separate tribes and their territories.

△ **THE DESERT CODE**
The code of the desert in offering food and drink to strangers is still strong. Traditionally a guest was welcome for exactly three-and-a-third days – the time it took for all traces of the host's food to pass through the body of the stranger.

◁ **BEST-DRESSED CAMEL**
Bedouin rugs and camel bags are some of Jordan's best buys – some of their patterns haven't changed since biblical times.

THE CAMEL CORPS GIVES AND TAKES

Perhaps the greatest move at integrating the Bedouin into modern society has been made by the army. As fighting and feuds were always a major part in the lives of tribesmen, it was natural that their warring heritage should be put to good use for the benefit of the kingdom. Thus the army has often given skills, training and opportunities to Bedouin who have missed out on basic education.

The value of having Bedouin as the backbone of the army, especially in the rugged "Hajaneh" camel corps, is acknowledged by Jordan's urban majority, many of whom harbour a romantic fondness for the perceived simplicity of desert life. Unfortunately when they leave the army, almost all the soldiers seek urban lives rather than return to their desert lands. Old ideals of the purity of the desert are slowly losing out to the dirt and pollution of city life.

▷ **CAMPFIRE CULTURE**
The *rababah*, a stringed instrument, has provided music around campfires for centuries. Most Jordanians are familiar with the more popular songs.

▽ **CAFFEINE SOCIETY**
Coffee, drunk in small, handleless cups, is a vital part of Bedouin culture.

△ **ALL THAT GLISTERS**
The designs for necklaces, headpieces and amulets often incorporate Islamic symbols or Koranic verses to bring good luck.

▷ **THE MANSAF**
At a *mansaf* feast ritual is as important as the food. Guests stand around the single dish, and using their right hand, may take only what is directly in front of them.

THE KING'S HIGHWAY

Twisting its way through a mountainous landscape, the ancient King's Highway connects some of Jordan's most spectacular historic sites, including Madaba, Karak, Shawbak and Petra

Map on page 222

The **King's Highway** winding south from Amman to Arabia is an ancient route, along which traders, armies and pilgrims have passed for more than 3,000 years. As early as 1200 BC, Moses addressed the Edomites: "Let us pass, I pray thee, through thy country: we will not pass through the fields, or through the vineyards, neither will we drink of the water of the wells: we will go by the king's highway, we will not turn to the right hand nor to the left, until we have passed thy borders." (Numbers 20:17).

The route's isolation from 20th century development soothes and inspires in turn. It plunges into major and minor *wadis* (valleys), the most spectacular of which is the formidable Wadi al Mujib. In spring and early summer, while winter rain water flows through the valley beds, the mountain slopes explode with dazzling flora. Around every corner in the winding road is either an archaeological or natural treasure, inviting travellers to stop and explore.

Heading south

Various options for the route south exist and which one you choose will depend on the time available: the winding but scenic King's Highway (250 km/155 miles between Amman and Petra), the duller but faster Desert Highway (265 km/165 miles; *see page 237*) or a combination of the two which takes advantage of the good east–west connecting roads. A popular option, which includes the best of the scenery and all the major sights, is to drive along the King's Highway via Madaba, Mount Nebo, Umm ar Rasas and Karak and then cross to the Desert Highway for more rapid driving. This route still takes about 12 hours if you intend to stop off and see the sights; two full days are recommended for a more leisurely tour.

There are government resthouses in Madaba and Karak, as well as several new hotels in the latter. The spa hotel at Zarqa Ma'in near Madaba provides alternative accommodation on the King's Highway, and further hotels are planned. Fuel and garage back-up are no problem as all the larger towns on the route have fuel stations.

Leaving Amman on the airport road, travellers can approach Madaba, 33 km (20 miles) to the south, either directly or via the ancient biblical site of **Hisban ❶**. To go via Hisban take the Na'ur exit about 10 km (6 miles) along the airport road, and the left fork when the road splits at Na'ur. The pools of Hisban are mentioned in the Song of Solomon: "Thy neck is as a tower of ivory; thine eyes like the fishpools in Heshbon [Hisban]…"(7:4). The only evidence of Hisban today are the archaeologists' trenches visible on top of a tell crowned by several impressive 19th-cen-

PRECEDING PAGES: Hammamat Ma'in. **LEFT:** the Land of Moab. **BELOW:** the Madaba map in St George's Church, Madaba.

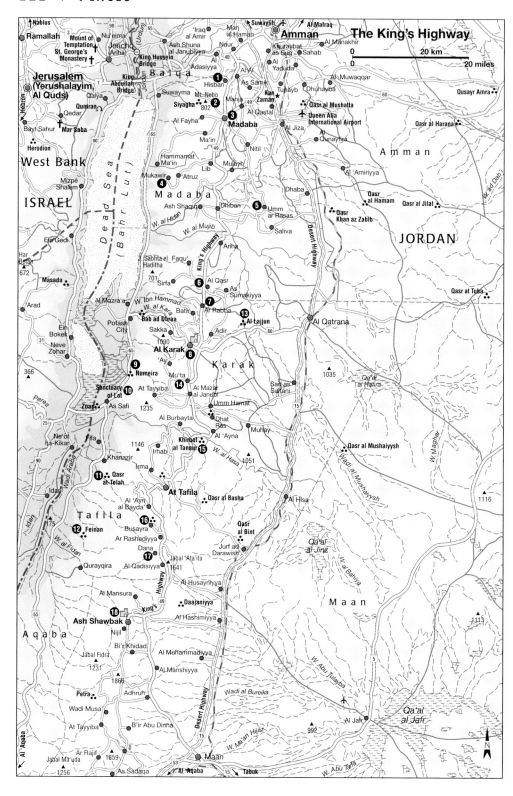

The King's Highway

tury village houses on the right-hand side of the main road. (Tells, formed by the accumulation of debris from successive cities and presenting a layer-cake effect when excavated, are common in Jordan.)

Map on page 222

Moses's mountain

"And Moses went up from the plains of Moab unto the mountain of Nebo, to the top of Pisgah, that is over against Jericho...And the Lord said unto him this is the land which I sware unto Abraham, unto Isaac, and unto Jacob saying, I will give it unto thy seed. I have caused thee to see it with thine eyes, but thou shalt not go over thither. So Moses the servant of the Lord died there in the land of Moab, according to the word of the Lord." (Deut.34:1, 4–5).

The cross on top of Mount Nebo.

Mount Nebo ❷ (Arabic: Jabal Siyagha), site of the death of Moses, has been a place of pilgrimage since the early days of Christianity. The standard pilgrimage route included Jerusalem, Jericho, Ain Moussa (the springs of Moses) and Mount Nebo, and ended with a restorative bathe in the **hot springs of Hammamat Ma'in**. (The facilities at Hammamat Ma'in are now more up-market – the four-star hotel with all spa facilities is signposted Zarqa Ma'in from Madaba – and allow this admirable example to be followed in comfort.)

In AD 394 the intrepid Roman pilgrim Egeria travelled from Jerusalem, over the Jordan River and up the Wadi Hisban and its tributaries to the **spring of Moses** (now marked by a large eucalyptus tree). She then scrambled further up to the **church of Moses**, erected by early Christians. By the 6th century the small, square chapel had expanded into one of the most extensive monastic complexes in the Middle East. Excavations started by the Franciscan Biblical Institute of Jerusalem in 1933 have exposed the three-apse basilica-church (still in use for services) and the monastic buildings surrounding it. (A modern monastery has been built to the southwest of the church.)

BELOW: mosaics at Mount Nebo.

The view from the platform in front of the church is stupendous and best seen early in the morning or at sunset. The Promised Land spreads out to the west, the dark-green mass of the Jordan Valley masking the ancient city of Jericho, the roofs of Jerusalem and Bethlehem glinting on the hills of Palestine, and the opaque expanse of the Dead Sea glinting below. The bronze snake on a cross outside the church was designed by Fantoni of Florence and symbolises the serpent lifted up by Moses in the desert and Jesus on the Cross.

The basilica itself dates from the 6th and 7th centuries, although the earlier chapels, baptistry and memorial to Moses are incorporated into the fabric of the building. The most significant mosaic, dating to AD 531, is that of the old baptistry to the left of the main entrance. The central field enclosed in a plait-border depicts hunting and pastoral scenes including exotic animals – zebra, zebu (humped ox), camel (spotted!), lion and ostrich, all present in Jordan until hunted to extinction in the early part of this century.

Most of the central aisle mosaics have been lifted for preservation and are displayed on the walls of the modern building. The memorial to Moses which the pilgrim Egeria reported probably survives as the

raised structure near the pulpit at the east end of the south aisle. Pieces of the mosaic which decorated this early church have been lifted and can be seen near the altar, including a simple cross. The tombs of early monks are near the chancel and are visible through metal trap doors in the nave.

The modern town of **Madaba** ❸ spills out over the rolling Madaba plain, a fertile land, planted with wheat, barley and tobacco. The tobacco crop is picked and dried by encampments of brightly-dressed Pakistanis, their vibrancy standing out amidst the wide open landscape. The town's skyline of church spires and minarets gives a clue to its history. In common with many of the settlements along the King's Highway, Madaba seems to have been abandoned in the 18th and 19th centuries, but was resettled by Christians from Karak at the end of the 19th century (it was these Christians who found many of the town's mosaics). Now the town is a thriving market centre for the local Bedouin tribes and it is not uncommon to see camels and sheep being brought to market.

Madaba has early origins in biblical times but it is as the seat of a Byzantine bishopric and the centre of a mosaic school that this "City of Mosaics" is most famous. The mosaics, inspired by pattern books circulating in the Byzantine world, were made from the local stone, *tesserae*. The pattern books ensured a certain amount of uniformity to the designs, although individual creativity on the part of the craftsman is always evident. Common motifs which look back to the Hellenistic/Roman world include scenes of hunting, fishing and pastoral pursuits; representations of buildings; mythological scenes; marine or riverine scenes; and, most commonly, depictions of animals, including exotic beasts from Africa and Asia, birds and plants. Such motifs are common to all the mosaics along the King's Highway.

A cockerel created in tiles at Madaba. Animals are a common motif of the mosaics.

BELOW: a surveyor using a theodolite to take measurements of the rocky desert terrain.

During the 7th–8th centuries, the figures of humans and animals in many of the mosaics were obliterated and replaced by carefully made patches of blank *tesserae*. This is more likely to be the result of the iconoclastic movement among Christian communities during the 7th and 8th centuries than the result of Muslim destruction of figural representation as is commonly claimed.

Map on page 222

The first stop in Madaba should be the 6th-century **Madaba Map** found during construction, in 1898, of the Greek Orthodox Church of **St George's**, itself on the site of a Byzantine church. The church stands near the government resthouse in the town centre. Between the gaudy icons of the modern church and covered by a dingy carpet when not on display (if the mosaic is not uncovered permission to pull back the carpet must be obtained from the attendant in the church) it portrays with delightful realism the physical characteristics of the Eastern Byzantine world, including rivers, valleys, the Dead Sea and its neighbouring hills and towns. The centrepiece is Jerusalem, including the Church of the Holy Sepulchre. The area depicted stretches from Tyre and Sidon to the Egyptian Delta and from the Mediterranean to the Eastern Desert.

Further along the main road, under an ugly hangar, lies the **Church of the Apostles**. The fine mosaic floors of the body of the church were completed in AD 578 by one Salamanios (whose name appears around the central medallion). This medallion depicts a personification of the Sea emerging against a background of jumping fish, open-jawed sharks and an octopus. Also housed here for display and safe-keeping are mosaics from Byzantine houses.

The centre of Madaba is the scene for long-term excavation of the main street of the city in classical and early Islamic times (a joint project between the Department of Antiquities and US AID). The various churches and private houses

BELOW: Mukawir, site of Herod's Palace.

The Land of Moab

The land through which the King's Highway passes south of Amman is often referred to by its biblical name Moab. Most of the Book of Ruth takes place against the background of this open limestone plateau of rolling rounded hills, which rises from about 900 metres (2,950 ft) to the peak of **Jabal Shihan** south of the Wadi al Mujib.

Dhiban, right on the King's Highway and situated between Mukawir and Umm ar Rasas, was the one-time capital of Moab. A black basalt stela, known as the Moabite stone, was set up in Dhiban, and on it is inscribed the exploits of the self-proclaimed King of the Moabites, Mesha. He liberated the Land of Moab from Israelite control, at a time when the region of modern-day Jordan was split into the Kingdoms of Ammon, Edom and Moab. The inscription at Dhiban is a rare trace of the Moabite language, and is therefore of great interest to linguists.

The plateau that forms the land of Moab

today is full of interest all year round, but it is most beautiful in spring (late-March to May), when there is a green fuzz over the hills and scarlet anemones, black irises, wild gladioli, yellow heavy-scented mimosa and fire-station-red poppies border the road, colour the fields and fill the **Wadi al Mujib**.

By summer, hollyhocks and caper-bushes take over, against a background of intense activity as first the harvesting (in many cases by hand), followed by the threshing, takes place. The tinkle of bells heralds flocks grazing the stubble – just one example of the way in which agriculture and pastoralism are intertwined in this region.

The same land is used by several interest groups: the nomadic tribes herding sheep, goats and, less commonly, camels, who live in black goat-hair tents; the semi-nomadic tribes who live in village houses for part of the year, but then exchange these for black tents in the spring and autumn when they follow the grazing and move out to the fields for harvest; and the villagers, who live mostly in concrete houses, but who used to build large stone abodes where at least half the space was used for storage of agricultural produce.

Occasionally, encampments of smaller sacking or canvas tents are seen on the outskirts of villages. These belong to the gipsies, who carry out "dentistry work" (putting in gold teeth) and sing and dance at weddings. Gipsies can be distinguished by the vibrantly coloured dresses of the women; for Moabite women traditionally dress in black. The latter are also known for their long braided hair, which falls down the front of their dresses while their heads are covered by tiny black tulle scarves.

The men of the region are less distinctive and opt for either Western dress or for a long, plainly coloured *dish-dash*. They reserve any form of sartorial individualism for their headcloth *(hatteh/keffiyeh)*, which varies in design from red-and-white check to snowy white and often worn at a rakish angle. On high days and holidays men wear an *abayeh* over the *dish-dash*, a finely woven cloak of wool or linen often trimmed with gold. The status of the man is indicated by his *agal*, the cord which holds the *hatteh* on the head. ❑

LEFT: spring flowers after rainfall.

on either side, including the church of the Virgin, the church of the Prophet Elias and the church of al-Khadr are being restored. The **Madaba Museum**, which is signposted, is worth visiting. It contains mosaics and artefacts removed from other buildings within the city and a large ethnographic section devoted to everyday objects and local traditional costume.

Twenty kilometres (12 miles) southwest of Madaba on the King's Highway is a signpost on the right indicating the direction of **Mukawir** ❹, the site of Machaerus, mentioned in the New Testament as the palace in which Salome danced in exchange for the head of John the Baptist (Mark 6:21–29). Mukawir lies on a stark promontory (700 metres/2,295 ft) overlooking the Dead Sea and protected on three sides by deep plunging ravines. The royal fortress on top of the steep hill is that of Herod the Great. It dates to 30 BC and is a replacement of an earlier structure. It is similar to Herod's other mountain-top abodes west of the River Jordan: Herodium, Alexandrum and Masada. The site is undergoing extensive restoration by the Department of Antiquities and the Franciscan Institute although few walls of any height remain standing and the view is the principal reward for the climb.

Umm ar Rasas ❺ is off to the east of the King's Highway, and can be reached from Dhiban or from the Desert Highway. This square walled town, full of a bewildering jumble of stone, was probably built in the Roman period. Two churches have emerged from the rubble in the southeast of the town, both floored with 6th-century mosaics depicting the familiar repertoire of fruit trees, animals, geometric and floral patterns. There are other discernible features, such as gates and towers, but the most dramatic churches and mosaics are outside the town perimeter, now sheltered under another ugly hangar.

Map on page 222

A black iris – the national flower of Jordan.

BELOW: a shepherd leads his flock.

The northern church was constructed in 586, and its mosaic depicts scenes of the church's benefactors carrying out daily tasks. The figures have been carefully patched during the iconoclastic movement so as to render them unrecognisable, but in the southeast corner a personification of a season was hidden by the stone base of a pulpit, and so has been preserved. The southern church was floored in two stages. According to an inscription, the mosaic of the presbytery was laid in 756 by Etaurachius of Hisban. The main mosaic of the central nave and small lateral nave was remade in 785. Both churches were obviously still in use well into the early Islamic period.

A grand descent

Nothing prepares one for the plunge into the gash across the plateau which is the **Wadi al Mujib**, Jordan's answer to the Grand Canyon. The King's Highway twists and winds its way down 900 metres (almost 3,000 ft) to a small post-office at the bottom of the *wadi*. There are Roman milestones on the southern edge marking the course of the Roman road. A dam is planned, which will detract from the *wadi*'s grandeur but help meet the country's water shortage. It is worth pausing at the vantage-point on the north side of the *wadi* to drink in the view and watch the buzzards soaring at eye level.

Emerging through walls of basalt rock at the top of the *wadi*, the road once again passes through a wide open plateau covered in grain. This is southern Moab, an area known for its independent spirit for centuries. The King's Highway passes through small but thriving villages, all boasting large schools to cope with the expanding population. Several of the villages have standing monuments close to the road. In **Al Qasr ❻** there is an early 2nd-century Nabataean

The man who runs the post office at Wadi al Mujib.

BELOW: apple orchards along the highway.

temple which has never been excavated. To the west of the main road through **Ar Rabba ❼** are the well-preserved remains of a Roman temple, probably converted to a church and then reused in the 19th century as a village house.

Map on page 222

Karak Castle

The site of **Karak ❽** has always been important because of its strategic position at the head of the Wadi al Karak leading west to Palestine. The visible remains of the castle date mainly from the Mamluke rather than the Crusader era, the cruder work of the knights having been refined at a later date.

Originally access was by small man-made tunnels through the rock and these are still visible under an impressive facade linking four square towers above a stone *glacis* (slope, often artificially strengthened), which is being reconstructed by the Jordanian and Czech governments. Now the entrance curls up to the government resthouse with its spectacular view down to the Dead Sea. Karak, like the other castles in Jordan, is a castle to be explored; there are many dark passages, cavernous holes and the occasional sheer drop (many of them unfenced, so beware). One problem for visitors and archaeologists alike is that the castle has been used and remodelled by successive governments right down to the brief Independent Republic of Moab in 1920, which makes it difficult to sift one period from another.

The steps down to the **Mamluke Lower Court** lead to a **museum** housed in one of the castle's many long galleries and containing artefacts from excavations and early photographs of Karak taken by England's Edwardian explorer Gertrude Bell. The inner wall of this Lower Court sits on Crusader foundations but is largely Mamluke, while the outer wall is Mamluke, dating to the time of

BELOW: looking towards the castle at Karak.

A natural hazard of the highway.

Sultan Baybars, who is also responsible for constructing the towers along the city wall inscribed with his emblem, the lion. Turning sharp left from the entrance, walk up into an impressive two-storey gallery which used to double as a football pitch for the local boys. Look through the narrow arrow-slits on to one of the original Crusader entrances, now a blocked-up doorway in the rough stone wall in a projecting bastion to the east.

Once through this gallery, turn right along a narrow passage past a relief of a male torso which many guides tell you is Salah-ad-Din, better known to the English-speaking world as Saladin, the famous opponent of Richard the Lionheart and Reynald de Chatillon. In fact, this is a fragment of a Nabataean sculpture which was found on the site when the Crusaders started building in 1142. There are side rooms leading off the passageway, including the castle bakery, crucial for sustaining the garrison in times of siege, as were the cisterns.

Emerging from the gloom of the passage, you will then find yourself in the ruined **Crusader chapel** just to the right, and ahead the three-storey Mamluke keep – there is a great view of the castle and its surroundings from this point. The keep lies at the southern end of the citadel and replaces an earlier Crusader construction. The crusader defences on this southern side would have been set up against the siege-engines of Salah-ad-Din, which were placed on the high ground opposite. Salah-ad-Din twice besieged the castle, then occupied by his arch-enemy Reynald de Chatillon, first in 1183 and then in 1184. Reynald had been harrying Muslim caravans and sailing vessels, and had managed to get within one day's march of Mecca. During the siege, Salah-ad-Din, in an extraordinary act of politeness, suspended his fire on the tower on account of it being occupied by the newly married Isabelle, sister of the King, and Reynald's step-

BELOW: restoration work at Karak.

Map on page 222

son. Both sieges were eventually relieved by Baldwin IV marching with a garrison from Jerusalem, and Karak did not capitulate until 1189.

Turning in the other direction and looking immediately down, you can see the excavated 14th-century reception-hall of al-Nasir Mohammed's palace. Here the Sultan would have received guests and supplicants. Its cruciform design with four *iwans* opening on to an unroofed courtyard is typical for that period and it mirrors a similar building at Shawbak.

The town of Al Karak, like Madaba, is a market centre for the surrounding Bedouin and villagers. Also like Madaba, it is a mixed Muslim and Christian town. Less than 4 per cent of the total population of Jordan is Christian; two-thirds is Greek Orthodox and one-third is Greek Catholic, Roman Catholic, Protestant, Syrian Orthodox or Armenian. To avoid the confusion of celebrating different feast days, the Catholic and Orthodox Christmas and Easter are celebrated alternately by everyone. The Christian population of the Karak area has a long history pre-dating the Crusades and several of the villages to the north of the town are 99 percent Christian. The Christians, being a minority, are determinedly Christian, and Karak also has its share of fundamentalist Muslims (recognised by their bushy beards and their disconcerting habit of not acknowledging female customers in their shops).

The main street of Karak is always bustling with fast-moving pedestrians and slow-moving cars. The modern *suq* is worth investigating; not only for the cool and tranquil interiors of the Ottoman shops but also for the useful items that can be purchased, such as threshing forks, sheep-skins, richly-roasted coffee beans, sacks of unidentified bark for medicinal purposes, goat-bells, blue-beaded Fatima's Hands for warding off the evil eye, rolls of tent-cloth and hand-stitched cotton- or wool-stuffed quilts, bolsters and mattresses. At the top of the main street several eateries offer very tasty *felafel*, *ful*, *hummus* and salad, while further down near the mosque the delicious smell of spit-roasted chicken tempts. On the first sharp bend on the road out of town, look out for the dyeing shop with its vats of colour and an Ottoman school built on the orders of Sultan Abdul Hamid in the late 1890s.

The Southern Ghors

West of the King's Highway and running parallel with it, a road runs through the **Southern Ghors**, an intriguing area along the southeast coast of the Dead Sea with many important historical associations. The road can be easily accessed from Karak. Bab ad-Dhraa and Numeira have been excavated in recent years and are plausible candidates for the sites of Sodom and Gomorrah. In the Genesis accounts, God destroyed Sodom and Gomorrah as a sign of His displeasure with the wickedness of their inhabitants. Abraham's nephew, Lot, was saved by fleeing to the hills with his daughters; his wife was less fortunate, however, and, merely for the crime of looking back upon the scene of devastation, was turned into a pillar of salt.

Bab ad-Dhraa (near the junction of the Dead Sea and Karak roads) was inhabited for about 1,000 years during the Early Bronze Age, around 3300–2000 BC;

TIP

There are very few places to stay in Karak, but a little south is a guest house in Wadi Dana nature reserve. The rooms are peaceful and the views exceptional (*see page 235 and Where to Stay in the Travel Tips*).

BELOW: the Sanctuary of Lot.

Mother and child watch the world from their doorway.

for much of that time it was also used as a cemetery by nomads who brought their dead for burial there in multiple shaft tombs and large charnel houses.

Numeira , 14 km (9 miles) to the south, is a large, hilltop walled town that lasted for about a century during the Early Bronze Age III period (c. 2750–2350 BC), before suffering a violent and fiery destruction (to judge from the compelling archaeological evidence of 40-cm/1-ft thick ash layers).

Together with Bab ad-Dhraa and Numeira, the remains of other Early Bronze Age sites in the area can be seen at **Fifa**, **Khanazir**, and **Safi** – suggesting to some that these five sites may be the best available candidates for the Five Cities of the Plain mentioned in the Book of Genesis, namely Sodom, Gomorrah, Admah, Zeboiim, and Bela (that is, Zoar).

Northeast of Safi is the **Sanctuary of Lot** ⓾. This Byzantine monastic complex had a church with mosaic floors, a reservoir, living quarters, burial chambers, and a cave that appears to have been presented to ancient pilgrims as the place where Lot and his daughters took refuge after the destruction of Sodom. Some ceramic artefacts found in the cave date from around 3000 BC – the assumed period of the destruction of Sodom. An inscription mentions Lot by name. The complex appears to have been used from the 5th to the 8th centuries. The site is identified on the Madaba mosaic map as the Monastery of Saint Lot.

Some 9 km (5 miles) south of Khanazir and nearly 2 km (1 mile) to the east are the extensive remains of **Qasr at-Telah** ⓫, a large Nabataean complex that includes a caravanserai, a reservoir, aqueducts, agricultural fields, and houses.

Fifteen minutes to the south by car brings you to the turn-off for **Feinan** ⓬, which is half an hour to the east and accessible only by four-wheel-drive vehicle. Feinan is a sprawling copper-mining complex that was one of the

BELOW:
Wadi al Hasa.

biggest in the ancient world. It has been associated with the biblical site of Punon. Several hundred shaft mines in the area were exploited for their rich ore during the 5½ millennia from the Chalcolithic to the Mamluke periods (*circa* 4000 BC–AD1500).

Map on page 222

Still visible above ground today are enormous slag heaps from several different periods, and remains of the large Roman-Byzantine town's water systems, agricultural fields, smelters, water-powered mill and at least two churches.

Military barracks

Returning to Karak, the next stop is the excavated legionary fortress of **Al Lajjun ⓭**, equidistant from the King's and Desert highways, and easily reached from Karak. The name Al Lajjun is very probably a corruption of the Latin *legio*; in this case the legion being Legio IV Martia. The square fortress was probably built in AD 302 during the reign of Diocletian and contains all the usual requirements of a garrison-town: the central *principia* (headquarters), the barracks, defensive towers and a monumental gateway within the wall.

Al Lajjun was one of the forts which guarded the Eastern *limes* of the Roman Empire, which ran north–south near the line of the Desert Highway. The buildings on the hill above the site belong to the late Ottoman period when a Turkish garrison was stationed here to guard the spring and the communication lines between Karak and Qatrana. The houses are now used by local Bedouin for storage of their winter tents.

Continuing south along the King's Highway from Karak, the road passes through the neighbouring towns of **Mu'ta ⓮** and **Mazar**, site of the first battle between the Muslims and Byzantium in 632 and of Jordan's third university. The

BELOW: the spectacular scenery of Wadi Araba.

Companions of the Prophet Mohammed who fell during the battle were buried at Mazar, and the town remains an important pilgrimage centre today, though the original commemorative mosque has been replaced by a 20th-century creation.

The road meanders on through rural landscape until reaching **Wadi al Hasa**, the ancient boundary between Moab and Edom. Edom was an Iron Age kingdom which differed from Moab in that it was made up of small stretches of cultivatable land between steep little valleys. The side valleys contain traces of the Nabataean terracing which harvested and exploited the water run-off.

On the southern side of Wadi Hasa, on top of a high isolated hill, lies the Nabataean temple of **Khirbet al-Tannur** ⓑ. The path to the summit is signposted and, if you make the treck, the sense of achievement at reaching the top is overwhelming. The temple was built between the 1st century BC and the 1st century AD, and is dedicated to the gods Hadad and Atargaris, local versions of the main Nabataean gods Dushara and Allat. The whole structure was richly decorated with fine sculpture, which is now in the Archaeological Museum in Amman (*see page 143*). Traces of the temple survive in low walls outlining the outer paved courtyard and altar in the northeast corner. A doorway leads to an inner smaller courtyard, in the centre of which stood the shrine and main altar. Animal sacrifices were made on these altars.

The King's Highway climbs out of the Wadi al Hasa onto the long plain of **Tafila** where Lawrence fought his only pitched battle against the Turks in January 1918. The region is famous for its olives, a fact readily appreciated when looking at the groves of olive-trees blanketing the side of the *wadi* leading down from Tafila.

After passing the ancient site of **Busayra** ⓰, ancient Bozrah and possible cap-

TIP

As well as larger animals, Wadi al Dana nature reserve is great for observing Middle Eastern and migrating birds. The RSCN can advise on the best times to visit to catch specific species.

BELOW:
the hilltop site of
Shawbak Castle.

ital of the Edomites, the road passes the ar-Rashadiyya cement works and, just below, the village of **Dana** , an enchanting honeycomb of tightly-knit roofs surrounded by fertile orchards. Dana nestles at the head of a magnificent *wadi* running west into the Wadi Araba which was the site of early copper-mines.

The area is a nature reserve, part of the Wadi Dana Project, initiated by the Royal Society for the Conservation of Nature (RSCN) and funded chiefly by the World Bank and UNDP. A research facility to study the local flora, fauna (including the rare ibex) and archaeology is underway, and old village houses are gradually being restored either as living quarters or as handicraft and organic foodstuffs centres.

Camping is the best way to enjoy this spectacular terrain, but for the faint of heart nine rooms at the Wadi Dana Guest House keep nature safely at bay; from the balconies there is a commanding view of the magnificent Wadi Araba. Backpackers will also feel at home here in the village hotel, which was designed specifically to cater to low-budget, environmentally conscious travellers.

Shawbak Castle

Shawbak Castle lies east of the main road running through **Shawbak** ⓲. The first sight of the castle on its isolated hill is quite breathtaking. As with Karak, most of the visible defences belong to post-Crusader times. Shawbak, or Montreal, was the first outpost of the Kingdom of Jerusalem in Outrejordain and constructed in 1115 by Baldwin I. It was later eclipsed by Karak when its commander, Pagan the Butler, realised the strategic value of the latter.

The castle shares a similar history to Karak. It was taken over by the Ayyubids and then the Mamlukes, whose extensive reconstruction is recorded in in-

Map on page 222

TIP

The women of Wadi Dana make excellent jams and preserves as well as striking silver jewellery, all of which are for sale at some of the country's best boutiques, handicraft stores and gift shops.

BELOW: the ruins at Shawbak.

Map
on page
222

The Shawbak area is particularly rich in shrines, some in good order, others tumbled down. Traditionally such shrines are the domain of women and children, who bring offerings of ornaments, stones, fossils and cloth.

BELOW: a school in Shawbak.

scriptions on the outer face of the towers. The original entrance to the castle was through a triple gate arranged on a bent axis as found at Ajlun.

The **Crusader church**, with its bird's-eye view of the old village, is above the entrance. Apart from this and several rooms along the arched corridor on the northeast side of the castle there are no other positively identified Crusader buildings. Although the water was usually brought up from springs at the base of the hill, in times of siege a deep and steep passageway within the castle walls led down to the spring. The passageway is still accessible but the steps are very worn and unlit.

A **palace/reception hall**, similar to the one at Karak, has been excavated. It was probably built by al-Mu'azzem Isa al-Adil, the Ayyubid governor of this area, at the end of the 12th century. The Ottoman village, including the old post-office and rebuilt rooms used by the village sheikh and more recently by a team of visiting archaeologists, is close to the entrance.

Below Shawbak Castle is the **shrine of Abu Suleiman al-Dirany**, probably Ayyubid/Mamluke in date. Hennaed hand-prints adorn the internal walls of the shrine, smeared there by women who come to offer prayers for the sick and for fertility.

From Shawbak the route on to Petra is straightforward. If you arrive towards sunset, you might consider taking a picturesque side road indicated to Hesha, on the right-hand side of the road shortly after the 20-km (12-mile) sign to Wadi Musa. The road wiggles up through the scrub-oak forest and emerges on the escarpment, giving a panoramic view of the rock-massif around Petra and Beidha, a particularly impressive sight in the setting sun. The road then snakes down to the modern villages. ❑

The Desert Highway

The alternative to the site-packed journey along the King's Highway is to take the Desert Highway (Tariq al-Bint in Arabic, or Maiden's Way). This is much faster, and a journey from Amman to Wadi Musa can be done in 3–4 hours, with a dual carriageway down to Ma'an. The road has its own appeal (mostly speed), but is less interesting.

This parallel route to the King's Highway, was a 16th-century Ottoman creation (Maiden's Way is thought to refer to an Ottoman princess's preference for this route over the King's Highway). The new road was intended to replace the ancient route, although water scarcity and the mood of potentially predatory tribes occasionally prompted recourse to the King's Highway.

Travelling down the Desert Highway during the Haj season today, you will encounter convoys of pilgrim-packed buses sporting flags from as far away as Turkey. Part of the Desert Highway's history lies in its role for conveying Muslim pilgrims from Damascus to Medina, and then later to Mecca.

The major truck-stops of Al Jiza, Qatrana and Al Hisa were also stops for the Haj caravan and each modern settlement hosts an Ottoman fort which guarded the cisterns and reservoirs so vital to the caravan. The fort at **Qatrana**, built in 1531, has been restored with financial help from the Turkish government. The Petra Resthouse at Qatrana always provides a welcome stop where good and hot meals are served.

Pervasive white dust heralds the phosphate mines at **Hisa**. Phosphate and potash from the Dead Sea are Jordan's most important exports, and the old Hejaz railway is still used to transport phosphate down to Aqaba. Apart from the luxurious mine-camp and truck stops, the only "villages" along the highway belong to recently settled Bedouin, who often use their concrete houses and tin shacks for storage rather than dwelling.

Petra is signposted near **al-Hashimiyya**

RIGHT: a lorry takes the fast route along the Desert Highway.

and again at **Ma'an**. The new road bypasses Ma'an where there is no longer much to see, apart from **Khoury's Resthouse** on the old road to the north of town. It is worth stopping for refreshment and a welcome by the patron, Khoury, whose pink palace is papered with photographs of himself as an actor.

From Ma'an, a scenic route to **Wadi Musa** takes you southwest for a little way before diverting to the right, via **Il** and **At-Tayyiba**, an old village perched on the edge of the escarpment overlooking Petra and the Wadi Araba. A slightly shorter alternative is via **Adhruh**, where the westerly route takes you to Wadi Musa and then on to Petra.

If, however, you are continuing down to Wadi Rum, you will notice that the dual-carriageway stops a little way south of Ma'an. The winding descent of the **Ras an-Naqab** offers stupendous views, though you will probably want to pay more attention to the oncoming over-laden trucks. In such circumstances, you may be hard-pushed to notice the Nabataean and Roman twin towns of **Al-Humayma al-Jadida**. ❑

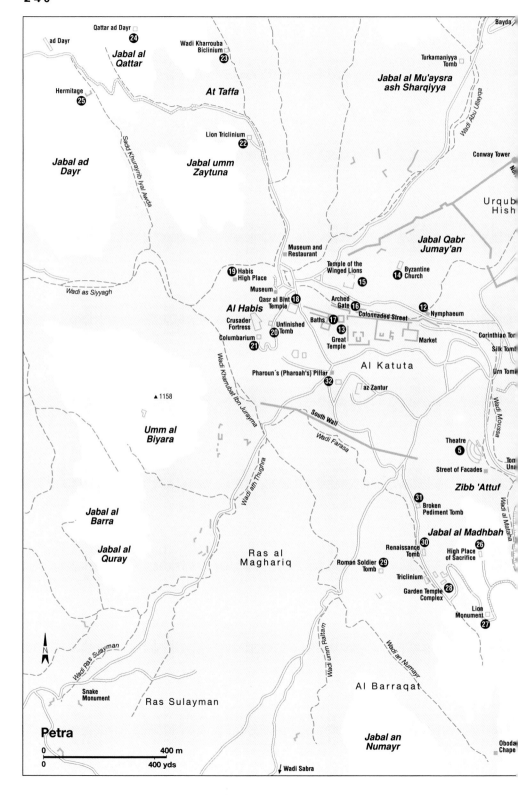

Petra

0 _____ 400 m

0 _____ 400 yds

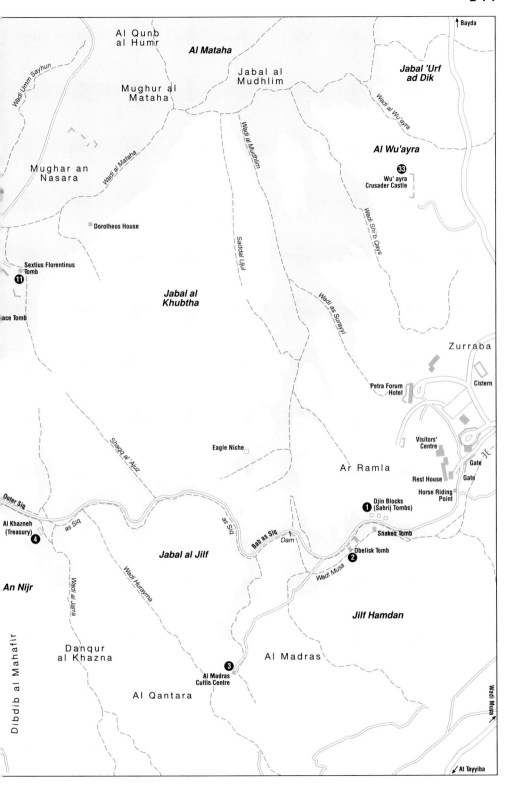

↑ Bayda

Al Qunb
al Humr

Al Mataha

Wadi Umm Sayhun

Jabal al
Mudhlim

*Jabal 'Urf
ad Dik*

Mughur al
Mataha

Wadi al Wu'ayra

Al Wu'ayra

Wadi al Mataha

Wadi al Mudhlim

㉝

Mughar an
Nasara

Wu' ayra
Crusader Castle

■ Dorotheos House

Wadi Shi'b Qays

Sadd al Ujul

■ Sextius Florentinus
Tomb

⓫

*Jabal al
Khubtha*

Zurraba

ace Tomb

Cistern

Wadi as Surayyi

Petra Forum
Hotel

Eagle Niche

Visitors'
Centre

Shaqq al 'Ajuz

Ar Ramla

Gate

Rest House

Gate

Outer Siq

Horse Riding
Point

as Siq

Djin Blocks
(Sahrij Tombs)

❶

Al Khazneh
(Treasury)

❹

as Siq

Bab as Siq

Dam

Snakes Tomb

Jabal al Jilf

Obelisk Tomb

❷

An Nijr

Wadi al Jarra

Wadi Hurayma

Wadi Musa

Jilf Hamdan

Danqur
al Khazna

Al Madras

Wadi Musa

D i b d i b   a l   M a h a f i r

❸

Al Madras
Cultic Centre

Al Qantara

↙ At Tayyiba

PETRA

There are only a few places in the world where the hand of God and the mind of man have joined forces to dazzle the human imagination. Petra in south Jordan ranks highly on the list

Map on pages 240–241

Petra is far and away Jordan's most spectacular touristic site, offering a powerful and always invigorating combination of Nabataean antiquities and sensational natural scenery. From sunrise to sunset, its footpaths bustle with curious tourists, yet an uncanny otherworldliness prevails. In the very midst of what was obviously a thriving city, the Nabataeans built a host of elaborate funerary monuments. These, combined with the intense glow of the rock and prolific references to gods, animals and mythological beings, create an almost supernatural aura.

The city was all but abandoned by the late 8th century, yet the architectural and artistic details of the monuments appear amazingly fresh. In many places, columns are as smooth and capital carvings as detailed today as they were 2,000 years ago. Such accomplished craftsmanship has shaped our impression of Nabataea as an enlightened civilisation, open to an amalgamation of cultural influences during its most glorious years. But details of both the birth of Nabataean culture and its eventual decline remain hazy, and archaeologists believe that further clues to Nabataean history may remain buried in the greater part of Petra that has yet to be discovered.

PRECEDING PAGES: the richly coloured rocks of Petra. **LEFT:** al-Khazneh (the Treasury). **BELOW:** a first glimpse as one approaches through the *siq.*

Carved in stone

Petra is best known for the dramatic tomb and temple facades that its Nabataean Arab inhabitants carved into the soft Nubian sandstone some 2,000 years ago. Since the city was "rediscovered" for the west in 1812 by Swiss explorer Johann Ludwig Burckhardt (*see page 255*), Western and Arab scholarship has identified over 800 monuments in the Petra area; all but a few dozen were carved into the red-hued cliff-faces.

A closer look at the monuments, however, quickly reveals their hybrid, trans-Mediterranean nature. Petra was a dynamic, peaceful meeting-place of people and ideas from the four corners of the earth, a timeless point of convergence of communication routes, mindsets, and cultural traditions from the leading occidental and oriental civilisations of the Mediterranean basin. Obvious Hellenistic and Egyptian architectural influences blend in with traditional Arab/Semitic local traditions, creating what we now refer to as Nabataean architecture. The Nabataeans also used a combination of languages, mainly their own Nabataean script, but also Greek, Aramaic and Latin languages that were common among trading cultures in the 300 years before and after the time of Christ.

This cross-fertilisation of ideas that characterises Nabataean architecture and culture reflects the single most important force that gave rise to Nabataean civilisation: the importance of international trade. Histor-

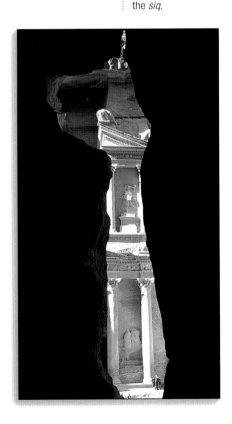

An imposing head stares out from the museum at Petra.

ical knowledge of the birth of Nabataea is hazy. Most scholars accept that the Nabataeans were a semi-nomadic people from the northern Arabian Peninsula who migrated to southern Jordan in the 6th and 5th centuries BC (to the lands of the former biblical kingdom of Edom). They were particularly successful in this semi-arid climate due to their ability to harness scarce water resources and to make maximum use of camels for transport.

By the 4th century BC, Petra was establishing itself as a centre of Nabataean culture, perhaps first as a combination of commercial entrepot and necropolis of a people whose economic base in southern Jordan relied on the income from regional trade in bitumen, aromatics, salt, copper and agricultural goods.

The importance of trade to the Nabataeans explains their developed sense of diplomacy; it compelled them to resolve disputes with neighbours without warfare, so that security could be maintained and trade continue flowing. The result: as Nabataean traders, professionals and public figures interacted regularly with nearby civilisations they absorbed elements of foreign culture into their own artistic repertoire (for example, a Roman Corinthian capital, a Hellenistic pedimented temple facade, an Egyptian obelisk funerary monument, an Assyrian cultic high place for spiritual purposes). At the height of its independence in the 1st centuries BC and AD, Petra was renowned for its sophisticated system of justice, humane monarchy and technological and commercial prowess.

After the Emperor Trajan formally annexed Petra and the Nabataean Kingdom into the Roman Empire in AD 106, Nabataean trade and culture continued to flourish for several hundred years. But Petra seems to have declined gradually after the 4th century AD, and was reduced to a shadow of its former urban splendour after a series of devastating earthquakes erupted between the 6th and the 8th centuries AD.

BELOW: the Obelisk Tomb.

Visiting Petra now

Today's visitors are awed by the magnificence and beauty of Nabataean tombs, temples, theatres, water works, and other monuments, many of which have eroded into fabulous natural striations of white, pink, red, blue and brown. A full week is required to see every important part of the Petra basin, which comprises nearly 100 sq. km (38 sq. miles) of rippled limestone mounds and undulating sandstone heights interspersed by narrow valleys and broad plains that are exploited for their agricultural potential today just as they have been for thousands of years.

Serious visitors should plan to spend at least one night and two full days to see the central Petra basin. From the start of the *siq* you must walk or take a horse carriage as horse riders are not permitted to enter.

A spate of new hotels has been built in the last few years, offering a wide range of accommodation from 4-star international hotel chains to small hostels catering to students and budget travellers. Booking ahead is a must in the spring and autumn high seasons. Those who can spare only a day can rent a car and make the round-trip on their own (about 2½ hours one way from Amman along the Desert Highway), or take an all-inclusive guided trip offered daily by the JETT bus company in Amman.

A walk through the antiquities

Even the area around the visitors' centre and ticket office is rich in remains: small graves and chambers are cut into the ground, a large Nabataean tomb, converted into a bar, is next to the rest house, and across from the Petra Forum Hotel there is a large water reservoir which fed the city centre through a rock-cut channel.

From the visitors' centre, the route descends into Petra through the **Bab as-Siq** area, passing three **djin ("ghost") blocks** ❶, early Nabataean tombs, on the right, and the stately **Obelisk Tomb** ❷, with its four obelisks, on the left. Facing it, on the other side of the path, is a large Greek/Nabataean bilingual funerary inscription. Just before the dam, you can walk up into the hills to the south to the **Al-Madras Cultic Centre** ❸, with its altars, inscriptions, rock-cut monuments, water installations and many niches.

Today, as in Nabataean times, the dam at the entrance of the *siq* prevents winter floodwaters from damaging the *siq* and the city centre, by diverting water through the al-Muthlim tunnel. The traces of the monumental arch just beyond the dam mark the start of the main route into Petra through the 1¼-km (¾-mile) long *siq* – a natural fissure in the mountain which the Nabataeans developed into the stately entrance into their capital city. It still sports remains of the paved Nabataean/Roman road, two water channels, and innumerable religious niches, stone god-blocks, and inscriptions.

The end of the *siq* opens suddenly to the drama of **al-Khazneh** ❹ ("the Treasury"), Petra's most famous monument; its name reflects the local legend that the urn on top of the monument held the pharaoh's treasure. This monumental tomb was probably built for the Nabataean King Aretas III in the 1st

Map on pages 240–241

Even as recently as the late 1960s, Petra was seldom visited. An expanding tourist industry has since crept up around what is one of the most dramatic and engaging sites of the Middle East, bringing the mixed blessing of home comforts and easy access.

BELOW: outside al-Khazneh.

Visitors dwarfed by the Treasury's mighty columns.

century BC. Its facade still shows a variety of classical and Nabataean architectural elements, including statues of gods, animals and mythological figures. The Outer Siq leads from here past the sand artists towards the theatre and the city centre, also passing several large tombs and tricilinia (singular: triclinium, a funerary banqueting hall with benches along three sides).

On the left just before the theatre are the 44 tombs that make up the eerie **Street of Facades**. The 7,000-seat **Theatre ❺** was first constructed by the Nabataeans, probably in the early 1st century AD, but was refurbished by the Romans soon after their conquest in AD 106; the Romans obviously did not respect the Nabataean tombs, which they sliced through to expand the theatre.

From the refreshment stands beyond the theatre, a rebuilt Nabataean staircase ascends to the **Royal Tombs**, a dozen large tombs thought to have held the remains of Nabataean kings. The stairs lead to the most striking one, the **Urn Tomb ❻** with its subterranean vaults and its large internal chamber that was converted into a Byzantine church in AD 446–47. The southernmost of the Royal Tombs is the very well-preserved **Tomb of Unayshu ❼**, a minister to Nabataean kings. North of the Urn Tomb is the heavily eroded but very colourful **Silk Tomb ❽**, set back in a recess.

Beyond it is the equally eroded but busy-looking **Corinthian Tomb ❾** (combining Nabataean and classical architectural styles, including a replica of the Khazneh in its upper storey). Immediately north of it is the huge, three-storey **Palace Tomb ❿**, with parts of its upper storey built rather than carved. Just north of the Palace Tomb is a large cistern into which flowed the water that came from the pool near the Petra Forum Hotel.

North of the pool is the **Sextius Florentinus Tomb ⓫**, built around AD 130

BELOW: the Street of Facades.

for the Roman governor of the province of Arabia (note the faint Latin inscription and imperial eagle on the facade). A sacred processional way of staircases and corridors started from here and wound its way up to several religious High Places on the summit of the mountain.

As you walk from the theatre towards the city centre, three minutes after passing the refreshment stands you come upon (on your right) the remains of the **Nymphaeum** ⑫, the public water fountain dedicated to the mythological nymphs who lived near rivers and water sources. Here you can pick up the remains of the ancient colonnaded street that was built around AD 106 along the line of an earlier Nabataean gravel-surfaced roadway lined with buildings (probably shops). The street was used well into the 6th century, from when the existing street-side shops date.

The Great Temple

The street leads directly to the arched gate that was the formal entrance into ancient Petra's most important temple precinct. Before you reach the arched gate, note a staircase leading south from the street towards an open area that scholars have called the "markets" of Petra. Also on the hill overlooking the street from the south is the collapsed **Great Temple** ⑬, under excavation since 1993. Some scholars think this might have been the city's forum or agora, the heart of its business and administrative dealings, but recent excavations have failed to confirm the theory. The 7,000-sq.-metre- (75,300 sq ft) temple complex, guarded from the front by four 40-metre- (130-ft-) tall columns (two of which remain intact in spite of the powerful earthquake that destroyed most of the temple), includes an upper and lower temenos and a temple. But further excavations unexpectedly revealed a small theatre – perhaps used for religious plays. The original colonnade was used to form an inter-columnar wall. This has led scholars to speculate that the site was originally home to a small shrine, although no supporting evidence has been found. Artefacts such as pottery shards dating from the early Nabataean era through to the Islamic period have further compouned the mystery surrounding the purpose and function of this enormous monument.

The slopes north and south of the colonnaded street are covered with broken pottery shards, cut stones, wall lines and architectural elements that indicate the presence of many unexcavated structures – most probably public buildings that once formed part of the city centre. Overlooking the colonnaded street from the north side of the *wadi* are two recently excavated structures. A triple-apsed **Byzantine church** ⑭, discovered in 1993, has stunning and well-preserved mosaic floors. Its elaborate decoration defies traditional assumptions about the fate of Petra during the 5th and 6th centuries, which claim the city had by then embarked on a steady period of decline.

Recent excavations here have uncovered dozens of papyrus scrolls; the only known written documents of Nabataen history in Petra. The scrolls, parallel in importance to the Dead Sea scrolls, were carbonised in a fire that destroyed parts of the church. Nonethe-

BELOW: hiking to the High Place.

TIP

Although some tours spend only a day at Petra, to appreciate some of the remoter sites, such as the Hermitage and the Lion Monument, you are advised to spend at least one more day, especially if you are visiting in the searing summer heat.

BELOW: overlooking the Royal Tombs.

less, researchers in 1998 completed the daunting task of unrolling and reading the scrolls, most of which document land ownership and dispute settlements. The scrolls have helped illuminate what is otherwise a blank page in Petra's history. They are stored under strict environmental control at the American Centre for Oriental Research in Amman while the Jordanian Department of Antiquities works to provide a permanent storage and display area.

Near the church and almost parallel with the Arched Gate is the **Temple of the Winged Lions ⓰**, first built around AD 27 and dedicated to a consort of the supreme Nabataean male deity Dushara. The **Arched Gate ⓰** – a common, three-entrance Graeco-Roman structure – had wooden doors that gave on to the temenos (the holy precinct) of the still-standing Qasr al-Bint Temple, the city's leading sanctuary. Note the small carved panels flanking the central doorway of the Arched Gate, with their human busts, soldiers, animals and geometric designs, and the capitals on the ground which bear animal head decorations. The **Baths of Petra ⓱** (these are not safely accessible to visitors) stand immediately above and south of the gate; opening on to the corner of the temenos, they may well have been used in association with religious rites conducted in the temenos.

The 200-metre (656-ft) long temenos, parallel to the *wadi*, originally included a low platform, shallow steps, a long double row of benches along its south wall, and fine stone paving, all dating from the early 1st century AD. The 23-metre (75-ft) high **Qasr al-Bint Temple ⓲** (or Qasr Bint Pharoun, "Palace of Pharaoh's daughter") is Petra's most impressive built (as opposed to carved) structure, and dates from just before or after the time of Christ. Its open-air altar was used for public religious ceremonies. The temple faces

north towards the Sharra Mountains, which gave rise to the name of the leading Nabataean god Dushara ("He of Shara"). The external walls were decorated with painted stucco, plaster panels, a Doric frieze, rosette medallions and bust reliefs, some of whose remains can still be seen. The temple was destroyed in the late 3rd century AD, perhaps when the forces of Queen Zenobia of Palmyra marched south to Egypt.

Map on pages 240–241

In high places

The small mountain overlooking Qasr al-Bint from the west is al-Habis. A winding staircase leads up to a small, impressive museum that reveals Nabataean skills in ceramics, hydrology, metalwork and sculpture. The museum is housed in an unusual Nabataean rock-cut structure with five windows over the door; it may have been associated with religious rites along the processional route that passed in front of it, leading to the **Habis High Place** ⓳, about 250 metres (275 yds) to the west. This is the easiest high place to reach for visitors who cannot make more demanding climbs on foot. Like most high places, this one has benches, a water basin or tank, an altar, an approach staircase and a dramatic, perch-like setting overlooking a *wadi*, in this case the Wadi Siyyagh (the site of a massive Nabataean rock quarry and the important Wadi Siyyagh spring).

On the east face of al-Habis (facing Qasr al-Bint) are two interesting monuments that are easy to reach. The large **Unfinished Tomb** ⓴ shows how the Nabataeans carved from the top down; the adjacent **Columbarium** ㉑, a former Nabataean tomb retooled with hundreds of small niches, was used either to hold cremation urns or to raise pigeons and doves. A small, 12th-century **Crusader fortress** on the summit of al-Habis can be reached easily in five minutes along a pathway and stairs from the south. The aerial view into central Petra is well worth the short climb to the fort's keep. The fort was a subsidiary lookout post for the bigger Crusader fortress at Wu'eira (near the Petra Forum Hotel).

Overlooking al-Habis from the southwest is the towering massif of **Umm al-Biyara** ("Mother of Cisterns"), whose east face sports a variety of Nabataean tomb styles. The trek to the summit along an ancient processional way is very demanding and requires a guide, but provides breathtaking panoramas of the entire Petra region. The summit retains the excavated remains of a small Edomite village from the 7th century BC Old Testament period, with impressive rock-cut water channels and cisterns. The Nabataeans also used the summit and built a small temple and other structures along its east rim.

The 45-minute ascent from the museum area to **ad-Dayr** is best made in the afternoon, when much of the route is in shade. On the way up, you can visit several interesting monuments amidst stunning scenery: the **Lion Triclinium** ㉒; the **Wadi Kharrouba Biclinium** ㉓ (room with two benches); the **Qattar ad-Dayr** ㉔ natural rock ledge and water source, which the Nabataeans used as a sanctuary; and the **Hermitage** ㉕, a perch-like chamber with many carved crosses. At the summit of the mountain is the open plain where the Nabataeans carved ad-

BELOW: the colonnaded street.

Dayr. This mid-1st century AD Nabataean temple or royal tomb has Petra's largest facade (45 by 50 metres/130 ft by 164 ft), and boasts some classical Nabataean capitals. Like Qasr al-Bint, it also has an open-air altar (just north of the courtyard, near the steps to the urn on top of the tomb, now blocked off). The name ad-Dayr ("the monastery") derives from the crosses scratched in its rear wall. The adjacent plateau has many other monuments, including tombs, water works, tricilinia, decorated niches, and a relief of two men with camels.

The High Place of Sacrifice

Petra's most important and perhaps oldest major cultic facility is the **High Place of Sacrifice ㉖**, or al-Madhbah in Arabic, located on top of Jabal (Mount) al-Madhbah, 200 metres (650 ft) above the theatre. Those who have the time should make the three-hour circular trip to the High Place, to complement their walk through the city centre. Such a trip is best made in the early morning. The route up via the Wadi Mataha starts near the theatre, and follows the Nabataean processional way that passes by two huge stone-carved obelisks (probably representations of deities) just before reaching the High Place. The remains of the fort you have to walk through to reach the High Place are probably those of a Nabataean defensive/lookout facility, or perhaps the stately entrance to the High Place of Sacrifice itself.

The Nabataeans may have inherited the High Place of Sacrifice from the Edomites. This important religious facility comprised two adjacent altars and associated cultic installations, an open central court with a small raised platform for offerings and shallow benches around three sides, and a nearby pool, water channels and drains – probably used for animal sacrifices.

BELOW LEFT: a tattooed lady in front of the Lion's Fountain.
BELOW RIGHT: the Renaissance Tomb.

From the High Place, you can return to the city centre via the **Wadi Farasa**, with its collection of fine monuments. You can see Nabataean inscriptions (near ground-level) in the rocks to your right just after starting down from the High Place. The first major monument you come upon is the **Lion Monument ㉗**, a 5-metre (16-ft) long, rock-carved cultic fountain; a few metres away is a small stone-cut altar. The water that emerged from the lion's mouth reached the city centre in a water channel that runs parallel with the staircase from the Lion Monument that winds down to the Wadi Farasa.

The first monument in the *wadi* is the **Garden Temple Complex ㉘**. It includes a small shrine, and an associated terrace complex above the temple with a once-arched room and a large plastered cistern. Water reached the city centre from here through a distribution system of cisterns, channels and ceramic pipes.

The next complex in Wadi Farasa is the **Roman Soldier Tomb ㉙** and its Triclinium. Note the three statues in Roman military dress in niches on the tomb facade. The Triclinium sports Petra's most spectacular interior today, due to the weathering of the rock. Further down Wadi Farasa on your right is the **Renaissance Tomb ㉚**, with its delicate facade of Nabataean capitals and six urns, and then the **Broken Pediment Tomb ㉛** perched on a raised recess.

The Wadi Farasa trail towards the city centre passes through an area full of rock-cut tombs and houses, crosses the low remains of a small gate within the South City Wall, and finally meanders through the area of **al-Katuta**, which is thought to have been used as the town rubbish dump in the 2nd century AD (that's why there is so much broken pottery on the ground).

The path then passes the rocky summit of az-Zantur before reaching **Pharoun's (Pharaoh's) Pillar ㉜**, one of two pillars which marked the entrance

Map on pages 240–241

A winged lion, chiselled from the red and honey-coloured stone at Petra.

BELOW: high views from the High Place.

The distinctive marbling of Petra rock.

to a Nabataean temple that lies unexcavated in the hillside. It is possible that this structure was located next to a road that entered Petra from the south and that brought camels and goods to the so-called "markets" above the colonnaded street. Recent excavations in this region have uncovered domestic and cultic structures, including a Byzantine church, dating from the 1st to the 6th centuries AD.

Further afield

From this area south of the city centre, the hardy can head off on foot or horseback to visit two distant sites, each requiring over two hours to reach. The Nabataean suburb of **Wadi Sabra** still shows the remains of a small theatre, several major buildings, a possible baths, a water catchment system, cisterns, tombs, niches and other remains from the Nabataean and Roman periods.

At the highest summit in the Petra region – 1,350 metres (4,430 ft) above sea level – is the shrine and 14th-century **mosque of Nebi Harun** (the Prophet Aaron), which enjoys a marvellous view of the region. The white dome of the mosque can be seen from most areas in and around Petra.

On the opposite, north side of the city centre, visitors can also explore slightly out of the way districts of Petra such as **Mughar an-Nasara** (the "Christian" or "Nazarene caves", so called because of the crosses that are carved into some tomb walls). This unspoilt area has many tombs, cisterns and altars, traces of the ancient northern entrance to Petra, a rare triclinium adorned with four shields and two Medusa heads, and some of Petra's most bizarre and colourful natural rock formations. (The adventurous and fit can exit Petra from Mughar an-Nasara by walking for about an hour to the north and then east, around Jabal

BELOW:
sunset over Petra.

Khubtha and parallel to the rock-cut water channel that linked the pools near the Petra Forum Hotel and the Palace Tomb.)

A kilometre (½ mile) north of Mughar an-Nasara is the new Bdul village at **Umm Sayhun**, near an ancient quarry, cultic altars, tombs and hydraulic installations. And 15 minutes by foot west of Mughar an-Nasara, on the other side of Wadi Umm Sayhun, is **Conway Tower** (al-Mudawwara in Arabic). This 25-metre (82-ft) diameter tower fortified the northwest corner of the Nabataean town walls and overlooks the entire region.

Two other outlying districts well worth visiting are located immediately west of Mughar an-Nasara. **Wadi Turkmaniyya** has the very important **Turkmaniyya Tomb**, whose upper facade boasts the longest known Nabataean inscription. It mentions the facilities that a proper Nabataean tomb complex should have: tomb, triclinium, cistern, courtyard, portico, gardens, houses, terraces and other facilities (most of which can be seen at the Roman Soldier Tomb or the Tomb of Unayshu). West of Turkmaniyya is **Jabal al Mu'aysra**, a rarely visited area full of tombs, water works, cultic installations, and processional ways.

Ten thousand years of history

Within half an hour's drive from Petra are several interesting archaeological sites that fill in important periods in the past 10,000 years of human civilisation in the Middle East. Three of these sites are located alongside the paved road that heads north from the visitors' centre and past the Petra Forum Hotel.

Wu'ayra Crusader Castle ㉝, west of the road about a kilometre (½ mile) north of the hotel, was built in the early 12th century and abandoned when

Map on pages 240–241

The crusaders who built the castle at Wu'eira would have been the last western eyes to rest upon Petra for over 500 years, until Burckhardt reawakened this sacred site to the attentions of Europe in 1812.

LEFT: pretty pictures in the sand. **BELOW:** a sand artist at work.

Map
on pages
240–241

Salaheddeen (Saladin) defeated the Crusaders in Jordan in 1189. The Crusaders called this region La Vallée de Moise (the Valley of Moses), a name that retains a link to the present Arabic name of the town of **Wadi Musa** (which also means the Valley of Moses). The dramatic entrance bridge over a precipitous moat (not for the fainthearted) leads into a roughly rectangular fortress, still sporting some of its defensive walls, towers, vaults, cisterns and internal structures, including a possible church.

Siq al-Barid, 10 minutes by car to the north, was a prosperous "suburb" of Petra located at the junction of ancient caravan routes that linked Petra with the Wadi Araba/Dead Sea region, Gaza, the Palestine coast, Egypt and the Mediterranean basin. Several immense cisterns carved into the rocks are still used today by local livestockers. The name Siq al-Barid comes from the miniature *siq* (fissure) that gives access to a splendid collection of tombs, temples, triclinia, houses, cisterns, water channels, niches, cultic installations, staircases and other structures. One small biclinium (room with two benches) still has the remains of 1st-century fresco paintings with floral motifs, birds, and classical mythological figures including Pan and Eros.

Five minutes to the southwest (by rough dirt track) is one of Jordan's most compelling attractions – the Neolithic village of **al Bayda**. This early farming and livestock settlement still retains standing walls, staircases, hearths, grinding stones, plastered floors, doorways and cultic installations dating from 7000–6500 BC, a period of transition for humans from nomadic hunter-gatherers to year-round settled farmers. Neolithic fans can also visit a similar excavated site at **Basta**, half an hour to the southeast.

Fifteen minutes by car east of Petra is the important ancient site at **Adhruh**, whose spring and strategic location were the main reasons for its almost uninterrupted settlement since the Iron Age, approximately 3,000 years ago. The main remains above ground today are the external walls and towers of a Roman legionary fortress, though the site was also important in the Nabataean and early Islamic eras.

Another Roman fortress can be visited at **Daajaniyya**, a 10-minute drive over a desert track southwest of the junction of the Desert Highway and the east–west road to Shawbak and Petra. Its standing fortifications and water system are particularly impressive. Like most of the forts along the southeastern frontier of the Roman Empire, it was probably built in the 2nd century AD, and abandoned during the decline of Roman power in this area between the 5th and 6th centuries.

The most recent historical period – the late Ottoman era of the end of the 19th/early 20th century – is well represented at **At Tayyiba**, a 10-minute drive south of Petra. This traditional Jordanian village has been recently renovated into a pleasant tourist village equipped with modern amenities but still retaining the buildings and atmosphere of turn-of-the-century Jordan. Similar traditional village architecture is visible throughout the Petra area; a good, easily accessible example is **Khirbet Nawafleh**, on the north side of Wadi Musa town. ❏

BELOW:
a tight squeeze.

Burckhardt

It was with some reticence that a young Swiss explorer summed up his visit, on 22 August 1812, to one of the legendary sites of the Middle East. "It appears very probable," he said, "that the ruins in Wady Mousa are those of the ancient Petra." Johann Ludwig Burckhardt was the first Westerner for 600 years to see the capital of the ancient Nabataeans.

Burckhardt was born in Basle in 1784, the son of a wealthy merchant. After university in Germany, he spent two years in London, with no work and dwindling finances, before a fruitful introduction to Sir Joseph Banks, a member of the Association for Promoting the Discovery of the Interior Parts of Africa. The association had hit on the idea of exploring caravan routes as a means of finding the source of the River Niger. Undeterred by the death or disappearance of everyone so far sent on this mission, Louis offered his services and was accepted.

After a crash course in Arabic at Cambridge University, he set off in March 1809 for Syria, where he perfected his Arabic and adopted the clothes and manners of his chosen alias, Ibrahim ibn Abdullah, a Moorish trader. Once master of the local dialect, he began travelling with the Bedouin. He explored large areas of Syria and Lebanon, taking copious notes as he went – secretly, for discovery could have cost him his life. So, too, could any inappropriate gesture. During interludes in Aleppo he studied Islam, wrote a treatise on Bedouin customs, a classification of the Bedouin tribes on the Syrian borders and notes on geography.

In spring 1812 "Ibrahim ibn Abdullah" finally left Syria for Cairo. En route he visited Jarash, Amman and Karak, where he was delayed for 20 days by the sheikh, who demanded protection money. At Tafila he detached himself from this "treacherous friend", and continued southward with a Bedouin guide called Hamid.

After leaving Shawbak, Burckhardt wanted to deviate from the route agreed with his Bedouin guide in order to see some ruins in the valley of Wadi Musa which the local people had spoken of with admiration. Knowing that this would arouse suspicion, he feigned a vow to sacrifice a goat at the shrine of Harun (Aaron) at the end of the valley. With a local guide and a goat for the sacrifice, he made his way through the ruins towards Jabal Harun (Mount Aaron), hiding his interest in the monuments lest he be taken for a magician. He went into the Treasury, passed the Theatre and observed the Royal Tombs, noting everything in his journal.

The sun was setting as they reached Jabal Harun, and the guide became agitated, so Burckhardt reluctantly agreed to sacrifice the goat there and then. The next day he resumed his journey south. He regretted not going to the top of the mountain – as he wrote, "a traveller ought, if possible, to see everything with his own eyes." He added, with characteristic modesty, "Whether or not I have discovered the remains of the capital of Arabia Petraea, I leave to the decision of Greek scholars." The Greek scholars confirmed that he had. ❑

RIGHT: a portrait of Burckhardt.

WADI RUM

Wadi Rum is one of the great natural landscapes of the world: a dramatic and inspiring terrain through which pilgrims, traders and herdsmen have journeyed for millennia

From the heights of Ras an-Naqab the land falls away abruptly to the south into the Quwayra plain, an expanse of pinkish sandy desert some 600 metres (1,970 ft) below. Pinnacles and broken ramparts of rock thrust upwards from the desert floor, stacked one behind another to a distant hazy vanishing point. Coming from the north, this is the first view of the vast tract of southeastern Jordan known as Wadi Rum. The forces of nature have colluded in sculpting a landscape designed to intimidate. The desert, the space, the sky and the silence thundering through the palisades are colossal, inspiring T. E. Lawrence in *Seven Pillars of Wisdom* to pen perhaps the best description of Rum: "vast, echoing and godlike."

What's in a name?

The area teakes its name from the largest and grandest of a whole networkof wadis (valleys) which for millennnia offered the easiest passage to the nomadic Bedouin and to trading caravans en route to or from the Arabian peninsula. Rum itself is believed to derive from the ancient Semitic word *irum*, meaning "high" or "heights", a probable reference to the enormous crags that erupted from the sands millions of years ago. More recent desriptions of Rum tend to focus on the "moonscape" of Rum, an allusion to both its erratic terrain – alternately shifting sand and parched, cracked earth – and, perhaps, its eternal, impenetrable repose.

Rum is also a window through which one can view the history of earth itself, for the stratification of some 600 million years has been identified here. Sharp eyes will also find traces of earliest life fossilised in the cliffs.

Although overwhelming, Rum is not foreboding, and there are several different ways to enjoy it, depending on personal taste and level of fitness – hiking, climbing, on camel back or by four wheel drive, under sun-hats or under the stars. There are dozens of bird species, the elegant but rare ibex and the dainty Arabian sand cat to be seen, as well as plants and herbs used in Bedouin medicine.

The Bedouin of the Howeitat tribe are likely to feature in your visit. They run many of the facilities in the area, and are the best guides.

Visiting Wadi Rum

There are various options for visiting the area. Ordinary cars can reach the village of Rum, the springboard for visiting the area, from the Desert Highway. Ten km (6 miles) south of the little town of Quwayra, and about 45 km (28 miles) north of Aqaba, a sign points eastwards along a narrow asphalt road which

PRECEDING PAGES: view above Rum. **LEFT:** ballooning, one of Rum's modern-day attractions. **BELOW:** time to make tracks.

reaches the **village of Wadi Rum** ❶ after 30 km (18½ miles) of increasingly spectacular scenery. The village has a small fort, one of a string built in 1933 by Glubb Pasha as an outpost of the Desert Patrol (now the Bedouin Police) and a government resthouse with a café, bar and basic camping facilities. It is possible to hire a pick-up, complete with Bedouin owner-driver, at the tourist office beside the resthouse to drive for an hour or more into the *wadi* system and see a few places of particular interest, or alternatively to hire a camel and guide. Even if you have your own four-wheel-drive vehicle, it is advisable to hire a guide. There are also walks, scrambles and climbs in the area (see the chapter on Hiking and Climbing, *page 110*).

Overnight camping under a brilliant starry sky is an unforgettable experience, and can be done independently by those with suitable vehicles, equipment, maps and an understanding of the terrain. Alternatively, a handful of companies in Aqaba specialise in arranging camping expeditions and can provide vehicles, drivers, camels, equipment, food and guides, who will also cook, for groups of all sizes. It is, however, best to book through a reputable travel company in Amman.

The geology of Rum

The valley floors are some 900–1,000 metres (2,950–3,280 ft) above sea level, and the great sandstone crags rise sheer a further 500–750 metres (1,640–2,460 ft). Jabal Rum, at 1,754 metres (5,755 ft) above sea level, is the highest peak in the area and the second highest in Jordan; but Jabal Umm Ishrin, just across the *wadi*, falls short by a mere metre.

The cataclysm which 30 million years ago created the Great Rift Valley – run-

TIP

If using a car and guide, establish the length of time, sites to be visited and cost at the tourist office before setting out – for example, the rock "bridge" featured on postcards and on page 265 of this book will take several hours.

BELOW: the sun sets on a desertscape.

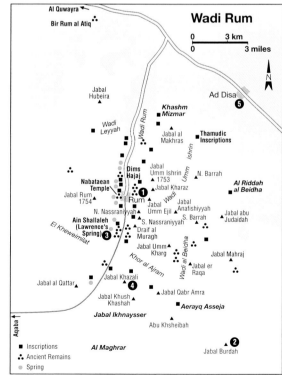

Wadi Rum

ning from southern Turkey through Syria, the Jordan Valley, the Dead Sea, Wadi Araba, the Red Sea and into East Africa – also tossed up the layers of rock here, the deposits of a wide range of geological periods. As the rocks settled, they were rearranged in the strange and complex formations that we see today, in a pattern of criss-crossing fault lines. Most lines run NNE–SSW, roughly parallel to the Wadi Araba rift, but these are traversed by counter-faults running NE–SW, NW–SE, E–W and N–S.

Map on page 260

Mostly hidden beneath the surface lies a crust of pre-Cambrian granites, at least 2,000 million years old. Above it is a vari-coloured mixture of early Palaeozoic sandstones of different periods, textures and colours – rich red Cambrian sandstones, 600 million years old, pale grey Ordovician and whitish Silurian – each separated by up to 100 million years of primitive life on earth. Between them are occasional bands of quartzite, shales, grits and conglomerates. Exposure to rain and wind has sculpted the sandstones into weird shapes that look at times like, giant mushrooms, organ-pipes or dripping candle wax. In **Jabal Burdah ❷**, this process of erosion has created an unbroken arch of rock over a canyon. There is another rock arch on **Jabal Kharaz**, in a remote area some 27 km (17 miles) north of Rum village.

A duty officer of the desert police at Rum.

The rocks were thrown up higher in the west, nearest the rift valley, and all the strata tilt down eastwards. In the western areas the granite rises above the *wadi* floor beneath a mantle of younger sandstones, and several springs are found here, particularly along the east face of Jabal Rum. These springs were created by winter rainfall penetrating the porous sandstone until hitting the sloping layer of impermeable granite, whence the water seeped down into the open and formed pools and waterfalls surrounded by lush foliage.

BELOW:
a parting shot.

Human influences

Today, Wadi Rum lies in the territory of the Howeitat, one of the largest Bedouin tribes in Jordan, who claim descent both from the Prophet Mohammed and from the Nabataeans. They are no longer fully nomadic, for they live in villages in winter, but in the long parched summers they still move around with their flocks and tents in search of pasture.

But early humans, late-comers on to the earth's stage, were in southern Jordan at least 400,000 years ago, in their most primitive Palaeolithic form. Water was plentiful from the springs in Wadi Rum, and they lived by hunting the abundant wildlife with stone-tipped weapons and by gathering fruits and roots in a savannah-like terrain dotted with trees. Very slowly, through the Palaeolithic millennia, the pattern of life evolved from one of almost perpetual motion to a nomadic lifestyle in which temporary camps were re-inhabited periodically, probably on a seasonal basis.

From 9000 BC on, some Neolithic families and groups introduced agriculture and the raising of domestic animals. Increasingly in the Chalcolithic period (4500–3300 BC) semi-permanent seasonal agricultural settlements were established throughout the complex network of *wadis*. Other groups adopted only the pastoral aspect, and continued their nomadic life in search of pasture for their flocks and herds. They ranged over a huge territory, in winter often penetrating deep into the Arabian peninsula. Some became traders, and travelled north, south, east and west, exchanging items of value with the more acquisitive sedentary groups.

The Nabataeans may have started coming here in the 6th century BC, but there is no concrete evidence of their presence until the late 4th century BC,

There are numerous fossil traces of marine creatures which once lived in the shallow tidal waters that recurrently inundated much of Jordan in the Palaeozoic and Mesozoic eras.

BELOW: a guide points out Thamudic inscriptions.

when they controlled all the trade routes through their territory in southern Jordan: frankincense and myrrh from Arabia Felix (modern-day Yemen), spices from India, purple cloth from Phoenicia. Through a subtle blend of trade and protection racket, the Nabataeans became immensely wealthy. Though their main centre was at Petra, they also had settlements in the Hejaz at Medain Saleh, in Sinai and the Negev, and here in Wadi Rum.

Map on page 260

The Nabataeans were not only inspired traders; these erstwhile nomads had acquired a mastery of water resources that enabled them to create settlements larger than many of their contemporaries might have deemed possible. To provide for their settlement in Wadi Rum, they built an aqueduct from the most abundant spring, Ain Shallaleh, to a reservoir in the valley below.

They also constructed three great dams, the largest at Bir Rum al-Atiq, just south of the road from Quwayra, about 6 km (4 miles) west of the Rum Ad Disa junction; another on the west face of Jabal Abu Judaidah; and a third just east of Jabal Mahraj. Towards the end of the reign of the last Nabataean king, Rabbel II (AD 71–106), they built a temple, dedicated to the goddess Allat. Its very tumbled remains lie a short distance due west of the resthouse.

A camel's brightly decorated saddlebag.

Lawrence's pool

Several springs in Wadi Rum have Nabataean rock-cut channels to divert the water into cisterns. T. E. Lawrence found some Nabataean inscriptions when he bathed in the **Pool of Ain Shallaleh** ➌. As Lawrence delighted in the clear, cool waters of the pool, a Bedouin came and peered at him. "After a long stare he seemed content, and closed his eyes, groaning, 'The love is from God; and of God, and towards God.' His low-spoken words were caught by some trick distinctly in my water pool. They stopped me suddenly… the old man of Rumm loomed portentous in his brief, single sentence… In fear of a revelation, I put an end to my bath."

BELOW: armed on patrol.

Coded messages

Something of the story of the nomads and settlers of Rum is inscribed on the faces of the mountains. Some are in the Nabataean script, an individual adaptation of the Aramaic that was current for many centuries throughout Syria; a few were written by Minaean traders from Ma'in in Yemen, in a bold angular script. (The Minaean kingdom flourished between the 5th century BC and the 1st century AD.)

Most common of all are the Thamudic inscriptions, hundreds of them, scratched on the rock faces by centuries of nomads and traders. The tribe of Thamud lived near Medain Saleh in the Hejaz from around the 5th century BC to the 7th century AD. Some inscriptions are simply a signature to a drawing; others are petitions to the Nabataean deities Allat and Dushara; yet others are messages of love or of grief.

For countless centuries, up to the present, the Bedouin have engraved on the rocks representations of the animals, people and events of their world. These images are as enigmatic in their meaning as their date. Outlines of hands and feet, elongated human figures dressed in tunics and hunting scenes

Map on page 260

"To clear my senses by a night in Rumm and by the ride down its dawn-lit valley towards the shining plains...Rumm's glory would not let a man waste himself in feverish regrets."

– T. E. LAWRENCE

BELOW: a great companion.
RIGHT: a natural rock arch.

are common; so too are drawings of ibex and camels; rarer are oxen, and local species of lion, wild ass and ostrich, which once flourished in Jordan. Some interesting and easily accessible drawings can be seen in a gully at the northern end of **Jabal Khazali ❹**.

Another curiosity is the "**topographical stone**" of Jabal Amud, a large stone slab in a cave formed by a rock fall on the south side of the mountain near **Ad Disa ❺**. It is scored with grooves and round depressions which appear to form a pattern. In 1978 some local Bedouin showed it to a team of scholars from Florence University, led by palaeontologist Professor Edoardo Borzatti von Löwenstern.

After several years of research, Borzatti concluded that the stone was a prehistoric map of the area, the depressions representing the positions of Neolithic and Chalcolithic settlements, or enclosures, while the grooves represented *wadis*. He further suggested that it may have been made by Bedouin of those distant times to keep a tally of the protection money, or taxes, that they extracted from settled farmers in return for not raiding their property. Seeing the outlines of the stone superimposed on a map of the area, it is hard not to be impressed with the similarities. However, many scholars remain unconvinced.

Wildlife and conservation

Although Wadi Rum does not teem with wildlife as it did even a few decades ago, if you sit still for a while you can usually see animals and birds appearing as if from nowhere. Hyrax, hares, fennec foxes, jerboas and gerbils come out at dusk, as does the Arabian sand cat, an elusive nocturnal hunter. Nubian ibex and gazelle, once abundant, now survive in residual herds.

Among the birdlife frequenting Rum are desert larks, crested larks, pale rock sparrows and bright pink male Sinai rosefinches with their dowdier wives. Chukar partridges can also be seen, along with Cretzschmar's bunting, redstarts, lesser whitethroats, white-crowned blackchats and yellow wagtails. Three kinds of vultures may be seen – in summer the Egyptian vulture, and at any time the griffon vulture and the lammergeier, the latter a rarity.

In the late 1980s Jordan's Royal Society for the Conservation of Nature (RSCN) proclaimed several new wildlife reserves, including 510 sq. km (197 sq. miles) of Rum. Within this area, it plans to make an enclosure of 75 sq. km (29 sq. miles) into which it will transfer some of the Arabian oryx at Shaumari near Azraq and ibex from the Wadi Mujib Reserve off the King's Highway. Another area of the same size will be designated as a park for tourism, and will include the historical and epigraphic sites, and climbing areas.

The RSCN encourages involvement by the local Bedouin, who know the animal habitats better than anyone. It promotes an approach to conservation that cares for the social and economic needs of the Bedouin as well as conserves the natural environment. It is hoped that the Bedouin will act as conservationists, responsibly managing and benefiting from their superb natural setting. ❑

THE GULF OF AQABA

The warm waters of Aqaba are a perennial draw for Jordanians and tourists alike, and beneath the rolling waves, container ships and pleasure boats is a serene world teeming with marine life

Map on page 270

● Amman

Aqaba

As Jordan's only outlet to the sea the port city of **Al 'Aqaba** evokes a feeling of freedom and a promise of relaxation to most Jordanians, who flock to their country's only real beach resort whenever possible. It is known for its clean, sandy beaches and agreeable climate, especially in the spring, autumn and winter. When the temperature in Amman is a chilly zero–10°C (32°–52°F), the temperature in Aqaba can be a pleasant 25°C (77°F).

But other visitors, especially the growing bands of Italian, German, English and Scandinavian tourists, come for the offshore attractions, for like its Israeli counterpart Eilat, a pebble's-throw across the bay, and Egypt's Ras Mohammed, Aqaba offers world-class scuba-diving on the coral reefs of the Red Sea.

Aqaba is situated on the tip of the Gulf of Aqaba, enclosed by barren, pink- and mauve-tinted mountains rich in phosphates. To the east a string of dark-golden beaches stretch about 20 km (12 miles) along the length of Jordan's coast to the Saudi Arabian border.

PRECEDING PAGES: sunset on the Gulf of Aqaba. **LEFT:** boats leaving the harbour. **BELOW:** a glass-bottomed boat awaiting takers.

Strategic value

Despite its holiday image, Aqaba's chief importance is as a port. It is Jordan's most strategically important city and has been crucial to other countries in the region. It served as a lifeline to Iraq throughout the eight-year Iran-Iraq War, which paralysed the Iraqi port of Basra, and has served as a main point of entry for goods moving into Iraq under the United Nations economic sanctions imposed after the 1990–91 Gulf War. As the number and variety of ships docking at the port and the massive truck-park on Aqaba's approach road testify, the city is the hub of sea-to-land transport routes in Jordan and beyond.

Jordan's economy bloomed during the 1980s, largely as a result of the transport activity that went through Aqaba's port. When the Allies almost closed access here during the 1990–91 Gulf War, the port came to a virtual halt except for ferrying people to and from Egypt. Jordan consequently suffered a crushing blow to its economy. The country still has not recovered from the impact of the crisis, and the port's activities are still slowed by the inspection of goods destined for Iraq.

There is now a fear that regional developments, such as the on-going peace process, the re-emergence of Lebanese ports, the beginnings of a rapprochement between Baghdad and Damascus, the opening and upgrade of ports in the Gulf and the gradual emergence of a Middle Eastern free trade area that will include Israel and its ports may further undermine the status of Jordan's only port.

To first-time visitors, Aqaba's proximity to the

TIP

You won't find much in the way of nightlife or bars in Aqaba, but the waters are a far cry cleaner than anywhere in the Med and beaches are much less crowded than those at Eilat.

Israeli port city of Eilat is astonishing. Indeed, at night the lights of the two cities seem to merge into one twinkling curve, and with the recent opening of the Wadi Araba border crossing between Jordan and Israel, just next to Aqaba, visitors to either country can easily visit the neighbouring port cities.

A long history

Aqaba's history goes back to biblical times at the very least. According to the Old Testament, King Solomon built a naval base at Ezion Geber, some 3 km (1¾ miles) north of modern Aqaba, next to the Jordanian-Israeli border.

From Ezion Geber the Old Testament king traded with the rulers of what is now Somalia and then used his new-found position to oversee trade with the old Kingdom of Sheba (Yemen) and Abyssinia (Ethiopia). The Romans (AD 106), who ruled the region from Bosra in Syria, used the town as one of their main trading stations en route to the sea. In the early 4th century the port city came under the rule of the Byzantine empire and was ruled on their behalf by the Ghassanides, Christian Arab tribes originating from south Arabia.

Ila (as Aqaba was then called) came under Islamic rule in 630–631, when the spread of Islam from the Hejaz reached the peoples of the Red Sea. Twelfth-century Crusaders wrested it from the Muslims and built a fort some 7 km (4 miles) offshore on Far'un Island – then called the Ile de Graye. When Saladin launched his counter-crusade against Western Christendom, he also captured Ila and the former Crusader castle then became known as Saladin's Castle. In 1182, the Crusader Reynald de Chatillon conquered the Island of Graye, but success was short-lived and it was retaken the following year.

With the rise of the Mamluke sultans in Egypt, Aqaba (as they renamed it)

BELOW: the waterfront at Aqaba.

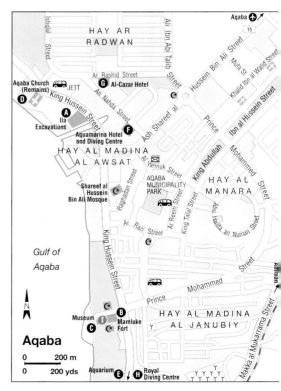

Aqaba

0   200 m
0   200 yds

Map
on page
270

came under Mamluke Egyptian rule. A Mamluke fort was built in the 14th century by Qansah Ghouri, one of the last sultans of the Mamluke era. After the Mamlukes, the Ottomans controlled Aqaba for some 400 years, during which the port declined to a relatively unimportant fishing town.

Aqaba's fortunes revived in the early 20th century. It was of key importance during the Arab Revolt, when Lawrence and the Arab forces prized the port from the Ottomans in 1917 and used it to receive arms shipments from Egypt.

Space is tight along the short Jordanian coast, and Aqaba has only a little room to expand. Already the demands of tourism, industry and shipping are clashing. When shipments of livestock bound for Saudi Arabia arrive from Australia or New Zealand every few weeks or so, they bring unpleasant odours, insects and fleas. So far, hoteliers have simply held their noses, but as tourism continues to develop complaints are likely to rise. Others have raised concerns that hotel construction and other tourism development will interrupt the beautiful views of the mountains surrounding the Gulf, as well as pose an environmental hazard. Environmentalists repeatedly warn of the threats posed by increased potash and phosphate production in the area, including the adverse effects heavy shipping and phosphate dumping are likely to have on the coral reefs.

Most of the port labourers in Aqaba today are Egyptians, Pakistanis or Indians. Prohibited under the restrictions of a migrant labour law from bringing their families with them, this expatriate community tends to be excluded from mainstream life in the town, which is deeply conservative, in spite of Aqaba's growing reputation as an international resort. Most of Aqaba's women wear the *hijab* (Islamic headdress) and strict social mores dictate a largely indoor life (evenings in Aqaba are a good deal more sedate than in Eilat opposite). Family beaches – in effect private or hotel beaches – are separated from male-dominated public beaches, where the Arab women who do swim invariably do so fully clothed.

Aqaba's sights

The remains of **Ila** Ⓐ, Aqaba's medieval forebear, can be visited, although travellers should keep in mind that what can be seen is probably a minute fraction of what existed. The majority of Ila's remains presumably extend far eastwards, buried under 20th century Aqaba. The excavations, begun in 1987, are opposite the Miramar Hotel in the centre of town. Signs in Arabic and English take visitors on a guided tour of the once high-walled city. Historically Ila was on important north–south and east–west trade routes, and even Chinese ships were known to dock here. Evidence of Egyptian, Syrian and Moroccan presence has been found.

At the southeastern end of the corniche don't miss the **Mamluke Fort** Ⓑ. The Hashemite coat of arms over the entrance was added after the Turks were ousted from Aqaba during World War I. Sherif Hussein ben Ali, the leader of the Arab Revolt, resided here. Just below the fort, in an attractively restored complex that also includes the **Department of Antiquities** and the **tourist office**, is a fine **museum** Ⓒ

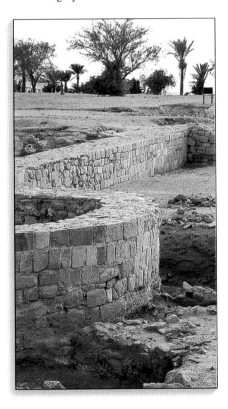

BELOW:
the remains of Ila.

dedicated to local finds, including fragments of lustreware from Samaria and Chinese ceramics. One of the rooms contains an exhibition on traditional Jordanian and Palestinian village architecture by the artist-cum-architect and historian Amar Khammesh.

Although Ila was known to flourish during the Nabataean, Roman and Byzantine periods, antiquities of the pre-Islamic period remained lost until mid-1998, when archaeologists unearthed what may prove to be one of the oldest churches on earth. In front of the JETT bus station, the mud-brick **Aqaba church**  is believed to date from the late 3rd century, making it slightly more ancient than the Church of the Holy Sepulchre in Jerusalem and the Church of the Nativity in Bethlehem, both dating from the 4th century. Most of the early churches in Jordan are thought to date from the late 5th or early 6th century.

The building measures 28 by 24 metres (92 by 79 ft), and walls stand about 4 metres (13 ft) tall around most of the perimeter. Trapped under the rubble of the earthquake that destroyed the church in AD 363 were several artefacts that convinced archaeologists that this had indeed been a church: of the 100 or more coins found on the floor, none were dated later than 360 AD, and a high concentration of oil lamps were identified as chandeliers common to early churches. A nearby cemetery containing a grave marked by a cross added further fuel to the theory that the structure was a church.

After the earthquake the church was filled with sand and never touched again. As early churches tended to metamorphose through long periods of use and reuse, archaeologists expect the Aqaba church to shed new light on the "model" 4th century church structure – that is, if present development plans don't consume this ancient monument first.

In 1965, King Hussein traded land with Saudi Arabia, exchanging about 6,000 sq km of Jordanian desert for 12 km (7½ miles) of valuable coastline.

BELOW: holidaying Jordanians.

Sand and sea

The main appeal of Aqaba is its offshore coral reefs. Deep water lies close to the Gulf coast, creating a fascinating marine environment where divers may encounter a wide variety of species, including the largest fish in the world, the whale shark. The marked diurnal tidal range also supports an interesting array of shore life that can be investigated at low tide, with rocks carpeted in creatures such as limpets, chitons and periwinkles that have adapted to survive the constant to and fro, from submerged world to the air and strong sunlight.

Map on page 270

Before venturing into the deep it is worth visiting the **Aquarium ⊖** in the **Marine Sciences Centre** (on the corniche southeast of town) in order to familiarise yourself with the exotic marine life you may encounter.

In town, the **Aquamarina Hotel and Diving Centre ⊕** offers the best facilities for water skiing, diving, scuba-diving, snorkelling, fishing and sailing, as well as trips in glass-bottomed boats. The **Al-Cazar Hotel ⊕** also organises dives, both during the day and at night – with cameras and lights.

Enjoying a quieter location 15 km (9 miles) out of town (4 km/2½ miles from the Saudi border) is the **Royal Diving Centre ⊕**, run by an English couple but set up by King Hussein. It offers scuba-diving lessons on a number of nearby reefs. The centre has a pool, changing facilities and expensive snack-bar, but no accommodation (the neighbouring holiday homes are for use by high-ranking police officers on vacation). However, a daily mini-bus service transports people to the centre from Aqaba's main hotels and taxis ply the route.

Independent private sailing is not allowed in Aqaba for security reasons – but arranged trips through one of the centres is possible. Boat trips to **Saladin's Castle** (which lies in Egyptian waters) run daily, providing the number of visitors is sufficient to make the journey worth the while of the boat captain; enquire at the Aquamarina Hotel for further details of sailings.

Aqaba's beaches are generally clean, especially the beaches belonging to the hotels. The public beaches are on the southeastern side of town. If you are not staying at a hotel with its own stretch of beach you will have to pay a fairly steep entrance fee to use a hotel's facilities. However, this may be worth it, especially for women travelling without male company. While nothing dangerous ever really happens in Aqaba, the prospect of staring, giggling men can ruin one's enjoyment.

The clear and shallow coastal waters are home to a vast array of aquatic and semi-aquatic life.

BELOW:
pupils of the Royal Diving Centre take the plunge.

In search of seafood

In spite of the great potential for seafood restaurants there are still only a few upmarket eateries in town. The Holiday Inn has a good Continental restaurant (at Continental prices) and a live band offers nightly entertainment in its air-conditioned bar – frequented by expatriates and wealthier Jordanians.

Otherwise, try **Ali Baba**, a fish restaurant which specialises in *masgoof* (grilled fish), and has an outdoor terrace, or **China Restaurant** in the commercial centre of town.

Below and to the east of the museum is **Mina House**, which was converted from an old tugboat and offers barbecued meats and fish. ❑

THE RED SEA – A WORLD APART

It takes little effort to appreciate the amazing diversity of Aqaba's aquatic life, whether in the coastal shallows or the depths of the Gulf

Almost any spot along Jordan's short Red Sea coastline offers a promising escape into an underwater world teeming with colour and life. For experienced divers, it is simply a matter of choosing an enticing section of coast, getting on their gear and climbing into Aqaba's calm waters, conducive to diving all year around. Newcomers to the sport can take guidance from the dive centres in town, and even those who don't want to do more than paddle in the shallows will find a wealth of marine life.

The most productive dives are to be had along the southern extremities of Aqaba, where aquatic life begins in the shallows, often replete with the tumbling, prickly sea urchins that demand some careful treading. A scintillating world of corals, sponges and sea fans thrives as little as 15 metres (49 ft) below the surface.

Other attractions include the shy globe fish – also known as the puffer fish for its amusing ability to swell its body into a near-perfect sphere when threatened – and the occasional whale shark, the largest fish in the world. This perfectly harmless fish is attracted by plankton in the northern shallows and, at certain times of the year, its mating call can be heard when diving or snorkelling around Aqaba.

▽ **SEA MONSTERS**
Divers find themselves in the company of clown fish, scorpion fish, Picasso trigger fish, goby, angel fish, surgeon fish and moray eels, like this one.

◁ A STING IN THE TAIL

Jellyfish drift with the sea currents, and carry a painful sting. Out of the water, the pain can be eased with a dousing of vinegar or, if necessary, urine.

△ HOT WATER

Rarely does the water drop below 20°C (68°F) and in summer it hovers at 26°C (79°F). Mild currents allow good visibility from May until February.

THAT SINKING FEELING

Diving centres in Aqaba recognise 14 dive sites, and favourites within the town's diving community include excursions to the *Cedar Pride* and to the *Gorgonian I*. The *Cedar Pride* was a Lebanese transport ship, which, having burned in the port, was deliberately sunk in 1985 to foster coral growth. It now lies pitched on its side in 27 metres (89 ft) of water. Although the corals are still in their infancy, the ship's body is well colonised and patronised by several shoals.

The profusion of hard and soft corals and brilliant reef fish has earned *Gorgonian I* a reputation as one of the finest dive sites in the Gulf of Aqaba, and it is recommended for both novices and experienced divers.

You needn't be an old hand to enjoy the reefs. The Aquamarina hotels, the Al Cazar hotel (in the town) and the Royal Diving Centre (on the south beach) are all accredited for tuition. They organise dives (including night dives and independently guided dives) and rent out equipment.

△ SUNKEN TREASURES

Roughly 100 metres/yards from the shore, submarine cliffs plunge towards a profusion of marine life, such as this angel fish.

◁ STAR FISH

The dramatic-looking Dragonfish, one of the stars of the coral reefs.

▷ ARABIAN HORSES

Jordan is renowned for the equine horses of the desert, but the beguiling form of the sub-aquatic sea horse has an appeal of its own.

BEYOND JORDAN

A brief guide to sites beyond Jordan's borders, across the river in the West Bank and north into Syria

Designed as a taster rather than as a comprehensive survey, the following chapters cover the West Bank cities of Jerusalem, Bethlehem, Hebron, Jericho and Ramallah – the highlights of any Holy Land tour – and offer an introduction to the best of Syria – an historic land of fabled cities and remote antiquities.

Tourism pays only passing attention to the politics of the Middle East, and many organised tours already hop between the banks of the River Jordan. If a state of Palestine ever becomes a reality, this traffic will increase enormously, boosting tourism for the whole region, including Syria and Lebanon (a factor which also puts archaeology on the bargaining table). In the meantime, anyone travelling independently to the West Bank from Jordan must contend with a certain amount of red tape and should heed any sudden political developments. (Advice on surmounting the bureaucratic hurdles and arranging transport is included in the *Travel Tips* section of this book.)

Straying into Syria is a natural extension for many travellers to Jordan, for, while the River Jordan creates a natural border to the west, the modern border with Syria is an arbitrary disruption to both geographical and historical realities. Though relations between Jordan and Syria have been decidedly frosty in the past, both countries now see their economic destinies best served through cooperation. This is already happening in their planning for tourism, where joint efforts are being made in site development, tour organisation and improved transport facilities.

Like Jordan, modern Syria is a 20th-century entity, created in the wake of World War I and the breakup of the Ottoman Empire. Prior to this, the name had historically referred to the whole area covered by Lebanon, Syria, Palestine and Transjordan, a unit whose frontiers were the Taurus Mountains, the sea, the Euphrates, and the deserts. Historical Syria was located geographically between the great civilisations of the east (Mesopotamia and Persia), the West (Europe), the north (Anatolia), and the south (Egypt). Syria, in the middle, was a true crossroads of civilisations and cultures, the natural battleground not only of armies but also of ideas. The result is a magnificent heritage of peoples, cultural expressions and monuments that has drawn the most eminent explorers and Orientalists. ❑

PRECEDING PAGES: the Church of the Holy Sepulchre; the Dome of the Rock.
LEFT: an elaborately embroidered dress from the West Bank town of Ramallah.

THE WEST BANK

The contested territory of the West Bank has been the scene of fierce religious devotion and conflict. This chapter concentrates on the West Bank's most notable sites

Map
on page
284

T he Old City of Jerusalem, Bethlehem, Hebron and Jericho lie just a couple of hours' drive from Amman, albeit across the Jordan River, a precious if unimpressive waterway that doubles as a formidable border. Together with their surrounding lands, these historic cities comprise the West Bank – part of the area earmarked for Palestine in the 1948 carve-up of the region, but annexed by Jordan in the subsequent Arab-Israeli War and then occupied by Israel after the 1967 war. The region's history under Israeli occupation, including the rise of the *intifada*, the Palestinian uprising that began in 1987, is recorded in the history section of this guide.

In 1993, the Oslo peace accords were signed by PLO Chairman Yasser Arafat and Israel's then-prime minister Yitzhak Rabin (who was subsequently murdered by a Jewish right-wing extremist), paving the way for gradual Israeli withdrawal from the West Bank. The agreement gave Palestinians real hope of attaining a state in the near future. Within a year Israeli troops had withdrawn from most of Gaza and Jericho. By 1995, the new Palestinian Authority's jurisdiction covered most major West Bank towns and eventually parts of Hebron, though Israel retained control over Hebron's holy shrine, the Tomb of the Patriarchs, and Jewish settlements in the heart of the city. At the same time, some 10,000 Palestinians in Hebron continue to live under Israeli military rule.

LEFT: inside the Damascus Gate. **BELOW:** a quiet corner of Haram al-Sherif.

A new Palestine

Autonomous, but not yet independent, Palestine now has its own postage stamps and international dialling code (still to come into effect), and its observer status at the United Nations has been upgraded. In 1996, the first democratic elections were held in the Palestinian Autonomous areas. Yasser Arafat was elected president (he now governs from Gaza), and the first Palestinian Legislative Council was elected that same year. In 1998 Gaza International Airport opened to great fanfare, its first plane arriving from Cairo, packed with Egyptian celebrities.

However, prospects for Palestine are not as glowing as they were when the Oslo agreement was signed. Since the election of the right-wing Israeli government led by Binyamin Netanyahu the peace process has been at a virtual standstill.

This does not bode well for a compromise on the most difficult issues of all, such as refugees, Israeli settlements and East Jerusalem, which will be the focus of final status negotiations between the two sides. At the same time, radical Jewish settlers and the anti-PLO Islamic movements Hamas and Islamic Jihad both reject the land for peace formula and remain committed to derailing the peace process.

A Palestinian waits by a border bus at the crossing from Jordan to the West Bank territory.

BELOW: the Western Wall in Jerusalem.

Tourist travel

Tourism pays only passing attention to politics and many organised tours hop between the banks of the Jordan River. It is also quite easy to travel independently to the West Bank from Jordan, although visitors must contend with a certain amount of red tape and should heed any sudden political developments. (Advice on surmounting the bureaucratic hurdles and arranging transport is included in the *Travel Tips* section at the back of this book.) Designed as a taster rather than as a comprehensive survey, the following chapter covers Jerusalem, Bethlehem, Hebron and Jericho – the highlights of the Holyland Tour – and Ramallah, a bourgeoning Palestinian city.

Jerusalem

Al-Quds, Yerushalayim, **Jerusalem ❶**. Whatever language one prefers to use, Jerusalem is one of the most resonant place names on earth. Closely associated with David, Christ and Mohammed, the city is central to the three monotheistic faiths, and contains many of their holiest shrines. Jews mourn the destruction of the First and Second temples at the Western Wall, Muslims revere the Dome of the Rock, the site of Mohammed's ascent to heaven, and Christians from all over the world make pilgrimages to the Church of the Holy Sepulchre, believed to be the site of Christ's crucifixion and burial.

Yet Jerusalem has witnessed some of the most brutal episodes in history. Since the first people of Jerusalem – the Canaanites (c.2000 BC) – ruled the city, it has been conquered 18 times by people as varied as the Israelites under King David (1,000 BC), the Muslims of Arabia (7th century) and the European Crusaders, at the end of the 11th century. In the 20th century alone, Jerusalem

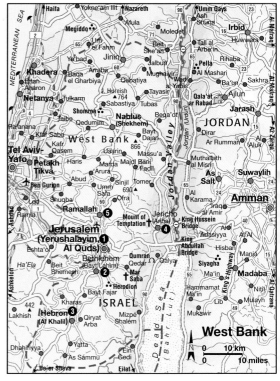

was ruled by Ottoman Turks, the British Mandate Government of Palestine, the Hashemite Kingdom of Jordan and the government of modern Israel. Divided into East (Arab) Jerusalem and West (Israeli) Jerusalem between 1948 and 1967, the city was reunited by Israel in the 1967 War. It remains disputed territory and the crux of any real Israeli-Palestinian peace agreement. While Israelis say Jerusalem is their undivided eternal capital, the Palestinians want a Palestinian state in the West Bank and Gaza, with East Jerusalem as its capital.

East Jerusalem

Home to the Old City, East Jerusalem is a congested maze of streets crammed with shops, street vendors, schoolchildren, foreign companies, consulates and would-be representatives to the "State of Palestine". A number of old neighbourhoods, such as **Wadi Joz** and **Sheikh Jarrah**, have many fine old houses built in the traditional Arab style, which are well worth closer inspection. Most of the action of East Jerusalem takes place on three main thoroughfares leading into the walled Old City: **Salahedin Street** (after Salah-ad-Din), **Nablus Road** and **al-Zahra Street**.

There are a number of interesting sights off these main streets. A short walk out of the Old City, along a tree-lined lane signposted off Nablus Road, for instance, brings you to the Protestant Golgotha, the **Garden Tomb**. British General Gordon, in 1883, identified this as the site of Christ's burial and Crucifixion (instead of the Church of the Holy Sepulchre); two small low rooms contain a 1st-century tomb.

Nearby, opposite the American consulate, is the **Palestinian Pottery Shop**, established by one of the Armenian families brought to Jerusalem in the 19th

Map on page 284

TIP

Independent travellers usually find it convenient to go to Jerusalem in a shared taxi (known as *serveece* in Arabic) which drops passengers off at Damascus Gate – the oldest and most magnificent entrance – on al-Zahra Street.

BELOW:
Damascus Gate.

century to produce the exquisite tile work of the Dome of the Rock. Today, Armenian pottery is sold at the shop, and can be made to order as well. Also here is **King Solomon's Quarry**, believed to have supplied the Jewish Temple of Jerusalem and the 5th-century mausoleum to the Unknown Soldiers of Armenia. A 10-minute walk from the quarry, on an unmarked road, is the **Armenian Convent of Polyeucte**. Once part of a private home, the convent contains one of the most impressive mosaic floors in Jerusalem.

Near the intersection of Salahedin Street and Nablus Road is the **Tomb of Kings** – once thought to be the burial site of the Kings of Judah. The subterranean tombs (take a torch if you want to explore) are believed to date from Babylonian times. To get an overview of the multiple layers of Jerusalem's history, the superb **Rockefeller Museum** (near Herod's Gate) provides information in a nutshell, while the **Palestinian Arab Folklore Centre**, on Obeid ibn Jarrah Street, displays further artefacts of historical and cultural importance.

David Ben Gurion, Israel's first prime minister, suggested razing the Old City walls to promote the unity of the city following his country's military victory in 1967. Needless to say, the proposal was rejected.

The Old City

Set in the middle of a wide plain, the Old City is contained by a wall as high as 12 metres (40 ft) in some places, built by the Ottoman Sultan Suleiman the Magnificent in 1537–40. The Old City walls are pierced by seven operational gates and one that has been blocked for centuries. A walk on the ramparts provides spectacular views and takes approximately half an hour. Admission tickets can be purchased at **Damascus Gate** (Bab al Amoud) and **Jaffa Gate** (Bab al-Khalil), and can be used several times over the course of two days. However, women are not advised to go alone. We begin a tour of the Old City with Jaffa Gate, closer to West Jerusalem.

BELOW:
Jerusalem from the Mount of Olives.

Jaffa Gate leads into a maze of mostly British-built churches and hospices, but just inside the gate is the **Citadel**, known as Phaesal's Tower, and one of only three remaining towers built by Herod. Burned down during the Jewish revolt of AD 66 and again in AD 70 when Titus razed Jerusalem, it was named David's Tower by the Byzantines. Suleiman the Magnificent is largely responsible for its present shape, although the minaret was added in 1635.

Map on page 284

Armenian Quarter

A right turn off Omar ibn Khattab Square leads to the Armenian Quarter, one of the most peaceful quarters in the city (also accessible through Zion Gate). The Armenian community, originally from the Caucasus, has lived in Jerusalem for over 1,000 years and still has its own language and alphabet. The first to adopt Christianity as a national religion (AD 310), the community has an important place in the history of Christianity and Jerusalem. Today, the quarter numbers some 4,000 people. This area is home to the **Armenian library** and the **Mardigian Museum of Armenian Art and History**, and at the centre of the quarter is one of the most beautiful structures in the Old City, **St James Cathedral**, which has existed in one form or another since the 5th century.

Exhibit in the Citadel Museum.

Beyond the cathedral stands the **Convent of the Olive Tree**, where Jesus was bound before his Crucifixion, while caretakers of the Assyrian Convent, on Ararat Street, claim that the Virgin Mary was baptised on the site of **St Mark's Church**, in the midst of their convent.

In addition to religious and historical sites, the workshops of the Armenian craftsmen located on the main road through the quarter are worth a visit. And the best place to stop for a moderately priced meal in this neighbourhood is

Follow the signs.

BELOW:
Orthodox Jews.

the **Armenian Tavern**, on the Armenian Orthodox Patriarchate Road. The mural by the well-stocked bar was painted by the owner's mother-in-law and the tiles are local work.

Jewish Quarter

East from the Armenian quarter is the Old City's Jewish Quarter, which has been repeatedly destroyed through the ages. Most recently, it was damaged during the Arab-Israeli War of 1948, when Jordanian forces demolished most of the synagogues. The Israelis repaired the buildings after they captured the city in 1967 and today the quarter looks clean and new, if a little sterile compared with the other quarters of the Old City.

Until 1948 most of Jerusalem's Jewish residents were Eastern or Sephardic Jews (today many are North American), and one of the most impressive sights in the quarter is formed by the four **Sephardic Synagogues**, originally built in the 17th century but altered and embellished numerous times since. The ancient Roman processional thoroughfare, the **Cardo**, is another magnificent site. Originally built by Hadrian (AD 117–138), it was extended by the Byzantines to link the Holy Sepulchre and the Nea Church. The Nea was built by Justianian in 543, but destroyed during the Persian conquest of 614; today, hardly anything remains of it.

Other highlights of this quarter include the **Ophel Archaeological Park**, often referred to as the Western Wall excavations, which contains finds dating from the Herodian, Byzantine and Arab periods. The site was recently expanded in honour of the controversial year-long Jerusalem 3,000 celebrations. The excavations border **Dung Gate**, its name a reminder that in past centuries the city's rubbish left via this gateway, though it is also known as the Moorish Gate (an allusion to the Moroccan community that traditionally settled around here). It is the only one of the seven open gates of the Old City that leads directly into the Jewish Quarter.

Just past the gate is the holiest site in Judaism: the **Western Wall** (known in Hebrew as Hakotel Hama' aravi) which is a retaining wall of the Temple (destroyed in AD 70). Over the centuries, Jews have come to pray at the wall to lament the destruction of their two temples, the reason many non-Jews refer to it as the Wailing Wall. Visitors leave notes of prayer in the cracks and crevices of the stone.

The Western Wall Plaza is especially crowded during the holidays of Sukkot, Passover and Shavuot – in keeping with an ancient tradition of pilgrimage to the Temple – as well as on the Sabbath when mainly Orthodox Jews come to "welcome the Sabbath bride". Young men from the nearby *yeshivas* (religious colleges) sing and dance in procession to the wall on Friday evenings.

Now considered an Orthodox synagogue, the Western Wall is divided into men's and women's prayer areas, and strictly adheres to conservative codes of dress. Men must cover their heads (cardboard skullcaps are supplied free of charge). Photographs and smoking are strictly forbidden on the Sabbath.

The plaza in front of the Wall was originally quite

small but after Israel captured the Old City in the 1967 war, the Moorish Quarter which was adjacent to the wall was bulldozed. The newest (and most controversial) feature is the 480-metre (1,550-ft) **Hasmonean tunnel**. The entrance, to the left of the Western Wall, sparked Palestinian riots when it was opened in September 1996 – many Muslims believe the excavations undermine the foundations of Islam's holy places.

Map on page 284

Muslim Shrines

To the right of the Wall is the entrance to the **Haram al-Sherif** (the Noble Sanctuary), known as the Temple Mount by Jews because it was the site of the First Temple (955–587 BC) and Second Temple (515 BC – AD 70). Eleven gates, two of which are permanently closed, lead to the Noble Sanctuary. Here is the **Dome of the Rock**, Islam's third holiest site, as well as the **Al-Aqsa Mosque** and the **Islamic Museum**.

As the site of Mohammed's ascension to heaven, Jerusalem was the place to which all Muslims turned to pray. The direction of prayer was later changed to Mecca.

The two mosques are among the most impressive shrines in the Muslim world. The rock enshrined by the Dome of the Rock is held to be the spot where Abraham prepared to sacrifice his son Isaaac and it is holy to Muslims and Jews alike. According to Muslim tradition, the Prophet Mohammed flew to Jerusalem from Mecca on his horse and from the Rock of Abraham ascended to heaven, only to return to Mecca at dawn. When Omar ibn al-Khattab, the Second Caliph (634–644), captured Jerusalem, he headed straight for the area around the rock, then used as a dump by the Byzantine Christians. Seeing the decay around it, the caliph had a small mosque built over the rock to protect it. The Dome of the Rock itself was built in 691 by Caliph Abd al-Malik ibn Marwan. Its shimmering 24-carat gilded dome was a gift from King Hussein of Jordan, who reportedly sold one of his London estates

BELOW: a dried-goods salesman in the Arab quarter.

to pay for its restoration. Apart from during prayer times and on Fridays, visitors are allowed inside (shoes must be removed). In a cave-like chamber beneath the rock are small tabernacles dedicated to Abraham and Elijah. The **Well of Souls** lies beneath.

The **Al-Aqsa Mosque**, first constructed in 715 by Walid ibn Abd al-Malik, has been repeatedly damaged by earthquakes and rebuilt. Its present form dates from 1033. During the Crusades it was known as Templum and both the Crusaders and the Knights Templar set up their administrative quarters in the mosque. It was on the steps of Al-Aqsa that King Abdullah of Jordan was assassinated in 1951, in front of his young grandson Hussein.

The **Golden Gate** (in fact, a double gate comprising the Gate of Mercy and the Gate of Repentance), the original entrance to Haram al-Sherif, has been sealed since 1530. Some believe that the Messiah will enter Jerusalem through this gate.

Leaving Haram al-Sherif from either the **Absolution Gate** (Bab al-Hitta) or the **Gate of Darkness** (Bab al-Atm) is the easiest way to enter the Muslim Quarter of Jerusalem (unlike the other quarters, this quarter contains both Muslim and Christian houses of worship). Another way to enter directly into the Muslim Quarter is through Damascus Gate or Herod's Gate (also known as Flowers Gate).

The Muslim Quarter is worth exploring mostly for its scenic Mamluke (1248–1517) architecture, which contributes so much to the colour of the Old City. It is full of *hammams* (public baths), *madrassas* (Islamic schools), libraries and the tombs of famous Muslims – including that of King Hussein of Jordan's great-grandfather, Sherif Hussein of Mecca. Palestinian families have lived here without interruption for 1,000 years or more. During the reign of Salah-ad-Din it was common for prominent Muslim families across the Islamic world to send a son and his family to Jerusalem to establish a branch of the family in the Holy City. Many Palestinian families from Jerusalem can trace their origins back 1,000 years to such places as Syria, Morocco, Samarkand and Sudan. During Ottoman rule the guards of the Haram al-Sherif were all Sudanese Muslims.

In Christ's footsteps

For Christian pilgrims, the highlight of a trip to Jerusalem is to follow the **Stations of the Cross**, along Via Dolorosa (Way of Sorrow) from the traditional site of Christ's condemnation by Pontius Pilate to the **Church of the Holy Sepulchre**, where Christ was crucified and buried. Although the Route of the Cross has been followed, more or less, since Byzantine times when Constantine's mother Helena traced what is believed to be the route, the number of stations has increased over the centuries. Several of the 14 stations were added as late as the 19th century. Each Friday at 3pm, priests lead a walking ceremony for pilgrims along Via Dolorosa. To trace the traditional route, start at the far eastern end of the Muslim Quarter, at **Lion's Gate**, which is also known as both St Stephen's Gate and the Gate of Our Lady Mariam. The nearby **Church of St Anne**, built for the mother of Mary, is a charming combination of Crusader, French and

BELOW: tourists follow the Way of the Cross during an Easter pilgrimage.

Muslim architecture. Groups of pilgrims from around the world come to take advantage of the church's dramatic acoustics designed for Gregorian chant.

The **First Station**, where Jesus was sentenced to Crucifixion by Pilate, is only 250 metres (273 ft) inside St Stephen's Gate. A little further along, on the right, are the chapels of Condemnation and Flagellation – the **Second Station** – where Roman soldiers flogged Christ and set a crown of thorns upon his head. Further down the street you stroll beneath the **Ecce Homo Arch**, said to have been built by Hadrian in the 2nd century. Right next to it is the **Convent of the Sisters of Zion**, believed by some to be the scene of Christ's trial.

Further down to the left of Via Dolorosa, on Al Wad Road (Valley Road), is the **Third Station**, at a small Polish chapel. This is where Jesus is said to have fallen for the first time. Just beyond the Armenian Orthodox Patriarchate is the **Fourth Station**, where Jesus met Mary, his mother. A right turn on Via Dolorosa leads to the **Fifth Station**, where Simon the Cyrene extended his help to a tired Jesus and carried the Cross. The **Sixth Station** is marked by what was once a large column; it was here that St Veronica wiped Christ's face with a cloth. Across the Khan al-Zeit Bazaar, a Franciscan chapel marks the **Seventh Station**, where Jesus fell for the second time. Up the street and up the steps of Aqabat al-Khanka, the Greek Monastery of St Charalamos marks the **Eighth Station**, where Jesus told the grieving women of Jerusalem: "Daughters of Jerusalem, do not weep for me, weep rather for yourselves and for your children" (Luke 23:28).

To reach the **Ninth Station**, return to the Khan al-Zeit Bazaar and climb 28 stairs to the Ethiopian Coptic Church, where Jesus fell for the third time. It is inside the complex of the **Church of the Holy Sepulchre** – identified by Queen Helena, Emperor Constantine's mother, in 326, as the site of the Crucifixion – that the last five Stations of the Cross are located. On the right near the entrance are two chapels, one Franciscan and one Greek Orthodox. The Franciscan Chapel marks the **Tenth Station**. Here Jesus was stripped of his clothing. At the far end of the chapel is the **Eleventh Station**, where he was nailed to the Cross. The Greek Orthodox Chapel commemorates the **Twelfth Station**, the site of Crucifixion, with a life-sized depiction of Jesus, surrounded by candles and icons. A life-sized statue of Mary, with a dagger in her heart, marks the **Thirteenth Station**, where Christ's body was taken from the Cross and given to his mother. Christ's tomb, the **Fourteenth Station**, is in the Church of the Holy Sepulchre itself, and is reached via the **Chapel of the Angels**.

Apart from the last five Stations of the Cross, the Church of the Holy Sepulchre contains at least a dozen points of interest even to the most secular of tourists. The complex – comprising some 60 chapels, altars and other places of worship – is divided between six denominations (Latin, Greek Orthodox, Armenian Orthodox, Syrian-Jacobite, Coptic and Abyssinian), each carefully guarding its turf and jealous of its neighbours. They have fought over issues of restoration and prayer times as well as who gets to put a candle where. It is said that one of the triggers to the Crimean War was a dispute over ownership of a

Map on page 284

Multilingual street signage on Via Dolorosa, the "Way of Sorow".

BELOW: the Church of the Holy Sepulchre.

Marking "The Centre of the World" in the Katholikon.

stair outside the church's entrance. A Technical Committee, set up in 1954, has attempted to ease some of the rivalry, but tensions still run high.

The **Monastery of the Sultan** – a cluster of mud huts on the roof of the church just above the Chapel of St Helena – is a case in point. This is where the Church of Ethiopia set up its headquarters after losing its right to a section of the church itself following the loss of its documents in a fire in 1808. The priests speak Amharic (Ethiopia's official language) and believe that King Menelik, the legendary son of King David of Israel and the Queen of Sheba founded their church, which has had envoys in Jerusalem since the 4th century. The church intends to stay, if only on the roof.

Other highlights of the church include the **Chapel of Adam**, officially the burial site for Crusader kings, and according to legend, the place where the skull of Adam was discovered, and the tiny **Chapel of the Copts**, full of exotic incense and colour. The **Syrian Jacobite Chapel**, next to it, leads into a 1st-century burial chamber. The Crusader church, the **Katholikon** (now a relatively large Greek Orthodox Chapel), was traditionally believed to stand at the centre of the world (the precise spot is marked by a chalice in the floor). Further down, the Armenian **Chapel of Helena** leads into the cavern where Queen Helena claimed to have found the remains of the True Cross.

If by this time you are ready for refreshments, try **Abu Shukri**, on Al Wad Street (near the Fifth Station of the Cross). It is popular with the locals and serves the best *hummus* and falafel in town. **Jaffar and Sons Pastry Café** in the Khan e-Zeit Bazaar, is guaranteed to satisfy any sweet tooth. It specialises in *kanafeh*, a layered pastry with mild sweet cheese, semolina, crushed pistachio nuts and lots of warm syrup.

BELOW: religious trinkets abound.

Christian Quarter

Jaffa Gate and David Street lead to a cluster of churches and *suqs*, including the oldest church in Jerusalem, **St John the Baptist Church**. (If you are coming from the Church of the Holy Sepulchre, walks towards the Armenian Quarter.) The **Church of the Redeemer**, now a Lutheran church, is believed to have been built in Byzantine times. The zodiac signs on its northern gate are typical of the designs employed by the Byzantines. The existing structure was built by the German Crown Prince Friederich Wilhelm, who bought the site during an official visit in 1869. The church's tower offers one of the best views over the Old City.

East of the Holy Sepulchre is **St Alexander Church**, where prayers for the late Tsar Alexander of Russia are held every Thursday. The **Mosque of Omar**, down the street from the Holy Sepulchre, commemorates the spot where the Caliph Omar prayed in what was then the courtyard of the Sepulchre Church.

Nearby, the **Arab Orthodox Society** runs a coffee shop/gift shop. Prices are not cheap but it is a good place for quality embroidered goods made by local Palestinian women. The Christian Quarter is also home to the **New Gate**, which was hammered into the wall of the Old City in 1887. It is the only gate that leads into the Christian Quarter. Across from New Gate, outside the Old City Wall, is the 19th-century **Notre Dame de France**. This grand complex houses the papal delegation to the city along with a monastery and a first-class French restaurant.

Outside the Old City

To the east of the Old City lies the famous **Mount of Olives**. It is said to be the site of at least a dozen biblical events. It is from here that Christ made his triumphal entry into Jerusalem, where he wept over Jerusalem, was betrayed and arrested and where he ascended into heaven. At the top is **A-Tur**, one of many Palestinian villages crowning the hills around Jerusalem. A-Tur is home to the quaint **Chapel of Ascension,** marking the spot where Christians believe Christ ascended to heaven 40 days after his resurrection. A petrified footprint marks the ground where he reputedly stood.

Across the road from the Chapel of Ascension is the **Pater Noster Carmelite Convent**, where Christ preached. The land around Pater Noster was bought by a French noblewoman in the 19th century. She had the Lord's Prayer inscribed on the walls in over 60 languages. Further down the mountain is the **Russian Monastery**, supposedly containing the head of John the Baptist, and the vast **Jewish cemetery** (the largest in the world) spreads towards the Golden Gate.

The sorrow of Christ is immortalised in the **Church of Dominus Flevit**, designed in the shape of a tear by the Italian architect Anton Barluzzi in 1953. Immediately below is one of the most picturesque churches in Jerusalem, the **Church of St Mary Magdalene**, with its seven onion-shaped domes. It adjoins the **Garden of Gethsemane**, where Jesus was betrayed.

At the foot of the Mount of Olives is the **Church of All Nations**, built in 1924, but containing the remains of at least two other older churches, one from the 4th

Map on page 284

TIP

Abu Shenab on Latin Patriarchate Street is a good place to grab an afternoon snack. Frequented by trendy Palestinians, it serves thick-crust pizzas, pints of cold beer and fresh salads.

BELOW: the Mount of Olives.

century and one from the 12th. To the right of the path at the bottom of the Mount of Olives is the **Tomb of the Virgin Mary**, next to the tombs of Crusader kings and their families.

South of the Old City is **Mount Zion**, a site associated with David, said to be buried on the hill, and with Jesus, who is said to have celebrated the Last Supper here. It can be reached through Zion Gate and Dung Gate. The site of Mary's death is marked by the **Dormition Abbey**, where a mausoleum, built in 1900, is surrounded by 12 columns. Virtually in the backyard of the abbey is the **Coenaculum** – the supposed setting of the Last Supper. Beneath is the Tomb of David; again, there is disagreement about whether David was buried to the east or to the south of Jerusalem; Jews nevertheless count the tomb as a holy shrine.

Christ's birthplace

The West Bank town of **Bethlehem ❷** lies 8 km (5 miles) from Jerusalem. Hundreds of thousands of pilgrims flock to this ancient village (known in Arabic as Bayt Lahim, "House of Meat", or in Hebrew as Beit Lechem, "House of Milk") to commemorate the birth of Jesus. The first basilica over the grotto said to be the birthplace of Christ was built by Constantine between AD 326 and 339. A Samaritan revolt in 529 destroyed most of Bethlehem, including the basilica, but the Emperor Justinian (527–565) repaired and enlarged the structure. In 614 the Persians destroyed almost every Christian house of worship, but left the Basilica of Nativity intact. In 638 the Second Caliph, Omar ibn al-Khattab, prayed in the southern part of the church, and while it has not become a place of prayer for Muslims it is revered as a symbol of Christian goodwill towards Islam.

BELOW: the Judaean Hills.

Map on page 284

The Crusaders renovated the basilica in 1099, and Bethlehem became a site where Crusader kings were crowned – Baldwin I was crowned in Bethlehem in 1100. In 1187 Salah-ad-Din captured Bethlehem but in 1229 the Muslim Sultan Malik al-Kamil returned the town to the Crusaders, which they held until finally ousted from the Holy Land in 1291. Many Bethlehemites claim to be descendants of either the Beni Ghassan (an ancient Christian Arab tribe from Arabia Felix, known today as Yemen) or the Crusaders, or both. Many are Catholics and have sought commercial, cultural and religious ties with other Catholic countries since the 19th century. In the first half of the 20th century, a large number of Bethlehemites settled in South and Central America, but more recently many have migrated to North America.

Every summer descendants of Bethlehemites return to their native town to find a bride or bridegroom for their children. Today, many of the town's residents are descendants of Palestinian refugees who fled their homes in northern Palestine when the State of Israel was created in 1948. Bethlehem's population is about 35,000, and the majority are Muslim.

Bethlehem's sites

The first sight as one approaches Bethlehem from Jerusalem is **Rachel's tomb**, set at the edge town. Rachel, the wife of Jacob, who died while giving birth to Benjamin (Genesis 35:19–20), is the only one of the four Old Testament matriarchs to be buried here rather than in Hebron. The current tomb was built by the Ottoman Turks in the 1620s, and the existing dome was added by the British-Jewish philanthropist Sir Moses Montefiore in 1841. With the redeployment of Israeli troops from Bethlehem, the site was fortified and an Israeli checkpoint

BELOW: carving in Bethlehem.

Manger Square,
nucleus of the
town of Bethlehem.

now stands in close proximity. The tomb is revered by both Muslims and Jews, and is open to visitors every day except Friday afternoons and Saturdays.

Manger Square is the centre of Bethlehem, and the hub of various pilgrim sites. (It is more commercial in character than the old *suq* on Star Street, just off Manger Square, which has a more authentic character and offers a greater variety of interesting goods.) The square is earmarked to become a serene garden with trees and fountains, say Palestinian Authority tourism officials. For better or for worse, the town has undergone significant renovation in preparation for the millennium celebrations.

The **Church of Nativity** (326–339), next to the Church of St Catherine on the square, encases the grotto where Christ is believed to have been born. Following a complex schedule of worship, more than half a dozen different churches – including Catholic, Protestant, Russian and Greek Orthodox, Armenian, Egyptian Coptic and Assyrian – manage to coexist in this grand basilica. Attempts by different denominations to control the church have created constant rivalry and even provoked war. It is believed that one of the causes of the Crimean War was Napoleon III's insistence that the complex be declared French property. Most of the existing structure, including the remaining mosaic floor, date from the time of Justinian, but the oak ceiling was a gift from King Edward IV of England. Most of the decorative icons around the main altar were gifts of the Russian imperial family in the 19th century.

At the front of the church, two sets of stairs on either side of the altar lead down to the **Grotto of the Nativity**, where Christ was born. Marked by a 14-point silver star, the site of Christ's birth is inscribed in Latin to the effect that Jesus was born here to the Virgin Mary. Silver-plated lanterns with precious

BELOW: Grotto
of the Nativity.

stones light the spot day and night. Next to the grotto is the **Chapel of the Manger**, where Mary placed her newborn son. Crosses etched into the walls and columns are the work of pilgrims and, in some cases, Crusaders.

The traditional Christmas Eve Mass that is televised all over the world is held next door in the Franciscan **Church of St Catherine** (1881). The church is dedicated to St Catherine in tribute to the vision of Christ that she, as Catherine of Alexandria, had here. Bethlehem's other great place of pilgrimage is the **Milk Grotto Church** (down Milk Grotto Street), where, according to legend, some of Mary's milk dripped on the ground and whitened the red floor.

Near Manger Square on King David street are **King David's Wells**. The site marks the place where David's men broke through a Philistine garrison to bring him water. The **Old Bethlehem Museum**, on Paul V1 Street, also near Manger Square, offers a glimpse of traditional Palestinian costume and architecture. The PA's centrally located **Ministry of Tourism** supplies free tourist maps noting other points of interest in and around the town. The map includes accommodation listings for those who wish to stay overnight in Bethlehem.

Nearby **Beit Sahur** (House of the Shepherd) is believed to mark Shepherds' Field, where angels announced the birth of Jesus to the shepherds. Jews also cherish this location, because tradition attests that this is where Boaz fell in love with the widowed Ruth. Their grandchild was David, King of Israel.

Hebron

Known in Arabic as Al Khalil, **Hebron** ❸ is one of the oldest towns in Palestine. It is 16 km (10 miles) south of Bethlehem and was inhabited by the Canaanites as early as 2000 BC. An envoy of Moses returning from an exploratory expedition described Hebron as the "land of milk and honey". In 1200 BC Moses's successor, Joshua, invaded and destroyed the city, killing all its inhabitants (Joshua:10:37).

A commercially active and industrially important town of 100,000 Palestinians, Hebron today is the hub of some four dozen villages. It is also home to 450 radical Jewish settlers, who live in a tiny enclave in the centre of the city, making it a regular trouble spot. The town is famous for its peaches, apples and grapes, and exports agricultural produce to neighbouring Arab countries. Its quarries are renowned – many refined homes in the West Bank are finished with Hebron marble – and so is its glasswork, a craft developed by monks from Italy. (Glass Junction, on the main road from Bethlehem to Hebron, is the place to shop for it.)

However, Hebron is best known for the **Haram al-Khalil** (known in Hebrew as Cave of Machpelah) or Tomb of the Patriarchs, where Abraham, Isaac and Jacob are believed to be buried. It is also thought to be the final resting place of Sarah, Rebecca and Leah, as well as Adam and Eve. According to Islamic tradition, Adam and Eve lived out their old age in Hebron. Muslims also revere Hebron because Mohammed is said to have visited the Haram al-Khalil on his way from Mecca to Jerusalem. It is a place of great religious importance to Muslims, Jews and Christians alike and has become a hotbed off religious zealotry.

Map on page 284

TIP

Tickets are required for St Catherine's Christmas Eve Mass, but monks outside the church often carry tickets under their cloaks, and may obligingly pass them on without charge to disappointed visitors.

BELOW: buying apples at a Bethlehem stall.

One of the worst examples of this was in 1994, when Jewish extremist Baruch Goldstein opened fired on Muslim worshippers in the Tomb of the Patriachs, killing dozens of Palestinians and wounding many others. Israeli forces withdrew from large chunks of Hebron in 1997, but they continue to control the Tomb. (Discreet dress for both men and women is recommended in this unsafe area.) The site is closed on Friday, except for Muslim worshippers.

In the opinion of some Jews, Abraham's purchase of the cave as his burial place made the site exclusively Jewish for all time. According to both Muslim and Jewish tradition, King Solomon is believed to have laid the groundwork for the Haram al-Khalil and, according to Muslim tradition, *djns* (spirits) helped Solomon's men build the edifice. In AD 70 the Jews revolted against the Romans and were expelled from Hebron until the city came under Muslim rule, when it was again open to all.

The site was converted into a church in 570 by the Byzantine rulers of Palestine. Under Islam in the 7th century the church was converted into a mosque, which was again transformed into a church in 1099 by invading Crusaders. The church replaced both the mosque and the adjacent synagogue, which marked the centre of the Haram at the time, and Jews and Muslims were banned. After the defeat of the Crusaders by Salah-ad-Din in the 12th century, the church was re-converted into a mosque, and Jews and Muslims were allowed to return to the city. It wasn't until 1967, when Israel captured the city, however, that Jews were permitted to enter the Tomb.

Entering the Tomb from the northwestern entrance, visitors climb a Mamluke staircase leading to the **Mamluke Mosque Djaouliyeh** (built in 1380). An adjoining courtyard leads to the synagogues, which house the 14th-century

Some scholars believe Hebron's Old Testament name, Qiryat Arba (village of the four) refers to the four important couples thought to be buried here; others say it alludes to the four Canaanite tribes that settled the town in pre-Biblical times.

BELOW: detail at Hisham's Palace.

cenotaphs of Jacob and Leah and of Abraham and Sarah, and the **Mosque of Isaac** (also known as the Great Mosque), which houses the cenotaphs of Isaac and Rebecca. A small Mamluke mosque situated in the southeastern part of the Haram is reserved for women; in one corner is a **petrified footprint**, which, according to legend, was left by Adam as he left the Garden of Eden. The exit leads through yet another mosque, which Muslims believe houses the cenotaph of Joseph.

Down the road from the Tomb is a vibrant market, where Palestinian residents of Hebron do their shopping. Beside the *suq* is **Beit Hadassah**, a Jewish enclave that has a small museum recalling the 1929 Arab massacre of the old Hebron Jewish community.

Jericho

Believed to be the oldest continuously inhabited town on earth (12,000 years), **Jericho ❹** is a green, desert city studded with palm trees, banana plantations and flowers. It was in Jericho that the Neolithic hunter turned settler-farmer, that the ancient Canaanites made fine pottery and that, at Mount Sultan near Elisha's spring, 23 consecutive cities rose and fell. This is where the prophet Elisha purified the water so the people would not die of thirst (Kings 2:19–22), and where Christ restored the sight of the blind beggar (Luke 18:34–43). Today it is a city of only about 7,500 people, but with another 10,000 living in the vicinity. Ancient Jericho, which was also known as Tel a-Sultan, goes back to the 10th millennium BC.

Located about 2 km (1 mile) from today's city centre, the existing *tel* (a hill formed by the layered accumulation of settlements) is today a heap of ruined walls. Archaeological excavation of Tel a-Sultan began in 1867, but the most significant work was conducted in 1952 by British archaeologist Kathleen Kenyon: she traced the transition of Jericho's inhabitants from hunter communities to settled farmers. The town still has a **Neolithic stone tower** dating from 7000 BC. Ten Neolithic skulls (now on display at the Rockefeller Museum in Jerusalem, *see page 286*) were uncovered during Kenyon's excavations. A centre for Canaanite trade as early as 3000 BC, in Roman times the city was one of Mark Antony's gifts to Cleopatra. Later Herod was awarded the town by the Emperor Octavian. In 550 BC the Persians used old Jericho as an administrative centre, and under Alexander the Great, in 332 BC, the town functioned as a royal resort.

The town fulfilled a similar purpose under the Muslims. **Hisham's Palace** (Khirbet al-Mafjar), Jericho's most impressive site, was built between 724 and 743 as a winter retreat from Damascus by Walid ibn Yazid, and named after his uncle, Sultan Hisham ibn Abd al-Malik. The ruins, 2.5 km (2 miles) north of Tel a-Sultan, bear traces of luxurious living-quarters as well as two mosques (in spite of the earthquake in 747, which destroyed most of the palace walls). The bath hall is decorated by elegant colonnades and a blue and pink mosaic floor. The *diwan* (reception hall) contains the famous tree of life mosaic, with 15 fruits (each rep-

Map on page 284

Hisham's Palace, built 724–743 as a winter retreat from Damascus.

BELOW: Yasser Arafat, a popular man in Jericho.

resenting a governate under the Sultan Hisham's rule). The two gazelles in the mosaic represent friends of the Sultan, while the gazelle being attacked by the lion symbolises the enemy.

About 1 km (½ mile) south of the palace is **Elisha's Spring** (Ain a-Sultan), where the prophet Elisha is supposed to have purified the spring's waters with salt. These spring waters have kept the town supplied since antiquity; today they provide water at a rate of up to 3,800 litres (1,000 gallons) a minute. A 20-minute walk – on carpets of wild flowers in spring – takes you up to the **Mount of Temptation** (Quruntul). This is the wilderness site where Christ spent 40 days and nights fasting, having previously suffered the devil's temptation. The **Greek Orthodox Monastery** houses the grotto where Christ is supposed to have sat during his fast. The Arabic name Quruntul is a local version of the old Crusader name of Mons Quaranta – "Mountain of Forty" (in commemoration of the 40 days and nights).

The existing monastery was built at the end of the last century, but was by no means the first to be built over the famous cave. Today's monastery didn't receive electricity until 1992, and water is still taken from half a dozen wells inside the monastery walls.

Just 8 km (5 miles) outside modern Jericho lies the **Mosque of Moses**, believed by Muslims to be the burial sight of Moses. Islamic tradition holds that God carried Moses's bones from the east side of the Jordan River, where he died on the mountain now known as Nebi Musa or Mount Nebo (*see page 223*), for burial in Palestine. The place is isolated and has a bleak feel about it. Some 10 km (6 miles) east of Jericho, **Al-Maghtas** by the Jordan River is the supposed site of Christ's baptism by John the Baptist.

BELOW: on the horizon, the Mount of Temptation.

Jericho today

Jericho today is a friendly and peaceful town, offering delicious fresh fruit juices and excellent Arabic cuisine. It also boasts lots of warm weather. In fact, when the winter chill permeates Jerusalem, Jericho is at its best. About 10 per cent of its inhabitants are descendants of Afro-Arabs who settled in the region over 1,000 years ago. In more recent times Jericho was home to some 185,000 refugees who fled Palestine after 1948. However, almost all these refugees fled to Jordan during the 1967 War.

As part of the Oslo Accords, Israeli troops withdrew from the city in 1994. The PA has attempted to pump new life into sleepy Jericho. In 1998 a new casino, called **Oasis**, opened its doors for business, much to the dismay of many of the town's strictly Muslim residents. Run by an Austrian company, the casino will eventually be part of a larger tourism complex that will include hotels, swimming pools and a world-class golf course.

From Jericho, a road leads 20 km (12 miles) down to **Qumran** on the Dead Sea. It was in a cave here, in 1947, that some local boys discovered the Dead Sea Scrolls. A visitors' centre at the site documents the story of the scrolls and their discovery. If you don't make it to Qumran, the history of the scrolls is also presented in the Archaeological Museum at the Citadel in Amman (*see page 143*).

Map
on page
284

Ramallah

Unlike the other towns that we have picked out in the West Bank, **Ramallah** ❺ is not packed with historical sites for the visitor to explore. It is, however, a good place to get a sense of the newly emerging Palestine. Since the PA took control of the city in 1995, it has become the centre of Palestinian commercial life and a hot spot for the towny crowd. The population of Ramallah (meaning Heights of God in Arabic) is estimated at 25,000, and is still growing. Before 1967, the town was predominantly Christian; today it is overwhelmingly Muslim. Nevertheless, churches of various denominations remain an important part of the town's skyline, and the Quakers continue to operate a prestigious school.

Many Palestinian-Americans who have returned to take part in the state-building process live in the affluent areas around Ramallah. According to estimates, up to 70 per cent of the residents of **Al Bira**, a sprawling suburb stretching from East Jerusalem to Ramallah, have lived in the US. It is also an area popular with members of the Palestinian Legislative Council, some of whom have apartments here.

Near the **municipal gardens** is a **folklore museum**, with examples of traditional Palestinian costume. You can sit in the gardens and relax with a tea and hubble-bubble in the evening. There is also a number of restaurants and cafés for a leisurely meal, such as **Bardouni** and the **Kit Kat**, both of which are listed in the *Travel Tips* section of this guide. Further afield is **Bir Zeit University**, the largest Palestinian university (during the Israeli occupation it was a hotbed of Palestinian nationalism). Nearby is the Palestinian Christian village of **Jifna**, which has managed to retain much of its ancient charm. ❑

BELOW: Qumran, site of the Dead Sea Scrolls' discovery.

SYRIA'S MAIN SIGHTS

Map on page 308

Syria, a land of fabled cities and remote antiquities, is a natural extension for many travellers to Jordan, for the border is merely an arbitrary disruption to geographical and historical reality

The order in which the following sights have been arranged presupposes an approach from Jordan. It thus begins with the sights closest to Jordan and then moves in a looping arc north to Damascus, anti-clockwise east to the Euphrates, north to Aleppo and its environs, west to the coast and finally south and southeast back to the starting point.

Land of the volcanoes

Having crossed Syna's southern border at Dir'a, follow the road due east across the red soils of the Hauran plain towards the rising heights of the **Jabal al-Arab** ❶, known until recently as the Jabal Druze, after the principal inhabitants of the region (and also called the Jabal Hauran, or Mount Bashan of the biblical Psalms).

The Hauran (classical Auranitis) is littered with basalt boulders from the volcanic activity of the Jabal al-Arab. The Jabal itself is not one but myriad volcanic cones which have spewed out lava in several phases over time. The accumulation of lava is sometimes more than 1,000 metres (3,280 ft) thick and the highest point on the Jabal is 1,860 metres (6,200 ft). In winter the Jabal is covered with snow and the higher rainfall catchment provides an important source of water for the Hauran settlements and for artesian basins to the south. Though it is a strange, bare and wild landscape, many sombre black villages dating back to Nabataean and Roman times perch on the edge of the desert to the east. On the eastern slopes, where nothing is grown today, the remains of ancient field systems are evident, attesting to a more populous and vital agricultural society in the past.

The overall use of black basalt building stone is typical of Hauran architecture. Lack of wood encouraged an idiosyncratic system of construction, whereby beams hewn out of basalt were placed on projecting corbels to span the roofs, and transverse arches necessary to support them were placed at frequent intervals. Stone was also used for doors and window screens.

Situated on the plain some 42 km (27 miles) to the east of Dar'a lies the ancient town of **Busra** ❷, still inhabited today, although the government is now relocating the population outside the city walls. Settlement dates from the Early Bronze Age, but the town rose to pre-eminence in the late 1st century AD when the last king of the Nabataeans, Rabbel II, moved his capital from Petra to Busra, which was better placed to take advantage of changing international trade routes. When the Romans established direct control over the region, Busra was made the capital of the Roman province of Arabia.

PRECEDING PAGES: the Roman Theatre, Busra; *norias* (water wheels) at Hama; **LEFT:** the Omayyad Mosque, Damascus. **BELOW:** idle chat.

*Playing a role in
Busra's Roman
Theatre.*

One can easily spend a whole day wandering through the extensive and well-preserved ruins dating from Nabataean, Roman, Byzantine and Islamic times, needing little imagination to picture the living city. The most surprising monument within this rich array is the **Roman Theatre**. Like a pearl within an oyster shell, it is completely hidden from view by the medieval citadel which fortified and surrounded it. Such protection has ensured its preservation as one of the most complete Roman theatres in the world. Clearance and excavation is ongoing, and the most recent discovery of note is an enormous Christian church of a centralised circular form, comparable in size to the great church of Hagia Sophia in Istanbul.

Museums are located in the citadel and in the **Hammam Manjak** (the restored Mamluke bath house). Other sites include impressive Corinthian columns and the Mosque of Omar. A new luxury hotel has recently made Busra the most attractive centre for exploring the Hauran and the Jabal.

The main regional centre of **As Suwayda** ❸ is 32 km (20 miles) northeast of Busra, on the mid-western flanks of the Jabal al-Arab. The populous modern town has now overrun the classical city of Dionysias, but it does have an excellent regional museum, along the road out to Qanawat.

Passing through the town, one is struck by the manner and dress of the local Druze population, where, as Robin Fedden, the author of *Syria and Lebanon*, observes, "even the poorest appear chieftains". A secretive religious minority, the Druze fled the Lebanon mountains in the mid-19th century after conflict with the Christians and sought refuge on the depopulated Jabal. They are noted for their beauty, courage, and fiercely independent spirit. The latter has continually brought them into conflict with authority, as the Turks, the French, and even the

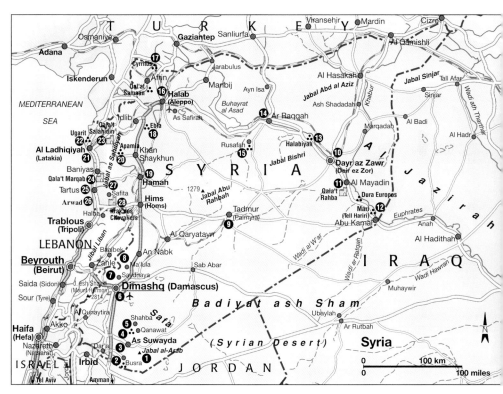

Map
on page
308

modern regime can attest. Many still wear traditional costume and the turbaned men take pride in their magnificent moustaches waxed at the tips. The women wear sweeping patterned dresses bunched into a high waist with a scooped neckline, striking quite a contrast to typical Arab attire.

A road northeast from As Suwayda leads to **Qanawat ❹** through rising terrain and the remnants of oak forests which once flourished on the Jabal al-Arab. Perhaps the prettiest area in the Hauran, Qanawat commands expansive views westwards across the plain to Mount Hermon/Jabal al-Sheikh (so-called in Arabic because of its year-round snow, which is likened to the white beard of a venerable sheikh). Qanawat was important from Hellenistic to Byzantine times and retains a charming but scattered collection of ruins. The main complex, the Seraya, is next to the central town square. It was originally a Roman temple and civic complex which was later appropriated to accommodate two Christian basilicas, with the addition of a monastery. Fifty metres/yards southwest of the town square are the remains of a small Temple of Zeus with a columned portico.

If one follows the road descending north from the front of the colonnaded courtyard of the "Seraya", access can be gained to the steep *wadi* on the right, containing a small theatre (odeon) and a nymphaeum set within a park of pine trees. Just off the road leading back to Suwayda, in the northwest of the town, is a temple dedicated to the sun-god, Helios.

It is a short, 3-km (2-mile) drive southeast of Qanawat to the hilltop sanctuary of **Sia**. Set on a narrow ridge, this beautiful site was originally a Semitic "high place", which later, under the Nabataeans and then the Romans, was embellished with temples and courts. An important place of pilgrimage for both

BELOW: Druze wedding, Shahba.

urban and pastoral dwellers, even the Safaitic nomads have left their inscriptions there. The remains of settlement, fortifications and a large gate spread along the ridge to the east.

The extraordinary product of a "local boy makes good" can be found at **Shahba**  (the Roman Philippopolis), 26 km (16 miles) north of Qanawat. When Philip the Arab gained the imperial crown of Rome in AD 244, he decided to glorify his roots (and himself) by creating an Imperial Roman city at his birthplace. Unfortunately his reign was shortened by his early and violent death and the major monuments in the town of Shahba can be dated to a few short years (about two, in fact, from 247 to 249), although a small Christian settlement lasted into the 4th century. Set beside black volcanic cones, the structures and streets that survived the 19th-century influx of Druze settlers are austere but beautifully built, nevertheless. A museum houses the best Syrian examples of late Roman (4th-century) mosaics, some of which are still in situ in the private house for which they were made.

To the northwest of Shahba lies a bizarre area of land called the **Ledja**. The Ledja is, in fact, a giant island of solid lava. A similar area of land (Safa, situated further to the east) was described by the indefatigable Gertrude Bell as being "like a horrible black nightmare sea, not so much frozen as curdled." And yet the Ledja contains many villages, some still inhabited and with origins dating back to Roman times. From its time as the classical Trachonitis until the early 20th century the Ledja has been feared as a lair for brigands and runaways. The Romans tried to tame it by building a dual-carriage way across the middle of the lava. This highway is still visible today, and even the central reservation can be identified.

BELOW: Azem Palace, Damascus.

The oasis capital

Passing the Ledja on the left, the eastern road heads north to **Damascus** (Dimashq) **❻**. Capital of modern Syria, once capital of the Omayyad caliphate whose borders stretched from Pakistan to Portugal, and earlier of biblical Aram, Damascus has risen and fallen with the tides of history since earliest times. It nestles at the foot of Mount Kassiun, on the eastern slopes of the Anti-Lebanon range, within a large basin watered by the Barada River and on the edge of the great Syrian Desert. By careful husbandry of the river, the rich soil of the basin has been irrigated and cultivated, creating a lush oasis (the Ghouta) which engirdles the city protectively. It is one of the traditional candidates for the location of the Garden of Eden, and the city itself has been lauded as the oldest continuously inhabited capital in the world. Legends they remain, as such uninterrupted and dense settlement has allowed for little systematic archaeological excavation.

The expansion of Damascus since Turkish times has largely occurred outside the walls, and the old city has retained its mixed medieval character. Artisans and craftsmen still ply their trade and the delights of shopping in the **Suq al-Hamediyeh** could result in a serious case of shopping fever. Silks, brocade, printed cloth, wooden inlay, glass, copper, rugs, gold, spices, sweets – and myriad more crafts and goods are located in their specialised areas. The crowd is dense and the hawkers are enthusiastic. Walk down the **Street called Straight** (where St Paul was lodged after his conversion on the road). It is, as Mark Twain quipped, "straighter than a corkscrew, but not as straight as a rainbow." The Eastern part of "Straight Street" brings you to the Christian quarter filled with monasteries and churches, both old and new. Nearby is what was once the Jewish quarter. Few of the original inhabitants have remained (most have emigrated to Brooklyn, New York or to Israel in the early 1990s) and today the area is mainly Christian. In between, visit the old khans (warehouses for trade and traders' accommodation), *madrassas* (schools), mausoleums (especially of Saladin and the Sultan Baybars) and, to appreciate the comforts and luxuries of urban life for the wealthy, visit the stunning black basalt and limestone **Azem Palace**, which houses the Museum of Popular Arts and Tradition.

It is a particular delight to get lost inside the Oriental maze of streets, covered alleyways, cul-de-sacs and courtyards lined by half-timbered houses of amazing variety and eccentricity. A walk around the recently renovated citadel, walls and the gates is for the interested but energetic. A major monument is the **Omayyad Mosque**, built on the site of the grand Byzantine cathedral of St John the Baptist (whose head is reputedly still inside), which replaced the Roman Temple of Jupiter (note the arch and columns at the end of the *suq* dating back to the 3rd century), which, in turn, replaced the Aramaean Temple of Haddad. The mosque is especially famous for its vast expanse of brilliant mosaics and patterned marble, although what survives is but a pale reflection of the original display. In keeping with modesty, women are required to wear an *abaya* – a head to toe black cloak

Map on page 308

Omayyad Mosque, Damascus.

BELOW: café habituees enjoying a smoke.

An Orthodox nun in Saydnaya, the most important place of Christian pilgrimage in the East after Jerusalem.

worn over clothing which can be obtained at the north entrance of the mosque for a few coins. Visitors must remove their shoes before entering the courtyard.

Beyond the old city, visit the **Hejaz railway terminus**, recently restored with a rich Damascene ceiling, and the **Tekkiyeh Mosque**, a beautiful 16th-century construction by the famous Ottoman architect Sinan. Adjacent to the mosque is the Military Museum, with a half dozen rooms displaying antique swords and armoury, as well as memorabilia captured in the 1973 War against Israel. Its impressive structure was built as part of a 400-year-old *caravanserai* for worshippers on their way to Mecca. Next to it, the handicrafts centre (added later, in similar style) is worth a visit. The **National Museum** contains a magnificent collection of archaeological and historical material, including 14th-century BC clay tablets bearing the 30 characters of Ugarit, the first known alphabet, and findings from Palmyra. The original murals of the Dura Europos Synagogue, dating back to the 2nd century, is one of the jewels of the collection. Across the river, on the lower slopes of Mount Kassiun, and surrounded by the wealthier section of the modern city, the atmosphericold quarter of **Salihiyyeh** contains many important monuments. Finally, one should not leave Damascus without a trip up **Mount Kassiun** itself, where the whole tapestry of the city is laid out for leisurely perusal.

Legends and Christians

Syria is a repository of many significant monuments and traditions relating to early Christianity. The picturesque village of **Saydnaya** ❼, on the edge of the Anti-Lebanon range 27 km (17 miles) north of Damascus, became the second-most important place of Christian pilgrimage in the east after Jerusalem. The

Map on page 308

convent dates from the time of the Emperor Justinian and contains an image of the Virgin said to be painted by St Luke and associated with many miracles.

A further 26 km (16 miles) north lies the village of **Ma'lula** ❽. Set in a dramatic ravine, its white and pale blue houses jumble around the lower slopes of the cliffs. The small upper monastery contains a chapel dating back to Byzantine times and the monks make a very acceptable wine. The gorge extending behind the village (beyond the Safir Hotel) narrows into a dramatic passage reminiscent of the famous *siq* at Petra. At the opposite end of the village is the chapel of St Thecla. The cave at the top of the steep stairs is a popular place for local Christians seeking inspiration from the legendary Thecla, a local female saint. The village has clung so tenaciously to its Christian identity that the inhabitants still speak Aramaic, the language spoken by Christ.

The caravan oasis

The oasis city of **Palmyra** (Tadmur) ❾ rises like a mirage from the barren waste, 243 km (150 miles) northeast of Damascus. Strings of honey-coloured colonnades interspersed with elegant ruins march across the vast plain, partially enclosed by bare hills to the north and west, with a backdrop of brilliant green from the palms and gardens of the springs to the south and east. As a source of water in the desert, midway between the coast and the Euphrates, Semitic Tadmur, as it was known, has been settled since Neolithic times.

However, it was not until the late Hellenistic and Roman period that the tribes of the desert organised to provide a safe route for traders from the eastern markets, shipping goods upriver to Dura Europos and cutting the shortest way across the desert to Damascus and the great Levantine trading cities on the

BELOW: the elegantly scattered ruins of Palmyra.

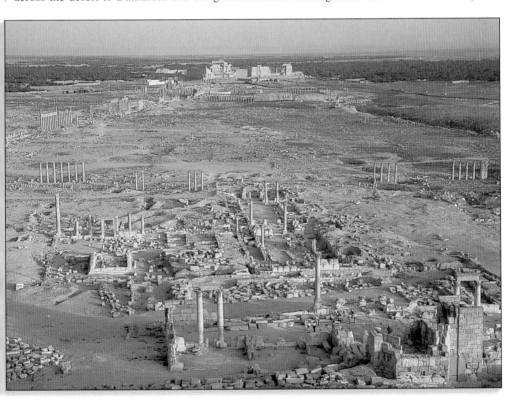

The horse is as much a canvas for artistic endeavour as a beast of burden.

Mediterranean coast. The Romans called it "Palmyra", the place of palms, and it grew rich from the taxes on the flourishing caravan trade.

As a buffer between Rome and its successive arch-rivals in the east, the Parthians and the Sassanians, Palmyran troops proved to be successful campaigners. But it was the remarkable Queen Zenobia who exerted such power and independence that she took on the might of the Roman Empire and captured Syria, Arabia, Egypt and Anatolia. This was the apogee of the city's fortunes as the centre of an Arab empire. However, it was all too brief – Zenobia was defeated and captured and the city was destroyed.

The site is vast but the layout easily visible. From the major complex of the Temple of Bel in the east the main monuments of theatre, baths, agora and other temples are scattered either side of the impressive main colonnaded street. At the western end lies the military camp of Diocletian, and a further climb up the northwestern hill leads to the later Arab castle of Qala't Ibn Maan. The glorious panorama is worth the effort, and one can see the full extent of the tower tombs stretching to the west as well as the southwest and southeast cemeteries. The modern town spreads to the east of the site and the museum contains many of the sculptures and objects which adorned the site and the tombs.

Along the Euphrates

Continuing to cross the desert to the east, you finally reach the mighty Euphrates and its fertile floodplain at **Dayr az-Zawr ❿**. There is little of antique interest in this town, apart from the riverscape itself and the town's role as a base for trips south and north. However, the museum has a good collection of material from the major sites of the region.

BELOW: local girl.

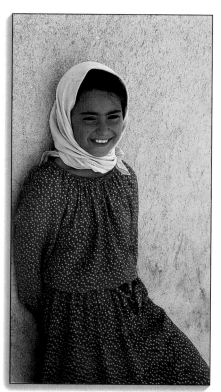

Travelling south, one can combine Dura, Qala't Rahba, and Mari in one trip. The small castle of **Qala't Rahba ⓫**, just off the main road south to Abu Kamal, is the first site. Built by the energetic Nur al-din in the 12th century, it contains a five-sided keep established to guard the Euphrates.

Further south, the massive mudbrick walls of the riverside garrison and caravan city of **Dura Europos** are clearly visible from the distant road. A chance discovery by British soldiers in 1920 led to the uncovering of a treasure-trove of wall paintings which revolutionised our understanding of early Christian and Judaic traditions and revealed a fascinating mixture of Parthian and Western art. These have been removed and taken to the safety of museums (including the Louvre and Yale University), but one can see the famous synagogue murals in the National Museum in Damascus.

Dura was established as a military colony by the Seleucids in the early 3rd century BC; it came under first Parthian and then Roman control and was destroyed forever by the Sassanian Persians in AD 256. The frantic thickening of the city walls was achieved by filling in the buildings adjacent to them. It ensured the survival of the unique representational paintings in the synagogue, various temples, and the house-church which is the earliest Christian cult centre found in Syria.

Twenty-four kilometres (15 miles) downriver the ancient city of **Mari**
(Tell Hariri) has produced crucial information on the history of Syria/
Mesopotamia in the third and second millennia BC. The 60-hectare (148-acre)
mound is surprisingly low and unprepossessing for the discoveries it has produced. The structures are predominantly mudbrick, dominated by the
labyrinthine palace of its last ruler, Zimri-Lim. Mari was destroyed by Ham-
murabi of Babylon in 1759 BC. Thousands of cuneiform-inscribed clay tablets
from the palace archives have revealed the political, social, religious and economic systems of its inhabitants and neighbours.

It is tempting to cross the river at Dayr az-Zawr and enter the most remote,
but agriculturally rich region of Syria, the Jazirah. It is a landscape riddled with
ancient tells, and well-watered by the Balikh and Khabur rivers. But time and
space restrict us to the Euphrates boundary, and we turn northwards to explore
the fortified garrison town of **Halabiyah** ⓭, less than an hour's drive from
Dayr az Zawr. Perched on the edge of the river, the great stone walls built in the
time of Justinian climb the hill westwards to a citadel built at the apex of a triangle. Much of the interior is buried or collapsed, but the magnificent walls, bas-
tions and associated vaulted rooms are largely intact.

The modern provincial centre of **Ar Raqqah** ⓮, on the east bank of the river
(86 km/53 miles north of Halabiyah), was historically important from Hellenistic to Ayyubid times, famed as the summer capital of Harun al-Rashid (the
caliph immortalised in *A Thousand and One Nights*) and from the late 12th
century a centre for the glazed ceramic industry. Remnants of this past can be
found in the Bab Baghdad (Baghdad Gate), the Qasr al-Banat (Palace of the
Maidens), the Great Mosque, and the museum.

Map on page 308

TIP

Before its destruction in 1758 BC, Mari had been a centre of artistic excellence. Most of the remains of this creative flowering – such as wall paintings and ceramics – have been removed, but they can still be seen in the museums of Damascus and Aleppo.

BELOW: roadside dates.

Continuing north, turn left at al-Mansura and cross a bare plain for 28 km (17 miles) to arrive at yet another impressively walled city in the middle of apparently nowhere. **Rusafah**  ⑮ was part of the Roman defences against the Sassanians and lies on a caravan route from Damascus, via Palmyra, to the Euphrates ford at Thapsacus. Its remarkable ascendancy in Byzantine times was due to the gruesome martyrdom and subsequent cult status of a Roman court official called Sergius, who refused to renounce his Christian beliefs during the persecutions of Diocletian in AD 305. After Constantine legalised Christianity, the city changed its name to Sergiopolis, and St Sergius eventually became the patron saint of Syria. Much of the city is collapsed and buried and pockmarked with treasure-hunting holes made by the Bedouin. Of the main monuments emerging above ground are three churches, a *khan* (market), and the magnificent cisterns, which held enough water to last two years.

The medieval bazaar

The culmination of a journey to north Syria must surely be **Aleppo** (Halab) ⑯. Set in a dry plain halfway between the Euphrates and the Mediterranean, Aleppo was one of the Near East's great commercial cities in the Middle Ages. It operated at the hub of world trade converging from Central Asia, India, Mesopotamia and Europe.

Political realignments strangled most of these trade routes and Aleppo has been largely bypassed by the 20th century. Herein lies our good fortune. Aleppo, even more than Damascus, is a hidden doorway into a fabled past. Its old walled city preserves medieval practices and trades and it richly repays a thorough exploration of its nooks and crannies. Be sure to seek out the specialist quarters

BELOW: blacksmith in Aleppo.

of its famous *suqs*, mosques, *khans* and *hammams* (baths) and, of course, its citadel, a military masterpiece set high in isolation like a cup face-down on the saucer of the surrounding city.

Map on page 308

The *suqs*, parts of which date from the 13th century, are a labyrinth of vaulted streets reaching 7 km (4½ miles) in length, unsurpassed in size and atmosphere. Quarters outside the old walls, such as Jdeide ("new", dating from the Mamluke period and now a mainly Christian area filled with churches) and the old *madrassas* (schools) to the south also charm the wanderer. The **Aleppo Museum** contains important collections from many periods and sites.

Aleppo is a melting-pot of Arabs, Turks, Kurds, Armenians and Assyrians and this is reflected in the wonderful variety of cuisine that can be sampled in the restaurants of the surrounding modern town. The faded grandeur of the Baron Hotel, opened in 1909 by the Mazloumians, two Armenian brothers, is a now famous landmark that once saw the likes of T. E. Lawrence, Theodore Roosevelt and Agatha Christie (it was here that she wrote *Murder on the Orient Express*). The bar still attracts interesting characters in the evening.

Of the "Dead Cities", **Qala't Samaan** (the Church of St Simeon), with its related monastery and pilgrimage centre, is perhaps the most striking. A great cruciform church was built around the pillar of the 5th-century ascetic Simeon Stylites, who chose to isolate himself from the world by living on top of a giant column for the final 40 years of his life. He was revered for his piety and wisdom all over the Byzantine world, attracting hordes of pilgrims, as well as many imitators. The remnants of the pillar form the centrepiece of the church today. The hilltop setting is dramatic and the honey-coloured buildings are extraordinary not just for their beauty but for their numerous architectural innovations.

Meeting on the road.

BELOW: Ottoman architecture, Aleppo.

THE DEAD CITIES

Aleppo is an excellent base from which to venture to the region of the "dead cities". This evocative term refers to the bare mountainous limestone region in the north, populated by the well-preserved ruins of elegant country villas, towns, monasteries and churches.

During the Roman and Byzantine periods they were the centre of a thriving olive oil and wine industry, which relied on the careful conservation of winter rains and commerce with the Mediterranean world. This economy collapsed with the disruptions of the Muslim conquest but the monuments remain, largely unpillaged and undisturbed except by earthquakes. The buildings, standing up to three storeys high, are of limestone, marrying Graeco-Roman architecture with an individualistic Syrian interpretation unique to this area.

Scattered remains at **Jeradeh** and **Ruweiha** are strewn across a desolate and inhospitable landscape: a 5th-century Byzantine cathedral at Jeradeh and the 6th-century Church of Bissos at Ruweiha. Nearby, at **Ma'aret an-Nu'aman**, is a collection of mosaics, which gives an indication of how the more affluent homes of the "dead cities" were decorated. The collection can be seen everyday, except Tuesday.

The ruins of the classical city of **Cyrrhus** 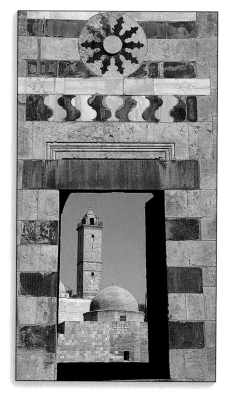, perched on the Turkish border, are not as well preserved as other such sites in Syria, but the location is one of the most romantic in its isolation and beauty. The approach to the site crosses two Roman bridges, both still in use today. Another site with less to see on the surface but of enormous significance in recent scholarship is **Ebla** (Tell Mardikh). South of Aleppo on the north Syrian plain, Bronze-Age Ebla was a major urban centre with international links at the time of the great cities of Sumer and Akkad in Mesopotamia. In 1975 Italian excavators discovered its archives, full of cuneiform tablets in the local language and a repository of information for archaeologists. Parts of the enormous tell have been excavated, revealing sections of the royal palace, sanctuaries, and city fortifications.

The Central Plains

A good base for visiting central Syria is the river town of **Hamah**, which straddles the curving banks of the Orontes. The town is famous for its wooden *norias* (waterwheels), which lifted water into aqueducts for town and agricultural supplies. Despite the destruction wrought on the old city by the internal troubles of 1982, some of its treasured buildings have survived and are being reconstructed. As well as the old mosques and khans, the museum in the gracious Beit al-Azem and the waterfront restaurants to the east are recommended. A new luxury hotel overlooks the 12th-century **Mosque al-Nuri** and some of the 17 waterwheels.

BELOW:
citadel, Aleppo.

The impressive ruins of Hellenistic-Byzantine **Apamia** are reached by an easy drive northeast of Hama. In contrast to the dramatic desertscape of Palmyra, its colonnaded streets, walls, and citadel are beautifully set in lush farmland, overlooked by the range of the Jabal as Sahiliyah to the west. A collection of superb mosaics have been recovered from the site and region, some of which are housed in the museum, a converted Ottoman caravanserai.

The Northern Coast

Since Syrian independence in 1946, **Al Ladhiqiyah** (Latakia) has grown from a modest fishing village to being the major Syrian seaport. The town has had a long and chequered history since its Seleucid foundation as Laodicea, but continual redevelopment has left little evidence of its glory. However, it now functions as a beach resort, with a number of large coastal hotels out of town, and forms a convenient base for visiting the surrounding area.

To the north lies the great Bronze-Age port of **Ugarit** (Ras Shamra). Unlike many contemporary Syrian cities, such as Ebla and Mari, which were built of mudbrick and vulnerable to erosion, Ugarit was largely built of stone. The layout is therefore far more comprehensible to the casual observer. It has been excavated by the French almost continuously for the last 50 years, and has provided a wealth of information and artefacts, including written records. Various palace complexes, temples and housing on the acropolis have been exposed amid an attractive setting of fruit and olive groves.

Crusaders and Saracens

The mountains of the **Jabal as Sahiliyah** stretching behind Latakia have long been a refuge of breakaway sects and minorities, and today contain populations of Alawites (whose members include Hafez al-Assad, Syria's president) and Ismaelis (once the feared Assassins of medieval times). Hiding within this wild and difficult landscape are myriad Crusader, Saracen and Assassin castles, the journeys to which are rewarding in themselves.

Map on page 308

One of the most splendid is **Qala't Salahidin** ㉓, 24 km (15 miles) east of Latakia. Set on a ridge between two precipitous ravines, it is one of the unchanged survivors of a number of early 12th-century Crusader fortresses. It was lost to Saladin in 1188 and never recaptured. Its history goes back to Phoenician times and covers the largest area of any castle in Syria.

Further down the coast, in the hills southeast of Baniyas, lies the black brooding mass of **Qala't Marqab** ㉔. It dominates the narrow passage of the coastal plain, and commands superb views of both sea and mountains. Built by the Muslims in the mid-11th century, it fell into Crusader hands and eventually went to the Knights Hospitallers. They applied novel concepts on a grand scale in their extensive refortification of the structure, pre-empting 13th-century developments in Europe.

Sarcophagus in Tartus Museum.

The coastal road continues south to **Tartus** ㉕, until recently a quiet, charming fishing town but now elevated to the second port in Syria. Originally a Phoenician foundation, it became important in Byzantine times and was the stronghold for the Knights Templar during the Crusades. Remnants of the multiperiod fortress can still be traced, and the Crusader cathedral, which is now the museum, is impressive in its simple, massive beauty.

BELOW: the stuff of legends – Krak des Chevaliers.

There is much character in the old city and port, and from here one can take the ferry to the island of **Arwad** ㉖. Arwad/Arados has a historical importance far exceeding its tiny size. It was a fortress, trading port and centre for ship-building. Today the harbourside fish restaurants are popular with daytrippers (making it hard to squeeze on to the ferries on Fridays and holidays).

Turning inland from Tartus, you can travel via the picturesque hill town of **Safita** ㉗, which has a fine luxury hotel with sea views and the remains of yet another Crusader castle, to reach what is undoubtedly the supreme monument to this extraordinary period of European intervention in the Levant.

The magnificent castle of **Krak des Chevaliers** ㉘ (Qala't al-Husn) is located on a hill near the vital east-west gap that runs through the ranges from the sea to Homs. Already an important defensive site before the Crusades, it was greatly expanded and remodelled by the Knights Hospitallers into the massive impregnable structure we see today. Attesting to the planning and engineering skills of the Crusader architects, the castle was never taken by force, and it remains, as T. E. Lawrence observed, "perhaps the best preserved and wholly admirable castle in the world." It requires a good three hours to explore the complex.

From here it's 50 km (31 miles) to complete the loop to Homs to take the highway to Damascus. ❑

INSIGHT GUIDES
TRAVEL TIPS

INSIGHT GUIDES

The world's largest collection of visual travel guides

Insight Guides – the Classic Series
that puts you in the picture

Alaska	China	Hong Kong	Morocco	Singapore
Alsace	Cologne	Hungary	Moscow	South Africa
Amazon Wildlife	Continental Europe		Munich	South America
American Southwest	Corsica	Iceland		South Tyrol
Amsterdam	Costa Rica	India	Namibia	Southeast Asia
Argentina	Crete	India's Western	Native America	Wildlife
Asia, East	Crossing America	Himalayas	Nepal	Spain
Asia, South	Cuba	India, South	Netherlands	Spain, Northern
Asia, Southeast	Cyprus	Indian Wildlife	New England	Spain, Southern
Athens	Czech & Slovak	Indonesia	New Orleans	Sri Lanka
Atlanta	Republic	Ireland	New York City	Sweden
Australia		Israel	New York State	Switzerland
Austria	Delhi, Jaipur & Agra	Istanbul	New Zealand	Sydney
	Denmark	Italy	Nile	Syria & Lebanon
Bahamas	Dominican Republic	Italy, Northern	Normandy	
Bali	Dresden		Norway	Taiwan
Baltic States	Dublin	Jamaica		Tenerife
Bangkok	Düsseldorf	Japan	Old South	Texas
Barbados		Java	Oman & The UAE	Thailand
Barcelona	East African Wildlife	Jerusalem	Oxford	Tokyo
Bay of Naples	Eastern Europe	Jordan		Trinidad & Tobago
Beijing	Ecuador		Pacific Northwest	Tunisia
Belgium	Edinburgh	Kathmandu	Pakistan	Turkey
Belize	Egypt	Kenya	Paris	Turkish Coast
Berlin	England	Korea	Peru	Tuscany
Bermuda			Philadelphia	
Boston	Finland	Laos & Cambodia	Philippines	Umbria
Brazil	Florence	Lisbon	Poland	USA: Eastern States
Brittany	Florida	Loire Valley	Portugal	USA: Western States
Brussels	France	London	Prague	US National Parks:
Budapest	Frankfurt	Los Angeles	Provence	East
Buenos Aires	French Riviera		Puerto Rico	US National Parks:
Burgundy		Madeira		West
Burma (Myanmar)	Gambia & Senegal	Madrid	Rajasthan	
	Germany	Malaysia	Rhine	Vancouver
Cairo	Glasgow	Mallorca & Ibiza	Rio de Janeiro	Venezuela
Calcutta	Gran Canaria	Malta	Rockies	Venice
California	Great Barrier Reef	Marine Life ot the	Rome	Vienna
California, Northern	Great Britain	South China Sea	Russia	Vietnam
California, Southern	Greece	Mauritius &		
Canada	Greek Islands	Seychelles	St. Petersburg	Wales
Caribbean	Guatemala, Belize &	Melbourne	San Francisco	Washington DC
Catalonia	Yucatán	Mexico City	Sardinia	Waterways of Europe
Channel Islands		Mexico	Scotland	Wild West
Chicago	Hamburg	Miami	Seattle	
Chile	Hawaii	Montreal	Sicily	Yemen

Complementing the above titles are 120 easy-to-carry Insight Compact Guides, 120 Insight Pocket
Guides with full-size pull-out maps and more than 60 laminated easy-fold Insight Maps

CONTENTS

Getting Acquainted

The Place

To the east of the Mediterranean and northwest of the Arabian Peninsula, Jordan lies between 29°11'–33°22' north and 34°59'–39°18' east parallels. It is bordered in the north by Syria, in the east by Iraq and in the south by Saudi Arabia. To the west lies the Israeli-occupied West Bank and Israel, with which Jordan has the longest ceasefire line of any Arab state. This fact has been of crucial importance in the modern history of Jordan.

Size

Jordan covers an area of 89,411 sq. km (55,900 sq. miles) excluding the West Bank which comprises 5,440 sq. km (2,100 sq. miles). (King Hussein formally renounced his claim to the West Bank in July 1988.) It is only 414 km (257 miles) from Ar-Ramtha at the border with Syria to Aqaba in the south and 387 km (240 miles) from the King Hussein Bridge on the Jordan river to the Iraqi border in the east.

Topography

The kingdom is divided into three natural regions from east to west, which converge in the south at Aqaba, Jordan's only outlet to the sea. The first consists of the eastern depression of the Jordan Valley from the southern end of the Sea of Galilee in the north, along the Jordan River, the Dead Sea (at about 395 m/1,300 ft below sea level the lowest point on earth) down to the Red Sea at Aqaba.

The second natural region is the upland area above the Jordan Valley, which begins at the Yarmuk River in the north. Stretching down to Aqaba, this region is intersected by *wadis* (valleys and gorges) that subdivide it into three distinct areas. The first lies in the area between the Yarmuk and Zarqa rivers, the second runs from the River Zarqa to the spectacular Wadi Mujib and the third consists of upland regions around Karak.

The "Badia" desert to the east of these uplands is the third and largest region, forming more than 75 percent of the total area. Azraq, whose black stone fort was for a short time the headquarters of Lawrence of Arabia, is the only major oasis in this inhospitable region. Throughout history, the line between the desert and the settled uplands has fluctuated according to the strength of central authority, local villagers and the Bedouin.

Geology

Soil types and climate vary between these different regions. Most of the Jordan valley to the north of the Dead Sea consists of alluvial soil and is very fertile. But low rainfall and high temperatures necessitate irrigation, which comes by way of a canal running through the valley from the north. Around the Dead Sea and to the south the soil varies between high salinity and a desert of gravel and sand.

The uplands to the east have attracted settlers throughout history. The dry temperate climate and soil, which varies from shallow and light to deep and rich, favour the production of grains and fruits. The desert to the east, which has almost no rainfall, is suitable only for animal husbandry. The cultivated area around the oasis at Azraq has shrunk in recent years as a result of excessive use of local water resources. In the north the desert region comprises grey basalt; further south granite and sandstone create the beauty of Petra and Wadi Rum. The area of Wadi Araba is rich in potash and

Nature Reserves

Shaumari Wildlife Reserve: near the eastern town of Azraq. Established by the Royal Jordanian Society for the Conservation of Nature to reintroduce animals that had become extinct in the region, such as the Arabian oryx (an antelope species), ostriches and gazelle.

Azraq Oasis: near Shaumari. Hosts many bird species migrating from Europe and Asia to Africa.

Wadi Mujib: Jordan's equivalent to the Grand Canyon. Supports a wildlife reserve spread along the eastern shore of the Dead Sea and Rift Valley escarpment.

Dana Wildlands Reserve: a little to the south of Tafila off the King's Highway, near the small towns of Qadisiyya and Busayra. One of the best areas to observe a great selection of Middle Eastern birds and animals. There is a small resthouse and the campsite is open from March to November, but it is best to book with the RSCN in Amman beforehand.

Wadi Rum: one of the most magnificent desert landscapes in the world and an amazing place for bird and animal watchers alike.

Gulf of Aqaba: this coastal reef is a protected marine area, with a huge variety of tropical fish and coral, offering world class scuba-diving.

● **RSCN** – The Royal Society for the Conservation of Nature, Amman. Tel: 533 3610 or 533 7931/2/3 e-mail: HYPERLINK mailto: rscn@nets.com.jo rscn@nets.com.jo

Wadi Hasa has phosphate: both are mined primarily for export.

National Parks

The **Dibbeen National Park**, between Jarash and Ajlun, has 48 km (30 miles) of pine woodland and a resthouse with bungalows and a picnic site. A Friday favourite with Jordanians, it is a great place for a picnic after a trip to Jarash and for walks, especially in spring when the wildflowers are out.

The **Zai National Park**, on the road from Salt to the Jordan Valley is also covered with pine trees and commands beautiful views of the valley. A small road winds through it and a resthouse (*istiraha*) offers fine views. Both parks have play areas for children and are ideal for half-day outings from Amman. Unfortunately litter collection is spasmodic and much of the green is littered with plastic containers.

Time Zones

Jordan is two hours ahead of Greenwich Mean Time and seven hours ahead of US Eastern Standard Time from the beginning of October to the end of March. It is three hours ahead of GMT from April until the end of September.

Climate

Jordan enjoys almost year-round sunshine and blue skies. Rain falls only from late autumn to mid-spring. Quantity is unpredictable, however, and when the time comes, farmers and other Jordanians often pray for rain. Aqaba, the south and the desert have negligible rainfall.

The best time to visit is in the spring (April–May), when the winter rains have turned the country green. In places, even the desert is a mass of colourful flowers. The next best time is autumn, October–November, when the hot summer has given way to milder weather perfect for outside dining.

Average temperatures: January:

Amman 7°C (45°F), Irbid 9°C (47°F), Aqaba 16°C (61°F); July: Amman 25°C (76°F), Irbid 25°C (76°F) and Aqaba 31°C (88°F).

The People

The population is about 4.6 million, half of whom live in Amman. Most sources agree that the majority are of Palestinian origin. Jordan lays great stress on national unity and officially no minorities exist. Christians have lived here since the dawn of Christianity. They make up about 5 percent of the population and are concentrated in and around Karak, Madaba, Salt and Amman. About two-thirds of these Christians are Greek Orthodox, who fall under the authority of the Patriarchate of Jerusalem. Their liturgy is in Greek and in Arabic. Most of the higher levels of the clergy are reserved for native Greeks.

Most of the remaining Christians are Greek Catholics, who broke with the Patriarchate in 1709. They have their own Patriarch and worship in Arabic. They recognise the authority of the Pope. There are also small numbers of Roman Catholics, Protestants, Assyrians (Nestorians), Armenians and Syrian Orthodox (Jacobites) in Jordan.

The Circassians (about 35,000) and Shishanis (about 4,000) are the only ethnic minority of any size in Jordan. They are Muslims (Sunni and Shia respectively), who originated in the Caucusus and Southern Russia. In the mid-19th century, the Ottomans in Istanbul, seeking to reassert their authority, encouraged the Circassians and others to settle parts of the empire which had broken away from central control.

The Economy

Jordan has few natural resources. Nowadays, agriculture accounts for about 7½ percent of GDP and phosphate and potash are among the kingdom's principal exports. Tourism and light manufacturing also figure; but until recently, Jordan's main natural resource and

earner was its highly-educated population. In the 1970s Jordan benefited from the oil boom in the Gulf and the civil war in Lebanon. Within a short time 28 percent of the labour force was working in the Gulf and their remittances were the largest single contributor to the balance of payments. At home the service sector expanded and became more efficient. Improvements in the infrastructure, in banking and finance permitted Jordan to take over Lebanon's role as the region's *entrepot*.

From the outset, Jordan has also relied heavily on foreign aid, first from Britain, then the US and the Arab states. The Jordanian economy enjoyed rapid growth between 1975 and 1983 at 13.9 percent per annum. However, the collapse in oil prices in the 1980s, among other things, reduced this figure to about 3 percent. More recently, the expulsion of more than 350,000 Palestinians and Jordanians from Kuwait following the 1991 Gulf War created further problems.

Jordan's economy is burdened by a huge foreign debt which in 1997 stood at US$6.5 billion. Nonetheless in the early 1990s the World Bank and the International Monetary Fund were talking about Jordan as a success story. The country has implemented many of the structural adjustment measures demanded of it and the US and other powers are beginning to forgive what they simplistically perceived as Jordan's support for Iraq in the Gulf War. In fact, 1992 was a boom year for Jordan, with GDP growth of about 11 percent.

Under a five-year IMF programme, from 1992 to 1997, inflation fell from 16 percent to around four percent and the budget deficit declined from 18 percent of GDP in 1991 to around 4.5 percent. However, the public began to debate the necessity of reforms when the government lifted bread subsidies in 1996, in spite of growing poverty, triggering riots in the south of the Kingdom. In 1998, the government was forced to concede that, under the reform programme, economic growth for the years 1996 and 1997 stood at only 0.8 and 2.7 percent respectively, instead of the 5.2 and 5.0 per cent it had boasted. Criticism of the government's privatisation programme, a main tenet of reforms, mounted as profitable state enterprises fell into the hands of establishment figures.

Government

Jordan is a constitutional monarchy and succession rests on male descent. The 1952 constitution is the basis for the political system. Jordan has a two-chamber National Assembly, comprised of a senate of 40 members who are appointed by the King and a Chamber of Deputies of 80 members which is elected by direct universal suffrage. The King has extensive powers. He appoints the prime minister and is Commander in Chief of the armed forces. He approves laws, convenes and adjourns the Chamber of Deputies and can postpone elections for up to two years.

The first free elections since the 1950s were held in 1989. In September 1992, a new law legalised political parties which had been banned in 1957. Twenty parties participated in the 1993 elections, and the most significant of these was the Islamic Action Front, in which the Muslim Brothers play the dominant role. In 1993 the first woman MP was elected. Christians, Circassians and Shishanis have their quotas in parliamentary seats.

The premier Kabariti was unpopular among many quarters because of his controversial decision to lift bread subsidies – a move which led to violent riots in the south of the country. The premier clashed with Prince Hassan (then the Crown Prince) over such matters as the bread policy, and was forced to resign in early 1997 to make way for the conservative government of Abdel Salam Majali. The main assignment of the Majali government was to oversee the

1997 parliamentary elections, which were boycotted by nine opposition parties (led by the Islamic Action Front), amidst claims of election rigging, corruption and anti-democratic behaviour. Several scandals involving the Majali government, including a major crisis concerning water pollution, led the ailing King Hussein to accept the government's resignation in the summer of 1998 from his sickbed at the Mayo Clinic in Minnesota, USA. The monarch then installed his chief of the Royal Court, Fayez Tarawneh, a Karaki, as prime minister, along with a new, youthful cabinet. He commanded them to put the stagnating economy back on track and mend fences with the public.

Islam

Islam, meaning submission in Arabic, is the religion propagated by the Prophet Mohammed in Arabia in the 7th century AD. For Muslims, Islam is the consummation and correction of its monotheistic predecessors, Judaism and Christianity. The basic principles of Islam are that there is one God who must be worshipped by man and that the Prophet Mohammed was the ultimate messenger of God's wishes to mankind. The *Koran*, the Word of God revealed to the Prophet Mohammed, and the *Hadith*, the words and actions of the Prophet, are the main sources of Islam.

As with other religions, practice and interpretation vary widely. There have been schisms from the Sunni (Orthodox) line. The most important of these are the Shia, who believed the leadership of the early Islamic community rightfully belonged to Ali, the cousin of the Prophet and the father of his grand-children through his daughter Fatima.

In the 19th century, Islam began to play a more political role, largely in response to the confrontation between European domination and local forces. For many Arabs Islam represents a form of cultural assertion and regeneration.

Jordan is overwhelmingly Sunni Muslim and Shiaism is largely confined to a small Shishan community numbering only 2,000. The royal family enjoys considerable prestige as Hashemites, descendants of the Prophet Mohammed, and has managed to contain political Islam. The Muslim Brotherhood, for instance – a movement of Sunni Muslims formed in the 1920s with the intention of creating a theocratic Islamic state – was co-opted by the Jordanian regime from the 1950s onward. However, shortly before the 1993 elections, the King changed the electoral law in a move which many observers said was directed against the power of political Islam in Jordan.

The Pillars of Islam

Every Muslim has five basic duties called the "pillars" of Islam. These are:
- testifying that "there is no god but God and that Mohammed is the messenger of God"
- praying five times a day (at dawn, midday, mid-afternoon, sunset and evening)
- setting aside a certain amount of money for the poor
- fasting from dawn to dusk in the month of Ramadan
- making the pilgrimage to Mecca at least once in a lifetime.

Planning the Trip

What To Bring

Comfortable, hard-wearing walking shoes are a must. In the cold months (November–March) bring warm and waterproof clothing. In the warm and hot weather you will need a pair of dark sunglasses, cotton clothes (avoid synthetic materials that do not breathe) and a hat. Even in the summer, the temperature drops significantly after sundown and you will need something to keep yourself warm in the evenings. If you plan to swim, bring a swim suit and suntan or sunblock lotion as these items are very expensive locally. Also bring insect repellent.

Jordan is a conservative country as far as dress code is concerned. You should avoid wearing tight clothes, sleeveless blouses, shorts, mini-skirts, and see-through materials, and refrain from exposing your back (see also the section on Women Travellers).

Jordan operates on a current of 220–240V. Most places have two-pin European-style plugs but a few have British-style three-pin plugs. You may find adaptors as well as transformers for American electrical goods in electrical stores.

Camera film and video cassettes cost a lot more than at home. Tampons are also expensive and not always easy to find.

Visas & Passports

All passports require an entry visa which is free of charge for some nationals and quite expensive for others. The price you pay usually depends on the amount your country charges for Jordanians to enter your country.

Apart from obtaining a visa from your nearest Jordanian consular authority you can get one upon arrival at any border entry, including the two new ones between Jordan and Israel, the Sheikh Hussein Bridge and the Wadi Araba border crossing. However, you still cannot obtain an entry visa at the King Hussein (Allenby) Bridge if you are entering from the West Bank, because Jordan does not recognise this to be a border. If you want to enter Jordan from the bridge you must already have a valid visa stamped in your passport (it doesn't need to be a multi-entry visa if you are re-entering).

Visas obtained in Jordanian consulates are valid for 3–4 months from the date of issue and can be issued for multiple entries. You will need to register at the nearest police station if you stay for more than two weeks in Jordan. Tourist visas allow a stay of up to one month initially; upon expiration this period can easily be extended for another two months. Beyond that date you should exit and re-enter the country or undergo the complicated immigration procedures. If your visa has not been renewed properly by the time you leave Jordan you will have to pay a fine at the border.

Animal Quarantine

There is no animal quarantine in Jordan. In fact there are no regulations about bringing pets into the country. At the very most you may be asked for a certificate of health for the animal.

Customs

Exempt from duty: personal effects such as cameras, clothes, typewriters and up to 200 cigarettes, 1 litre of spirits and 2 litres of wine and 200 grams (7 oz) of tobacco.

Both departing and arriving passengers can buy duty-free items at Queen Alia International Airport. The Mall duty-free shop is open from 8am to midnight.

Cars and electrical equipment, from household goods to personal computers etc, are subject to duty in Jordan, and this can be very high. If you are bringing in taxable goods such as a laptop computer, ask the customs officials to enter details in your passport to avoid paying tax. Upon exit you will be asked to show that your goods were tax exempted.

Books, as well as videos, are subject to censorship in Jordan. If, you bring large numbers of books into Jordan, do not be surprised if they fall under scrutiny. Books with a political content that is deemed hostile to the interests of the state of Jordan, as well as sexually explicit material, are likely to be confiscated.

Recommended Maps

Maps are available in most hotels, bookshops and shops geared towards the tourist trade.

You can purchase the quite cheap and very adequate Arabic/English maps produced by the **Royal Jordanian Geographic Centre** (RJGC): The Tourist Map of Amman, The Road Map of the Hashemite Kingdom of Jordan with city plans of Amman, Aqaba, Irbid, Jarash and Karak, and The Tourist Map of Petra.

The RJGC also prints the Map of Jordan (in Arabic, English, French, German and Italian).

Jordan, the map produced by GEO Projects (Lebanon), is adequate but its roads badly need updating. If you want the most reliable and frequently updated information on roads in Jordan you should purchase Bartholomew's map of **Israel with Jordan** which unfortunately omits the eastern tip of Jordan bordering Iraq. Foreign maps of Jordan are not available in Jordan.

● In Britain, try **Stanfords Maps**, 12 Long Acre, London WC2E 9LP. Tel: 020-7836 1321.

Health

If you come from a country infected by epidemic diseases such as cholera and yellow fever, you will have to show a certificate of inoculation. It is advisable to be inoculated for hepatitis (Gamma Globulin), polio, tetanus and typhoid.

Jordan is one of the cleanest countries in the region, but it is advisable to take some precautions at least until your system adjusts.

Hotels rated 4-star and up have their own filtering systems and their tap water is safe to drink. Elsewhere you should use bottled water which is widely available and, outside hotels, cheap. All fruit and vegetables that you buy should be washed thoroughly. During the warmer months avoid salads and cold meats that have been sitting for a long time on hotel buffets.

Money Matters

The Jordanian currency is called the Jordanian Dinar (JD) and it is divided into 1,000 fils or 100 piastres (or 'irsh). It appears in paper notes of 20, 10, 5, 1 and 0.5JDs. Coinage includes several mints slowly being taken out of circulation (100, 50 and 25 fils silver coins and copper coins of 10 and 5 fils) and new coins being introduced (1JD, 0.5JD and 250 fils brass coins, a brass and silver commemorative 0.5JD coin, and new, smaller silver coins of 100, 50 and 25 fils, which are denoted as 10, 5 and 2.5 piastres)

Since the 1988 devaluation of the Jordanian Dinar Jordan has become a relatively cheap country for Westerners to visit.

1 US$	=	0.7 JD
1 £	=	1.2 JD
1 DM	=	0.40 JD
1 FF	=	0.12 JD
100 Yen	=	0.54 JD
100 IL	=	0.04 JD

You can change foreign cash or traveller's cheques in any bank in Jordan; only for traveller's cheques will you be charged a commission (this varies from bank to bank).

Visiting During Ramadan

Although Ramadan is not a good time to come to Jordan for business, it is a great time to enjoy local customs and the special atmosphere that the shared hardship of fasting creates among Muslims.

You should avoid eating, drinking or smoking in public during the hours of fasting: it is illegal and it can provoke strong reactions. At sundown everyone breaks the fast with *iftar* and then relaxes until long into the evening. Just before dawn the last meal is eaten before the next day's fasting resumes. Huge amounts of food and sweets are prepared and devoured after dark. As a result most people look exhausted at work next day and government officials may often use this as an excuse to provide a much reduced service!

When you change traveller's cheques you will be asked to show your sales receipts for the cheques despite the fact that you are not supposed to keep them together.

There are authorised money-changers in Amman, Aqaba and Irbid and generally speaking you get better deals at moneychangers downtown. Exchange rates between banks and moneychangers vary slightly. Hotels of three stars or more will also change money but at a less favourable rate. Foreign currency restrictions have been dropped, in line with IMF reforms.

Credit cards are acceptable in several hotels, restaurants and shops; the most widely accepted being American Express, Visa, Diners Club and Mastercard (in this order). You can also use your cards to draw cash (up to 500JDs only) at any bank linked with your credit card network at no extra charge. Automatic cash machines outside banks in Amman are generally limited to Jordanian bank account holders. However, some machines in the capital's more affluent areas – Abdoun, Sweifiyeh or Shumaysani – are equipped to handle credit cards with international PIN numbers.

Public Holidays

Friday is the weekly holiday when government offices, banks and most offices are closed. However, some airline offices and travel agents stay open with a reduced service and some shops also open.

Most businesses and banks have a half-day on Thursday and some take Sunday as a half-day or a complete holiday.

Fixed public holidays

1 January	Christian New Year
15 January	Tree Day (Arbor Day)
22 March	Arab League Day
1 May	Labour Day
25 May	Independence Day
10 June	Arab Renaissance Day, commemorating the Arab Revolt; also Army Day
11 August	King Hussein's accession to the throne
14 November	King Hussein's Birthday
25 December	Christmas Day

Holidays that are not fixed

Muslim holidays follow the lunar calendar, moving back each year by 11 days. The first two holidays in the list below last three days, during which Friday services are encountered. The remaining holidays in the list are one-day public holidays.

Ayd Al-Fitr: the feast that marks the end of Ramadan, the month of fasting.

Ayd Al-Adha: the feast of sacrifice, which falls at the end of the month of the pilgrimage to Mecca (*Haj*). It commemorates Abraham's offering of Isaac for sacrifice. Families who can afford to slaughter a lamb share the meat with their poorer co-religionists. The richer the family the more lambs it slaughters and

distributes to the poor.
1st of Muharram: Muslim New Year
Mawoulid An-Nabawi: the Prophet
Mohammed's Birthday.
Ayd Al-Isra wa Al-Miraj: the feast
celebrates the nocturnal visit of the
Prophet Mohammed to heaven.

Christian holidays
If you happen to visit Jordan during
Easter bear in mind that the local
Protestant and Catholic churches
celebrate Easter at approximately
the same time as the local Greek
Orthodox. Three out of every four
years the timing will vary by a week
but in the other year by a whole
month. Eastern (Orthodox)
Christians regard Easter as a more
significant feast than Christmas.

If you plan to visit Jordan during
Christmas don't be put off by the
fact that this is a predominantly
Muslim country because, thanks to
Western commercialism and the
local foreign community, Christmas
and the New Year are celebrated in
some splendour. There are also
many opportunities for children to
enjoy themselves during these
times.

Getting There

By Air
Jordan's national airline, Royal
Jordanian (RJ), flies direct to Amman
from numerous European and
Middle Eastern destinations, North
America, India and Southeast Asia.
RJ has offices in even more
destinations including almost every
European capital. Here are a few of
their addresses concentrating on
the UK, North America and the
Middle East:
Bahrain: Ground Floor, Chamber of
Commerce Bldg, King Faisal
Highway, Manama.
Tel: 292 293/4/5.
Cairo: Zamalek Sporting Club Bldg,
26 July Street, Mohandeseen.
Tel: 344 3114 and 346 7540.
Chicago: 6 North Michigan Ave.,
Suite 803, Chicago, Illinois 60602.
Tel: (312) 236 1702.
Damascus: 29 Ayyar Street.
Tel: 221 1267 and 221 8681.
Detroit: 6 Parklane Blvd, Suite 122,

Dearborn, Michigan 48126.
Tel: (313) 271 6663.
Dubai: Dubai Pearl Bldg, Ground
Floor, Dayra Side.
Tel: 232 855.
Dublin: Chepman Freeborn (Ireland)
Ltd, 3 Clyde Road, Ballsbridge,
Dublin 4.
Tel: 842 3144.
Houston: 3336 Richmond Ave,
Suite 216, Houston, Texas 77098.
Tel: (713) 524 3700.
Istanbul: Merkez Apt No 163, 2nd
Floor, Elmadag, Istanbul.
Tel: 212-230 4074 and 232 8269.
Karachi: Hotel Metropole,
Mereweather Road, Karachi 75520.
Tel: (21) 566 0458/9/60.
London: 32 Brook St,
London W1Y 1AG.
Tel: 020-7878 6333.
Los Angeles: 6033 West Century
Blvd, Suite 760, Los Angeles,
California 90045.
Tel: (310) 215 9627.
Manchester: Suite 3, 3rd Floor,
Lancaster Bldgs, 77 Deansgate,
Manchester M3 2BZ.
Tel: 0161-832 4847.
Miami: 7200 Corporate Center
Drive N.W., 19th Street, Suite 401,
Miami, Florida 33126.
Tel: (305) 599 0800.
Montreal: 1801 McGill College Ave,
Suite 1050, Montreal, H3A 2N4.
Tel: (514) 288 1647;
toll-free: 1-800-363-0711.
New York: 535 Fifth Avenue,
New York, NY 10017.
Tel: (212) 949 0060.
Riyadh: Mashael Al-Riyadh Bldg,
Altamaneen St, Olaya,
Riyadh 11462.
Tel: 462 5697 and 462 6405 and
465 4991.
Sydney: Concorde International
Travel PTY Ltd, 403 George Street,
Sydney, NSW 2000.
Tel: 029 321 9222.
Toronto: 45 St Clair Avenue West,
Toronto, Ontario M4V 1K9.
Tel: (416) 962 3955;
toll-free: 1-800-363-0711.
Washington: 1660 L Street N.W.,
Suite 305, Washington DC 20036.
Tel: (202) 857 0401.

For bookings in Amman, tel: 6
567 8321.

For special meal requirements,

Queen Alia Airport

International flights use the
modern and very secure Queen
Alia International Airport, which is
32 km (20 miles) south of Amman
on the highway to Aqaba.

place your order through the
reservation system at the time of
booking or contact Royal Jordanian
Catering Services directly at Queen
Alia International Airport, Amman,
tel: (00962) 8 53105; fax: (00962)
8 53367.

Royal Jordanian is now on the
internet, offering further and
updated information at:
www.rja.com.jo

Other airlines operating flights to
Jordan are: Air France, Air Algerie,
Austrian Air, Alitalia, Air Ukraine, Air
Yemen, Aeroflot, El Al, British
Airways, Cyprus Airlines, Emirates
Airlines, Egypt Air, Gulf Air, Kuwait
Airlines, KLM, Lufthansa, Middle
East Airlines, Olympic Airlines,
Pakistan International Airlines,
Qatar Airlines, Royal Wings, Saudia,
Sudan Airways, Tarom and Turkish
Airlines

By Train or Bus
By train from Syria: The Hejaz
railway train runs once a week
between Amman and Damascus on
the same single track that was built
by the Ottomans at the beginning of
the 20th century. A train leaves
Damascus every Sunday
at 7.30am, arriving at Amman at
5pm. Tickets cost 2.500JD and can
only be purchased on the day of
travel.

**By bus or service taxi from
Syria:** Karnak, the Syrian bus
company, runs an air-conditioned
bus service between Damascus
and Amman twice daily (early
morning and in the afternoon) which
takes about five to six hours
counting the time taken to complete
formalities at the border crossing,
from Dir'a, 100 km (62 miles)
south of Damascus on the Syrian
side, to Ar-Ramtha 88 km (55
miles) north of Amman on the

Jordanian side. Buses leave from the Karnak bus station and arrive at the JETT bus station near Abdali. Book well in advance. One-way tickets cost about $6.50 in Jordan, where bookings are handled by Jordan Express Tourist Transport Co Ltd (JETT), Abdali, Amman (tel: 569 6151 or 556 4146).

Service taxis (pronounced *servees*) are shared taxis and they run throughout the day. The taxi rank is near the Karnak bus station. The trip takes almost as long as on the bus.

By bus and ferry from Egypt: There is a bus service between Cairo and Amman run by JETT and Superjet of the Arab Unity Co, Sharikat Al-Ittihad Al-Arabi, Cairo (tel: 290 9013). The bus leaves Cairo every Saturday, Monday, Tuesday and Thursday at 5pm from the bus station in Masr Al-Gedida, arriving in Amman the next day at around 10pm. One-way tickets cost US$59 for non-Arabs and include the Nuwayba-Aqaba ferry fare.

By bus from Saudi Arabia: JETT runs a bus service from Jeddah to Amman three times a week and the trip lasts around 22 hours.

By bus or service taxi from Israel and the Occupied Territories: In East Jerusalem service taxis

(*sherouts*) leave from just opposite Damascus Gate (Bab Al-Amoud) for the King Hussein (Allenby) Bridge and fill up from 7.30am onwards. You can reserve a seat at the nearby office or you can ask your hotel to call the taxi company and organise for you to be picked up from your own hotel at a prearranged time. You should try to book in advance and ensure that they will take you all the way to the check-point. Start your trip early as the bridge crossing can take a long time, especially during the high season. The fare is 26 shekels per person if the 7-seat taxi is full. If you cannot get a shared taxi you will need to pay up to 100 shekels for a private taxi that takes four passengers.

The trip takes 40 minutes to the bridge check-point on the Israeli-occupied side. Upon exit from Israel or the West Bank you will have to pay an exit tax of approximately US$26, payable in dolars, shekels or dinars. From there you have to join the JETT bus that shuttles every hour between the Jordanian and Israeli check-points from 8am, when the bridge opens, until 8pm, when it closes. The JETT bus ticket costs 1.500JD and must be paid in JDs or US dollars.

Once you are on the Jordanian side you have to pass through passport control and your bags will be checked by customs officers. For Amman, pick up a shared taxi at the nearby rank where you should pay no more than 2.000JD. The taxi will drop you at Abdali bus station. You can also catch the cheaper public minibus that will drive you straight to Abdali.

As well as the King Hussein (Allenby) Bridge there are two new border crossings between Jordan and Israel, the Sheikh Hussein Bridge at the north of the Jordan Valley near the Israeli town of Bet Shean and the crossing at Wadi Araba near Aqaba and Eilat. These two entry points are open Sun–Thur from 8am to 10pm, and on Fridays from 8am until 8pm.

Exit tax from Israel is the same (*see above*) and you will get your passport stamped automatically on both sides of the border – so , clearly, this is not the way to enter Jordan if you plan to make your way to Syria. (See *On Departure, To Syria*.) There are bus services operated by the Israeli state company Egged (for information, tel: 03-527 1223 – Tel Aviv) that can take you to Bet Shean and Eilat, and from there you can take a

Women Travellers

Sexual harassment in Jordan is less common than in other parts of the Arab world with high numbers of tourists. However, there will be moments when you will feel uncomfortable – as men try to touch you on the street or by the way they stare at you.

The city centre of Amman, where men far outnumber women on the streets, may make you feel particularly uncomfortable. One tip is to avoid looking into people's faces and to concentrate on where you are going. This won't save you from harassment but it will make you less upset. When choosing a place to sit for a coffee or tea, look first to see how many other women are present to give you an

indication of how comfortable you will be. However, even if you venture into a café full of men without realising, you won't experience any hostility – Jordanians are too polite for that.

It is sensible to dress modestly, but this should be regarded as a gesture of respect for local culture rather than a safeguard against harassment by men. If you happen to see young Jordanian women in mini-skirts, consider the fact that they are more aware of social confines than you are likely to be and would rarely dress in such a way if they were about to go downtown or to make use of public transport.

Although Jordan is a relatively

safe country and crimes against women travellers are practically unheard of, be alert and careful. If you take a taxi to a remote area on your own, take the name of the driver and the number of the taxi before you get in. Do not sit in the front seat of a taxi. In the countryside and when visiting archaeological sites, try to be in view of other people at all times. Hitching will invite the inevitable unpleasant encounter so avoid it.

Take special care at hotels of two stars and below, making sure that there are no peeping holes in the walls or door and that your bedroom door locks. As a general recommendation, it is safer for women to travel together.

sherout or private taxi to the borders. Massada Tours in Israel (tel: 02-255453 and 03-5444454) runs a bus service from Jerusalem to Jordan via Tel Aviv.

Israelis have to travel in groups of at least five people when entering Jordan. All travellers entering Jordan through these points must spend at least one night in Jordan.

By Car

To bring your car into Jordan you will need an international driving licence (*carnet de passage en douane*) and insurance, both of which should be obtained before leaving home. You may also have to pay for a local third-party car insurance, which costs very little, or you may want to buy local comprehensive insurance, the cost of which varies according to the make of the car. Your car is free of import duty for up to one year unless you decide to sell it to tax-paying residents, in which case you have to pay the duty.

From Syria: Drive to Dir'a and cross into Ar-Ramtha.

From Egypt: Drive to Nuwayba and take the Egyptian or Jordanian ferry to Aqaba, which leaves in the morning and in the afternoon (check precise timings before you travel). You can buy tickets at the port office in Nuwayba and you must pay for each passenger as well as the car. The ferry journey should take three to four hours but it can take much longer, depending on traffic and weather conditions.

From Israel and the Occupied Territories: The peace treaty between Israel and Jordan stipulates that there will be private car traffic beween the two countries and preparations are under way to allow cars to cross the three crossing points.

Special Facilities

Children

The Middle East in general does not have any of the Western hang-ups about children. Travel in Jordan for children will be as easy and pleasurable as it is for adults.

Jordanians take their children everywhere and you will often see them up until late in the evening at parties and in restaurants. Crime against children committed by strangers is unheard of. Jordan is so safe from this point of view that busy parents are known to leave their children to roam around Safeway supermarket on their own for hours instead of hiring a babysitter.

Most restaurants can cater to children's needs and a few in Amman have a play area for children. Some hotels have playrooms and can easily arrange baby-sitting. Amman hotels that cater readily to children's needs include the Amra Hotel, which has a special playroom and organises weekly puppet shows and story-telling, the Marriott which, among other things, arranges entertainment for children over Friday brunch and at Christmas and Easter, and Al-Maqsura apartment hotel which has a small playground. Almost all hotels of 3-star and up have baby cots. Babies up to two years of age travel free on planes, and up to the age of 12 for half price.

Students

Non-Jordanian students will get no concessions at museums or on public transport in Jordan, but all airlines give discounts on airfares. Royal Jordanian gives discounts of 45–60 percent of the full fare to holders of an international student card. Discounts are also available to students under 31 years old for routes in Europe, to students under 26 for Europe and the Middle East and to students under 25 for Europe, the Middle East and the United States. Young people between 12 and 24 years old qualify for discounts of around 45 percent of the full fare. Jordan has no travel agents specialising in youth/student travel.

Disabled

Although special facilities for the disabled are very rare, Jordanians are always willing to help. You are advised to enquire with your travel agent or your hotel before booking. Disabled visitors to Petra can reach the main sites by horse-driven carriages, and the new Taybet Zaman Village there promises to have ramps throughout the public areas. As a rule, Royal Jordanian provides wheelchair service when they receive prior notice.

Jordan Tourism Board

The Jordanian Ministry of Tourism has no offices outside Jordan. However, the private sector Jordan Tourism Board has offices in the US, UK and France, and all Royal Jordanian offices can supply information and a few brochures.

Jordan Tourism Board Offices Abroad
JTB – USA,
3504 International Drive NW, Washington D.C. 20008.
Tel: 202-244 1451.
Fax: 202-966 3110.
e-mail: SeeJordan@aol.com
JTB – UK,
Representation House,
11 Blades Court,
Deodar Road,
London SW15 2NU.
Tel: 020-8877 4524.
Fax: 020-8874 4219.

Tour Operators

UK TOUR OPERATORS
Abercrombie & Kent,
Sloane Square House,
Holbein Place, London SW1W 8NS.
Tel: 020-7730 9600.
Bales Worldwide,
Bales House, Junction Road,
Dorking, Surrey RH4 3HL.
Tel: 01306-885991.
British Museum Traveller,
46 Bloomsbury Street,
London WC1B 3QQ.
Tel: 020-7323 8895.
Cox & Kings Travel,
4th Floor, Gordon House,
10 Greencoat Place,
London SW1P 1PH.
Tel: 020-7873 5000.
Dragoman, Camp Green,

Debenham, Stowmarket, Suffolk
IP14 6LA. Tel: 01728-861133.
Exodus Expeditions,
9 Weir Road, London SW12 0LT.
Tel: 020-8675 5550.
Explore Worldwide,
1 Frederick Street, Aldershot,
Hants GU11 1LQ.
Tel: 01252-319448.
Goodwood Travel,
St Andrew's House, Station Road
East, Canterbury, Kent CT1 2WD.
Tel: 01227-763336.
Guerba Expeditions,
Wessex House, 40 Station Road,
Westbury, Wilts BA13 3JN.
Tel: 01373-826611.
Holts Tours,
15 Market Street, Sandwich,
Kent CT13 9DA.
Tel: 01304-612248.
Jasmin Tours,
53-55 Balham Hill,
London SW12 9DR.
Tel: 020-8675 8886.
Jordan Travel Service,
Devon House, Wellesley Road,
Wansted, London E11 2HF.
Tel: 01628-483550.
Kuoni Travel,
Kuoni House, Dorking,
Surrey RH5 4AZ.
Tel: 01306-743000.
Martin Randall Travel,
10 Barley Mow Passage, Chiswick,
London W4 4PH.
Tel: 020-8742 3355.
Noble Caledonia,
11 Charles Street,
London W1X 8LE.
Tel: 020-7491 4752.
Page & Moy,
136-140 London Road,
Leicester LE2 1EN.
Tel: 0116-250 7979.
Prospect Music & Art Tours,
36 Manchester Street,
London W1M 5PE.
Tel: 020-7486 5704.
Saga Holidays,
Saga Building, Middleburg Sq,
Folkestone, Kent CT20 1AZ.
Tel: 01303-857000.
Swan Hellenic,
77 New Oxford Street,
London WC1A 1PP.
Tel: 020-7800 2300.
The Imaginative Traveller,
14 Barley Mow Passage, Chiswick,

London W4 4PH.
Tel: 020-8742 3113.
Travelbag Adventures, 15 Turk
Street, Alton, Hants GU34 1AG. Tel:
01420-541007.
Travelsphere, Compass House,
Rockingham Road, Market
Harborough, Leics LE16 7QD. Tel:
01858-410818.
**Voyages Jules Verne/Serenissima
Travel**,
21 Dorset Street,
London NW1 6QG.
Tel: 020-7616 1010.

Natural History
Avian Adventures,
49 Sandy Road, Norton,
Stourbridge DY8 3AJ.
Tel: 01384-372013.
Naturetrek
Cheriton Mill, Cheriton, Alresford,
Hants SO24 0NG.
Tel: 01962-733051.

Diving
Aquatours,
Shelletts House, Angel Road,
Thames Ditton, Surrey KT7 0AU.
Tel: 020-8398 0505.
Regal Diving,
22 High Street, Sutton, Ely,
Cambs CB6 2RB.
Tel: 01353-778096.

Pilgrimage Tours
Fairlink Christian Travel,
The Mews Office, Devon House
Wellesley Road, Wansted,
London E11 2HF.
Tel: 020-8989 0331.
Maranatha Tours,
Trafalgar House, Horton Road,
Horton, Berks SL3 9NU.
Tel: 01753-689568.

Steam Train Tours
LCGB (Locomotive Club of Great
Britain),
2 Manston Avenue, Norwood Green,
Middx UB2 4HE.
Fax: 020-8843 1556.
TEFS,
77 Frederick Street, Loughborough,
Leics LE11 3TL.
Tel: 01509-262745.

US TOUR OPERATORS
Carrefour Tours, 2530 N Lincoln
Ave. Street 266, Chicago, Illinois
60614. Tel: (773) 525 2305.
Calvary Tours, 1559 Post Road,
Fairfield, CT 06830. Tel: (203) 256-
1234.
Catholic Tours,
7301 Sepulveda Blvd, Van Nuys,
California 91405.
Tel 818 909-9910
Consolidated Tours,
1675 Virginia Avenue, Suite 200
Atlanta, GA 30337.
Tel: 404-767-2727.
DAIT (Destinations & Adventure
International Travel),
8489 Crescent Drive, Los Angeles,
CA 90046.
Tel: (213) 650 7267.
DTA Tours,
11825 Preston Road, Dallas,.
TX 75230.
Tel: (214) 701-9944.
General Tours,
53 Summer St, Keene, New
Hampshire 03431.
Tel: (603) 357 4548.
Golden Horn Tours,
PO Box 207, Annapolis, MD 21404.
Tel: (800) 772-7009.
Great Touring Adventures,
1515-B Gregg Street, Philadelphia,
PA 19115.
Tel: (215) 677 8574.
Group Wholesale Tours,
200 Main Street, Hackensack,
NJ 07601.
Tel: (201) 343-3929.
Heavenly International Tours,
6944 N. Port Washington Road
Milwaukee, WI 53217
Tel: 414-352-8622
Intrav,
7711 Bonhomme Avenue, St Louis,
MO 63105-1961.
Tel: (314) 727 0500.
Journeys Unlimited,
500 Eighth Avenue, Suite 904,
New York, NY 10018.
Tel: 212-736-2028.
Marantha Tours,
13825 N. 32nd Street, Suite 24,
Phoenix, AZ 85032.
Tel (602) 788 8864.
R. Crusoe & Son,
566 W Adams Street # 505,
Chicago, Illinois 60661.

Tel: (312) 980 8000;
e-mail: jhutton@rcrusoe.com
Rothschild Tours,
900 West End Ave, New York,
NY 10025.
Tel: (212) 662-4858.
SOLREP International,
3271 West Alabama, Suite 200,
Houston, Texas 77098.
Tel: (800) 231-0985.
Special Expeditions,
720 Fifth Avenue, New York,
NY 10019.
Tel: (212) 765 7740.
Speikermann Travel Service,
31363 Harper, Street Clair Shores,
Michigan 48082.
Tel: (810) 415 9550;
e-mail: goegypt@ earthlink.net
Sunny Land Tours,
166 Main Street, Hackensack,
NJ 07601.
Tel: (201) 487 2150
TFI Tours,
401 S. Milwaukee Avenue
Wheeling, IL 60090
Tel: 1-800-446-5952
Travel Plans International,
1200 Harger Road, Oak Brook,
Illinois 60521.
Tel: (630) 573 1400;
e-mail: travelplans@aol.com
Tri-Star Tours,
3432 Richmond Road, Staten
Island, NY 10306.
Tel: (718) 987-3900.
TTI,
401 South Milwaukee Ave,
Wheeling, IL 60090.
Tel: (708) 520-8087.
World Pilgrimages,
2300 Henderson Mill Road, Suite
325, Atlanta, GA 30345.
Tel: (404) 491-0532.

Practical Tips

Emergencies

Security and Crime

Jordan is a very safe country to
travel in but obvious precautions
should be taken; keep your money
in a hotel safe if available and keep
an eye on your belongings in public
places. It is common wisdom that
women travelling alone should stick
to places where other people are
present and should avoid isolating
themselves. If you want to
guarantee your complete safety,
talk to people in the place you are
visiting and establish a relationship
with them. From then on Jordanians
will take care of you better than one
of their own.

If you run into serious trouble
and need legal advice or
representation contact your
embassy which may be able to
recommend local lawyers. The vast
majority of lawyers and doctors
speak English. In case of a car
accident, go to the police station
with the other party involved and
obtain the necessary documents for
your insurance claim.

Loss of Belongings

Report any lost belongings to the
nearest police station and ask for a
certificate of loss for insurance
purposes. If you lose your passport
you should also contact your
embassy/consulate as soon as
possible.

Medical Services

All treatment including emergency
treatment must be paid for – a
certificate of treatment will be
issued to enable you to claim back
the expenses from your insurance.
It is therefore wise to buy health
insurance from your travel agent
before travelling.

Generally speaking Jordan has
good medical care and there is a
medical centre or clinic in every
town and village. Amman has a
large number of hospitals and high
quality specialists. Outside Amman
there are hospitals in Aqaba,
Ma'an, Karak, Madaba, Zarqa, Irbid
and Ar-Ramtha, and there are
clinics with a small number of beds
in the Jordan Valley.

There are three classes of
hospital beds and prices are
standardised. Contact your
embassy to enquire about hospitals
and doctors they can recommend.
To find a doctor or pharmacist that
is open outside normal hours
consult the free monthly *Your Guide
to Amman*, which lists doctors and
chemists on night duty and
hospitals. *The Jordan Times* (Page
2) also lists duty doctors and
pharmacists in the capital.

Tipping

In Jordan you will certainly not be
pressed anywhere near as much
as in Egypt for what is known in
Arabic as *baqsheesh*, but it is
nonetheless a good idea to leave
a small tip. The better hotels and
restaurants may add 10–12
percent service charge to your
bill but waiters do not always get
this. Other establishments
expect you to leave a tip for all
staff or give something to those
that worked for you most. Taxi-
drivers are generally not tipped
but it is customary to pay the
nearest round figure to the price
on the meter. Anywhere else tip
according to will, bearing in mind
that tips are always appreciated.
Note: One place where you will
be pressed very hard to tip is
Petra, particularly when you rent
a horse. You need not tip more
than 10 percent of the price you
paid for the horse and in any
case no more than 2JD. If you
are harassed for more, complain
to the Tourist Police at the
Visitors' Centre.

Weights & Measures

Jordan employs the metric system. Length is counted in metres, distances in kilometres, weight in kilograms and volume in litres.

1 inch = 2.54 centimetres (cm)
1 foot = 0.30 metres (m)
1 yard = 0.91 metres (m)
1 mile = 1.61 kilometres (km)
1 acre = 0.40 hectares (ha)
1 ounce = 28.35 grams (g)
1 pound = 0.45 kilograms (kg)
1 British ton = 1016 kilograms
1 American ton = 907 kilograms
1 imperial gallon = 4.55 litres (l)
1 American gallon = 3.79 litres (l)

Business Hours

Government offices: Open 8am–2pm. Closed Friday. During Ramadan: 9.30am–2pm.
Businesses: Open winter (November–April) 8/8.30am–1/1.30pm, 3/3.30–6.30pm and summer (May–October) 4/4.30–7.30pm. Most businesses close Friday and some close Sunday all day or half-day. Some travel agencies stay open during the lunch break. During Ramadan: 9am–3/6pm.
Banks: Open winter 8.30am–12.30/1pm, 3.30–5/5.30pm; summer 8.30am–12.30/1pm, 4/4.30–6pm; closed Friday all day, Thursday and Sunday afternoons. During Ramadan: 9am–1/2pm.
Museums: Generally open 8am–5pm, closed Friday. Consult the *Museums* section under *Attractions: Culture* as times vary.
Shops: Open winter 9am–6.30/7pm, summer 9am–8/9pm. Most shops close in the afternoon for about two hours any time between 1pm and 4pm. They also close Friday, except for Amman's downtown *suq* and some close Sunday. During Ramadan: 9am–1pm and after the break of fast most will reopen until 9 or 10pm (see *Shopping*).
Post Offices: Open winter 8am–5pm, summer 7am–7pm. During Ramadan: 8am–3/4pm. Some post offices in Amman and around the

country open on Friday mornings 8am–1.30pm.

Religious Services

There are several churches and monasteries of a variety of denominations in Amman and the rest of the country, including St George's in Madaba, which has the famous mosaic map of Palestine. Amman has Greek Orthodox, Anglican, Roman Catholic, Evangelical Lutheran, German-speaking Evangelical, Armenian Catholic and Orthodox, Coptic, Syrian Orthodox and interdenominational churches. Churches and their telephone numbers are advertised daily on page 2 of the *Jordan Times* and you should ring to find out the times of services. In the same place you will also find information about the times of Muslim prayers (see also *Public Holidays* for Easter timings).

Media

Newspapers and Magazines
Jordan has a rather large number of newspapers in circulation in comparison with its population. The press body boasts four major Arabic dailies: *Al Arab Al Yawm* (Arabs Today) and *Al Aswaq* (The Markets) are fully independent papers, while *Al Dustour* (The Constitution) and *Al Ra'i* (The Opinion) are owned 32 and 61 per cent, respectively, by the state. Along with these, about 20 rowdy weeklies circulate each week.

There are two English language papers. The *Jordan Times*, a daily which covers events in Jordan and the region quite well and reproduces analytical pieces from the international press (internet: http://www.access2arabia.com/jordantimes). *The Star* is a weekly with good feature articles on local news and a French section (internet:http://star.arabia.com/). Investors in *Al Arab Al Yawm* hope to have a second English language daily up and running in 1999.

Many Amman news agencies also stock a good selection of

foreign newspapers and magazines in English, French, German, Italian and Arabic. Imported publications are very expensive and subject to censorship, which means that copies carrying articles deemed offensive to Jordan's leadership and the government are not available.

Radio and Television
Jordanian television broadcasts in two channels, Channel 2 being international with English- and French-language programmes. The quality of imported series and feature films varies greatly. The Channel 2 TV programme is advertised daily on page 2 of the *Jordan Times*. In Jordan you can also receive Syrian and Israeli television, the latter being watched very widely. The Jordan Radio and Television Corporation and private companies also sell subscriptions to satellite TV networks like CNN, BBC World Service TV, MTV, TV5 (French), as well as MBC (Middle East Broadcasting) and LBC (Lebanese Broadcasting Corporation), both in Arabic. Radio Jordan broadcasts in Arabic as well as in English and French. The English programme is transmitted at 99kHz VHF FM stereo and 350.9 Mhz and 855kHZ medium wave and has news bulletins every hour on the hour. The BBC World Service radio broadcasts to Jordan in English at 1323 kHz, 227 MHz medium wave (3–7.30am and 9am–11.15pm GMT) and 639 kHz, 469 MHz medium wave (3–3.30am, 6–8.15am, 10.30am–12.45pm GMT).

Postal Services

Post offices open winter 8am–5pm, summer 7am–7pm, and during Ramadan 8am–3/4pm. Postal services in Jordan are generally reliable although there have been reports of parcels going missing. Mail is not delivered to addresses but to post office boxes, so if you send letters to an address without a post box number the letter will be returned to you. Registered or express mail sent from Jordan is relatively cheap, but parcels are very expensive to mail and they have to be left open so that they may be inspected by customs officials.

Poste restante service is available at some post offices but you should enquire first. *Poste restante* letters are kept for only one month from the date of their arrival at the post office.

Telecoms

Jordan has a very good telecommunications system that is continuously updated; but, as a consequence, phone numbers are frequently changed. Public telephones exist inside post offices, but many shopkeepers will let you use their telephone for local calls (100 fils). Pay phones have recently mushroomed around the Kingdom, but require a phone card. Cards can be purchased at most small grocers around the capital as well as at bookstores and news kiosks. Some pay phones also now accept credit cards. Additionally, mobile phones can be rented at major hotels. Internet services can be found in dozens of cafés around the capital and other major cities. International calls are expensive as post offices charge for a minimum three minutes and hotels charge a good percentage more than the actual rates. Faxes are very widely

available in hotels and even many of the 1-star hotels have them. Many hotels also have telex facilities. The new telecommunications shops offer the best rates.

Actual rates of telephone calls, ie what you will have to pay at the post office and on private telephones (not hotels) per minute, are as follows:

Category one rates (U.S.A, Canada, Australia, Japan, Iran, Germany, Switzerland, Denmark, Sweden, Norway, Austria, Greece, Italy, Belgium, Poland, Turkey, Romania, Hong Kong, Portugal, Spain, France, Holland, Yugoslavia, Thailand, Taiwan, Singapore, South Korea and India): 8am–10pm 750 fils, 10pm–8am, Fridays and national holidays 525 fils.

Category two rates (United Arab Emirates, Bahrain, Saudi Arabia, Iraq, Kuwait, Yemen, Oman, Qatar, Syria, Lebanon, Libya, Egypt, Sudan, Somalia, Morocco, Tunisia, Djibouti, Mauritania and Israel): 8am–10pm 500 fils, 10pm–8am, Fridays and holidays 350 fils.

Category three rates (all countries not already listed): 8am–10pm 1JD, 10pm–8am, Fridays and national holidays 0.75JD

To increase the number of lines, many six figure numbers are becoming seven figure numbers, but not in any regular way. The main numbers affected are those with area codes 03, 06 and 08. All the

codes are remaining the same, but the individual numbers are being expanded. For example, in the Amman (06) area, all six figure

Local codes

02 Irbid, Umm Qays, the North
03 Wadi Musa region
  (Aqaba, Petra, Maan, Karak)
04 Jarash, Ajlun, Mafraq
05 Salt, Jordan Valley
06 Amman
07 Yaduda (Kan Zaman), Umm Al-Amad
08 Airport, Madaba
09 Zarqa

numbers formerly beginning with 60, 66, 67, 68 and 69 now begin 560, 566, 567, 568 and 569. For numbers starting 61, 63, 64 and 65, add a 4 at the beginning. But 70 becomes 562! 84 is 534, 831 is now 5331 and 837 is 5337.

In the south of the country (code 03) numbers beginning 330 become 2130; 331 is 2131; 332 is 2132; 333 is 2133; 334 is 2164; 335 is 2165; 336 is 2156; 337 is 2157; 339 is 2150. Bear in mind that it will be some time before printed contact information incorporates such changes.

The international network access code is 00. If you want to call a number outside Jordan you have to dial 00 + country code + local code + number.

Directory enquiries: 121 or 4640444 for Amman numbers and 0132 for international numbers. Some English is spoken but the service in general leaves a lot to be desired.

Amman Tourism Services

There are no tourist information offices but the public can visit the **Ministry of Tourism** in Amman near Third Circle, which can be contacted at:
PO Box 224, Amman 11118.
Tel: 4642 311; fax: 4648465;
e-mail: mota@amra.nic.gov.jo
Open 8am–2pm.
It operates like a tourist office, supplying visitors with a free map, a few colourful brochures and information.

They also run a **Tourist Complaints service**, which deals

with complaints about resthouses, hotels and restaurants.

There is also the **Jordan Tourism Board** at:
PO Box 830688, Amman 11183.
Tel: 4647951; fax: 464 7915;
e-mail: jtb@nets.com.jo
Also at:
www.arabia.com/Jordan
Information can also be obtained from the many new **web sites** on the internet, such as:
www.iiconnect.com/jordan/
www.iiconsulting.com/jordan/
index.html

Tourist Information

Jordan Today, published monthly as a complementary booklet, is distributed throughout all the major entertainment centres, cafés, four- and five-star hotels, fitness and cultural centres. It usually publishes short, timely features on travel and tourism of interest to both locals and foreigners, and includes a comprehensive guide/listing of all relevant tourism facilities. In addition to the obvious places and events, it includes a listing of churches, fitness centres, banks and the latest in literature available at some of Amman's upmarket bookstores.

Outside Amman, there are four visitor centres that are intended to serve the same purpose as those in the capital city:

Queen Alia International Airport.
Tel: 4451680 or 4452680 or 4452700.
Jarash.
Tel: 04-451272.
Near the South Gate of the archaeological site. Open daily winter 7.30am–7pm, summer 7.30am–8.30pm.
Petra.
Tel: 03-336020.
At the entrance of the site. Open daily winter 7am–4pm, summer 7am–5pm.
Aqaba.
Tel: 03-201 3363.
Near the castle. Open winter 8am–2pm, summer 8am–5pm.

Tour operators in Amman and Aqaba organise **independent package tours** which are generally expensive for individual travellers but worthwhile and convenient for groups and families. If you would like to do something unusual you could enquire about camel caravan trips, desert racing, ballooning (see also *Sports*) or staying with a Bedouin family in the desert, all of which can be catered for in one way or another. It pays to shop around, but if you don't have the time to spare then try any of the following:
International Traders.
Tel: 5607014
Fax: 5669905.
They also have an office in Aqaba.
Tel: 03-316324
Fax: 03-315316.
Shumaysani represent American Express in Jordan. Amongst other things, they can organise a Hejaz railway trip, which involves a mock Bedouin camel raid and a meal in a tent in the desert near Amman.
Bisharat Tours.
Tel: 4641350 or 4644355.

Intercontinental, Amman and in Aqaba. Friendly staff organise a number of more conventional trips around the country, accommodation, flights and land travel.
Renaissance Tours.
Tel: 4643661.
Near Third Circle, Jabal Amman. For package tours to Aqaba and Wadi Rum.
Guiding Star.
Tel: 4654251.
Emir Mohammed Street, Jabal Amman. Guiding Star also has an office in Jerusalem and are therefore ideal for booking hotels ahead of your trip to the West Bank.

Embassies

All the diplomatic missions listed below are in Amman. Egypt also has a consulate in Aqaba. Other diplomatic missions are listed in the monthly *Your Guide to Amman*, available free at hotels and travel agents in Amman.
American Embassy, Abdoun.
Tel: 5920101
Fax: 5923759 or 5927653.
Open 9am–noon, closed Friday and Saturday.
Australian Embassy, between Fourth and Fifth circles, Jabal Amman.
Tel: 5673246
Fax: 5673260.
Open to general public 9am–noon Monday and Wednesday only, but for Australian citizens 7.30am–3pm daily except Friday and Saturday.
British Embassy, opposite Orthodox Club, Abdoun.
Tel: 5923110 or 5923100.
Open 8am–3pm, closed Friday and Saturday.
Canadian Embassy, Philadelphia Bank building, next to Pizza Hut, Shumaysani.
Tel: 5666124
Fax: 5689227.
Open 8am–4pm, closed Friday and Saturday.
Danish Embassy, Abdel Hamid Sharaf Street, Shumaysani, behind UNESCO.
Tel: 5603703
Fax: 567 2170.
Open 8am–1pm, 3–5.30pm, Friday

8am–1pm, closed Sunday.
Egyptian Embassy, near First Circle, Jabal Amman.
Tel: 5605202
Fax: 5604082.
Open 9am–2pm, closed Friday.
Egyptian Consulate, Al-Wihdat Al-Gharbiya, Aqaba.
Tel: 03-2016171.
Open 9am–2pm, closed Friday.
French Embassy, near Third Circle, Mutanabi Street, near Ministry of Tourism, Jabal Amman.
Tel: 4641273
Fax: 4659606.
Open 8am–2pm, closed Fridays. Visas only on Saturday.
German Embassy, Benghazi Street, behind mosque on Fourth Circle, Jabal Amman. Tel: 5689351; fax: 5685887. Open 8am–4pm, closed Friday and Saturday.
Irish Consulate, near Ministry of Finance, King Hussein Street (known as Sharia Salt), downtown. Tel/fax: 5625632.
Open 9.30am–1pm, closed Friday.
New Zealand Embassy, Khalas Stores building, King Hussein Street (Sharia Salt), downtown.
Tel: 4636720 (shared with Khalas stores)
Fax: 4634349.
Open 8am–1pm, closed Friday.
Syrian Embassy, Haza al-Majali Street (behind Ministry of Foreign Affairs), near Third Circle, Jabal Amman.
Tel: 4641076
Fax: 5698685.
Open 9–11am, closed Friday.

Getting Around

On Arrival

Getting from the Airport to Amman

The Queen Alia airport, 32 km (20 miles) south of Amman, has a bus service to Amman every half an hour which arrives at Abdali bus station and costs 0.750JD. There are also plenty of taxis. They charge a fixed fare of 8JD on top of which you could add another 1JD as tip. The journey to Amman takes 30–40 minutes.

Getting from Aqaba to Amman

There are six JETT buses every day and the fare costs 4JD. The JETT bus station in Aqaba is on the Corniche opposite the archaeological site of Ayla and is a well-known location. The trip takes approximately four hours. There is also a much cheaper public minibus service that leaves from the main bus station, where you will also find service taxis for Amman, but you will have to wait until one fills up to set off.

Royal Jordanian has six to seven flights a week to Amman. These take 45 minutes and cost approximately 25JD one way and 50JD return. Royal Wings Airlines also fly from Amman to Aqaba, as well as Tel Aviv and certain Red Sea charter destinations. Tel: 4875201; fax: 4875656. Website: www.royalwings.com.jo E-mail: info@royalwings. com.jo

Getting from the King Hussein Bridge to Amman

See Getting There, page 328.

Public Transport

There are four types of public transport in Jordan: the big blue buses of the JETT company, which are air-conditioned and reliable but require booking well in advance; the white large public buses and the public minibuses, which are very cheap and go everywhere in the country; the white shared taxis that cover fixed routes and are called service taxis – they leave when they are full – and the yellow taxis that are not for sharing.

By Bus

JETT runs daily services between Amman and Petra (one way 5JD, round trip 11JD, excursion with horse hire and packed lunch 32JD). You should book well in advance and can ask to be picked up from your hotel. There are six daily services to Aqaba. Be warned that the JD4 ticket you purchase at the Abdali JETT station is a one-way ticket; there is no round trip ticket available. Tickets to Amman must be purchased in Aqaba, and if you plan to stay just for the afternoon, buy your return ticket immediately after deboarding the arriving bus. JETT also travels daily to the King Hussein Bridge – departing from the JETT Abdali station at 6:00 am every day – and travels to Hammamat Ma'in Hot Springs south of Madaba, each day at 8 am (round trip JD10).

There are two main bus stations in Amman: Abdali and Wahdat. Buses from Abdali go to Ajlun, Beqa'a, Dayr Alla, Fuhays, Jarash, Irbid, Suwaylah, Wadi As-Seer and the King Hussein Bridge. Most fares cost less than half a dinar. The Hejazi bus company, whose buses leave from the top end of Abdali, runs a very frequent and cheap non-stop service to Irbid and Yarmuk University. Buses from the Wahdat station go to Aqaba, Madaba, Petra, Ma'an, Wadi Musa, Karak and Hammamat Ma'in. If you want to go to Azraq you must first get a bus to Zarqa. Fares do not exceed 2JD.

The Dead Sea is hard to get to without private transport as no JETT or public buses go there. You could take a public bus from Ras Al-Ain in Amman for Shuneh and from there take your chance. Destinations on the front of public buses are always in Arabic, so you may need to be shown the right bus.

Taxis

Unless your budget is very tight, the yellow private taxis are a fast and fairly cheap way of getting about Amman. You will rarely have to wait long to get one. They are obliged to use their meter, which starts at 0.150JD. Most rides will cost between 0.400 and 1.500JD. Beware of taxis in ranks outside big hotels: they refuse to use their meter and will ask an inflated flat rate. You will be better off walking a short distance away from your hotel and hailing one of the many passing taxis. Jordanian women never sit in the front of a taxi next to the driver, so it is wise for women travellers to follow suit and sit in the back in order to avoid a misunderstanding.

Private Transport

Jordan has an excellent road infrastructure, which is expanding and improving. Driving is on the right-hand side. There are highways from the King Hussein Bridge to the Iraqi border and from Ar-Ramtha to Aqaba. From Amman to Aqaba the four-lane Desert Highway is faster

Service Taxis

Service taxis from a number of locations in downtown Amman and from Abdali will take you almost anywhere in Amman. Likewise chances are that any service taxi passing by can take you to either of these two places. Like buses, service taxis also post their destinations in Arabic so you may find it difficult to familiarise yourself with their routes. If you cannot read Arabic hail a passing service taxi, shout your destination and it may just stop to pick you up. Fares are between 80 and 120 fils.

than the two-lane King's Highway but less interesting.

Driving in the city can be hair-raising as Jordanian drivers rarely indicate. They are very responsive to horns, however. If you have to go through one of the "circles" be patient and, when you can, move steadily. On the highway it is easy to miss the turning you want because signs give little warning. Most signs are in English as well as Arabic.

If you decide to drive in the desert ensure that your car has the right type of tyres and a 4-wheel drive and take a container with extra petrol/gas and plenty of water. Before you venture into the wilderness inform the nearest Desert Police Patrol station.

There are several petrol stations in the capital and major towns but not many on the open road. Petrol/gas is called *benzeen* and super is called *khas*.

Car Hire

Car hire in Jordan is expensive in comparison to Europe and the US, but there are plenty of choices in Amman and the airport, and to a lesser extent in Aqaba. Rental cars are distinguished by their green number plates with yellow writing.

The free publication *Your Guide to Amman* advertises several car rental companies. When you ring around to compare prices ask whether they require a deposit, which can be very high. Prices range from around 25JD to 35JD per day for a medium size car and mileage limits vary from 100–200 km (62–124 miles) a day, after which you pay extra.

Apart from international car hire companies, such as like Avis (tel: 5699420), Europcar (tel: 5601350, 5601360, 5674267) and Budget (tel: 5698131/2), there are plenty of cheaper local companies, which are just as reliable, such as Amin Jarrar (tel: 5603500), Atlas (tel: 5697469), Dallah (tel: 827082), Jarash (tel: 5603233), Sabri (tel: 5693026) and Safari (tel: 5605080).

On Foot

You can walk and hitch everywhere in the country except in the security area at the Dead Sea and between the Jordanian and Israeli checkpoints on the King Hussein Bridge. It is usually easy to get picked up by cars unless you are in a very remote area. Drivers will often expect a small contribution towards their petrol, especially if you travel with them a long way. From Amman, you can hitch from the Seventh Circle to anywhere in the south and west, from Suwaylah for west and north and from the road to Zarqa to the north and east. Women should not hitchhike on their own. Summertime is not recommended for hitching but if you do hitchhike at this time at least ensure that you are well equipped to cope with the heat and the sun.

On Departure

Departure tax is 10JD at the airport, 6JD in Aqaba going to Egypt, and 4JD at the land borders going to Syria, Iraq, Israel and the West Bank. If you have not renewed your visa you will also have to pay a fine (also see *Entry Regulations*).

Fast Track

If flying out of Amman with Royal Jordanian you can take advantage of the new City Terminal at the 7th Circle. You can check in your baggage, get your boarding pass and pay the departure fee between 7.30am and 10pm; then you will be driven to the airport, where you are whisked straight through to immigration control.

To Egypt

JETT buses run between Amman and Cairo every Saturday, Monday, Tuesday and Thursday, leaving at 5am and arriving in Cairo in Masr Al-Gedida at around the same time the next day. A one-way ticket costs US$46 for non-Arab nationals and it includes the fare on the ferry between Aqaba and Nuwayba but

Getting into Syria

● You must obtain a visa for Syria before travelling, preferably from a Syrian consulate in your own country, as the Syrian embassy in Amman often refuses to handle visa applications for those not permanently resident in Jordan.

● Procedures in Amman can take only a few hours, but you will be asked whether you have ever visited Occupied Palestine – the answer should be "no".

● If your stated occupation is writer or journalist, your visa application will take considerably longer to be processed as it has to be vetted by the Ministry of Information in Damascus.

● You will be denied a visa or entry into Syria if your passport carries any Israeli stamp or an Egyptian or Jordanian stamp from the border crossings with Israel. Therefore, if you plan to visit Syria from Jordan, do not enter Jordan from Wadi Araba or the King Hussein and Sheikh Hussein bridges. You may, however, enter from the King Hussein/Allenby Bridge (with a valid visa to Jordan) provided that you politely, but firmly, ask the Israelis not to stamp your passport.

not the exit tax. For information and reservations call JETT in Amman (tel: 664146/7). Book at least two days in advance. Also try the Alpha Tourist Bus Company (tel: 5698223). Royal Jordanian and Egypt Air run almost daily flights between Amman and Cairo. You must obtain a visa for Egypt at the Egyptian consulate in Amman or Aqaba before entering Egypt.

To Syria

There are buses from Amman to Damascus twice daily. JETT, the Jordanian bus company, departs at 7am and 3pm; Karnak, the Syrian bus company runs a similar service.

Both depart from the JETT bus station in Abdali and arrive at the Karnak station in Damascus approximately five hours after departure. Buses are air-conditioned and one-way tickets cost 4.500JD For information and reservations call JETT in Amman Tel: 5664146. Service taxis leave Abdali and the one-way trip costs 6.000JD. For roughly 3 times that price a service taxi can take you a far as Beirut (if you have a visa). For the more adventurous there is also the Hejaz railway service that leaves Amman (Mahata) at 7.30am every Monday arriving in Damascus at 5pm. The quickest way to get there is to fly. Royal Jordanian and Syrian Airways each operates flights several days a week at 46JD one way and 92JD return.

To Israel and the Occupied Territories

JETT buses run between Amman and King Hussein Bridge every morning at 6.30am and they will collect passengers from their hotels. The fare is 6JD – more expensive than service taxis, which cost no more than 2JD at any time of the morning, or the public bus that leaves from Abdali and charges 1JD. However, apart from comfort, the important advantage of the JETT bus is that it guarantees you a crossing as soon as the bridge has opened at 8am and, moreover, it secures a place on the only means of transport allowed across the bridge itself, namely a bus that shuttles between the Jordanian and Israeli check points every hour between 8am and when the bridge closes, at sunset (4pm in winter and 6pm in summer) Sunday to Thursday and at 11am on Friday.

If you take a taxi it will drop you at the Jordanian check point, where you must wait for a place on the next available shuttle bus. The fare is 1.500JD and the last bus leaves the Jordanian check-point half an hour before the bridge closes.

The bridge is closed Saturday, on Jewish holidays and some Muslim feasts. Check with the Department of Bridges and Borders or your hotel before planning your travel as it can

close at short notice sometimes.

From the bridge (called Allenby on this side of the river) you can share a service taxi (called *sherout*) to Jerusalem for a rate advertised on a board inside the checkpoint building. There are also less frequent *sherouts* to Ramallah and there is a bus service to Jericho and from there to Jerusalem.

It is advisable to make advanced reservations for accommodation in Jerusalem, especially in the Christmas and Easter periods when hotels in the city are heavily booked.

There are two new crossings into Israel since the peace treaty was signed: the Sheikh Hussein Bridge at the north of the Jordan Valley, between the Jordanian town of Irbid and the Israeli Beit Shean, and the Wadi Araba border crossing between Aqaba and Eilat in the south. You can reach the Sheikh Hussein Bridge from Irbid in a service or private taxi. On the Israeli side you will have to take a taxi or *sherout* to Bet Shean and from there public (Egged) buses will take you to other Israeli towns. The Wadi Araba border can be reached from Aqaba in service taxis. Also a JETT bus leaves Aqaba daily at 8.30am to the border. **Trust Tours** in Amman (tel: 5813427) run a bus service Sun–Fri to Tel Aviv, departing Amman at 7am, and another to Nazareth-Haifa at 7.40am.

By Bus to Saudi Arabia

JETT runs a bus service to Jeddah on Monday, Wednesday and Friday, leaving from the JETT bus station near Abdali at 11.30am and arriving in Jeddah at 6–7pm the next day. For information call JETT in Amman (tel: 5664146). Getting the bus is the easy part – you will first have to get a visa and that can be very, very difficult.

By Bus and Service Taxi to Iraq

Service taxis leave from Abdali as they fill up. A cheaper way is to get the public bus from Wahdat station. A more comfortable way is to hire a private car and driver – enquire at the Intercontinental Hotel.

Where to Stay

Jordan

There are no "Bed and Breakfasts" in the British sense in Jordan and no motels, but in Amman alone there are over 3,000 five-star beds and 2,500 four-star beds.

All hotels are open to some wheeling and dealing over prices, especially during the low season (October–March) and for longer occupancies; smaller hotels are particularly flexible. All hotels except one-star hotels charge an additional 10 percent government tax and 10 percent service charge. If you are a foreign resident in Jordan enquire about favourable rates. Many hotels have different rates for Jordanians and foreigners, but would charge foreign residents the same rate as Jordanians.

Prices quoted below may vary according to season. Unmarried couples may be prohibited from sharing a room. Proof of marriage may be required if the surnames on a couple's passports are not the same. Hotels may even complain if a man visits a woman's room for a short while.

The resthouses included in the list below provide adequate and clean accommodation for the budget traveller, and tend to be very popular, so book ahead.

AMMAN

✩✩✩✩✩ (deluxe)
Intercontinental Hotel (also known as the Jordan Hotel). Jabal Amman, near Third Circle.
Tel: 4641361
Fax: 4645217
A favourite among journalists and media hacks. The hotel boasts an efficient business centre, press office, and Reuters wire service.

Almost every summer night is filled with joyous sounds of bagpipes and drums as another bride and groom celebrate their wedding. **$$$$**.
Marriot Hotel. Shumaysani district.
Tel: 5607607
Fax: 5670100
Well located and with the most extensive sports and health club facilities of any hotel in Amman. Enquire about special rates. **$$$$**
Meridien (formerly Forte Grand). Shumaysani district.
Tel: 5696511
Fax: 5674261
Attached to the Housing Bank Centre and home to over 100 shops and businesses. **$$$$**
Al Yasmin Suites. Jabal Amman, off Third Circle.
Tel: 4643216/8
Fax: 4643219
Ten luxurious suites exquisitely furnished and equipped with every convenience, including a kitchenette. Rates comparable to five-star hotels but the facilities are superior to what is offered anywhere else in town. In-house business centre and private faxes can be installed in executive suites upon request. Guests have free access to the Intercontinental Hotel swimming pool. **$$$$**
Radisson SAS Amman. Shumaysani, near 3rd Circle.
Tel: 5607100
One of the best new hotels. **$$$$**
Regency Palace. Queen Alya St, Sports City Road.
Tel: 5607000
Fax: 5660013
Located in central Shumaysani. Business centre, health club, sauna and swimming pool. Thirty per cent

Price Brackets

$$$$ = over 100JD
$$$ = 50–100JD
$$ = 20–50JD
$ = under 20JD
Prices are for a double room per night.
For rock bottom prices, see page 339.

discount for Royal Jordanian ticket holders. **$$$$**

☆☆☆☆
Amra Forum Hotel. Sixth Circle.
Tel: 5510001
Fax: 5510003
The best hotel in its class with services that compete favourably with five-star hotels. **$$$$**

☆☆☆
Marmara. On Mecca Street before Mujama'a Jaber.
Tel: 5530480
Closer in style to a four-star hotel, with tasteful rooms and a fantastic restaurant.At the lower end of its price range. **$$$**.
Shepherd Hotel. Behind the Islamic College, near Second Circle.
Tel: 4639197
Fax: 4639198
Rooms are comfortable and rates include breakfast. Hotel staff are helpful. It has three popular bars and a quaint restaurant known for its fondues. **$$**
Hisham Hotel. Near Third Circle.
Tel: 4642720
Fax: 4647540
In a green and quiet neighbourhood

of Jabal Amman this hotel has a loyal clientele. Small but always busy. Its summer terrace bar and restaurant are a big bonus. **$$$**
Al Qasr Hotel. Shumaysani, opposite Peking Chinese Restaurant.
Tel: 5666140
Fax: 5689673
A charming hotel situated on a quiet residential street. Reasonable rates and an unpretentious ambience. **$$**
Al Maqsura. Shumaysani, opposite Safeway.
Tel: 5698222
Fax: 5690671
The only hotel in Amman that would pass as a motel, but the standard is superior to the American equivalents. Kitchenette, satellite TV and in-house movies; suites have sofa beds. There's a small play area for children behind the hotel on the edge of a secure parking lot. Front terrace and restaurant. Alcohol-free zone. Not well known amongst the Western crowd but good value for money. **$$**
The Commodore Hotel. Shumaysani, around the corner from Safeway.
Tel: 5607185
Fax: 5668187
On the lower end of 3-star scale, and so are the rooms. Hodge-podge decor, all standard conveniences and access to neighbouring Middle East Hotel outdoor swimming pool free of charge. **$$$**
Ambassador Hotel. Shumaysani, opposite American Express.
Tel: 5605161
Fax: 5681101

Holiday Flats

A selection of what's available in Amman:
Turino. Suwayfiya. Tel: 818637, fax: 5679304. Flatlets are slightly ostentatious by Western standards but management offers every convenience. Services include babysitters, business centre and newspaper delivery, valet parking, AT&T international dialling, and free use of local health club.

Apartments average 80JD for two beds.
Darotel. Shmaysani. Tel: 5607193, fax: 5602434. Short-let apartments with hotel services. Prices vary according to standard and space. Ice machine, shoe-shine and small fitness room on premises. Discounts of up to 50 percent during the winter season. Apartment 50JD for two people.

Olympia. Abdoun. Tel: 810150, fax: 827113. One-bedroom apartments are surprisingly modest for such a swanky neighbourhood. King-size sofa-bed in living-room offers extra sleeping space. Check the apartment allocated as some need minor repairs. Coffeeshop in lobby doubles as bar in evening. Single apartment (only) 40JD.

Offers 97 rooms and suites tastefully decorated and equipped with all standard conveniences, although a bit pricey for a 3-star establishment. Babysitters can be arranged. Nice coffee shop in addition to bar and restaurant. Tourist office and rent-a-car right outside the hotel. **$$$**

Carlton Hotel. Off Third Circle across from the International.
Tel: 4654200
Fax: 4655833
Former home of the US embassy in Amman, now a clean little hotel with classy roadside Café de la Paix. Very convenient location. **$$$**

Amman International. Jubayha area.
Tel: 5841712
Fax: 5841714
Modest comfortable rooms and suites. Rates include breakfast. Facilities: outdoor swimming pool, billiard room, restaurant and bar. Good for those who want to be in the university area or who have their own transportation. **$$$**

☆☆

Canary Hotel. Jabal Al-Luwaybida, opposite Terra Sancta College.
Tel: 4638353
Fax: 5661196
Offers 21 comfortable rooms equipped with en suite bathroom, TV and balcony overlooking one of the oldest neighbourhoods in Amman. A couple of larger rooms for four persons and with attached dining alcove are available. Homey communal dining area opposite lobby and pleasant front garden. A good place for single travellers as well as families on a budget. **$$**

Caravan Hotel. Jabal Al-Luwaybida, opposite the King Abdullah Mosque (also known as the Blue Mosque).
Tel: 5661195/7
Fax: 5661196
Pleasant rooms, most with standing shower only. Small sitting areas outside rooms, cheery lobby and communal dining area. Use of kitchen for light meals with advance notice. Light sleepers beware – the call to prayer is highly audible! **$$**

Hotel Al Remal. Abadali, opposite police station.
Tel: 4615585.

Although it doesn't look very appealing from the outside, it is actually not bad inside. TV can be arranged for longer occupancy. Fax and telex. Hotel cafeteria through separate entrance next door. A bit noisy during the day. **$$**

☆

Cleopatra Hotel. Abdali, opposite bus station.
Tel: 4646959
Rooms are drab but adequate. Bathrooms en suite (Turkish toilets without toilet paper). Hot water in afternoon only. Not the best value, but bearable if you're just passing through and need a cheap place to flop, close to bus station. **$**

Al Monzer. Abdali, opposite the bus station (one flight above Cleopatra).
Tel: 4639469
Fax: 4657328
Same price as the Cleopatra but slightly more inviting thanks to brighter lobby. European-style toilets and hot water 24 hours a day. No alcohol on premises. **$**

Sunrise Hotel. Abdali, opposite the bus station.
Tel: 5621841.
Rates are slightly cheaper and the standard is a little better than in neighbouring hotels. Bathroom facilities vary enormously. If the hotel is not packed, guests may use hotel facilities to prepare light meals. **$**

New Park Hotel. Downtown, on King Hussein Street.
Tel: 4612144/5
Fax: 4648145
A bit more expensive than the other places on this street but some rooms are worth it. First and second class rooms available. **$**

The Lord Hotel.
Downtown, near New Park Hotel.
Tel: 4654167.
Decent for its price range. Most rooms have bathrooms, although same rates apply for those without bathroom facilities. Unless privacy is a priority, use the showers off the corridor; these tend to be larger and considerably cleaner. Communal fridge. **$**

Palace Hotel. Downtown, opposite Haifa hotel.
Tel: 4624327
Fax: 4650603
One of the largest hotels downtown and probably the most decent in its price range. Rates are comparable to the Cleopatra and Al Monzer, but it is much cleaner and brighter. **$**

Rock Bottom Prices

Cliff Hotel. Downtown, opposite Khalifah stores.
Tel: 4624273
Most popular among backpackers and budget travellers and has the closest thing to a youth hostel atmosphere. Rates are charged per bed and showers cost extra. Shared bathroom facilities. Free storage. If you're really broke you can sleep on the roof in summer. Sometimes single men are turned away. 8JD (roof 2JD).

The Baghdad Hotel. Downtown, near the Cliff. The hotel lacks character and is slightly more expensive than the Cliff for roughly the same standard. Showers are included, but water is hot only in the morning. Those travelling with sleeping bags or spare sheets might find their stay here more comfortable. Bed 3JD.

The Farouk Hotel. Downtown, opposite Arab Bank. Keep climbing up the stairs until you come to a door which looks as though it leads to the roof – which is exactly what it does. The lobby of this place is literally the roof, definitely a plus during the warm summer months. Overall, it's small and a bit creepy. Women are best off avoiding this place altogether. Double 5JD.

The Yarmuk. Downtown, near the Farouk Hotel. The price depends on nationality and appearance. If you fit the bill (it's unclear what is ideal) you may get the lowest rate in town. Shared bathroom and no lobby area. Bed 2–4JD.

Haifa Hotel. Downtown, opposite the Yarmuk. This hotel has seen better days but it still bears traces of past grandeur. Rooms are larger and sunnier than other places in the budget range. Bed 2JD.

Youth Hostels

YWCA. Jabal Amman, near Second Circle.
Tel: 4621488.
Priority given to Arab women residing in Amman but space is sometimes available for travelling foreign women. Smoking is forbidden in the rooms and guests must abide by YWCA rules. The 10.30pm nightly curfew is extended to midnight every Thursday. It is advisable to call in advance to check availability.

Campsites

The only site that could qualify as a fully serviced campground is located in **Dana**, south of Tafila. It has clean, architecturally designed toilets that make a big impression on every visitor. The location is beautiful, inside the Nature Reserve.

Pensions

La Bonita (tel: 4615061, fax: 4615060) and the **As-Sabeel** (tel: 4630571, fax: 4630572), both near Third Circle. Both offer pension-style accommodation above their popular restaurants, and also give good rates for people staying for long periods. Frequented by employees of international organisations and diplomats. Tax is only 10 percent, instead of 20 percent in hotels. **$$**

AJLUN
☆☆
Qala'at Ar-Rabad.
Tel: 02-6420202.
Near the castle. Rooms are simple, with bathrooms, hot water and balconies; the view is beautiful. **$$**
Ajlun Hotel.
Tel: 02-6420254.
Rooms with bathroom, TV, central heating and balconies. **$–$$**

AQABA
☆☆☆☆
Coral Beach.
Tel: 03-2013521.

Price Brackets

$$$$ = over 100JD
$$$ = 50–100JD
$$ = 20–50JD
$ = under 20JD
Prices are for a double room per night.

One of the nicest hotels in Aqaba, suitable for those who want to relax in peace rather than indulge in sports and nightlife. **$$$**
Radisson SAS Aqaba.
Tel: 03-201 2426.
Formerly the Holiday Inn, it offers excellent facilities but is the most expensive. **$$$$**

☆☆☆
Aqaba Hotel.
Tel: 03-2014091/2.
Situated on the beach with air-conditioned rooms and bungalows, it offers a very good service. There is also a night club and some watersports. **$$–$$$**
Aquamarina I, II, III.
Tel: 03-2016250.
This group of hotels specialises in watersports. The best facilities are provided by Aquamarina I, the only one on the beach, but these are freely available to guests at the other two hotels. All three are popular, so book in advance. **$$–$$$**, depending on the hotel and the view.
Nairoukh II.
Tel: 03-2012980.
This hotel is not on the beach but it has free access to the beach of the Aqaba and Aquamarina hotels. Rooms have TV, fridge and telephone. **$$**

☆
Al-Jameel Hotel.
Tel: 03-2014118.
Located in the city centre of Aqaba. Air-conditioned rooms (rare in its price range), with hot water and balcony. **$**

AZRAQ
Azraq Resthouse.
Tel: 681028 ext. 6.
All 24 rooms have their own

bathroom, mini-bar, and TV and are air-conditioned – a major consideration. **$$**
Hunter Hotel (Al Sayed).
Tel: 06-647611 ext: 94.

WADI DANA
A little way north of Shawbak, but south of Karak, is Wadi Dana and the Dana Nature Reserve – a beautiful area for walks and climbs:
Wadi Dana Guest House.
Tel: 03-368497/8
Fax: 03-368499
Perched on the edge of Wadi Araba with stunning views from all rooms, which are clean and peaceful; nearby craft workshop and lodge. **$$**
Wadi Dana Village Hotel.
Tel: 03-368537.
Located in the Wadi Dana village, with indoor or outdoor (Bedouin tent) accommodation; outdoor communal showers. **$**

DEAD SEA
Dead Sea Spa Hotel.
Tel: 08-546101, fax: 08-546108.
The ideal place for a quiet health retreat. It has a private beach as well as a swimming pool, fitness and anti-stress programmes, whirlpool, vegetarian menu, special diet plans, mud packs. **$$$–$$$$**

HAMMAMAT MA'IN
Ashtar Hotel.
Tel: 08-54500.
Prices include use of the outdoor cold-water swimming pool, sauna, indoor hot water pool and gym. Health clinic with its hydro and mud-therapy and massage, is extra. Jordanians and residents in Jordan can take advantage of special three-night half-board packages. **$$$–$$$$**

IRBID
☆☆☆
Ar-Razi Hotel.
Tel: 02-275515.
Near Yarmuk University. It has a coffee shop, bar and restaurant and rooms have TV and fans. **$$**
Al Hejazi Hotel.
Tel: 02-279500
Fax: 279520

Well located in Irbid, with small but well-equipped rooms. Four-star facilities. The downstairs café has music and is very popular with students. **$$**

JARASH

Dibeen Resthouse. Tel: 04-452413. Has 19 bungalows in the heart of the National Park a few kilometres from Jarash and is ideal for those who want to go walking. All the rooms have private bathrooms, telephone, fridge, TV and portable heaters and there is a play area for children. However, it has no restaurant, only a snack bar. Not suitable for those without private transport. **$**

KARAK

Resthouse.
Tel: 03-351148.
There are 13 rooms with private bathrooms heated in the winter as well as a restaurant and bar and a TV lounge. **$$**
Castle Hotel.
Tel: 03-352489.
Basic, but really the only option if the resthouse is full. **$**

PETRA

Over the last few years many new hotels have been set up in Petra. This small selection concentrates on the more established ones:
Taybet Zaman Village.
Tel: 03-2150111
Fax: 03-2150101
This brand-new holiday complex, built by the owners of Kan Zaman near Amman, is located 9km (5½ miles) south of Petra. It claims to be environment-friendly using natural toiletries and chemical-free fruits and vegetables. Mid-19th century village houses have been transformed into bungalows with magnificent views of the Petra mountains. They have underfloor heating and cooling, minibar, satellite TV, direct dial telephones and fax upon request. The village has its own bakery, steam bath, swimming pool, fitness room and town square. **$$$$**
Petra Movenpick.
Tel: 03-2157107

Fax: 03-2157112
Facilities include continental and Mediterranean restaurants, a rooftop bar with nightly live entertainment and a pool and billiards room. **$$$$**

✫✫✫✫
Petra Forum Hotel.
Tel: 03-2156977
Fax: 03-2156266
Situated next to the entrance of the site, this was for many years the most comfortable hotel in Petra but also the most pricey. It offers air-conditioned, centrally heated rooms, all with bathrooms, telephone and mini-bar. There is also a pool overlooking the mountains and a restaurant inside the site. **$$$–$$$$**

✫✫✫
Palace Hotel.
Tel: 03-2156724.
Near the entrance to the site. New facilities include a bar, a pool and satellite television. **$$**

✫✫
Petra Resthouse.
Tel: 03-2156011
Fax: 03-2156686
Budget accommodation with or without air-conditioning, but all rooms have private bathrooms. Advisable to book well in advance during the busy season. **$$$**
Flower City Hotel.
Tel: 03-2156440
Fax: 03-2156448
Near the square, 15 minutes' walk from site entrance. All rooms with central heating, TV, fridge and hot water. Some also have air-conditioning. Price negotiable in summer. **$$**

Syria

The only hotel chain covering the whole of Syria is Cham Palaces and Hotels, which has hotels in all the main tourist destinations, including four hotels in Damascus. Their designation "palace" signifies large, luxurious hotels with all facilities. Their "hotels" tend to be comfortable but smaller.

ALEPPO

Chahba Cham Palace. Damascus Road, Aleppo. Tel: (21) 248572/215272. Aleppo's only five-star hotel. **$$$**
Baron Hotel. Downtown on Baron Street, Aleppo.
Tel: (21) 0880.
While this hotel has seen better days, some of its old charm remains. Facilities include basic rooms, a bar and a restaurant. The proprietor, Armen, is a great source of information about the surrounding area. **$$**

BOSRA

Bosra Cham Palace. PO Box 7570 Damascus.
Tel: (151) 23502.
New hotel in the heart of the city. Tennis courts and swimming pool. **$$$$**

DAMASCUS

Le Meriden. Choukri Kouatly Road. Tel: 371-8730.
Well situated in the heart of the city. Close to the National Museum. All facilities including swimming pool, tennis courts and nightclub. **$$$$**
Cham Palace. Maysaloun Street, Damascus.
Tel: 223-2300.
In the heart of the city. Its many facilities include the only Chinese and revolving restaurants in Syria. **$$$$**
Ebla Cham Palace. Airport Road, Damascus.
Tel: 224-1900.
Set in extensive grounds halfway between the city centre and the airport. Offers horse riding and golf. **$$$$**
Techrine Cham Hotel.
Tel: 11-225077/225142.
Damascus. Relatively small hotel, with air-conditioned rooms, one restaurant and bar. Access to nearby tennis courts and swimming pool. **$$$**
Jallaa Cham Hotel. PO Box 9067. Damascus.
Tel: 11-664946/47.
Pleasant small hotel in Mazzé area of town. Access to nearby tennis

courts and pool. Squash court. **$$$**
Omar Khayam Hotel. Off Martyrs' Square, Damascus.
Tel: 221-1666.
Moderately priced and close to the Old City. The 1920s Art Deco style makes this hotel one of the more pleasant places to stay. **$$**
Orient Palace Hotel.
Tel: 11-2220501
Comfortable older style hotel near the Hejaz railway station. Cheaper than any of the above. **$$**
Sultan Hotel. Moussallam Baroudy Road.
Tel: 222-5768.
More basic, but clean and pleasant and also near the Hejaz railway station. **$$**
Venezia Hotel. Near Yousef al Azmeh Square.
Tel: 222-1224.
Inexpensive and very close to the Old City. Television and fridge in each room. **$$**

Other medium range hotels include the **New Omayyad Hotel** (Tel: 11-2217700), **New Semiramis**, (Tel: 02-894455), and the lower end has a jewel, the **Al-Bassam Hotel**, opposite the Hamadiya market

DAYR EZZOR

Furat Cham Palace. Aleppo Road, PO Box 219.
Tel: 51-25418/25126.
At the city entrance, on the banks of the Euphrates river. Every luxury. **$$$$**

HAMA

Apamee Cham Palace. PO Box 7570 Damascus.
Tel: 331-27429.
Five-star hotel overlooking the Orontes river. Swimming pool and tennis courts. **$$$$**

LATAKIA

Le Meridien. BP 473.
Tel: 41-229000/3/4/5.
Situated in woodlands on the coast about 7 km (4 miles) from the city centre. Offers windsurfing and jet ski. **$$$$**
Cote d'Azur de Cham. PO Box 1079.
Tel: 41-26333/34.

Price Brackets

$$$$ = over 100JD
$$$ = 50–100JD
$$ = 20–50JD
$ = under 20JD
Prices are for a double room per night.

On the beach about 10 km (6 miles) from the city centre. A less expensive hotel with self-catering facilities, the Cote d'Azur de Cham Residence, is attached. **$$$$**

MA'LULA

Asfir Hotel. Beside the monastery.
Tel: (012) 770250.
Pleasant hotel with 4-star hospitality. Superb restaurant and bar, a playground for children, and a spectacular view of the village. **$$$**

PALMYRA

Palmyra Cham Palace. PO Box 7570.
Tel: 31-37000.
Luxury hotel right next to the ruins, about 2 km (1 mile) from the city. Facilities include an ancient cave bath with sulphuric waters.

SAFITA

Safita Cham Hotel. PO Box 25.
Tel: 321-25980.
Small hotel overlooking the rolling valleys of this mountain resort. Swimming pool.

Jerusalem

East Jerusalem has hotels to suit all budgets. At the top end of the range there is:

American Colony. Nablus Road
Tel: 02-6279777.
A small but very attractive renovated 19th-century villa, established by American Christians. Outdoor swimming pool, and lunch and tea are served in a fragrant courtyard. Ibrahim's garden bar is the ideal place for a quite drink in colonial style. **$$$–$$$$**
Addar Suites. Opposite the American Colony.
Tel: 02-6263111.

Each suite has a kitchenette, small sitting area, bedroom, balcony and bathroom with whirlpool. Pricey, but elegant. **$$$$**
Ambassador Hotel
Tel: 02-5828515/6.
Nablus Road in Sheikh Jarrah. Popular with tour groups. Adjacent to the hotel is the Palestinian Needlework Shop supported by the Mennonites. **$$$**
Seven Arches. Situated on the Mount of Olives.
Tel: 02-6277555.
Offering beautiful views (especially sunsets) of the Old City. **$$$**
YMCA East (also known as **Capitolina Hotel**). Nablus Road.
Tel: 02-6286888. Facilities include dining room, snack bar, playground and outdoor garden. It also a swimming pool, gym and squash courts on the premises but guests pay extra. **$$**
St George's Cathedral Pilgrim Guest House. Nablus Road.
Tel: 02-6283302. Offers quiet accommodation on the grounds of the cathedral. Good value. **$$**
There is also the pleasant

Other medium price options include **Jerusalem Inn** (Tel: 02-6283282), the **National Palace** (Tel: 02-6273273), the **Christmas Hotel** (Tel: 02-6282588), **Ritz** (Tel: 02-6273233) and the quaint **al-Zahra Hotel** (Tel: 02-6282447), all in the same vicinity.

For budget travellers, very clean and cheap accommodation can be found with religious establishments, such as the **Lutheran Hospice** (Tel: 02-6282120) and **Armenian Catholic Patriarchate Hospice** (Tel: 02-6284262), as well as in a number of youth hostels in the Old City and outside Damascus Gate.

RAMALLAH

Grand Park Hotel.
Tel: 02-2986194.
On the upper end of the price scale, away from the hustle and bustle of downtown Ramallah. Nice terrace in the evening. **$$$**
Al Bireh Tourist Hotel. On the main road from Jerusalem to Ramallah.
Tel: 02-2986803.
Very basic, but pleasant. **$–$$**

Where to Eat

What To Eat

In culinary terms Jordan is bracketed with Syria, Lebanon and Palestine. (Few dishes are unique to Jordan, but look out for *mansaf*.) If you have been in other parts of the Arab world you will already know that food is a very important part of Arab culture and used to express hospitality and generosity. Jordanian people are very hospitable and usually proud to host you at home no matter how modest their means. A Jordanian invitation means that you are expected to bring nothing and eat everything.

At home all dishes, main course and appetisers, are served together but in restaurants the appetisers, which are known as *mezze* or *muqabalat*, are brought first; then, if you are still hungry, you will be asked to order your meat or fish. A meal usually ends with seasonal fruit. Some people eat with their hands at home and some dishes, like *masakhen*, are also eaten with hands at restaurants.

Mezze or Muqabalat

Hummus: a purée of chick-peas blended with *tahina* (pulped sesame seeds), lemon and garlic. This is the most common of the *muqabalat* and for many people constitutes a meal in itself.

Baba ghanoush: a dip made of the pulp of cooked aubergine which is at its best when it has been cooked over charcoal and has a wonderful smokey flavour. When mixed with *tahina* it is called *moutabbal*, but the distinction is not always made.

Ful moudames: a pauper's meal which somehow made its way to the table of the better-off. You will come

across it in the Arabic breakfast served at your hotel and at street restaurants. It consists of boiled brown beans served with crushed garlic and lemon juice and topped with olive oil. Dip your bread in it and enjoy.

Koubba (or kibbe) maqliya: a deep-fried oval-shaped ball with a meat and bulgar wheat paste as its crust and an aromatic filling of minced meat and pine nuts in the middle. It must be eaten hot to be enjoyed. Making *koubba* requires a lot of skill and talent so the smaller their size and the thinner their crust, the more skilled the cook that made them. You'll find the best *koubba* at home and not at a restaurant. It is sometimes served in a warm yoghurt-based sauce.

Vine leaves: stuffed with rice and/or meat, herbs and spices.

Fattayer and sambusak: small baked pastries filled with minced meat, or with a white salty cheese from Nablus and herbs, or with spinach and *soummak*, a slightly sour dark-red powdered seed.

Tabouleh: a salad of freshly chopped parsley, tomatoes, spring onions and fresh mint mixed with soaked bulgar wheat and sprinkled with lemon juice.

Main Course

Nothing can beat the taste of Middle Eastern grilled meats cooked on skewers over a charcoal fire. Some of the most common grills available in restaurants are: **shish taouk**, a delicious low-fat dish of boneless chicken pieces served with lemon juice and garlic; **kofta kebab**, spicy minced lamb; and **shish kebab**, cubes of boneless lamb or beef.

Jordan's national dish *par excellence* is **mansaf** and it is a real privilege to be able to taste it in a Jordanian home. It consists of big chunks of stewed lamb in a white yoghurt-based sauce served with rice. In a Bedouin household it is placed in one large dish on a low round table with the guests and family gathered around it. Each person eats with the right hand, and only takes the food on the part of

You will find a wide variety of cheap, delicious Middle Eastern fast food is sold at street stalls and restaurants.

Shawaramah: thin cuts of beef, lamb or chicken cooked on the spit and stuffed into pitta bread with *tahina* and pickles.

Felafel: small deep-fried balls of dried white broad beans crushed and mixed with chopped onions, garlic, parsley and spices. It is often served as a sandwich inside a hot pitta bread with *tahina* and salad, but can be eaten on its own. This is often regarded as pauper's food and is rarely served in upmarket restaurants. You'll enjoy it best on the street where it's served hot and fresh out of the pan.

Ma'ajanat: meaning pastries made with dough (*ajin*), such as *fattayer, sambusak* and also *manaeesh* (flat bread with powdered oregano and sesame seeds), or *sfeeha*, a flat dough spread with spicy minced meat.

the dish in front of him or her.

If your hosts happen to be of Palestinian origin they are more likely to serve **mussakhan**, chicken quarters baked and served on pieces of flat soft bread covered with chopped onions, pine-nuts and plenty of *samak;* or **maqhloubeh**("upside-down"), which is made of rice mixed with large chunks of chicken, lamb, or fish and vegetables moulded and turned upside down to serve.

A good supply of fresh fish is a relatively new phenomenon in Amman. As a rule, it is prepared on a charcoal fire, fried or cooked according to traditional recipes such as the famous **sayadiya**, boiled fish served on a bed of rice topped with a lemon sauce.

Sweets

Sweets, home-made or bought, are prominent and devoured in huge quantities during Ramadan, Muslim and Christian feasts and, of course,

at weddings. However, beautifully arranged trays of sweets are on display at patisseries all year round and they can be packed especially for you to take back home (see *What to Buy*). The most common type of sweet all over the Middle East, albeit with many variations, comprises layers of pastry filled with cream or chopped nuts, such as almonds, walnuts or pistachios, and soaked in a thick syrup.
Baklava: thin layers of *filo* pastry spread with chopped nuts and covered with syrup.
Konafa: shredded dough which looks like very fine *vermicelli,* filled with nuts or slightly salted white cheese.
Ataif: a medieval recipe for small, deep fried pancakes stuffed with nuts or white cheese and coated with syrup. Eaten during Ramadan only.
Ma'amoul: baked pastries with nuts or dates perfumed with rose water.

Other sweets are based on milk, like **mahalbiyya,** a pudding made of milk thickened with rice flour and perfumed with rose or orange-flower water, and the elastic **mastic ice-cream,** which is made with the powdered sahlab root and flavoured with mastic or Arabic gum, a resin that gives it its texture. It's usually coated with chopped nuts.

Sahlab is hot milk drink made with the powdered sahlab root and served with chopped pistachios, cinnamon and rose water.

Where To Eat

Amman has many restaurants that serve top quality Arabic food. When Jordanians go out to eat they expect at least the same high standard of cooking that they would have at home. Unfortunately, the same is not the case with the foreign cuisine available locally. Here quality varies and it is very rarely exceptional, even though Amman has a host of Italian, Far Eastern and "Continental" restaurants.

Although it is difficult to generalise about the standards of restaurant hygiene in Jordan as a whole, it is safe to say that Jordan is one of the cleanest countries in the region as far as food is concerned. However, it may be wise to enquire about the reputation of an eating establishment in advance and to go easy with uncooked vegetables. When you are faced with a buffet meal, check the freshness of the salads and cold meats and refrain if they look as if they have been sitting there for a while. The restaurants listed below are generally known to be safe choices in this respect.

Vegetarians will have a real feast with Arabic food (most of the many appetisers are suitable) and it is perfectly acceptable to have only a selection of starters (*muqabalat*) rather than a full meal. You can also have excellent vegetarian meals in Amman's Italian restaurants.

Price Guide

Based on the average cost of a meal, comprising appetiser and main course, per person:
$ – Inexpensive: 4JD and under
$$ – Medium: 5JD–9JD
$$$ – Expensive: 10JD and over

Note: If you order a selection of *muqabalat* only, the price will be lower.

During the hot months many restaurants move their main dining area to their outdoor terraces and gardens. Establishments with summer facilities are indicated in the list that follows. Outdoor eating is between May and October. Jordanians tend to eat late, with lunch at around 2pm and dinner at 9pm. However, restaurants open earlier, at 12.30pm for lunch and at 7.30pm for dinner.

All the restaurants listed below serve alcohol except for lower range restaurants. During Ramadan many restaurants close for the whole month because they are not allowed to sell alcohol and their profits are low. Those that do open serve food only after sunset when the fast is broken; some of these offer fantastic Ramadan specials.

Amman and other towns in Jordan are relatively small and restaurants are generally known. Because of this we give only the general area where restaurants are located, as precise addresses would be of no help – no one understands or uses them.

Amman

Middle Eastern & Jordanian
Reem Al Bawadi. End of Gardens Street after the Waha Circle. Tel: 5343733. Enormous dining room, and in the summer you can dine under a Bedouin tent. Offers generous portions of good Arabic cuisine. **$$$**
Fakhreddine's. Behind 2nd Circle. Tel: 465 2399. The interior decoration is exquisite and it serves the best Arabic, particularly Lebanese, cuisine around, albeit at quite a high price. Indoor and outdoor dining. Excellent service. **$$$**
Tannoureen. Ameerah Street near the Cordoba Hotel. Tel: 551 5987. Authentic Lebanese cuisine in intimate, quiet dining atmosphere. **$$$**
Al-Bustan. University Road, near Jerusalem Hotel. Tel: 5561555. This is probably the best known restaurant in Amman and definitely the best Arabic food in town. Lebanese and Jordanian cuisine at its best served with freshly baked bread. Outdoor verandah in the summer. Best to book in advance. **$$**
Kan Zaman Restaurant. Yaduda, 12 km (7 miles) south of Amman off the Desert highway. Tel: 412-8392/3. A popular restaurant inside the renovated stables of an old house serving Arabic food from an impressive buffet. Bread is made in front of you and the waiters join up for a brief dance, the *dabkeh.* **$$**
Al-Waha. Al-Waha Circle, at the end of Gardens Street. Tel: 5343734. Excellent Arabic food eaten at low brass tables with traditional decor. Offers a log-fire in the winter and outdoor Bedouin tent in the

summer. **$$**

Sakhan Ad-Dimashq. Shumaysani, opposite Jordan Gulf Bank. Excellent cheap Arabic food served in a Damascene interior. So clean, you could eat off the floors. Famous for its *shawarma* which attracts long queues. **$**

Mata'am Hashem. Downtown, in a small alleyway off the main street. A favourite with local Egyptian labourers, it serves excellent *ful moudames*, *felafel* and *hummus* with lots of oil. No alcohol. **$**

Ma'atouq. Third Circle, Jabal Amman. Fast-serving Arabic *mezze*, grills and sweets, which dishes up superb *hummus*. One of the best cheap restaurants. **$**

Okaz Restaurant. Intercontinental Hotel. Tel: 4641361. Lunchtime Lebanese buffet for Friday lunch and a mixture of continental and Middle Eastern buffet daily for lunch and dinner. **$$$**

Jabri. Shumaysani (Tel: 5688111) and Gardens Street (Tel: 5681700). A good chance to taste a wide selection of local dishes served fast in hearty portions cafeteria-style. Packed during the holidays and excellent value for money. No alcohol. **$**

Ana Amman. Above the Roman amphitheatre, downtown. Tel: 4787833. Grilled meats and *mezze*. The main attraction here is the view rather than the food. **$$**

La Terrasse. Shumaysani, opposite Jabri's on second and third floors. Delicious Arabic starters and Continental main courses. Outdoor terrace in the summer. **$$–$$$**

Abu Ahmad's. Two branches: the **Orient** at Basman Street, downtown

(Tel: 4636069) and the **New Orient** at the Third Circle, Jabal Amman (Tel: 4641879), both known as Abu Ahmad's. During the warmer months the Third Circle branch offers the advantage of a garden setting. Arabic food served with freshly baked bread; good grilled meats but *muqabalat* portions are relatively poor in both size and quality. **$$**

Qasr Snober. Off the Desert Highway 10 km (6 miles) from Amman and well signposted. Good Arabic food combines with a nice outing into the countryside. **$$**

Filfila. Shumaysani, next to Kentucky Fried Chicken. A small, inexpensive place serving a limited range of delicious dishes. Grilled meats are recommended. Also take-away. No alcohol. **$**

Zuwadeh. Al Fuhays, to the northwest of Amman. Tel: 079 32413 (mobile). An original restaurant located in the restored 19th-century village of Al Fuhays. Go early enough to shop in some of the quaint antique and handicraft stores. Owners of this restaurant relie on their mother's recipes to bring you some of the tastiest Arabic food around. Truly original selection of *fatteh*. Best time to enjoy is spring and autumn with dinner on the terrace capped by a smooth *arjeelah*. **$$**

Italian

Romero's. Opposite side of the road to the Intercontinental Hotel, near the Third Circle, Jabal Amman. Tel: 4644227. A popular choice with elegant locals and great for its social scene. The food is very good, the service is excellent and the

interior decoration is very tasteful. Its home-made *nociolla* (hazelnut) ice-cream is the best in town. Outdoor eating in the summer. **$$–$$$**

Leonardo Da Vinci. Shumaysani, next to the Islamic Bank. Tel: 5562441/5606281. Excellent food with a salad bar. The only drawback – for tall people – is the low ceiling. **$$–$$$**

Turino. Located in the Suwayfiya district. Excellent Italian food, served within a neoclassical-kitsch setting. **$$–$$$**

Cheers. Next to Turino. Tel: 5863944. Good Italian and American food in an informal atmosphere. Satellite TV. **$**

Milano. Shumaysani. The best pizza in town. Delicious sandwiches and salads. Very popular with well-heeled Jordanian youths. **$–$$**

Nouroz. Third Circle, Jabal Amman. Tel: 4642830. Italian only in so far as it makes delicious pizza. It also serves fast meat grills, salads and basic Arabic *mezze*. **$**

Bonita. Near the Third Circle. Tel: 4615060. Some Italian food, Spanish *paella* and other good international cuisine. Also a bar and outdoor eating in the summer. **$$**

La Cucina. Abdoun, behind the traffic lights leading to Swayfiyah. Tel: 593 3344/593 3355. Well-lit, classy interior. **$$**

French

L' Olivie. Abdoun. Tel: 5929564. The finest cuisine in one of the most expensive restaurants in town. Also the most popular in its price range. Live music. Book in advance. **$$$**

Internet Cafés

Internet cafés are springing up all over Jordan, but especially in the capital. Costs vary from around 1JD to 5JD per hour of internet usage.

In Amman **Books@Cafe**, located near the First Circle off Rainbow Street, is Jordan's original internet cafe. Situated inside a funky, remodelled Ottoman home, it is a bookstore, craft shop and internet

café rolled into one There are also two outdoor terraces with views of east Amman.

A host of others cluster around the university on University Road, such as **Culture Café**, **Ur Internet**, **University Internet Café** and the **International Internet Café**. A few others are in the Shmaysani district, including **Time Internet Café**, **Cyber**

Tunnel and **News Café**.

Outside the capital, there are cafés **Apollo**, **Shuleh** and **Haroun** in Irbid on University Road, near Yarmuk University campus, and in Mafraq there is the student-owned **Prisim Computer House**. **MafNet** and **Al AL Bayt Internet Café**, which is one of several cafés open 24 hours a day.

Drinking Notes

Most restaurants and hotel bars in Amman and outside serve alcohol except during Ramadan, when alcohol sales and drinking are banned. Jordanians can be seen drinking in many central locations in Amman. Jordan has its own beer, the excellent Amstel, brewed locally under licence. A big bottle costs just over 1JD to buy in a shop and 50–200 per cent more in bars and restaurants. Wine is imported from the "Holy Land", Tunisia, Cyprus and France. The best Palestinian wines are the Domaine de Latroun wines, and especially the Sauvignons and Pinots, as well as Caregnano. Alcohol can be purchased at many grocers and supermarkets. Safeway stocks the widest selection in foreign wines.

Indian

Bukhara. Jordan Intercontinental Hotel, near the Third Circle, Jabal Amman. Tel: 4641361. Wide range of Indian dishes including vegetarian, in a pleasant atmosphere. **$$$**

Mankal Chicken. Gardens Street and Abdali. Chicken tikka and Arabic starters. **$**

Clay Oven. Rabia, next to the Bonita Café. Tel: 5535322. Set within a lavish interior that is quiet and comfortable. **$$$**

Mexican and South American

Mama Juanita. At the Jordan Intercontinental Hotel. Tel: 464 1361. A fun-loving Mexican restaurant/bar. Not the best Mexican you'll have, but the closest thing you'll find in Amman. **$$$**

Latinos. Located in the Meridien. Tel: 569 6511. Sizzling South American dishes in a fun atmosphere of vibrant decor and live music by a Latino trio. Divided into a bar and restaurant. **$$$**

Far Eastern

Taiwan Tourismo. Opposite the Akileh Hospital, near the Third Circle, Jabal Amman. Tel: 4641093. Probably the best Chinese food in town in a very modest setting. No air-conditioning, only fans. **$$**

Peking. Opposite the Al-Qasr Hotel, Shumaysani. Tel: 5660250. The decor is more impressive than the cuisine but it is one of the most tasteful Chinese restaurants in its price range. VIP lounges for special occasions. **$–$$**

China Town. At the Meridien Hotel, Shumaysani. Tel: 5696511. Good food and variety. Beautifully decorated individual rooms (enclosed by Chinese screens) for private parties. **$$$**

Restaurant China. Opposite Ahliya school, near First Circle. Tel: 4638968. The first Chinese restaurant in town and still one of the most popular. **$$**

Miscellaneous

Rozena. Part of the Sabeel Hotel suites, near the Second Circle, Jabal Amman. A homely interior and a pleasant summer terrace. Very good food, except for dessert. Excellent service and a friendly atmosphere thanks to its manager. **$$**

Merlin's. On Mecca Street in the Marmara Hotel – keep your eye out for the huge, red lighted sign. Tel: 553 0480. The food here is simply superb: fondue or homemade ravioli are good choices, made all the better by Earnest Linger, Merlin's exceptionally friendly and concerned chef. **$$$**

Champion's. Located in Amman's Marriott. Tel: 560 7607. American sports bar and grill with occasional pasta dishes thrown in along with tex-mex appetisers. Music, spun by resident DJ, can be too loud for a comfortable dining atmosphere. Best avoided on Thursday evenings if you are looking for quiet dining. **$$$**

Houston's. Shumaysani. Tel: 562 0610. The name pretty much says it all. Serves the best in the way of American burgers, several sizzling tex-mex dishes, Huge salads and appetisers along with some tasty pasta dishes. **$$$**

Hard Rock Cafe. Amman had to have one. Palatial establishment in Abdoun, you can't miss it. Serves the usual Hard Rock dishes. Occasional cover charge. **$$$**

Patisseries & Cafés

In Amman you find Arabic as well as French-style coffee house: cafés where you can enjoy a cake or ice-cream or enjoy a *argheelah* (water pipe) and Arabic coffee while watching the world go by. There is a concentration of Western-style patisseries in Shumaysani.

Babiche. Shumaysani and Abdoun. The best treat for a sweet tooth that you are likely to find in Amman. Enjoy its splendid fruit tarts and chocolate mousse cake in a nice ambience enhanced by the gentle rhythms of Greek music. Also sandwiches and *ma'ajanat*.

Café Mokka. Abdoun, next to MegaTech store and across from Galleria Cinema on the road leading to the Orthodox Club. Cosy, and certainly the best pastries in town.

Café de Paris. Abdoun, off Abdoun Circle, beneath the Galleria Cinema. Outdoor Terrace. If you're a budget traveller, Café de Paris is probably too sexy for your wallet – no seat for less than 5JD. Unfortunately mediocre coffee, sweets and service, but the best place in town to observe the trendiest of Amman's youth.

Jabri. Downtown, Shumaysani and Gardens Street. Cakes and ice-cream including mastic ice-cream.

Coffee House El-Farouki. Shumaysani and Jabal Al-Hussein. It grinds its own coffee.

La Patisserie. The Marriott Hotel, Shumaysani.

Vienna. Amra Hotel.

Phoenik. Gardens Street. A hang-out for young returnees from Kuwait, where you can eat, drink and see an exhibition.

The Arab League Café. Faces the King Hussein Mosque. A true Arabic café but a man's domain.

Frosti's. Shumaysani and Swayfiyah. Ice-cream parlour serving the only frozen yoghurt in the country.

Snack Bars & Pubs

The Irish Pub. Located between the 4th and 5th Circles, neighbouring the Egyptian Consulate and beneath the Dove Hotel. True to form: just a pub, and that's why it's great. You can catch the football here on ESPN, prices are reasonable and the crowd youthful.

Rovers Return. Swayfiyah, underneath Comfort Suites. The typical English pub, smack in the middle of Amman, modelled on the British soap opera *Coronation Street*. Serves surprisingly good fish and chips, and homesick Englanders can find compatriots here most any night of the week. Good service and better prices. Tends to be very crowded Monday and Thursday evenings.

Ciro's Pizza Pomodoros. Off Abdoun Circle on the road to the Othodox Club. Tricky to find as entrance is at the side and there are no signs facing the street. You'll know you're in the vicinity by the number of Mercedes and BMWs parked outside. A favourite among Amman's young and wealthy, so rather expensive, but you can get some great pasta and pizza here.

Yesterday's. Jabal Amman, by 4th Circle. Again, very expensive, and Thursdays can see long queues and steep cover charges. But the food is good and there's a dance floor.

Tropicana. On top of the Middle East Hotel. Open during the summer. Reasonable prices and generally not too crowded.

Salute. Second Circle (near Rozena restaurant). Salute offers an exotic menu of alcoholic and non-alcoholic cocktails and coffee liqueurs. Best to book on Thursday nights.

Mama Juanites, Intercontinental Hotel. Expensive drinks but a great meeting place. Also famous for its Wednesday night quiz. There is a 3JD minimum charge. Satellite TV.

After Eight. Attached to the Amigo Nabeel restaurant, near First Circle. Very small but with a good atmosphere. A hang-out for local journalists.

Hisham Hotel Bar. Near Third Circle. Particularly nice in the summer when you can sit outside.

Tapas Bar (Bonita). Near Third Circle. Live music in the winter and outdoor terrace in the summer.

Outside the Capital

In addition to the following, there are many other places where one can eat clean, decent food in Irbid, Ajlun, Petra town and at the Azraq and Wadi Rum resthouses.

Ajlun

Bonita Restaurant. On the incline to your left as you descend from the Ajlun Castle. Tel: 02 642 0981. If you can, sit on the terrace for a spectacular view of the castle and its environs. Mostly Arabic food. Serves alcohol. **$$**

Aqaba

Ali Baba. Known for its fish and Arabic food. Wines are wrapped up in green paper due to local sensitivities. **$$**

Chinese Restaurant. There are two of these in town; both are good, but the most recent is one of the best of its kind in the country. **$$**

Club Murjan. Outdoor terrace or indoor dining. Menu packed with seafood dishes and Arabic *mezze*.

Mina House. In an old tug boat moored past the Mamluke fort. Fresh fish and barbecued meat. **$$**

Jarash

Lebanese House (also known as **Um Khalil's**). Half a kilometre south of the hippodrome, off the road to Ajlun. The best Arabic food in Jordan, bar none. A favourite with Jordanians and other visiting Arabs who will drive up from Amman just to lunch or dine here. **$$**

Ya Hala. Inside the town itself and near the northern end of the archaeological site. A good second to Um Khalil's. Large garden with a water pool and artificial streams. **$$**

Abu Yehia's. On the road to Amman, marked only with a 7-Up sign. Excellent meat dishes. **$**

Green Valley Restaurant. On the Jarash-Amman road. Excellent shish and kofta kebabs, supported by great bread and dips. Alcohol served. **$$**

Madaba

Haret Ajdoudnah. Turn left when exiting St George's church and within a short walk you'll come across this restaurant at a road on the right. Tel: 08 548650. This turn-of-the-century home of the Jumean family serves mezza and pizza; alcohol is also sold. Take time to wander through the shops selling high quality handicrafts. **$$–$$$**

Pella

Resthouse in Pella. Run by Romero's in Amman, it is nicely decorated and serves snacks and beverages including alcohol. Wonderful view of the Jordan Valley. **$$**

Umm Qays

Restaurant at Umm Qays. Tel: 02-217210 or 02-217081 ext. 59. Run by the owner of Romero's in Amman, it offers delicious Arabic food with the most spectacular view of the ruins of ancient Gadara, Lake Tiberias and the Golan Heights. Advisable to book in advance. **$$**

The West Bank

Here's a brief list of recommended restaurants you might like to try in East Jerusalem and Ramallah:

East Jerusalem

Pasha Restaurant in Sheikh Jarrah. Tel: 02-5825162. Serves Arabic mezze and barbecued meats. Nice outdoor garden, and is right next to Al Wasati gallery. **$$**

Kan Zaman, near the Old City on Nablus Road. Tel: 02-6283282. Serves Arabic mezze, barbecued meats, soups and sandwiches. Lovely outdoor garden in the summer and cosy indoor seating in the winter. Traditional Arabic music every Thursday; it is a good idea to make a reservation. **$$$**

Askadinya, in Sheikh Jarrah. Tel: 02-5324801. Named in Arabic after the sprawling loquat fruit tree in the middle of the restaurant. A tasty selection of fish, pizza and pasta. **$$**

Ramallah
Bardouni on Jaffa Street, near the city centre. Tel: 02- 2951410. A popular eatery with the locals. Serves traditional Arabic food and has a nice outdoor garden.
Kit Kat. Just off the municipal gardens square. Tel: 02-2987312. The café is known for its fine selection of freshly ground coffee, but also serves good pizza, pasta and American ice-cream.
Angelos Pizza, in the centre of Ramallah, is a popular hang out for the Bir Zeit University crowd.

Syria

In Damascus, unlike Amman, restaurants are rather hard to find if you don't know where to look. So, here are a few to get you started.

Damascus
Omayyad Palace Restaurant. Tel: 2220826. in a narrow alleyway on the south side of the Omayyad Mosque. Offers a delicious lunch and dinner buffet amidst an eclectic assortment of antiques and plenty of atmosphere. Live music and whirling Dervishes every evening. Moderately priced, but no alcohol is served. Excellent value for money.
The Piano Bar. On Hanania Street. Tel: 5430357. Serves European cuisine in a lovely outdoor area. Spaghetti, fish, chicken, soups and salads. Good place for cold beer. Atmospheric bar.
Ali Baba on Fardoos Street. Serves mezze and grilled meats.
Nofara Café behind the Omayyad Mosque is a popular spot to have coffee and tea served the traditional way, or a *nargeelah* (hubble-bubble pipe). Unlike similar cafés, women are welcome too.

Culture

Jordan has a rapidly developing fine art scene and, to a lesser degree, this is true of theatre and poetry indigenous to the country and the Middle East region. Music, ballet and film are imported and, this being a relatively poor and small country, appear irregularly and often under sponsorship. Many of the cultural activities in Amman take place at the theatres and exhibition halls of the Royal Cultural Centre. Foreign cultural centres are also active in organising exhibitions, films, plays and recitals for Jordanian and other Arab artists.

Archaeological Sites

Some of the archaeological sites are open all the time and can be visited during daylight hours without paying an entry fee. Others are fenced off and access is confined to set hours which apply throughout the country (except for Petra): namely, every day, even on feasts and during Ramadan, from 8am to 5pm in winter and 8am to 6pm in summer. At some of these sites the Department of Antiquities charges an entry fee which is different for Jordanians and non-Jordanians. The prices listed below apply to non-Jordanians. It is forbidden to spend the night at any of the sites.

Entry Times and Fees
Open sites are: the Citadel; the Roman Amphitheatre; Nymphaeum; Nuwayjis; Rujm Al-Malfouf and Ain Ghazzal (all in Amman); the Desert Castles; Um al-Jimal and the castle and Ayla in Aqaba.
Open standard hours with free entry are: the Suwayfiyya mosaic, Quwaysima and the Cave of the Seven Sleepers in Amman; Ajlun Castle; Shawbak; Madaba, Mount Nebu, Um Ar-Rasas and other sites in the Madaba region; and churches of St George and the Apostles, Madaba (except closed Sunday).
Open standard hours with an entry charge are: Jarash (2JD); Karak Castle (1JD, including museum) and Umm Qays (1JD).

Museums

Amman
Jordan Archaeological Museum. Citadel. Tel: 4638795. Finds from excavations all over Jordan dating from prehistoric times to the 15th century. Open 9am–5pm. Entry 2JD for non-Arabs.
Jordanian Museum of Popular Tradition. At the Roman amphitheatre. Tel: 4651760. Probably the most impressive little museum in Jordan, with fragments of Byzantine mosaics, costumes and jewellery well displayed. Open 9am–5pm. Entry 1JD for non-Arabs.
Jordanian Folklore Museum. Next to the Amphitheatre. Tel: 4651742. An effort to recreate traditional life in Jordan with various artifacts, such as a tent, home furnishings, musical instruments and crafts. Open 9am–5pm. Entry 1JD.
Jordan University Archaeological Museum. On University Campus. Tel: 843555, ext. 3412. Artifacts dating from the Bronze Age to the Islamic period. Open 8am–5pm, closed Thursday and Friday. Free.
Jordan University National Folklore Museum. On University Campus. Tel: 843555, ext. 3739. Open 8am–5pm, closed Thursday and Friday. Free.
Jordan University Biology/Medical Museum. University Campus. Tel: 843555, ext. 2300. Open 8am– 5pm, closed Thur and Fri. Free.
Jordan Postal Museum. Ministry of Communications, on

Eighth Circle, Jabal Amman).
Tel: 5624301.
Old and new Jordanian stamps.
Open 8am–2pm, closed Friday. Free.
Coin Museum.
Central Bank of Jordan, King
Hussein Street, downtown.
Tel: 4630301.
Ancient and modern Jordanian coins.
Open 9am–2pm, closed Tue and Fri.
**Military Museum (Martyrs'
Memorial).**
Sports City (Medina Riadhiya)
University Road.
Tel: 5664240.
Military memorabilia from the Great
Arab Revolt of 1916 to more recent
wars. Museum open 9am–4pm,
closed Saturday. Free.
**Children's Heritage and Science
Museum.**
Haya Arts Centre, Shumaysani.
Tel: 5665195.
Open 9am–1.30pm, 3.30–5.30pm,
closed Friday. Free.

Aqaba
Museum of Aqaba's Antiquities.
Near the Mamluke fort.
Tel: 03-2013731.
Displays from Ayla's excavations.
Open 8am–1pm and 5pm–7pm
(3pm–5pm in winter). Closed
Tuesday. Entry 1JD.
The Aqaba Marine Science Station.
Aquarium for marine life in the Gulf
of Aqaba.
Tel: 03-2015144/5.
Open daily 8am–5pm except Monday.
Entry 0.500JD for non-Jordanians.

Irbid
Archaeological Museum.
Tel: 02-277066.
Open 8am–5pm, closed Friday. Free.
**Museum of Archaeology and
Anthropology.**
Institute of Archaeology and
Anthropology, Yarmuk University.
Tel: 02-271100, ext. 3746.
Open 10am–3pm, closed Friday.

Jarash
Archaeological Museum.
On the site, off the cardo.
Tel: 04-452267.
Open winter 9am–5pm, summer
8.30am–6pm, public holidays
10am–4pm. Closed Friday. Free.

Petra

Opening times: daily winter
7am–5pm, summer 7am–6pm.
Entry fee: (for non-Jordanians
and non-resident foreigners)
20JD for one day, 25JD for two
days and 30JD for three days; for
resident foreigners and
Jordanians: 1JD. This price
includes access to the two
museums but not horse rental.
Horse rental: 6JD for the return
journey, excluding tip. Horse
rental is optional. You should buy
a ticket at the nearby kiosk which
will give you the rota number of
the horse you will be renting. You
may also rent a horse for the
return leg only but beware: you
may be asked outrageous rates
– don't settle for anything more
than half to two-thirds of the
official round trip price (it's a
good opportunity to try out your
bartering skills).
In the past it was possible to
ride horses down the *siq* (and
you will still see photographs of
this), but now only horse carts
for the disabled are allowed in.
Horse riders must stop at the *siq*
entrance and walk down the
narrow corridor of the *siq*.

Karak
Archaeological Museum.
Tel: 03-351149.
Open winter 8am–2pm, summer
8am–5pm, closed Tuesday. Entry
included in entrance fee to the
castle.
Mazar Islamic Museum.
Mazar, near Karak.
Tel: 03-371042. Islamic antiquities.
Open 8am–2pm, closed Tuesday.
Free.

Madaba
Archaeological Museum.
Tel: 08-544056.
Open 9am–5pm, closed Tuesday.
Entry 3JD for non-Arabs.

Petra
Archaeological Museum.
Tel: 03-83029.
Open daily 8am–4pm.

Salt
Archaeological Museum.
Tel: 05-555653.
Open 8am–2pm, closed Friday and
public holidays.

Umm Qays
Archaeological Museum.
The building itself is as interesting
as the Roman, Hellenistic and
Byzantine exhibits inside. Open
8am–5pm, closed Tuesday. Free.

Cultural Centres

Royal Cultural Centre.
Tel: 5661026 or 4641993.
Shumaysani, near the Sports City,
Amman. Opening hours depend on
activity.
American Centre.
Abdoun, Amman.
Tel: 5920101.
Inside the American embassy
complex. Open: office and video
library 8am–5pm; library 8am–7pm,
closed Friday; feature films Sunday
and Thursday 7pm; documentaries
Tuesday 7pm.
Goethe Institut.
Near Third Circle, Jabal Amman,
Amman.
Tel: 4641993.
Reference library, films, exhibitions
and concerts. German lessons also
given here. Open 9am–12.30pm,
closed Thursday and Friday.
French Cultural Centre.
Jabal Al-Luwaybida, Amman.
Tel: 4637009.
French, Arabic, music, exhibitions,
lectures and film presentations.
Office open: 9am–1pm, 4–7pm,
closed Friday; library (books, video,
tapes) 9am–1pm, 4–7pm, closed
Friday and Saturday mornings.
British Council.
Abu Bakr As-Siddiq Street (known
as Rainbow Street) near First Circle,
Jabal Amman.
Tel: 4636147/8, 4638194,
5624686.
English teaching, library, exhibitions
and films. Office: 8am–3pm
Sun–Thur, 7.45am–1.45pm, 3–6pm
Wed. Library: 10am–6pm. Language
Centre 11am–6pm Sat–Wed.
Abdel Hamid Shoman Foundation.
Near First Circle. Exhibitions and

Music, Ballet & Theatre

Recitals, concerts (classical or pop) and, less frequently, ballet performances take place at the Royal Cultural Centre, the foreign cultural centres and occasionally are organised by the upmarket hotels in Amman.

The **Jarash Festival**, held every summer (often in July) attracts national and international drama, ballet, folklore shows and singers.

lectures (Arabic), a library in Shumaysani with periodicals and books in English and Arabic; also several foreign newspapers. Free.

Art Galleries

The Jordan National Gallery of Fine Arts. Montaza, Jabal Al-Luwaybida, Amman. Tel: 4630128.
Paintings and some sculpture and ceramics by contemporary Arab artists. The 19th-century Orientalists collection is not always on display. Open 9am–5pm, closed Tuesday. Free, except for special exhibitions.

If you are interested in buying as well as seeing art, check the listings in the *Jordan Times* for current events at these galleries:
Darat Al-Funun (Little House for the Arts). Tel: 4643251/2.
The most impressive, attractive and interesting of all Jordan's galleries. It is housed in a beautifully restored old house in Jabal Al-Luwaybida. Open 10am–7pm, closed Friday.
Baladna. Gardens Street, near Safeways, Amman. Tel: 5696010. Specialises in local artists. Open daily.
Riwak Al-Balka'a for Arts. Near the Municipality building, Fuhays, near Amman. Tel: 4720677.
Exhibitions by foreign and Arab artists, poetry readings, outdoor theatre in the summer and music performances in an old house with a lovely courtyard (the *riwak*). Also has a small complex of craft shops. Open daily 10am–1pm, 3–8pm.
The Gallery. Jordan Intercontinental Hotel, Amman. Tel: 4641361, ext.

2183. Paintings and photographs by local and foreign artists, pottery, cards, old prints, books on Jordan and many other ideas for gifts. Open 8am–7pm, closed Friday.
Alia Art Gallery. Abu Bakr As-Siddiq Street (known as Rainbow Street) near First Circle, Jabal Amman. Tel: 4639350. Open 9am–1.30pm, 3.30–6.30pm, closed Friday.
Orient Gallery. Shumaysani. Tel: 5681303.
Features Arab artists from Asia and North Africa. Open 9.30am–1.30pm, 3.30–8.30pm.
Jarash Art Gallery. On the main road, halfway between the Tourist Visitors' Centre and Hadrian's Arch (*see p172*), Jarash. Open daily 9am–4.30pm.

In Jerusalem a visit to **Gallery Anadiel**, 27 Salah Eddin Street, is a must. A small gem of a gallery presenting and selling the work of contemporary Palestinian artists. Open daily 9am–2pm, 4.30–7pm except Sunday 10am–2pm. The gallery may also open on special request (tel: 02-288750).

Cinema

There are three modern cinemas in Amman: the **Galleria** at Abdoun Circle, the **Philadelphia** at the Tower building, Emir Mohammed Street, near Third Circle, and the **Concord**, near the Housing Bank Centre in Jabal Al-Hussein. They all show popular films from the West, albeit rather later than in the States or Europe. Shows are advertised in the *Jordan Times* daily. Tickets costs vary around the 3JD to 5JD figure, and films are censored for kissing and sex scenes.

The fastest way to see the latest Western releases is to hire videos but these may also be censored. Other cinemas downtown show karate and low-quality action movies. The foreign cultural centres organise film shows regularly and advertise in the *Jordan Times*.

The Amman **Film Festival** is held in May. During the festival European films are shown at the Royal Cultural Centre for free and in some of the major cinemas for a fee.

Shopping

Shopping Areas

Gift and souvenir shopping in Jordan can be an exciting experience. If you do not have much time to devote to it, head for **Al-Aydi** ("The Hands"), which ccupies the ground floor of a house behind the Lebanese Embassy on Second Circle, Jabal Amman. Tel: 4644555. Look out for the sign with the palm of a hand, logo of the Jordan Craft Development Centre (established in the early 1970s to provide a living for craftspeople and to salvage craft skills). Fixed prices. Open winter 9am–1pm, 3–6pm, summer 9am–1pm, 4–7pm, closed Friday and public holidays.

There are a number of well-stocked souvenir shops with a great variety of goods and negotiable prices:
Al-Shami Bazar and Gifts. Between Third Circle and Intercontinental. Oriental Souvenirs Stores. Emir Mohammed Street, near Third Circle.
Boys' Town. At the Intercontinental shopping arcade.
Al-Afghani. In Jabal Al-Luwaybida, opposite the post office near Al-Hawouz Circle.
Gallerie Mesopotamia. Ground floor of Jordan Insurance building, off Emir Mohammed Street, near Third Circle.
Arabic and Islamic Heritage House, Baouniya Street, Jabal Al-Luwaybida.

There are also plenty of souvenir shops near all major tourist attractions. However, Jordanian crafts deserve some attention and you should sample the best available. Two projects, the **Noor Al-Hussein Foundation** (near Safeway) and the **Jordan River Designs**, in the Save the Children building on

Jabal Al-Luwaybida, produce a huge variety of beautiful and high quality crafts hand-made by local women. Prices are fixed but high.

The **Nazik Al-Hariri Centre for the Handicapped**, near Eighth Circle on the way to Fuhays, has a nice selection of rugs and basketwork. **Kan Zaman** has many craftshops stocking a variety of work sold at fixed prices; in particular look out for the **Bridal Chest** shop. Finally the **airport duty-free shop** is an excellent last minute choice.

The **downtown suq** is a typical Middle Eastern market, where you can buy almost anything. But, generally, shopping in Amman is less concentrated than it used to be, with new neighbourhoods developing with their own shopping areas. The following areas should cover almost all your shopping needs: downtown, **Emir Mohammed Street** (from Third Circle to the city centre), **Abu Bakr As-Siddeeq Street** (known as Rainbow Street), **Wasfi Tell Street**, known as Gardens Street (from Safeway to Al-Waha Circle) and the upmarket areas of **Suwayfiyya** and **Shumaysani**

Bargaining is gradually losing ground in Jordan as more shops stick to fixed prices. You should, however, attempt it in souvenir shops and in the *suq* downtown.

What to Buy

Palestinian Ceramics
For mugs, plates, bowls, cups and tiles try **Boys' Town** and **Al-Shami Bazar** in Amman. Jerusalem, however, can offer better variety and prices. The **Palestinian pottery workshop** beside the American Consulate in East Jerusalem has some of the most artistic (and pricey) ceramics. Other ceramicists are to be found in the Arab and Armenian quarters of Jerusalem's Old City.

Palestinian Embroidery
In Amman, search out the shop called **Zakaria Ar-Ramadi's** (tel: 5629719, 4647719), which has low prices and excellent quality

work. It specialises in embroidered cushion covers, jackets, dresses, slippers and hair bands. It is at No. 10, Alleyway 2, off Omar Al-Khayyam Street, where the service taxis for Jabal Al-Luwaybida have their taxi rank.

Another place where you can actually pick your design and be fitted for items of clothing is the **Olive Branch** opposite the French Cultural Centre in Jabal Al-Luwaybida. Also try **Al-Dalal Co** (tel: 5603217), inside the Forte Grand Hotel, **Boys' Town**, **Al-Aydi**, the **airport duty-free shop**, and **Kan Zaman**. Prices for small embroidered cushions range from a low 12–15JD to a high 20–25JD, and dresses cost 100–200JD. Quality varies so be careful.

Pottery
Bowls, vases, plates and lamp-bases. The common pattern of pale-coloured pottery with Arabic script designs is produced mainly by two workshops. The first is **Silsal Pottery** (tel: 5680128). Its products are on sale at the workshop (third turning right between 5th and 4th circle) as well as at Al-Aydi, the Noor Al-Hussein Foundation (near Safeway), the Marriott souvenir and newspaper shop, The Gallery at the Intercontinental Hotel and at the airport duty-free. The second workshop is **Hazem Zoubi's gallery and studio** (tel: 5680908), in Shumaysani behind Safeway – call the shop for directions – where you can find bowls and plates, as well as ceramic wall pieces with abstract designs.

Bedouin Kilims
Bani Hamida House (tel: 4658696) is just off Abu Bakr As-Siddiq Street (Rainbow Street), near First Circle, Jabal Amman. The shop sells the famous Bedouin-made rugs to modern designs. Open 8am–6pm, closed Friday. **Al-Aydi** also has a large stock of Bedouin rugs in authentic patterns and colours. There are a number of shops in Madaba where many rugs are actually produced.

Hebron Hand-Made Glass
Look out for carafes, bowls, jars, vases and mugs made in Jordan by a family originally from Hebron, who now live and work in Na'ur, near Amman. Apart from the traditional dark-blue glass there is also clear glass, light brown, green and yellow. It is sold at **Al-Aydi**, but many souvenir shops also stock it. For the best prices go to the workshop in Na'ur where you can see the glass-blowers at work.

Basketry
This is produced in Mukhayba, north of the Jordan Valley. Available at **Al-Aydi**, where you will find some of the finest new and old pieces, and also at the museum shop in Umm Qays.

Gold
Cheaper here than in the West and there is a huge variety of quality available in the *suq* downtown. Know your stuff and bargain within reason. Look out for silver jewellery and amber. Silver from Yemen is particularly attractive.

Sand-Filled Bottles
These are bottles containing various designs and pictures in coloured sand. They are made in Aqaba and Petra and sold everywhere. Quality varies.

Oriental Sweets
These will keep fresh if packed airtight. The patisserie **Jabri** has branches in Shumaysani, Gardens Street, on the main street in Jabal Al-Hussein, on the main road between Fifth and Sixth circles as well as downtown. **Zalatimo** is another famous brand in oriental sweets. They have several outlets around the capital; the most accessible are in the Amra Hotel shopping arcade and in Abdali, across from the bus station in the Al Quds building, ground floor.

Wood Inlaid with Mother of Pearl
In most souvenir shops you will find boxes with Dome of the Rock designs, on mirrors and picture frames and sometimes chairs and

chests of drawers, most of which are produced in Palestine and Syria.

Olivewood
From kitchen utensils to Christmas Nativity scenes, eggs and other miscellaneous kitsch. On sale all over the country as well as in the West Bank where it is produced.

Copperware
Stocked at most souvenir shops.

Antiques
Try **Al-Afghani** (tel: 5625992, 5635758, 5676670). Branches in Jabal Luwaybida, off the Al Hawuz Circle, across from the post office. Alternatively, a smaller shop, often with the best antiques, is located behind the Stop and Shop Grocery. Best place for people who know their Middle Eastern antique jewels and lanterns. other branches in Jabal Hussein and Gardens street.

Art
See *Art Galleries, page 350.*

Exporting Purchases

There are no export restrictions except for antiquities, i.e. items more than 100 years old. Shopkeepers can post your purchases to the US and Europe.

Complaints

After you have tried to reason with the shopkeeper, go to the police. Take a receipt, otherwise you will have no evidence of how much you have paid.

Sport

Participant Sports

Sports City (Al-Medina Ar-Riadhiya), on the University Road, Amman. An impressive complex of sports facilities with a gym, indoor and outdoor swimming pools, tennis and squash courts.
Orthodox Club, Abdoun. This has indoor and outdoor swimming pools, basket and volleyball grounds, tennis and squash courts and a gym.

Tennis and Squash
There are tennis and squash courts at Sports City, the Royal Automobile Club and the Orthodox Club. The YWCA (near Third Circle), the Meridien, Crown, Jordan Intercontinental, Marriott, Philadelphia and Amra hotels also have tennis courts.

Weight-Training and Aerobics
Gyms are mushrooming all over Amman; also health clubs offering sauna, steam bath, whirlpool and massage. You can pay per visit, which can be expensive, or get a short-term or long-term membership, which works out a lot cheaper. The best value for money in this field are **Body Must Fitness and Beauty Centre**, at the Amra Hotel, **Fitness One**, on Mecca Street and the **Plaza Fitness centres** in the Housing Bank building and in Suwayfiyya, which offer a wide range of aerobics classes. Good facilities are also available at the Intercontinental's new InterFit Spa (the most luxurious but also the most expensive), the Marriott Hotel Health Club, Regency Palace Hotel Health Club, Power Hut in Shumaysani, Sports City and the Orthodox Club.

Bowling
Brunswick Bowling Centre, Abu Bakr As-Siddiq Street (Rainbow Street) near First Circle, Jabal Amman.

Swimming
Most outdoor swimming pools open at the beginning of May and close at the end of September. Most hotel pools are open to non-residents but you must pay an entrance fee. Sometimes monthly and season tickets are available. The best swimming pools are at the Jordan Intercontinental, the Orthodox Club and Sports City, but they all get overcrowded on holidays and Fridays. Other hotels with outdoor swimming pools of varying sizes include the Marriott, Meridien, Amra, Philadelphia, Crown Hotel, Amman International, Grand Palace, Crown Hotel, Middle East and Al-Manar. Many of these places have children's pools.
In the winter you can swim at various indoor pools, including those at the Intercontinental Health Club, the Marriott Hotel Health Club, Regency Palace Hotel Health Club, the Plaza Health Club in Suwayfiyya, the Orthodox Club and Sports City, where you can pay by the visit or, if you're staying for a while, get membership.

Jogging
The Hash-House Harriers meet on Monday evenings. A jog is followed by hearty drinking and eating. For details of upcoming venues, contact the British Embassy or British Council in Amman and the Al-Cazar Hotel in Aqaba.

Scuba Diving and Snorkelling
Aqaba offers some of most spectacular diving in the world on the coast towards Saudi Arabia. Larger hotels also offer trips in glass-bottom boats. Try to avoid March and April when the water contains a lot of algae. Shop around the following diving centres (they offer instruction at all levels and rent out gear):
Aquamarina I Hotel.
Tel: 03-2016250.
Offers snorkelling, diving from a

boat or the beach, water-skiing, windsurfing, fishing trips and half-day boat trips to Far'un Island and its coral reef. Also pedalo, speed-boat, marine camera and other equipment hire **Al-Cazar Hotel.** Tel: 03-2014131. For diving trips, instruction and equipment. **Royal Diving Centre.** Tel: 03-2017035. Situated outside Aqaba, en route to the Saudi border. For snorkelling, diving and marine photography equipment hire, and instruction. **Red Sea Diving Centre.** Tel: 03-2018969. Professional but friendly, with reasonable prices. Situated near the Aqaba Gulf Hotel. **Club Murjan.** Tel: 03-2018335. Full beach club. Outdoor terrace, swimming and wading pools, bar, restaurant, snorkelling and scuba diving equipment available along with other water sports. Situated on south beach.

Hiking, Climbing and Trekking

Wadi Rum and Petra are ideal locations for all these, but avoid the summer months. In Wadi Rum aim for the rock bridge. Two useful books on the subject are: Tony Howard's *Treks and Climbs in the Mountains of Rum and Petra*, Jordan Distribution Agency/ Cicerone Press, 1987 (new edition 1993); and Tony Howard & Diana Taylor's *Walks and Scrambles in Wadi Rum*, Al-Kutba, Amman, 1993. Bring your own gear for climbing.

Spectator Sports

Apart from **football** and **basketball** matches you can watch **horse-** and **camel-racing** in spring and summer in Marka (east of Amman city centre) under the supervision of the Royal Racing Club.

Language

Few things please Jordanians more than meeting a foreigner who can speak their language, so it's well worth a try.

Greetings

Hello *Márhaba, ahla*n
(reply) *Marhabtáyn, áhlayn*
Greetings *As-salám aláykum* (peace be with you)
(reply) *Waláykum as-salám* (and to you peace)
Welcome *Áhlan wasáhlan*
(reply) *áhlan fíkum*
Good morning *Sabáh al-kháyr*
(reply) *Sabáh an-núr* (a morning of light)/*Sabáh al-wurd* (a morning of the smell of flowers)
Good evening *Masá al-kháyr*
(reply) *Masá an núr*
Good night *Tisbáh al-kháyr* (wake up well)
(reply) *Wa ínta min áhlu* (and you are from His people)
Good bye *Máa Saláma* (with peace)/*alla Máák* (God be with you)/*Ya'atik aláfia* (may God give you health)
How are you? *Káyf hálak?* (to a man)/*Káyf hálik?* (to a woman)
well, fine *mabsút* or *mneeh* (for a man)/*mabsúta* or *mneeha* (for a woman)
please *min fádlak* (to a man)/*min fádlik* (to a woman)
After you *Tafáddal* (to a man)/ *Tafáddali* (to a woman)/*Afáddalu* (to more than one)
Excuse me *Samáhli* or *Idha láwu samánt* (to a man)/*Samáhili* or *Idha láwu samánti* (to a woman)
Sorry *Áfwan* or *mutaásif* or *ásif* (for a man)/*Áfwan* or *mutaásifa* or *ásifa* (for a woman)
Thank you (very much) *Shúkran (jazilan)*

Thank you, I am grateful *Mamnúnak* (to a man)/*Mamnúnik* (to a woman)
Thanks be to God *Al-hámdu li-llá*
God willing (hopefully) *Inshá allá*
Yes *Náam* or *áiwa*
No *La*
Congratulations! *Mabrúck!*
(reply) *Alláh yubárak fik*

Useful Phrases

What is your name? *Shú ismak?* (to a man)/*Shú ismik?* (to a woman)
My name is... *Ismi...*
Where are you from? *Min wáyn inta?* (for a man)/*Min wáyn inti?* (for a woman)
I am from... *Ána min...*
... England ... *Ingíltra*
... Germany ... *Almánia*
... the United States ... *Amérika*
... Australia ...*Ustrália*
Do you speak English? *Btíhki inglízi?*
I speak... *Bíhki...*
... English ... *inglízi*
... German ...*Almámi*
... French ...*Fransáwi*
I do not speak Arabic *Ma bíhki árabi*
I do not understand *Ma báfham*
What does this mean? *Ya'áni esh?*
Repeat, once more *Kamán márra*
Do you have...? *Ándkum...?*
Is there any...? *Fí...?*
There isn't any... *Ma fí...*
Never mind *Ma'alésh*
It is forbidden *Mamnú'a*
Is it allowed? *Masmúh?*
What is this? *Shú hádha?*
I want *Bídi*
I do not want *Ma bídi*
Wait *Istánn* (to a man)/*Istánni* (to a woman)
Hurry up *Yalla* or *bi súra'a*
Slow down *Shwáyya*
Finished *Khalás*
Go away! *Imshi!*
What time is it? *Adáysh as-sáa?/kam as-sáa?*
How long, how many hours? *Kam sáa?*

Vocabulary

General
embassy *sifára*
post office *máktab al-baríd*

stamps *tawábi'a*
bank *bank*
hotel *otél, fúnduq*
museum *máthaf*
ticket *tádhkara*
ruins *athár*
passport *jiwáz as-sáfar*
good *kuwáys*
not good, bad *mish kuways*
open *maftúh*
closed *musákkar, múghlik*
today *al-yáum*
tonight *hadhi-l-láyl*
tomorrow *búkra*

Eating/Drinking Out
restaurant *máta'am*
food *ákl*
fish *sámak*
meat *láhma*
milk *halíb*
bread *khúbz*
salad *saláta*
delicious *záki*
coffee *áhwa*
tea *shái*
cup *finján*
with sugar *bi súkkar*
without sugar *bidún súkkar*
wine *nibíd*
beer *bíra*
mineral water *mái ma'adaniya*
glass *kubbaiya*
bottle *ázaja*
I am a vegetarian *Ána nabbáti* (for
a man)/*nabbátiya* (for a woman)
the bill *al-hisáb*

Getting Around
Where...? *Wáyn...?*
downtown *wást al bálad*
street *shária*
Amir Mohammed Street *Shária al-
amir Mohammed*
car *sayára*
taxi *táxi*
shared taxi *servís*
bus *bas*
aeroplane *tayára*
airport *matár*
station *mahátta*
to *íla*
from *min*
right *yamín*
left *shimál*
straight *dúghri*
behind *wára*
near *aríb*
far away *ba'id*

petrol, super *benzín, benzín khas*

Days of the Week
Monday *(yáum) al-itnín*
Tuesday *at-taláta*
Wednesday *al-árba'a*
Thursday *al-khamís*
Friday *al-júma'a*
Saturday *as-sábt*
Sunday *al-áhad*

Numbers
zero *sifir*
one *wáhad*
two *itnín*
three *taláta*
four *árba'a*
five *khámsa*
six *sítta*
seven *sába'a*
eight *tamánia*
nine *tísa'a*
ten *áshara*

Shopping
market *súq*
shop *dukkán*
money *fulús*
cheap *rakhís*
expensive (very) *ghái (jídan)*
receipt, invoice *fatúra, wásl*
How much does it cost?
  Adáysh?/bi-kam?
What would you like? *Shú bidak?*
  (to a man)/*Shú bidik?* (to a
  woman)/*Shú bidkum?* (to more
  than one)
I like this *Buhíbb hádha*
I do not like this *Ma buhíbb hádha*
Can I see this? *Mumkin ashúf
  hádha?*
Give me *A'atíni*
How many? *Kam?*

Looking for a Room
a free room *ghúrfa fádia*
single room *ghúrfa munfárida*
double room *ghúrfa muzdáwija*
hot water *mái súkhna*
bathroom, toilet *hammám, tuwalét*
shower *dúsh*
towel *bashkír*
How much does the room cost per
  night? *Adáysh al-ghúrfa al-láyl?*

Further Reading

General

A History of the Arab Peoples, by
Albert Hourani. London, 1991. A
landmark history of the Arabs, by
the 20th-century doyen of Middle
East studies. It spent several
months on the US bestseller lists.
The Arabs, by Peter Mansfield.
Penguin, 1976. A good survey by
ex-London *Times* journalist.
The History of the Middle East, by
Peter Mansfield. Penguin, London,
1991. A very readable introduction
for the lay person.
*Heart-Beguiling Araby – The
English Romance with Arabia*, by
Kathryn Tidrick. I.B. Tauris,
London/New York, 1989. A must if
you nurture romantic ideas about
the Arab world.
The Bedouin, by Shelagh Weir.
British Museum Publications,
London, 1990.
*On the Banks of the Jordan: British
and Nineteenth Century Painters*,
by Jordan National Gallery & the
British Council, 1987. Available in
English and Arabic.

Biblical

If your visit whets your appetite for
some controversial theories about
Jesus and the New Testament you
should read:
The Dead Sea Scrolls Deception,
by Michael Baigent & Richard Leigh.
Corgi Books, England. A fascinating
account of the controversy
surrounding the ancient scrolls
discovered in caves by the Dead
Sea in the late 1940s.
*Who was Jesus? A Conspiracy in
Jerusalem*, by Kamal Salibi. I.B.
Tauris, London/New York, 1986/9.
The Bible Came from Arabia, by
Kamal Salibi. I.B.Tauris,
London/New York, 1986/9.

History

Nomads and Settlers in Syria and Jordan, 1800–1980, by Norman Lewis. Cambridge, 1989. A fascinating look at the land and people of the area. Scholarly, but also a good read by the man who introduced the concept of a "frontier of settlement".

Pioneers Over Jordan: The Frontier of Settlement in Transjordan, 1850–1914, by Raouf Abu Jaber. London, 1989. A scholarly work on settlement in Transjordan in the 19th century.

Jordan: Crossroads of Middle East Events, by Peter Gubser. Colorado, 1983. One of a series of books which provide profiles of countries in the modern Middle East. Gubser is an old Jordan hand and covers all facets of life in Jordan in less than 150 pages. The statistics are a little dated now, but still the best all-round book on Jordan for the newcomer. Scholarly style.

The Making of Modern Jordan, by Kamal Salibi. London, 1993. The best history of Jordan, by one of the most eminent historians in the Middle East. Very readable and informative. Cheaper in Jordan.

Jordan's Palestinian Challenge, 1948–1983: A Political History, by Clinton Bailey. Colorado, 1984. A look at one of the most sensitive political questions in Jordan today by an Israeli academic. Scholarly rather than a good read.

Biography & Autobiography

King Abdullah, Britain and the Making of Jordan, by Mary C. Wilson. Cambridge, 1987. A scholarly book covering the period from the founding of the Emirate to the assassination of King Abdullah. Wilson's book looks more closely at the controversy surrounding King Hussein's grandfather than does Kamil Salibi.

Hussein of Jordan: A Political Biography, by James Lunt. London, 1989. The most recent biography of the King. Sympathetic and very readable.

Memoirs of King Abdullah of Transjordan by H. M. King Abdullah of Jordan. London, 1950. The Emir's (and later King's) account of Jordan's early days.

Uneasy Lies the Head: An Autobiography, by H. M. King Hussein of Jordan. London, 1962. Particularly interesting about the King's early life. The King also wrote his account of the run-up to the 1967 war in **My War with Israel**, London, 1968. A later autobiography is **Mon Métier de Roi** (1975), in which the King brings the story up to and beyond Black September. Surprisingly, this book does not seem to be available in English.

Glubb Pasha: A Biography by James Lunt. London, 1984. A sympathetic account of the life of the British commander of the Jordanian army, by one of the officers who served under him.

Glubb Pasha: The Life and Times of Sir John Bagot Glubb, by Trevor Royle. London, 1992. A good read.

A Soldier with the Arabs, by Sir John Bagot Glubb. London, 1957. Autobiography of the British commander of the Arab Legion. A good read which gives Glubb's perspective on Jordan.

Lawrence of Arabia: The Authorised Biography of T.E. Lawrence, by Jeremy Wilson. London, 1989. The definitive account of Lawrence's life.

Travel Literature

Walks and Scrambles in Wadi Rum, by Tony Howard and Diana Taylor. Al-Kutba, Amman, 1993.

Famous Travellers to the Holy Land, by Linda Osband. Prior, 1989. Ranges from William Makepeace Thackeray to Gertrude Bell and Mark Twain.

Archaeology

Al-Kutba Jordan Guide Series in English and French on Petra, Wadi Rum and Aqaba, and in English only on Jarash, the Desert Castles, Amman, Umm Qais, Pella, Umm Al-Jimal, Madaba and Mount Nebo,

Karak and Shobak, and The King's Highway. Written by experts but an informative and easy read.

Petra, by Ian Browning. Chatto & Windus/Jordan Distribution Agency, 1989.

Jarash and the Decapolis, by Ian Browning. Chatto & Windus/Jordan Distribution Agency (1982) 1991.

The Art of Jordan – Treasures from an Ancient Land, by Piotr Bienkowski (ed.). National Museums & Galleries on Merseyside, 1991.

The Antiquities of Jordan, by G. Lankester Harding, Jordan Distribution Agency, Amman (1967) 1990.

Archaeology of Jordan: Essays and Reports, by Khair Yassine. University of Jordan, Amman. For the specialist only.

Crafts

Palestinian Embroidery, by Shelagh Weir & Serene Shahid. British Museum Publications, London, 1988.

Weaving in Jordan, by Widad Kawar. The Jordan Crafts Centre, Amman, 1980.

The Crafts of Jordan, by Meg Abu Hamdan. Al-Kutba, Amman, 1989.

Palestinian Costume, by Jehan Rajab. Kegan Paul International, 1989.

Traditional Palestinian Embroidery and Jewellery, by Abed Al-Samih Abu Omar. Al-Shark Arab Press, Jerusalem, 1987. English and Arabic.

For Children

Dig Cats, by Carol Meyer. Al-Kutba, Amman, 1989. A pet cat visits the sites in Jarash.

Colouring Jordan, Al-Kutba, Amman. English and Arabic.

Books on the Butterfly Series of Librairie du Liban, Stories from the Arab World Series: **Prince Jamil and Leila the Fair**, **Ma'arouf the Cobbler**, **The Man Who Never Laughed**, and, from the Stage 2 series, **Handicrafts of the Arab World**, **Farming the Desert**, and **Deserts**.

Middle Eastern Cooking

A New Book of Middle Eastern Food, by Claudia Roden. Penguin, 1985. The most comprehensive work of its kind and unique for its culinary history of the region.

The Complete Middle Eastern Cookbook, by Tess Mallos. Peter Ward, England, 1993. Illustrated and divided into country/regional sections.

Wildlife

Birds of Jordan, by Arslan Ramadan Bakig & Dr Hala Khiyami Horani. Amman, 1992.

Photographic

Amman Yesterday and Today, by Arslan Ramadan Bakig. Amman Photographs from the *Jordanian and Palestinian Heritage*, by Ibid. The Arab Institute for Research and Publishing, Amman, 1991. English and French.

High Above Jordan, by Jane Taylor. Amman, 1991. Aerial photographs of the major sites in Jordan with brief commentary, published in English, German, French and Italian; also **Petra**, Autumn Press, 1993. A tour of the famous site with photographs.

Aqaba: Under-Water Paradise, with photographs by C. Petron and text by J. Jaubert. Editions Delroisse/Jordan Distibution Agency. For scuba fans.

Old Houses of Jordan, published by TURAB (Jordan's Ever Lasting Heritage), a cultural charity. Forward by Queen Noor Al Hussein. 1997. A documentary of some of Jordan's most notorious landmarks, old family homes (such as the Mango, Abdo and Bisharat homes). Photography by Bill Lyons; text by Mohammed Al Asad.

Holy Sites of Jordan, published by TURAB in 1996. Photography by Fakhry Malkawi, Father Michele Piccirillo and Ammar Khammash. Text by Sheikh Hassan Saqaf and Father Michele Piccirillo. Documents some lesser-known holy sites.

Jordan – A Land for All Seasons, published by the Queen Alia Fund. Spectacular photographs, by Zohrab Markarian, of some of the country's most magnificent landscapes and monuments.

Journey Through Jordan, published by Willetts and Kiley. Photography by renowned international photographer Mohammed Amin. Photos are accompanied by well-written and descriptive text.

Fiction

There is no fiction in English that deals with Jordan alone and what is available draws from the experience of the Palestinian-Israeli conflict.

Nisanit, by Fadia Faqir, King Penguin. The harrowing story of a young Palestinian refugee woman living in Jordan, who falls in love with a Palestinian guerrilla in the West Bank, runs parallel to the story of her boyfriend's Israeli torturer.

Pillars of Salt, also by Fadia Fakir. Interlink Books, 1997. A journey into the hearts of Maha, a Bedouin, and Um Sa'd, from Amman. The two meet in Fuhays Mental Hospital, where they were both placed after going "insane" after suffering the abuse permitted in a conservative male dominated society. They alternate the telling of their tales, interspersed with narrative of a third voice; a male who sees their stories from an entirely different perspective.

Arab Folktales, by Inea Bushnaq (ed.). Pantheon Books, New York, 1986. A superb and delightful read with insight into popular Arab wisdom.

Blood Brothers, by Elias Chacour. Kingsway Publications, England (1984) 1987. The effort of a Palestinian in Israel to bring about reconciliation between Arabs and Jews.

Other Insight Guides

Other Insight Guides which highlight destinations in this region include *Egypt, The Nile, Israel* and *Jerusalem*. They all contain full colour photographs, background essays, detailed maps and full coverage of all the sites.

In addition to the main Insight Guides series, Insight publishes Pocket Guides and Compact Guides. Insight Pocket Guides are selective, itinerary-based guides written by a local host. They are supported by a large fold-out map. Compact Guides are easy-reference guides, with full colour photographs and maps.

ART & PHOTO CREDITS

Photography by Lyle Lawson unless otherwise stated
AP Photo/Enric Marti 61
AP Photo/Santiago Lyon 75
Gonzalo M. Azumendi 254, 273T
Chris Bradley 108, 109, 111, 118, 144, 147T, 172, 212, 213, 214, 215, 237, 252,
Rami Khouri 174
Bill Lyons 2B, 54, 60, 98, 99, 110, 119, 210/211
Mansour Mouasher 106
Mary Evans Picture Library 23, 30, 31, 32, 33, 34, 36
Christine Osborne Pictures 101, 206, 226, 227T, 270, 290
Jane Taylor 104, 105, 107
Topham Picturepoint 35, 47, 48, 51, 52, 53, 55, 56, 57R, 59

Picture Spreads

Pages 96/97
Top row left to right: Bill Lyons; Lyle Lawson; Gonzalo M Azumendi; Lyle Lawson
Bottom row: Lyle Lawson; Lyle Lawson, Bill Lyons; Bill Lyons; Gonzalo M Azumndi

Pages 154/155
All pictures by Amy Henderson except
top right: J. Worker/Christine Osborne Pictures
Pages 216/217
Top row left to right: Christine Osborne Pictures; Bill Lyons; Christine Osborne Pictures
Bottom row: Christine Osborne Pictures; Bill Lyons; Christine Osborne Pictures; Lyle Lawson; Lyle Lawson
Pages 274/275
All pictures Terraqua except top right: Bill Lyons; *bottom centre left*: E. Bjurstiom/Christine Osborne Pictures

All small pictures on cover by Lyle Lawson, except bottom spine: Chris Bradley

Map Production Berndtson & Berndtson Productions
© 1999 Apa Publications GmbH & Co. Verlag KG, Singapore.

INSIGHT GUIDE
JORDAN

Cartographic Editor **Zoë Goodwin**
Production **Stuart Everitt**
Design Consultants
Carlotta Junger, Graham Mitchener
Picture Research **Hilary Genin**

Index